Petrarch's War

This revisionist account of the economic, literary, and social history of Florence in the immediate aftermath of the Black Death connects warfare with the plague narrative. Organized around Petrarch's "war" against the Ubaldini clan of 1349–1350, which formed the prelude to his meeting and friendship with Boccaccio, William Caferro's work examines the institutional and economic effects of the war, alongside literary and historical patterns. Caferro pays close attention to the meaning of wages in context, including those of soldiers, revising our understanding of wage data in the distant past and highlighting the consequences of a constricted workforce that resulted in the use of cooks and servants on important embassies. Drawing on rigorous archival research, this book seeks to stimulate discussion among academics and offer a new contribution to our understanding of Renaissance Florence. It stresses the importance of short-termism and contradiction as subjects of historical inquiry.

William Caferro is Gertrude Conaway Vanderbilt Professor of History and Professor of Classics and Mediterranean Studies at Vanderbilt University. He has held fellowships at the Institute for Advanced Studies in Princeton, Villa I Tatti in Florence, and the Italian Academy at Columbia University and, in 2010, he received a Simon R. Guggenheim fellowship. He has written widely on medieval and Renaissance Italy, including *Mercenary Companies and the Decline of Siena* (1998), *The Spinelli of Florence: Fortunes of a Renaissance Merchant Family* (2001), *John Hawkwood: An English Mercenary in Fourteenth Century Italy* (2006), which won the Otto Gründler Award from the International Medieval Congress, and *Contesting the Renaissance* (2010).

Petrarch's War

Florence and the Black Death in Context

William Caferro

Vanderbilt University

CAMBRIDGE
UNIVERSITY PRESS

CAMBRIDGE
UNIVERSITY PRESS

University Printing House, Cambridge CB2 8BS, United Kingdom

One Liberty Plaza, 20th Floor, New York, NY 10006, USA

477 Williamstown Road, Port Melbourne, VIC 3207, Australia

314–321, 3rd Floor, Plot 3, Splendor Forum, Jasola District Centre,
New Delhi – 110025, India

79 Anson Road, #06–04/06, Singapore 079906

Cambridge University Press is part of the University of Cambridge.

It furthers the University's mission by disseminating knowledge in the pursuit of
education, learning, and research at the highest international levels of excellence.

www.cambridge.org
Information on this title: www.cambridge.org/9781108424011
DOI: 10.1017/9781108539555

© William Caferro 2018

First published 2018

Printed in the United Kingdom by Clays, St Ives plc.

A catalogue record for this publication is available from the British Library.

ISBN 978-1-108-42401-1 Hardback

Contents

Figures, Maps, and Tables

Preface and Acknowledgments

This is not the book I intended to write. But archives are subversive and often tell us what we do not want to know. The present volume began as a study of the effects of war on the Florentine economy from 1336 to 1402. I hope to complete that project, now two decades old, soon. But I encountered documents along the way relating to a "war" that I knew nothing about and that coincided with the immediate aftermath of the Black Death. The material connected Petrarch and Boccaccio, added details to their historical portraits, and raised an array of political, institutional, diplomatic, and above all economic questions about Florence that I did not have answers for, nor had even considered.

This book is an attempt to interpret the evidence. It is, at base, a case study of war, the most overlooked aspect of fourteenth-century Italy, for which no justification is needed. Although I had hoped to mechanically add my findings to existing assumptions about Florence, the addition of war altered the assumptions. The evidence forced me to reexamine and revise many of my own hypotheses. The decision to restrict the study to two years was a difficult one, but the material warranted the approach. The book is thus unapologetically revisionist. It argues against the false distinction between long-term "usable" history and the short-term irrelevant form, and it speaks to the dangers of teleology embedded in historical study, particularly with regard to economic data. It takes as its fundamental tenet that contradiction and anomaly are a part of history, and acknowledgment of them ultimately tells a more useful and interesting tale.

The project has taken a long time to research and write. It has been stopped several times by illness, vision troubles, and studies of Dante. I have accrued substantial debts to numerous colleagues, students, and institutions that have supported my work, helped me fashion my ideas, and urged me to render them in this manner. I want to thank first the Institute for Advanced Study, where the project began and I first presented my "contradictory" data to the economic history seminar organized by Nicola di Cosmo and to the medieval table organized by

Caroline Walker Bynum. I am deeply grateful to both scholars for their generosity, friendship, advice, and encouragement along the way. I wish to thank the Simon R. Guggenheim Foundation for a fellowship to pursue further the research for this book, and to Carolyn Dever, the Dean of Arts and Sciences at Vanderbilt University, for allowing me leave from academic duties to take the fellowship. I am similarly indebted to the Italian Academy for Advanced Study at Columbia University and the weekly seminars led by Achille Varzi and Barbara Faedda. I thank the participants for their critiques: Elisabetta Benigni, Lorenzo d'Angelo, Anna Galeotti, Edward Goldberg, Sarah Goler, Stefano Lorenzetti, Anna Loretoni, Daniele Maras, Eleanora Pistis, Karin Schlapbach, and Marissa Span. I wish, above all, to thank Joel Kaye of Barnard College and Neslihan Senocak of Columbia University for taking time from their busy schedules to attend my presentation and comment on a penultimate version of this book. Their help altered the shape and content of the manuscript. The shortcomings were then and remain my own.

I acknowledge the guidance and friendship of the fellows at the Institute for Advanced Study, especially Richard Abels, Susan Boynton, Luigi Capogrossi, Martin Eisner, Barbara Kovalzig, Jens Ulff-Moller, Glen Peers, and Giacomo Todeschini. I am grateful to Eric Maskin for discussing aspects of economy with me. I thank Luigi Capogrossi and Giacomo Todeschini for ongoing debates about economic history (ancient and medieval) and Susan Boynton for her friendship and support way beyond the call of duty, and her invitation to present my work at the medieval colloquium at Columbia University. I thank the community of economic historians whose counsel I rely heavily upon: Lawrin Armstrong, Judith Brown, Steven A. Epstein, Richard Goldthwaite, Maryanne Kowaleski, John Padgett, Tony Molho, and John Munro. This book was inspired in the first instance by the work of Professor Munro, whose recent death leaves our field with an unfillable void. I am grateful also to my medievalist and Italianist colleagues Alessandro Arcangeli, Daniel Bornstein, Samuel K. Cohn, Bill Connell, George Dameron, Bob Fredona, Tim Kircher, Julius Kirshner, Tom Kuehn, John Law, Lauro Martines, Edward Muir, John Najemy, Dennis Romano, Dan Smail, Sharon Strocchia, and Susan Stuard for their advice and critique. I want to single out Steven Epstein and Sue Stuard, who helped at every stage, both with personal and professional issues. I wish to express my thanks for the mentorship of four outstanding scholars who are greatly missed by us all: William Bowsky, Gene Brucker, Benjamin Kohl, and Ronald Witt.

I owe a special scholarly debt to Teodolinda Barolini and Giuseppe Mazzotta for their generous advice and soaring intellectual example. I am similarly grateful to Albert Ascoli, Todd Boli, Martin Eisner, Warren Ginsburg, Victoria Kirkham, Ron Martinez, Kristina Olson, Lino Pertile, and Justin Steinberg. I thank Will Robbins for our conversations about literature and history dating back almost two decades now.

My greatest debt is to Francesca Trivellato, whom I admire more than I can express here and without whom there would be no book. I thank her for her detailed critical reading of the text and for her friendship. I also thank her, Naomi Lamoreaux, and Tim Guinnane for an invitation to the economic history seminar at Yale University. I thank Jay Rubinstein and Tom Burman for inviting me to the University of Tennessee to present an early version of this work, and for their continuing collegiality and friendship for our "Tennessee medieval group." I am indebted to Marcus Meumann and Matthias Meinhardt for their invitation to participate in the seminar *Die Kapitalisierung des Krieges* in Berlin, where I presented initial findings. I thank my colleagues/*amici* in Italy, especially Maurizio Arfaioli, Andrea Barlucchi, Lorenz Böninger, Franco Franceschi, Luca Mola, and Alessandro Monte. I am grateful to Andrea Barlucchi and Alessandro Monte for inviting me to participate in the *convegno* on the Ubaldini clan in both Florence and Scarperia, and for encouraging me to present my work in Italian, to the general amusement of all. I have relied on the unparalleled expertise of Professor Barlucchi for help throughout the entire project.

At Vanderbilt, I am grateful for the support and close friendship of my colleagues William Collins in the Economics department, Elsa Filosa in Italian and French literature, Phil Lieberman in Jewish Studies, and Joe Rife in Classics. I wish to thank the participants in our Pre-Modern Cultural Studies Group at the Robert Penn Warren Center: Annalisa Azzoni, Barbara Bowen, Katie Crawford, Jessie Hock, Peter Lorge, Leah Marcus, Tracy Miller, Elizabeth Moody, Lynn Ramey, Samira Sheikh, and Kathryn Schwarz. I thank also the wonderful director of the Warren Center, Mona Frederick, who has made study groups like this possible. I thank my colleagues in the department of History for their advice and support, particularly David Carlton, Julia Cohen, Katie Crawford, Lauren Clay, Leor Halevi, Catherine Molineux, Moses Ochonu, Matt Ramsey, and David Wasserstein.

I wish to thank also my undergraduate research assistants David Gaffney and Hunter Guthrie, who helped manage data and draw maps. I acknowledge the outstanding support of my graduate research assistant Pedro Gomez, now professor of history at the University of Wisconsin, and Laura Hohman, now of Trivecca Nazarene. They not only tracked down sources and arranged data, but helped me interpret it all as well. I thank my former graduate student, Megan Moran, now of Montclair

State, for discussions on Italian history that have taught me a great deal, and my current graduate students Katherine McKenna and Hillary Taylor, who continue to do the same. I thank Hillary Taylor for her help with the final stages of the manuscript and J'Nese Williams for getting the annoying lines out of the text and listening to my rants against technology. I wish to thank Liz Friend-Smith of Cambridge University Press for her kind and generous support in seeing this manuscript through the many stages.

Finally, I want to acknowledge formally the mentorship of Michael Mallett, who introduced me to the topic of Italy and war in graduate school, and to Tony Molho and John Najemy, whose support has allowed me to have a career. It is their intellectual example that so many of us try to follow.

I dedicate this book to my wife Megan Weiler, who transferred her love of Italy to me and with whom I have spent the greater part of a lifetime in the very same parts of the Mugello discussed in this book. Her intelligence and work ethic are my most immediate models. The research for the book coincided with difficult times for both of us, and I dedicate this volume also to friends and family members whom we have loved and miss dearly.

Introduction: The Plague in Context: Florence 1349–1350

Stories of the long-term ... have the powerful effect of banishing myths and overturning false laws. This and not the appreciation of mere antiquities is the reason that universities have history departments and the reason for history's classical mission as *magistra vitae*, the teacher of all aspect of life.

Jo Guldi and David Armitage, *The History Manifesto*[1]

Out of useless activity there come discoveries that may well prove of infinitely more importance ... than the accomplishments of useful ends.

Abraham Flexner, "The Usefulness of Useless Knowledge"[2]

I

If, as recent historiography suggests, the Middle Ages was a period of "alterity," difficult to relate to current times, it may also be said that it was a time of contradiction and of conflicting forces operating at once.[3] In this it resembles all eras.

Contradiction is the subject of this book, which takes as its title, *Petrarch's War*, as a way of emphasizing that fact. The author of "Italia mia," the famous pacific poem, ending with a threefold call for peace on the peninsula, wrote a letter to Florentine officials in June 1349 demanding that the city wage war even while it was still suffering the immediate effects of the devastating plague of the previous year. Francesco Petrarch's call to arms appears in the same collection of epistles (book VIII of *Rerum familiarum libri*, or *Familiares*) that also contains his famous lament about the pestilence. Petrarch sent his bellicose letter, *Familiares*

---

[1] Jo Guldi and David Armitage, *The History Manifesto* (Cambridge: Cambridge University Press, 2104), p. 37.

[2] Abraham Flexner, "The Usefulness of Useless Knowledge," *Harper's Magazine* 179 (June 1939), p. 549.

[3] Paul Freedman and Gabrielle Spiegel, "Medievalisms Old and New: The Rediscovery of Alterity in North American Medieval Studies," *American Historical Review* 103 no. 3 (June 1998), pp. 677–704.

VIII 10, to the Florentine priors. It was transcribed by Giovanni Boccaccio, a long-time admirer of Petrarch, who had recently returned to his native city and was then writing the *Decameron*.[4] Shortly thereafter Florence sent out its army. The target was the Ubaldini clan of the upper Mugello, who had attacked two of Petrarch's closest friends as they traveled through the mountainous region.[5]

"Petrarch's war" ended on 27 September 1350, the day before Boccaccio returned from his embassy to Dante's sister in Ravenna and a week before Petrarch traveled to Florence, where he first met Boccaccio, on his way to the papal jubilee in Rome (October 1350).[6] The conflict thus frames the incipient friendship between the two men and casts new light on their relationship, and on the relationship between the poets, the city, and their famous forebear Dante – subjects of keen interest to literary scholars.[7]

The connection may account for the abundant and detailed material that has survived in the Florentine state archives. Indeed, no contemporary conflict is better documented. The material includes two of the earliest extant *balie*, containing the acts of the ad hoc committees that oversaw the day-to-day management of the war; budgets of the *camera del comune*, which handled the city's income and expenditure; diplomatic dispatches (Signori, Missive, I Cancelleria, 10) to ambassadors and city council legislation.[8] The very first *consulte e practiche* (1) register, relaying the debates of the executives who ran the city, deals extensively with the war. Indeed, the discussion of Ubaldini misdeeds fills the first twenty pages of the volume, which makes no mention of the plague.[9] The war is

---

[4] Francesco Petrarch, *Rerum familiarum libri, I–VIII*, translated and edited by Aldo S. Bernardo, vol. 1 (Albany, NY: State University of New York Press, 1975), pp. 429–435. On Boccaccio writing the *Decameron*, see Vittore Branca, *Giovanni Boccaccio. Profilo biografico* (Florence: Sansoni, 1997), p. 80.

[5] For a preliminary discussion of the war and its economic and literary implications, see William Caferro, "Petrarch's War: Florentine Wages at the Time of the Black Death" *Speculum* 88 no. 1 (January 2013), pp. 144–165, and " Le Tre Corone Fiorentine and War with the Ubaldini," in *Boccaccio 1313–2013*, edited by Francesco Ciabattoni, Elsa Filosa and Kristina Olson (Ravenna: Longo editore, 2015), pp. 43–55.

[6] Giuseppe Pelli, *Memorie per servire alla vita di Dante Aligheri* (Florence: Guglielmo Piatti, 1823), p. 30.

[7] Todd Boli, "Boccaccio's Trattatello in laude di Dante, Or Dante Resartus," *Renaissance Quarterly* 41 (1988), pp. 395–398; Jason M. Houston, "Boccaccio at Play in Petrarch's Pastoral World," *Modern Language Notes* 127 (2012), pp. 47–53; Giuseppe Mazzotta, *The Worlds of Petrarch* (Durham, NC: Duke University Press, 1993); Martin Eisner, *Boccaccio and the Invention of Italian Literature: Dante, Petrarch, Cavalcanti and the Authority of the Vernacular* (Cambridge: Cambridge University Press, 2013).

[8] The sources in the Archivio di Stato di Firenze (ASF) include balie 6, 7; Consulte e pratiche (CP) 1; Camera del comune, Scrivano di camera uscita 5, 6, 7, 8, 9, 10; Provvisioni, registri 36, 37, 38; and Signori, Missive, I Cancelleria 10.

[9] The discussions go from 18 April 1349 to 22 June 1350. ASF, CP 1 fols. 1r–19r.

recounted in detail by the chronicler Matteo Villani and by his younger contemporary Marchionne di Coppo Stefani. It is also discussed by the famous diarist Donato Velluti, who, as we shall see, took a leading role in executive councils and served as an ambassador during the conflict.

The war, in short, mattered. As far as military engagements go, it was nevertheless unremarkable. Florence fought frequently with the Ubaldini clan, a prominent and obstinate Ghibelline family, whose patrimony lay along important trade routes to Bologna, a key outlet of Florentine goods to and from the north (Maps I.1 and I.2). The most famous instance of violence between the two occurred just after Dante's exile in 1302. The poet, along with other "white Guelfs," allied with the Ubaldini against the city. They were quickly defeated, but battles between Florence and the clan continued throughout the fourteenth century.

From a purely political perspective, the conflict in 1349–1350 may be viewed as an instance of what Paolo Pirillo has called the "successiva fiorentinizzazione" of border regions that accompanied the city's expansion into a territorial state. More immediately, it served as a prelude to the bitter interstate war with Milan (1351–1353) – the first of several contests between the two from which scholars have seen the roots of a civic humanism that formed part of Florence's self-definition during the Renaissance.[10] The relation between magnate families and the ruling *popolo* is part of a venerable debate, recently reinterpreted by Christiane Klapisch-Zuber, who stresses the complex and ambiguous role of the clans in Florentine affairs.[11] The area of conflict, the upper Mugello, is associated in modern times with the *linea gotica* (Gothic line) set up by the Nazis in the late stages of World War II to stop the Allied advance though Italy. Every year battle reenactors assemble at Giogo, the mountain pass

[10] Paolo Pirillo, "Signorie dell'Appennino tra Toscana ed Emilia-Romagna alla fine del Medioevo," in *Poteri signorili e feudali nelle campagne dell'Italia settentrionale fra Tre e Quattrocento: fondamenti di legittimità e forme di esercizio*, edited by Federica Cengarle, Giorgio Chittolini, and Gian Maria Varanini (Florence: Florence University Press, 2005), pp. 211–220. For the larger trajectory of the Florentine territorial state, see William Connell and Andrea Zorzi, eds., *Florentine Tuscany: Structure and Practices of Power* (Cambridge: Cambridge University Press, 2000); Giorgio Chittolini, "City-States and Regional States in North-Central Italy," *Theory and Society* 18 no. 5 (1989), pp. 689–706; Samuel K. Cohn, *Creating the Florentine State: Peasants and Rebellion* (Cambridge: Cambridge University Press, 1999). For civic humanism at the end of the century, see Hans Baron, *The Crisis of the Early Italian Renaissance* (Princeton, NJ: Princeton University Press, 1966).

[11] On the magnates and their relation to the *popolani*, see Gaetano Salvemini, *Magnati e popolani in Firenze dal 1280 al 1295* (Florence: G. Carnesecchi, 1899); Nicola Ottokar, *Il comune di Firenze alla fine del Dugento* (Florence: Vallecchi, 1926) and John Najemy, *Corporatism and Consensus Florentine Electoral Politics, 1280–1400* (Chapel Hill, NC: University of North Carolina Press, 1982). See now Christiane Klapisch-Zuber, *Ritorno alla politica: I magnati fiorentini, 1340–1440* (Rome: Viella, 2007).

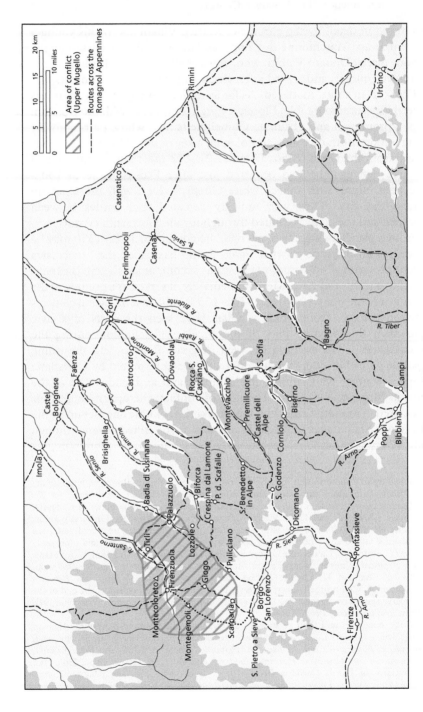

Map I.1 Florence and routes across the Romagnol Apennines

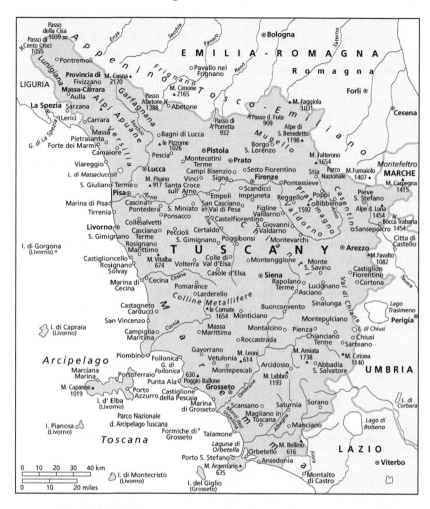

Map I.2 Tuscany

that separates Scarperia and Firenzuola, to refight the decisive encounter (September 1944) between the Nazis and Allies. The region lies in the heart of what was previously Ubaldini territory.

The application of the term "war" to the conflict in 1349–1350 is done with caution. The definition was not so clear then as it is today. The sources alternately refer to the engagement as a *cavalcata*, implying more of a police action, and as a *guerra,* a more formal war. The distinction may derive from the fact that the conflict involved two campaigns, the second on a larger scale than the first. But the language of the documents is imprecise, with frequent alternation of terms. For the purposes here, the distinction is irrelevant since both required the mobilization of a substantial military force, economic resources, and the appointment of special committees to oversee activities.

In either case, infra-state contests such as that of 1349–1350 have been consigned to scholarly obscurity in the Anglophone academy.[12] The status quo reflects a general lack of interest in warfare as a field of academic inquiry. It is a messy and disconcerting subject, which, as Jay M. Winter asserts, poses "intractable problems" for researchers, owing to uneven evidence, ideological bias, and, paraphrasing Fernand Braudel, the tendency of each generation to construct its own understanding of war.[13] This is particularly true of medieval Italy, where scholars, following the famous example of Niccolò Machiavelli, have too often treated war in moral terms, stressing the lack of "native martial" spirit and reliance by Italian states on greedy, "useless," "unreliable," and "disloyal" mercenaries.[14] Machiavelli's depiction has encouraged scholars to separate Italian warfare from its societal milieu.[15] This is particularly true for the middle years of the *trecento*, the era of the "companies of adventure," bands of mercenary soldiers, which included foreigners from outside the peninsula, who arrayed themselves into

---

[12] C. C. Bayley, among others, does not mention these in his oft-cited account of Florentine warfare in the *trecento*. He mentions only the interstate war and the conflict with the Visconti. C. C. Bayley, *War and Society in Renaissance Florence: The De Militia of Leonardo Bruni* (Toronto, University of Toronto Press, 1961), p. 18.

[13] Jay M. Winter, ed., *War and Economic Development: Essays in Memory of David Joslin* (Cambridge: Cambridge University Press, 1975), p. 2. Fernand Braudel, *The Mediterranean and the Mediterranean World in the Age of Philip II*, translated by Sian Reynolds (New York, NY: Harper Books, 1966), p. 891.

[14] Machiavelli famously condemned mercenaries as "useless," "unreliable," "dangerous," "disloyal," and "undisciplined," in addition judging them "cowards." See *The Prince* (books 12 and 13), *The Art of War* (book 1), and *The Discourses* (book 2, discourse 20). Niccolò Machiavelli, *The Prince*, translated and edited by David Wootton (Indianapolis, IN: Hackett Publishing Co., 1995), pp. 38–45; *The Discourses*, translated by Leslie J. Walker and edited by Bernard Crick (New York, NY: Penguin, 1970), pp. 339–341; *The Art of War*, translated by Christopher Lynch (Chicago, IL: University of Chicago Press, 2003), pp. 13–32. Machiavelli's views shaped nineteenth- and early twentieth-century Italian scholarship and remain influential. Ercole Ricotti, *Storia delle compagnie di ventura in Italia*, 4 vols. (Turin: Pomba, 1844–1845); Giuseppe Canestrini, "Documenti per servire alla storia della milizia italiana dal XIII secolo al XVI," *Archivio storico italiano* 15 (1851), pp. 347–446; Piero Pieri, "Alcune quistioni sopra fanterie in Italia nel periodo comunale," *Rivista storica italiana* (1933), pp. 561–614 and *Il Rinascimento e la crisi militare italiana* (Turin: Einaudi, 1952).

[15] See William Caferro, "Warfare and Economy of Renaissance Italy, 1350–1450," *Journal of Interdisciplinary History* 39 (2008), pp. 167–209 and more recently "Individualism and the Separation of Fields of Study: Jacob Burckhardt and Ercole Ricotti," in *The Routledge History of the Renaissance*, edited by William Caferro (Abingdon: Routledge Press, 2017), pp. 62–74.

marauding armies during times of ostensible peace.[16] For all the literature devoted to the development of the Florentine territorial state at this
time, warfare has not been properly integrated into the discussion.

The scholarly inattention to Petrarch's war in 1349–1350 owes most of
all, however, to the Black Death that occurred immediately prior to it.
The cataclysmic nature of the event and its role as an historical turning
point has crowded out consideration of other contemporaneous phenomena. In F. A. Gasquet's famous formulation, the pestilence brought
nothing less than the "close of the medieval period and the beginning of
the Modern Ages." G. G. Coulton described the plague as a "gateway" to
the Renaissance and Reformation.[17] More recent literature has avoided
simplistic pronouncements, but the notion of the plague as a turning
point and all the baggage that goes with it remains. The subtitle of
David Herlihy's book on the Black Death is "The Transformation of the
West."[18] Bruce Campbell calls his recent integrated study of the contagion the "Great Transition."[19] A. B. Falsini's detailed investigation of
Florence, still an important starting point for examination of events in the
city, argues that the Black Death brought an entirely "new economic and
social reality."[20] Bruno Dini asserts in his study of the Florentine wool
cloth industry (*arte della lana*) that the plague of 1348 not only changed
that business, but the "general economic organization" of Florence.[21]
The art historian Millard Meiss notes a basic shift in Florentine artistic

[16] Maria Nadia Covini, "Political and Military Bonds in the Italian State System,
Thirteenth to Sixteenth Century," in *War and Competition between States*, edited by
Philippe Contamine (Oxford: Oxford University Press, 2000), p. 14; Brucker's list of
Florence's wars in the *trecento* are intercity ones, notably with Pisa and Milan.
Gene Brucker, *Florentine Politics and Society, 1343–1378* (Princeton, NJ: Princeton
University Press, 1962), pp. 84–130. Brucker does not mention the conflict with the
Ubaldini, although he mentions the papacy's request for troops in 1350, which Florence
denied on account of the war with the Ubaldini. Brucker, *Florentine Politics and Society*,
p. 141; William Caferro, *Mercenary Companies and the Decline of Siena* (Baltimore, MD:
Johns Hopkins University Press, 1998).

[17] F. A. Gasquet, *The Great Pestilence* (London: G. Bell, 1893), p. xvi; G. G. Coulton, *Black
Death* (London: Ernest Benn, 1929); Thompson compared the Black Death to World
War I, the real transformative event of his own day. James Westfall Thompson,
"The Aftermath of the Black Death and the Aftermath of the Great War," *American
Journal of Sociology* xxvi (1921), pp. 565–572.

[18] Herlihy called the contagion "Europe's greatest known ecological disaster."
David Herlihy, *The Black Death and the Transformation of the West* (Cambridge, MA:
Harvard University Press, 1997), p. 17.

[19] Bruce Campbell, *The Great Transition: Climate, Disease and Society in the Late Medieval
World* (Cambridge: Cambridge University Press, 2016).

[20] A. B. Falsini, "Firenze dopo il 1348: Le conseguenze della pesta nera," *Archivio Storico
Italiano* (1971), pp. 437–482.

[21] Bruno Dini, "I lavoratori dell'Arte della Lana a Firenze nel XIV e XV secolo" in *Artigiani
e salariati. Il mondo del lavoro nell'Italia dei secoli XII–XV, Pistoia, 9–13 ottobre 1981*
(Bologna: Centro Italiano di Studi di Storia e d'Arte, 1984), p. 33.

styles in 1350: from a realistic/optimistic emphasis on humanity to a brooding/religious conservatism.[22] Louis Green, examining the Florentine chronicle tradition, sees a "radical re-dimension" in the pre-plague writing of Giovanni Villani (who died of the plague) and the post-plague writing of his brother and successor as chronicler Matteo – a shift from religious devotion and general optimism to pessimism and greater acceptance of the natural world,[23] and Katharine Park has outlined the decline of the medical profession after 1348.[24]

The present study seeks to add war to the plague narrative on the basis of the extant sources. Indeed, it follows precisely the lead of Petrarch himself, whose account of the Black Death (*Familiares* VIII 7) is not only in the same book of letters as his advocacy of the war, but was, in its original version (which has survived), part of the *same* letter that describes the attack by the Ubaldini on his friends.[25] Petrarch did not distinguish between the violent death of a friend at the hands of robbers and the death caused by the epidemic (which took his beloved Laura). Both brought "insufferable loss." The war thus casts light on the Black Death; the Black Death casts light on the war.

The coincidence of plague and violence is itself noteworthy. Common sense, or perhaps common decency, suggests that the plague, as some scholars have argued, caused a "cessation of all activities" in its immediate aftermath. Doubtless this was true of *some* activities, but it was not true of violence. Indeed, Florence saw a quickening of the pace of both internal and external unrest. The problems with the Ubaldini coincided with more general difficulties with magnate families in the countryside.[26] And armed conflict was not restricted to the Florentine state. There was unrest in the papal lands in the nearby Romagna and Marche. An anonymous chronicler from Rimini wrote that although the Black Death killed "two of every three people," it did not do away with "contentious tyrants and great

---

[22] Millard Meiss, *Painting in Florence and Siena after the Black Death: The Arts, Religion, and Society in the Mid-Fourteenth Century* (Princeton, NJ: Princeton University Press, 1979).

[23] Louis Green, *Chronicle in History* (Cambridge: Cambridge University Press, 1972), pp. 86–87.

[24] Katharine Park, *Doctors and Medicine in Early Renaissance Florence* (Princeton, NJ: Princeton University Press, 1985), pp. 42–45.

[25] Aldo S. Bernardo, "Letter-Splitting in Petrarch's Familiares," *Speculum* 33 no. 2 (April 1958), pp. 236–241.

[26] ASF, Provvisioni, registri 36 fols. 63v–64r; Provvisioni, registri 37 fol. 7v; *Capitoli del Comune di Firenze, inventario e regesto*, edited by C. Guasti, A. Gherardi, vol. 2 (Florence: Cellini, 1893), p. 61 note 7; 257–266, 311–314. Matteo Villani, *Nuova Cronica*, vol. 1, edited by Giuseppe Porta (Parma: Fondazione Pietro Bembo, 1995), pp. 48–49; Demetrio Marzi, *La Cancelleria della Repubblica Fiorentina*, Rocca San Casciano: Cappelli 1909), pp. 667–669, Samuel K. Cohn, *Creating the Florentine State* (Cambridge: Cambridge University Press, 1999), p. 140.

lords" of the region.[27] In May 1350, Francesco degli Ordelaffi, lord of Forlì, attacked nearby Bertinoro, a town that was part of the papal state.[28] The Malatesta of Rimini moved on the Marche in 1349–1350.[29] Hungarian and French branches of the Angevin family fought in Naples in 1349.[30] The two commercial republics, Genoa and Venice, battled on the Black Sea in August 1350. The Visconti of Milan and the Church were at odds.[31] Siena and Orvieto quarreled over rights to castles in bordering territories.[32] And Matteo Villani spoke of war also in Tunis in northern Africa and the ongoing "Hundred Years War" between England and France.

The inclusion of war alters the current portrait of post-plague Florence delineated by scholars, and raises important questions that are not easily answered. It affords an opportunity to cross subfields and even disciplinary boundaries and to reevaluate literary and historical trends that are usually treated separately.

The sources cast new light on the friendship between Petrarch and Boccaccio, their political activities, their connection to the establishment of the new university in Florence, and their attitude toward, and appropriation of, Dante, who, as Simon Gilson and others have argued, served as literary intermediary in the developing amity between the men.[33] At the same time, the documents reveal a Florentine army that, contra Machiavelli and the scholarly consensus, was not "ad hoc," "backward," or lacking a native component, but built around a small cadre of "faithful" mercenaries and professionalized local infantrymen, some of whom worked over the long run for the city, even invested in the public debt and lent money to the city for the war! Florentine officials appropriated revenue from pious bequests of plague victims to the confraternity of Orsanmichele, Florence's main charitable institution, to help pay for

---

[27] *Cronaca malatestiane*, edited by Aldo Massèra, *Rerum Italicarum Scriptores*, vol. 15 (Bologna: Zanichelli, 1922–1924), p. 17.

[28] Albano Sorbelli, *La Signoria di Giovanni Visconti a Bologna e le sue relazioni con la Toscana* (Bologna: Forni, 1902), pp. 2–4.

[29] P. J. Jones, *The Malatesta Lords of Rimini* (Cambridge: Cambridge University Press, 1974), p. 65; ASF, Missive I Cancelleria, fol. 2v; Capitoli, registri 27 fol. 40r; Demetrio Marzi, *La Cancelleria della Repubblica Fiorentina*, pp. 653–657.

[30] ASF, Capitoli 27 registri, fols. 40r–54r; Demetrio Marzi, *La Cancelleria della Repubblica Fiorentina*, pp. 653–654.

[31] Frederic C. Lane, *Venice: A Maritime Republic* (Baltimore, MD: Johns Hopkins University Press, 1973), pp. 175–176; Mario Brunetti, "La battaglia di Castro (1350)," *Rivista marittima*, 43 (January–March 1910), pp. 269–282.

[32] Demetrio Marzi, *La Cancelleria della Repubblica Fiorentina*, p. 663.

[33] Hannah Chapelle Wojciehowski, "Petrarch and His Friends" in *The Cambridge Companion to Petrarch* (Cambridge: Cambridge University Press, 2015), pp. 16–34; Simon Gilson, *Dante and Renaissance Florence* (Cambridge: Cambridge University Press, 2005).

the war, using one form of misery to fund another. Infantrymen recruited from the mountainous regions of the state recycled war money back to their rural communities.

The documents provide an especially close look at Florence's public labor force – and, above all, its army, a large part of that labor force – whose wages have never been studied, but behave differently from current plague models. Demographic contraction enabled workers to do more than one job – evidence that, along with careful consideration of their terms of employment, calls into question scholarly attempts to posit modern notions of occupation into the distant past. Meanwhile, the shortage of labor had profound and unexpected institutional and diplomatic consequences. Florence employed men of low rank, members of the so-called family (*famiglia*) of the priors – bell ringers, servants (*donzelli*), and cooks (whom Petrarch notes were traditionally considered the "most vile" of men) – on long-term embassies to the most important diplomatic destinations, including the papal court in Avignon, the Holy Roman Empire, and Hungary.[34] Thus, while the city projected itself, in Nicolai Rubinstein's famous formulation, as a "bastion of republicanism" in these years, it appears to have conducted vital foreign policy matters by means of personal retainers of the executives of the city in a manner similar to the tyrannies it condemned. Florentine bureaucratic structures were porous and personal, and, like medieval notions of occupation, difficult to apprehend in modern terms.

The war with the Ubaldini even affected the physical landscape of the city. Master builders (*capomaestri*) hired in 1349 to build the church of Sant'Anna in honor of plague victims were sent to the town of Scarperia in the Mugello in 1350 to oversee the building of trebuchets – machines of war – and the destruction of Ubaldini castles. The church project was halted on account of this, and indeed was never completed.[35]

II

Contemplation of the periphery, in short, alters our apprehension of the center, and close consideration of an all too pedestrian war connects literary and historical trends. This volume follows Teodolinda Barolini's eloquent plea to better "historicize" great literary figures, whose lives and material circumstances remain insufficiently

---

[34] Gene Brucker, "Bureaucracy and Social Welfare in the Renaissance," *Journal of Modern History* 55 (March 1983), p. 4; Petrarch, *Familiares* VIII, 4, vol. 1.
[35] Saverio La Sorsa, *La Compagnia d'or San Michele, ovvero una pagina della beneficenza in Toscana nel secolo XIV* (Trani: V. Vecchi, 1902), pp. 110–111, 240–250.

understood.[36] The need is particularly urgent with respect to Petrarch, one of the most steadfastly deceptive figures of the era, who, as Albert Ascoli and Unn Falkreid remind us, rendered the realities of his own life "effectively invisible" from modern view despite sharing his many emotions and "notions of the Renaissance self" embedded therein.[37]

It is important to emphasize the economic implications of the present study. The plague has been the subject of many works in this regard, most notably in terms of wages and prices, by both historians and economists. The portrait for the years 1349–1350 was settled long ago. James E. Thorold Rogers, in his pioneering studies of England, saw in these years the "fullest effect" of the plague, which produced "panic and compulsion" in markets, whose immediate consequence was "to double the wages of labour."[38] Similar conclusions have been reached by modern day economists including Robert C. Allen, Sevket Pamuk, and Gregory Clark, who take "the long view" and position their data in terms of European industrialization, using estimates of nominal and real wages and standards of living to gain greater understanding of the "great divergence" that separated the West and East economically.[39] The excellent,

---

[36] Teodolinda Barolini, "'Only Historicize': History, Material Culture (Food, Clothes, Books), and the Future of Dante Studies," *Dante Studies* 127 (2009), pp. 37–54. See also the recent critical guides to the work of Petrarch and Boccaccio, which seek to contextualize the poets. *Petrarch: A Critical Guide to the Complete Works*, edited by Victoria Kirkham and Armando Maggi (Chicago, IL: University of Chicago Press, 2009); *Boccaccio: A Critical Guide to the Complete Works*, edited Victoria Kirkham, Michael Sherberg, and Janet Levarie Smarr (Chicago, IL: University of Chicago Press, 2013). See most recently, Kristina M. Olson, *Courtesy Lost: Dante, Boccaccio and the Literature of History* (Toronto: University of Toronto Press, 2014).

[37] Albert Russell Ascoli and Unn Falkeid, "Introduction" in *Cambridge Companion to Petrarch* (Cambridge: Cambridge University Press, 2015), p. 1.

[38] James E. Thorold Rogers, *A History of Agriculture and Prices in England from the Year after the Oxford Parliament (1259) to the Commencement of the Continental War (1793)*, vol. 1 (Oxford: Clarendon Press, 1866), p. 265. Thorold Rogers says that in 1349 the "demand for labor was at its height" (p. 272). See also James Thorold Rogers, *Six Centuries of Work and Wages: The History of English Labour*, vol. 1 (London: Swan Sonnenschein and Co., 1894).

[39] Robert C. Allen, "The Great Divergence in European Wages and Prices from the Middle Ages to the First World War," *Explorations in Economic History* 38 (2001), pp. 411–447; Süleyman Özmucur and Sevket Pamuk, "Real Wages and Standards of Living in the Ottoman Empire, 1489–1914," *Journal of Economic History* 62 (2002), pp. 292–321; Sevket Pamuk, "The Black Death and the Origins of the 'Great Divergence' across Europe, 1300–1600," *European Review of Economic History* 11 (2007), pp. 289–317, in particular 292. See also in this regard, Jan L. Van Zanden, "Wages and the Standards of Living in Europe, 1500–1800," *European Review of Economic History* 2 (1991), pp. 75–95. Gregory Clark, *A Farewell to Alms* (Princeton, NJ: Princeton University Press, 2007), p. 102; Clark deals also with farm labor for England in "The Long March of History: Farm Wages, Population and Economic Growth, England 1209–1869" *Economic History Review* 60 (2007), pp. 97–135. Campbell compares building wages in Spain, Tuscany,

but more circumscribed studies of Florentinists such as Charles de La Roncière, Richard Goldthwaite, and Sergio Tognetti have outlined similarly steep rises in nominal and real wages and standards of living from 1349 to 1350 in the city. The years were ones of "fort dynamisme," according to La Roncière, characterized by "spectacular" rises in rates.[40] Goldthwaite pointed to the "sharp impact of the demand/supply mechanism" on the labor market at this time.[41]

The difficulty with the approaches to wage patterns is that they have typically involved the study of day wages from the building industry, judged the "most available" and most "usable" for comparison across time and space (Chapter 4). La Roncière pointed out that wage data of building workers from the Hospital of Santa Maria Nuova in Florence had many gaps, but he chose them for study instead of the Florentine wool cloth industry because they were "most suited" to modern apprehension. Christopher Dyer has spoken of "the inevitability" of using building crafts for England.[42] Pamuk saw craft wages as the basic means by which scholars could compare developments in Europe with those in the Ottoman Empire.[43] He pointed to the doubling of wages in the immediate aftermath of the plague as a key economic turning point.[44]

The data for such studies is taken from private institutions (Chapters 4 and 5; Epilogue) and is not only limited in sample size (far smaller than the data that exist for soldiers), but ringed with qualifications that are often lost in the quest for "big" and "relevant" conclusions. The methodology is deeply rooted in the historiography. It reflects the "second phase" *Annales* school interest in quantification as a means of "getting below the surface" of historical narratives and the concurrent Cliometric economic school that champions the "empirical" quality of

and England and adds data on farmers from Clark, showing divergent patterns but clear increases. Bruce Campbell, *The Great Transition*, pp. 311–312.

[40] Charles M. de La Roncière, "La condition des salariés à Florence au XIVe siècle" in *Tumulto dei Ciompi: un momento di storia fiorentina ed Europea*, edited by Atti del Convegno internazionale (Florence: Leo S. Olschki, 1981), pp. 19, 21–24.

[41] Richard Goldthwaite, *The Building of Renaissance Florence* (Baltimore, MD: Johns Hopkins University Press, 1980), pp. 335–338, 342–343. Goldthwaite notes that the standard of living for Florentine workers improved immediately after 1348 as "a dramatic fact in the social history of the city."

[42] La Roncière, "La condition des salariés à Florence au XIVe siècle," pp. 14, 17; Dyer, *Standards of Living*, p. 220.

[43] Pamuk, "The Black Death and the Origins of the 'Great Divergence' across Europe, 1300–1600," p. 292.

[44] Pamuk, "The Black Death and the Origins of the 'Great Divergence' across Europe, 1300–1600," pp. 289–317.

numbers and the utility of counterfactual questions.[45] The great *Annaliste* historian, Emmanuel Le Roy Ladurie, created in his essay "Motionless History" a bridge between the two schools, with his ringing affirmation of Cliometricians for their ability to use statistics to get at "uncomfortable truths" and to show "the way the world is turning."[46] "Statistics are not merely the sulky handmaidens of a concept," wrote Le Roy Ladurie. On the contrary, it is from the evidence of figures that the concept emerges."[47] The economic historian David Landes put the issue succinctly when, in his critique of Ernest Labrousse, a founding father of the statistical approach in the 1930s, he noted that "modern man is reassured by numbers, which possess a quality of precision that mere words cannot give." "Their mathematical character," he argued, "discourages criticism."[48]

But archives are subversive. They care little for modern economic theory and still less for notions of numerical empiricism. As Marc Bloch, a founder of the *Annales* school, asserted back in 1934, archives move scholarly research toward "le concret et particulier."[49] They often tell us precisely what we do not want to know and add variables that we do not anticipate.[50] This is the case with the present study, which reveals unexpected stagnation in wages and alternate movements for public employees for 1349–1350, in the face of "panic and compulsion in markets" and the heightened effects of supply and demand. The "sticky" wages include those of mercenary cavalrymen, a workforce, as Machiavelli famously noted, synonymous with greed for money. In general, Florence had diverse arrangements with its employees, whose pay was figured by day, month, semester (six months), or year. The patterns vary such that extrapolation from a single type of wage data is problematic. Like Thomas Kuhn's "normal science," current economic models are "eminently successful in their aims," but they do not

---

[45] On the *Annales* school, see Peter Burke, *The French Historical Revolution, 1929–2014* (Cambridge: Polity Press, 2015), pp. 87–132. Initial interest in quantification goes back to Simiand and Labrousse. See François Simiand, *Le salaire, l'évolution sociale et la monnaie*, 3 vols. (Paris: Felix Alcan, 1932) and Ernest Labrousse, *Esquisse du mouvement des prix et des revenus en France au XVIIIe siècle*, 2 vols. (Paris: Librairie Dalloz, 1933).

[46] Emmanuel Le Roy Ladurie, "Motionless History," *Social Science History* 1 no. 2 (Winter 1977), p. 135.

[47] Le Roy Ladurie, "Motionless History," pp. 120, 121.

[48] David S. Landes, "The Statistical Study of French Crises," *Journal of Economic History* 10 no. 2 (November 1950), p. 196.

[49] Marc Bloch, "Le salaire et les fluctuations économique à longue periode," *Revue Historique* 173 (January 1934), p. 2.

[50] Hatcher has argued for contemporary England that the "pursuit of internally consistent wages series" misses a basic reality that such endeavors are likely impossible (see Chapter 4). John Hatcher, "England in the Aftermath of the Black Death," *Past and Present* 144 (August 1994), pp. 12–19, 21–25.

account for contradictory data.[51] As Kuhn argued, "assimilating a new sort of fact demands a more than additive adjustment of theory."[52]

Numbers give the appearance of "empirical" surety, but they are in fact open to interpretation like texts. The quality of conclusions depends on the quality of the evidence. It is necessary to sift carefully through sources to understand more completely what occurred. As Joan Scott said in an entirely different context, historians "need to scrutinize their methods of analysis, clarify their operative assumptions," and replace the search for single origins by conceiving of "processes so interconnected that they cannot be disentangled."[53] "I do not think we should quit archives," she added, "and abandon study of the past, but we should change some of the ways we have gone about working some of our questions, replacing general causality with meaningful explanation."[54]

It is "meaningful explanation" that is sought here. The focus on two years and on an infra-state conflict is intentionally provocative and revisionist. This volume follows the micro-history credo, articulated by Giovanni Levi, that reduction of the scale of inquiry can reveal previously unobserved factors.[55] It makes no claim, however, to being micro-history proper as traditionally understood in the Anglophone academy. The study does not use legal sources to uncover and explore an intriguing character or event, or attempt to see "the world in a grain of sand."[56] The form of this work is, to paraphrase Thorold Rogers, "necessarily repulsive," owing to the need to relay "dry details" that "hold little charm for the general public."[57] But if the purpose of history is, as Jo Guldi and David Armitage argue in *The History Manifesto*, to answer big questions and provide "pragmatic counsel" to modern day readers and government policy makers, then it is all the more important that historians get their

[51] Thomas S. Kuhn, *The Structure of Scientific Revolutions* (Chicago, IL: University of Chicago Press, 1996, 3rd edn.), p. 52.

[52] Kuhn, *The Structure of Scientific Revolutions*, p. 53.

[53] Scott cites the work of the anthropologist Michelle Rosaldo. Joan Scott, "Gender as a Useful Category of Historical Analysis," *American Historical Review* 91 no. 5 (December 1986), p. 1067.

[54] Scott, "Gender as a Useful Category," pp. 1066–1067.

[55] Giovanni Levi, "On Microhistory" in *New Perspectives on Historical Writing*, edited by Peter Burke (Cambridge: Cambridge University Press, 1991), pp. 95–97; see Francesca Trivellato, "Is There a Future for Italian Microhistory in the Age of Global History?" *California Italian Studies* 2 no. 1 (2011) http://escholarship.org/uc/item/0z9 4n9hq (last accessed February 2017) and "Microstoria/Microhistoire/Microhistory," *French Politics, Culture & Society* 33 no. 1 (2015), pp. 122–134.

[56] This is the microhistorian paraphrase of William Blake's poem *Auguries of Innocence*. See Jill Lepore, "Historians Who Love Too Much: Reflections on Microhistory and Biography," *Journal of American History* 88 (June 2011), pp. 129–144.

[57] Thorold Rogers, *A History of Agriculture and Prices in England*, vol.1, p. vi.

facts straight.[58] Intellectual discoveries are, as the scientist and educator Abraham Flexner famously noted, not made by those in search of utility, but by those following their own intellectual curiosity, which often "lacks an obvious relevance."[59] And the greatest mistakes in the public arena have been made by those who take too facile a view of the past, derived from, as Marc Bloch warned years ago, "a-priori opinions pillaged from imperfect descriptions of the present."[60] The need to contextualize is manifest, and this invariably involves coming to terms with, or at least attempting to come to terms with, contradictory and problematic evidence as will be presented here.

Contextualizing the Black Death does not of course detract from its cataclysmic nature. But a life lived is different from a life viewed in historical perspective, just as an event experienced in real time differs from one examined at a distance of centuries. In apprehending the past, we invariably add order and structure that is, to be sure, the essence of the historical method. But the contention here is that the historian, like Clifford Geertz's ethnographer, needs to assay carefully the multiplicity of layers "superimposed or knotted into one another, which are at once strange, irregular and inexplicit."[61] Guldi and Armitage's call to replace "short-termism" with long-termism misses the mark. Short-termism is neither a "spectre" nor a "disease," as they call it, and its opposition to long-termism is artificial.[62] Indeed, the short-term assertions presented here are specifically intended to lay out a methodology for a longer-term study of institutional, economic, and literary trends in Florence.

A reinterpretation of the use of numbers is particularly needed for the city of Florence. Numbers have loomed large in studies. Jacob Burckhardt set the precedent already in the nineteenth century, when he described Florence as "the home of statistical science" and as a city with a "statistical view of things."[63] The Swiss historian cited Giovanni Villani's chronicle and his famous statistical breakdown of the city for

---

[58] Jo Guldi and David Armitage, *The History Manifesto* (Cambridge: Cambridge University Press, 2104), p. 19.

[59] Flexner, "The Usefulness of Useless Knowledge," pp. 544–553.

[60] Marc Bloch, "Le salaire et les fluctuations économique à longue period," *Revue Historique* 173 (January 1934), p. 30.

[61] According to Geertz, ethnography is like reading a manuscript – "foreign, faded, full of ellipses and incoherent." Clifford Geertz, "Thick Description: Toward an Interpretive Theory of Culture" in *The Interpretation of Cultures* (New York, NY: Basic Books, 1973), p. 7.

[62] See also the *American Historical Review* exchange on the *Manifesto*. Deborah Cohen and Peter Mandler, "The History Manifesto: A Critique," *American Historical Review* (April 2015), pp. 530–542.

[63] Jacob Burckhardt, *The Civilization of the Renaissance in Italy*, translated by S. G. C. Middlemore (New York, NY: Penguin, 1954), pp. 61, 63.

1338, which has since been adduced in countless studies. David Herlihy and Christiane Klapisch-Zuber (*Tuscans and Their Families*) used numbers taken from the famous Florentine *catasto* of 1427 to reconstruct social and economic life in the city and countryside in the early fifteenth century. La Roncière makes clear in the introduction to his study of salaries and prices (*Prix et salaries à Florence au XIVe siècle, 1280–1380*) that he took his inspiration from the *Annales* school.

The "statistical view" of Florence has been accompanied by the teleological impulse to position Florence in terms of modernity. Werner Sombart and Alfred Doren saw the precocious stirrings of economic modernity and notions of "capitalism" that went with it in the Florentine textile industry.[64] Fernand Braudel described Florence as the "forerunner of modernity" in his *Civilization and Capitalism*. He noted the precocious use of the word "capital" in the works of Giovanni Villani, Velluti, and Boccaccio – all key figures in this study.[65]

These tendencies remain in the literature, though stated less overtly. By contrast, the analysis in this volume follows Karl Polanyi's injunction that statistics, like the economies for which they serve as indicators, are embedded in a social culture specific to that place and time.[66] It adheres to Joseph Schumpeter's methodological statement in *History of Economic Analysis* that "nobody can hope to understand economic phenomena of any, including the present epoch, who has not an adequate command of historical facts." Schumpeter added, as if anticipating the work of medievalists, that Latin paleography "is one of the techniques of economic analysis."[67] Statistics are of "vital importance" to economic inquiry, but it is "impossible to understand statistical figures without understanding how they were compiled."[68] The implicit linkage between numbers and modernity deserves closer scrutiny.

---

[64] Werner Sombart, *Der Moderne Kapitalismus* (Leipzig: Verlag von Dunker und Homblott, 1920), p. 129; Alfred Doren, *Die Florentiner Wollentuchindustrie* (Stuttgart: Cotta, 1901), pp. 220–234, 259–256. See also Charles M. de La Roncière, *Prix et salaries à Florence au XIVe siecle, 1280–1380* (Rome: Palais Farnese, 1982), p. 258, and Richard Goldthwaite, *The Economic History of Renaissance Florence* (Baltimore, MD: Johns Hopkins University Press, 2009), p. xii.

[65] Fernand Braudel, *Civilization and Capitalism: The Wheels of Commerce*, translated by Sian Reynold, vol. 2 (New York, NY: Harper and Row, 1979), pp. 232–233.

[66] Karl Polanyi, *The Great Transformation* (Boston, MA: Beacon Press, 2nd paperback edn., 2001), p. 46.

[67] J. A. Schumpeter, *History of Economic Analysis* (Oxford: Oxford University Press, 1954), pp. 12–13.

[68] Schumpeter, *History of Economic Analysis*, p. 14; Hatcher points out the often substantial difference between written accounts and archival material for England. Hatcher, "England in the Aftermath of the Black Death," pp. 12–19, 21–25.

III

The plague and Petrarch's war may be contextualized still further. A careful reading of Matteo Villani's account of the contagion shows in fact that he devoted at least as much attention to the contemporary civil war between the rival Hungarian and French branches of the Angevin family in the kingdom of Naples. If the amount of space given to an event reflects its significance, then it must be noted that seven of the first twenty-five chapters of the first book of Villani's chronicle are about the plague, but eight chapters are about the Hungarians. The historian Gene Brucker found Florence's interest in the Hungarians "curious."[69]

But the civil war to the south had important implications for the city, which had economic interests in the region and stood in the path of armies and mercenary companies traveling to and from there. Matteo Villani specifically refers to his brother Giovanni's account of events in Naples, recapitulating for the reader the earlier description of a situation that had effectively not changed.[70] In this respect, Matteo's work, seen as contrasting sharply with Giovanni's, demonstrates a continuity between the writers and their depictions of pre- and post-plague events. The war in Naples was a constant. Giovanni Villani devoted thirteen of the last twenty-seven chapters of his chronicle to the war in 1347, by far the largest amount of space he affords any event.[71] Matteo even follows Giovanni in interrupting his narrative with a digression about the ongoing war in Muslim Tunis, which Giovanni describes as an example of the effects of "superbia, avarizia and lussuria" evident in Italy at the time[72] – traits that Matteo then applies to post-plague Florence.[73] There is, in short, a literary transmission between the works that stands apart from the cataclysmic "break" supposedly brought about by the plague. Moreover, Matteo does not connect the events in Naples with the plague. The contagion was not, as some scholars argue, the measure of all other contemporary difficulties.

This is particularly clear with respect to the earthquake that struck Italy in September 1349. Its epicenter was at l'Aquila, the site of a devastating

---

[69] Gene Brucker, *Florentine Politics and Society, 1343–1378* (Princeton, NJ, Princeton University Press, 1962), pp. 144–145.

[70] Matteo Villani, *Nuova Cronica*, p. 18.

[71] Giovanni Villani complained that civil war endangered the movement of grain to Florence from that region. Grain was already scarce. Giovanni Villani, *Nuova Cronica*, pp. 526–558.

[72] Giovanni Villani, *Nuova Cronica*, p. 518.

[73] Matteo Villani, *Nuova Cronica*, pp. 23–24; Giovanni Villani, *Nuova Cronica*, pp. 514–518.

modern *terremoto* on 6 April 2009 (and not far from the one at Amatrice in 2016).[74] It destroyed much of the famous Benedictine abbey of Montecassino, brought down towers in Rome, and fractured the buttresses erected for the nave of the proposed "super" cathedral in Siena.[75] The damage in fact stopped Siena's ambitious project, which is still attributed solely to the plague and the economic difficulties resulting from it.[76] Campbell has restated this view, calling the unfinished Sienese cathedral "Europe's most tangible monument to the human devastation wrought by the Black Death."[77] In actuality the earthquake exposed the faulty architectural principles that lay behind the structure, which is too large for the hill it is on.

The earthquake, like Petrarch's war, has been overshadowed by the Black Death, or, more precisely, understood only in terms of it. But contemporaries treated it as its own phenomenon. Petrarch spoke of the quake in *Familiares* XI 7, addressed to Ludwig van Kampen ("Socrates"), the same man to whom he wrote about the attack on his friends by the Ubaldini and the outbreak of the Black Death. Petrarch feared that by hitting so close to Rome, "the holy and eternal city," the earthquake announced the "destruction of peace and liberty" for that city and with it, all of Italy.[78] But he made no mention of the recent plague in the letter, and indeed placed the epistle in a wholly different part of his *Familiares* (book XI) than his description of the plague (book VIII). Matteo Villani, for his part, drew again directly – and incongruously – from his brother Giovanni when describing the earthquake that struck Friuli in Northern Italy and Bavaria in southern Germany in 1347/1348, just prior to the plague.[79] Writing of the disaster in Umbria, Matteo referred to the condition of the town of Villaco, "a fertile land near Slavonia," which Giovanni had described in 1347/1348 as completely destroyed by the quake, its fields rendered sterile and with cracks formed in the local piazza in the shape of a cross. Matteo tell his readers that Villaco was now

[74] A team of scientists has examined the evidence related to the earthquake. Paolo Galli and José Alfredo Naso, "Unmasking the 1349 Earthquake Source (Southern Italy): Paleoseismological and Archaeoseismological Indications from the Aquae Iuliae Fault," *Journal of Structural Geology* 31 (2009), pp. 128–149.

[75] Matteo Villani, *Nuova Cronica*, p. 70.

[76] Agnolo di Tura, "Cronaca senese" in *Rerum Italicarum Scriptores*, edited by Alessandro Lisini and Fabio Iacometti (Bologna: Nicola Zanichelli, 1931–1939), pp. 556–557.

[77] Bruce Campbell, *The Great Transition: Climate, Disease and Society in the Late Medieval World* (Cambridge: Cambridge University Press, 2016), pp. 310–311.

[78] Francesco Petrarch, *Letters on Familiar Matters*, translated by Aldo S. Bernardo (Baltimore, MD: Johns Hopkins University Press, 1982), vol. 2, pp. 99–101.

[79] Matteo Villani, *Nuova Cronica*, p. 54.

restored to its former beauty, going out of his way to connect his tale to that of his older brother.[80]

IV

The broader point and central aim of this book is to stress the importance of context, to acknowledge that the historical "edges" are important, and that there is a place for contradiction and anomaly in historical study. If the short term is, as Guldi and Armitage assert, a "disease" that invariably leads to irrelevance, then the long term is a technique that risks oversimplification and may in fact reify errors. If close documentary study risks "fetishizing" archives, then steadfast adherence to *Annales* methodology and other advocates of the long-term risks "fetishizing" our scholarly forebears, or a handful of them – a still greater sin.

The book has five chapters and an epilogue. The first chapter examines Petrarch's and Boccaccio's involvement with the war against the Ubaldini, their relationship to Florence, and the establishment of the new university there. It uses archival evidence to show the political activities of the men, and literary evidence to reveal how the conflict formed an important part of their friendship and dialogue, believed to have begun only after their physical meeting in October 1350. The chapter argues that the war was connected to Florence's (and Boccaccio's) desire to gain Petrarch's service for the new studio – a goal with strong economic motivations, and was perhaps the most egregious instance of faculty recruitment in western history (it did not work). The chapter gives close reading to Petrarch's letters in book VIII of his *Familiares*, the most reedited and reworked of the poet's epistolary, and to Boccaccio's invitation to Petrarch to join the university, his *Trattatello in laude di Dante* and *Epistle* 10. I argue that they form a dialogue that contains echoes and inversions of Dante, whose *Commedia* Petrarch purportedly did not yet possess (he would later receive a copy from Boccaccio).

The second chapter deals with the most unexplored aspect of Florentine history: the practice of war and the nature of the Florentine army. It examines the specifics of how Florence fought in the Apennine mountains, the interplay of communal institutions, the composition of the Florence force, and the employment of the wide range of "faceless" noncombatants, who helped sustain the army in the field. The chapter emphasizes the blurred lines between Florence's military and pacific spheres, and raises questions about the nature of the city's institutions,

---

[80] Giovanni Villani, *Nuova Cronica*, pp. 562–566.

which appear more porous, personal, and mobile than expected. Even the monks in charge of the *camera del arme*, the communal office that maintained the city's arsenal of weapons in the palace of the priors, traveled with the army in the field.

The third chapter looks closely at public finance and how Florence paid for the war. It assesses the impact of the conflict on the Florentine economy and the unexpected role of plague bequests from the confraternity of Orsanmichele in financing the war. It traces the effect of the conflict on merchants and the recycling of money back to the mountain communities from which many of the infantrymen came. The chapter also highlights the importance of the *dirittura* tax, a hitherto unstudied impost, that was used to convert communal expenditure (of which war was greatest) into the public good, by beautifying the cathedral and paying for the new university. The evidence gives insight into a Christian ethos that lay behind Florentine public finance, which involved monks in the role of chamberlain of important fiscal offices.

Chapter 4 examines the wages of soldiers and compares them with the wages of other Florentine public employees. The evidence does not correspond to current scholarly models, and the chapter attempts to explain the divergence, which necessarily involves reexamining the meaning of the term "mercenary," the most misunderstood of all medieval professions. It highlights the often glaring difference between "professional" wages and actual income, and the numerous Florentine workforces that behaved differently in response to the plague.

Chapter 5 deals more closely with the Florentine public workforce, exploring the details of currency and taxation, and factors such as skill, danger, and status that, beyond market forces, went into the configuration of rates. It connects the evidence of public workers to that of other Florentine workforces, notably the wool cloth industry. It argues for the variable nature of occupation during plague-era Florence and explores the implications of this for the political and institutional makeup of the city. The chapter stresses the inherent difficulty of transferring medieval notions of occupation to the present day and shows how the constricted work force encouraged Florence to use bell-ringers, cooks, and servants of the Signoria for long-term embassies to its most important and problematic allies.

A brief epilogue argues for the importance of short-term study in the face of current calls for a return to a *longue durée* approach. It asserts the necessity of closely examining our sources to "banish myths and overturn false laws" that Guldi and Armitage attribute to short-termism. It argues for the importance of undertaking historical study with an open mind and a willingness to avoid the urge to uncritically fit information into soothing preexisting models, even if the payoff for our scholarly careers is greater. Short- and long-term studies are not contradictory, but must necessarily coexist, a point that Fernand Braudel, whom Guldi and Armitage use as their models, would himself have agreed with.[81] To reinforce the point, the epilogue prospectively extends the wage data to ten years.

[81] Trivellato, "Is There a Future for Italian Microhistory in the Age of Global History?"

1   Petrarch's War

See, noble lord, from what trivial causes comes such cruel war the hearts that proud fierce Mars make hard and closed ... Song, I bid you to speak your message courteously ... You shall try your fortune among the magnanimous few ... I go crying peace, peace, peace.

Petrarch, *Italia mia* (1344)[1]

Consider what has happened ... A very pleasant and deservingly dear citizen of yours and friend of mine while returning from France to Florence, having gone through many annoyances and dangers ... practically on the very threshold of his own door and of your gates was cruelly killed, so to speak in your very bosom.

Petrarch, *Familiares*, VIII, 10 (1349)[2]

It was late in the day, and the light was already waning when, returning from my long exile, I was received within my native walls by you with respect and reverence far beyond my deserts.

Petrarch to Boccaccio, *Familiares*, XXI, 15 (1351)[3]

The plague of 1348 interfered with the basic functions of the Florentine state. Officials had difficulty distributing grain and collecting taxes.[4] But the contagion did not slow the impetus toward violence.[5] In 1349 the city council complained of unrest ("novelle") both inside and outside the city.[6] Civic struggle centered on the feud between the rival Albizzi and

---

[1] *Petrarch's Lyric Poems*, translated by Robert M. Durling (Cambridge, MA: Harvard University Press, 1976), pp. 256–263.

[2] Francesco Petrarch, *Rerum familiarum libri, I–VIII*, translated and edited by Aldo S. Bernardo, vol. 1 (Albany, NY: State University of New York Press, 1975), p. 429 (cited hereafter as Petrarch, *Familiares*).

[3] Francesco Petrarch, *Rerum familiarum libri, XVII–XXIV*, translated and edited by Aldo S. Bernardo, vol. 3 (Ithaca, NY: Italica Press, 2005, 2nd edn.), p. 207.

[4] ASF, Provvisioni, registri 36 fol. 20r (October 1348); A. B. Falsini, "Firenze dopo il 1348: Le consequenze della peste nera," *Archivio storico italiano* 129 (1971), pp. 438–439.

[5] Samuel K. Cohn, "After the Black Death: Labour Legislation and Attitudes towards Labour in Late-Medieval Western Europe," *Economic History Review* 60 no. 3 (2007), p. 467.

[6] In April 1349, ASF, Provvisioni, registri 36 fol. 81r. For July, Provvisioni, registri 36 fol. 132v; Provvisioni, registri 36 fol. 95v. Civil strife is noted in the legislation of May and June 1349. The city elected men to try "to make peace, truces and concords"

Ricci clans. External strife converged around the activities of magnate families in the countryside and at the boundaries of the Florentine state.[7] Lack of personnel to oversee roads, walls, and defend fortresses encouraged armed conflict.[8]

The most troublesome of the rural clans was the Ubaldini of the upper Mugello. Their patrimony lay above the towns of Borgo San Lorenzo and Scarperia, along Florence's northern boundary with Bologna, from the Sieve river to the high valley of the Santerno river.[9] The Ubaldini ruled the region, known as the "Alpes Ubaldinorum (Alpi Ubaldini)," since Ottonian times and claimed independent status by means of imperial diploma from Emperor Frederick II Hohenstaufen.[10] They were Ghibellines and remained so when Florence had become a Guelf city. The clan sustained itself on feudal dues, taxes on pastures and woods, tolls (*pedaggi*) on the roads, and, on occasion, by robbery of merchants and travelers who passed by.[11] The importance of the Ubaldini derived primarily from the fact that their lands lay on key trade routes to Bologna and the Romagna.[12] The roads were used to transport grain to Florence

---

("circa paces, treguas et concordias") in June. ASF, Provvisioni, registri 36 fols. 95v, 105v. On the Ricci-Albizzi feud in the city, see Gene Brucker, *Florentine Politics and Society, 1343–1378* (Princeton, NJ: Princeton University Press, 1962), pp. 124–129.

[7] On Florence's relations with magnate families, see Christiane Klapisch-Zuber, *Ritorno alla politica: I magnati fiorentini, 1340–1440* (Rome: Viella, 2007).

[8] ASF, Provvisioni, registri 36 fol. 10r, Falsini, "Firenze dopo il 1348," p. 438; on 16 January 1349 the city council cited a lack of infantry and stipendiaries to defend forts "on account of the plague." Provvisioni, registri 36 fol. 47r.

[9] Laura Magna, "Gli Ubaldini del Mugello: una signoria feudale nel contado fiorentino" in *I ceti dirigenti dell'età comunale nei secoli XII e XIII* (Pisa: Pacini, 1982), pp. 13–16, 18–22; Daniele Sterpos, *Comunicazioni stradali attraverso i tempi: Bologna-Firenze* (Novara: De Agostini, 1961), pp. 28–29, and "Evoluzione delle comunicazioni transappenniniche attraverso tre passi del Mugello," in *Percorsi e valichi dell'Appenino fra storia e leggenda* (Florence: Arti Grafiche Giorgi e Gambi, 1985). G. C. Romby, ed., *Una terra nuova nel Mugello: Scarperia: popolazione, insediamenti, ambiente, XIV-XVI secolo* (Scarperia: Comune di Scarperia, 1985); N. Galassi, *Dieci secoli di storia ospitaliera a Imola*, 2 vols. (Imola: Galeati, 1966–1970); *Commissioni di Rinaldo degli Albizzi per il comune di Firenze (1339–1433)*, edited by Cesare Guasti (Florence: Tipi di M. Cellini, 1867–1873), vol. 1, pp. 13–14; Paolo Pirillo, "Tra Signori e città: I castelli dell'Appennino alla fine del Medio Evo" in *Castelli dell'Appennino nel medioevo*, edited by P. Fosci, E. Penoncini, and R. Zagnoni (Pistoia: Società Pistoiese, 2000), pp. 15–29. The Ubaldini family ranked relatively low in terms of financial potency with respect to other magnate families according to Klapisch-Zuber, who uses the *estimo* of 1352; see Klapisch-Zuber, *Ritorno alla politica*, p. 88.

[10] David Friedman, *Florentine New Towns: Urban Design in the Late Middle Ages* (Cambridge, MA: Harvard University Press, 1989), pp. 39–46; Magna, "Gli Ubaldini del Mugello," p. 27.

[11] Magna, "Gli Ubaldini del Mugello," p. 32.

[12] John Larner, "Crossing the Romagnol Appennines in the Renaissance" in *City and Countryside in Late Medieval and Renaissance Italy: Essays Presented to Philip Jones*, edited by Trevor Dean and Chris Wickham (London: Bloomsbury, 1990), pp. 147–170.

and grew in significance in the late thirteenth and fourteenth centuries as Florence expanded.[13] They were critical during the famous wars later in the century between Milan and Florence (1390–1392, 1402). Milan tried to cut off Florence's access to these roads as a means of "starving out" the city.

Florence devoted a great deal of effort to defending the routes. In the early fourteenth century, the city constructed so-called new towns, a species of conscious urban planning for defense, which, according to David Friedman, reveals much about the city's architectural self-perception.[14] The "new" towns included Scarperia, a former Etruscan colony (25 kilometers from Florence), built astride the mountain passes through the Apennines along the ancient Roman Faentina road. The town, completed in 1306, was expressly intended to divert traffic from the previous route, which ran directly through the heart of Ubaldini lands and the family headquarters at Monteaccianico, the formidable castle made famous by Dante's resistance there, alongside the White Guelfs, against the city shortly after his exile. In 1332, Florence built the town of Firenzuola directly across the Apennines from Scarperia, beyond the Giogo pass, to further facilitate the safe passage of goods to and from Bologna.[15] Firenzuola was laid out on a Florence–Bologna axis. Its main street is oriented toward the two cities, with the *porta* Fiorentina in the south pointing to Florence and the *porta* Bologna in the north directed toward Bologna.

Petrarch's War

The spring of 1349 was an opportune moment for the Ubaldini to strike. In March, Florentine officials cited their inability to find castellans to protect forts in the countryside, and in April officials complained that they had no money with which to pay infantry and cavalrymen, who had "not been paid in many months."[16]

The deliberations of city executives in *consulte e practiche* records make clear that in April the Ubaldini began causing trouble. Donato Velluti, a member of the executive councils and author of the famous diary the *cronica domestica*, spoke out against the "inurias violentias et robbarias" committed by the clan against Florentine citizens.[17] He called for the city

---

[13] Giovanni Villani underlined the importance of grain trade through the Romagna just prior to the plague. Giovanni Villani, *Nuova Cronica*, edited by Giuseppe Porta, vol. 2 (Parma: Fondazione Pietro Bembo, 1991, 1995), p. 558.

[14] Friedman, *Florentine New Towns*, p. 41.

[15] Magna, "Gli Ubaldini del Mugello," pp. 32, 52–53.

[16] ASF, Provvisioni, registri 36 fol. 81r.

[17] ASF, Consulte e Pratiche (CP) 1 fol. 1r (18 April 1349). The problems with the Ubaldini are also mentioned in Provvisioni, registri 36 fol. 82r (24 April).

to move "manfully" against the clan.[18] The chronicler Matteo Villani caustically recounted how the Ubaldini "robbed and killed travelers first during the day," and then, "to make amends," by night.[19] Marchionne di Coppo Stefani confirmed Villani's assessment. He highlighted the economic aspect of Ubaldini misdeeds, noting that Ubaldini attacks on merchants led to reprisals against Florentine merchants abroad, "in France, Lombardy and Germany."[20]

The criminal activities had a profound effect on Francesco Petrarch, who was in Italy at the time, having traveled there just after the onset of plague in 1348. On the very same day that Velluti first spoke out against the Ubaldini (24 April), Petrarch received a lucrative benefice in Padua that helped secure his residency in the peninsula.[21] In May, Petrarch anticipated the arrival from Avignon of two close friends: Mainardo Accursio, whom he called Simplicianus, and Luca Cristiani, whom he called Olimpius. The three men had gone to the university at Bologna together and had enjoyed the patronage of the Cardinal of Colonna at the papal court. Petrarch hoped, in the face of the plague and the death of so many of his friends, to live together with the men and another close friend, Ludwig van Kempen, a Flemish chanter, whom Petrarch called Socrates.

The plan was ruined by Ubaldini aggression. Mainardo and Luca were attacked as they traveled from Avignon through Ubaldini territory in the Apennines. The two were robbed and beaten. Mainardo died of his wounds. Luca, who came to Mainardo's defense, withstood the blows of numerous attackers and proceeded unsteadily forward.[22]

The incident may be taken as a typical instance of Ubaldini brigandage, of which there are many examples. But the brazen act shocked Petrarch. He recorded Mainardo's death in his copy of Virgil, now in the Ambrosiana library, the same manuscript in which he noted the death of his beloved Laura a year earlier (April 1348) from the plague.[23] Petrarch recounted the attack on his friends in detail in letter 9 of book

---

[18] ASF, CP 1 fol. 4r; *La cronica domestica di Messer Donato Velluti*, edited by Isidoro del Lungo and Guglielmo Volpi (Florence: G. C. Sansoni, 1914).

[19] Matteo Villani, *Nuova Cronica*, edited by Giuseppe Porta, vol. 1 (Parma: Fondazione Pietro Bembo, 1995), pp. 48–49.

[20] Marchionne di Coppo Stefani, *Cronaca Fiorentina*, edited by N. Rodolico. In *Rerum Italicarum scriptores: Raccolta di Storici Italiani dal cinquecento al millecinquecento*, edited by L. A. Muratori, tomo XXX (Città di Castello: S. Lapi, 1910), p. 234.

[21] Ernest H. Wilkins, *The Life of Petrarch* (Chicago, IL: University of Chicago Press, 1961), pp. 82–84.

[22] Petrarch, *Familiares* VIII, 9, vol. 1, pp. 412, 425; Ernest H. Wilkins "Petrarch's Last Return to Provence," *Speculum* 39, no. 1 (January 1964), p. 78. Also on Petrarch's life, see Aldo Foresti, *Annedoti della vita di Francesco Petrarca* (Padua: Antenore, 1977, originally published in 1928).

[23] Wilkins, *The Life of Petrarch*, p. 96.

VIII of his *Familiares* [*Rerum familiarum libri*], addressed to Kempen (Socrates), to whom he dedicated the entire epistolary collection:[24] "We were four persons with a single mind[,]" but "we appeared too happy ... Most cruel fortune envied us and because she had not yet cast down all the victims of the world's tragedy, she was indignant."[25]

The hope for shared friendship and a joint life together constitute the central theme of book VIII of the *Familiares*, which also includes Petrarch's famous letter recounting the Black Death. Seven of the ten letters relate to the theme: four are addressed directly to Luca Cristiani, two to Socrates (Kempen), and one to the city of Florence.[26] Petrarch tells of the intended meeting of the men: how his friends had crossed the Alps from Avignon, "suffering all the hardships of the roads," and had stopped at Parma to see Petrarch only to find that he was not there. They searched the house and the garden, spent the night, and left a letter. They then proceeded on their fateful journey through the Apennines into the Florentine Mugello region. Accursio intended to go to Florence; Cristiani to Rome. Petrarch blamed his absence from Parma – from which he had not strayed for more than a year – for their unfortunate choice of route and their demise. The detour caused Accursio and Cristiani to alter their itinerary and proceed through Ubaldini lands, to the "straight road to destruction," as Petrarch called it, in the "summits of the Apennines."[27]

The letters convey a palpable sense of dramatic tension. In the epistles to Cristiani (*Familiares*, VIII, 2–5, dated 5 May to 19 May), Petrarch meditates on the details of their future life together. He weighs carefully where to stay, judging Parma the best place owing to its access to Bologna (where the men had been students) and to other "worthy places," including Venice, the Treviso, Milan and Genoa, and Padua. Petrarch assesses (letter 3) the relative merits of his secluded life in southern France at Vaucluse on the banks of river Sorgue, with its peaceful mountains and woods, with those of Italy, with its "open valleys and spectacular springs," the "talents and customs of the people," and "attractive and flourishing cities." Petrarch says immodestly that Vaucluse was known "as much for my name as for its extraordinary springs."[28] In *Familiares* VIII, 4, the

---

[24] Kempen was in Provence. The news of the death of Mainardo reached Petrarch on 26 May 1349. Giuseppe Billanovich, *Petrarca Letterato: Lo scrittoio del Petrarca* (Rome: Edizioni di Storia e letteratura, 1947), pp. 92–93.

[25] Petrarch, *Familiares* VIII, 9, vol. 1, pp. 422–423.

[26] Petrarch, *Familiares* VIII, 1–10, vol. 1, pp. 396–412; Vittorio Rossi, *Le familiari*, 4 vols. (Florence: G. C. Sansoni, 1933–1942).

[27] Petrarch *Familiares* VIII, 9, vol. 1, pp. 423–424.

[28] Petrarch, *Familiares* VIII, 3, vol. 1, pp. 399–400. *Familiares* VIII, 5, vol. 1 is briefer than letter 3 (letter 5 is four pages in Bernardo, pp. 409–412). It again expresses the desire to live together.

longest letter to Cristiani, Petrarch reflects on broader issues of friendship and life: "We must seize happiness forthwith . . . When we have assembled in a single place: what is there to prevent us from enjoying our future?"[29]

Literary critic Gur Zak has stressed how Petrarch used the story of his friends as an "exemplum about the dangers of worldly attachments."[30] Giuseppe Mazzotta has pointed out Petrarch's "politics of the self" and the multiple moral strands embedded in the letters, including Petrarch's consideration of the importance of place.[31] Hans Baron has interpreted the letters as a precocious moment in the evolution of Petrarch's overall thought, in which Petrarch shows his first interest in the "active" rather than solitary life, a transformation that would occur later in Petrarch's career with fateful consequences for the history of humanism.[32]

But book VIII of *Familiares* also reveals Petrarch's bellicose side. To letter 9 to Kempen outlining the crime against his friends, Petrarch attached a copy of another epistle, dated 2 June, that he sent to the priors in Florentine.[33] In it, Petrarch demands that the city seek retribution from the Ubaldini for the attack. Petrarch condemns the clan in the strongest terms as "a bunch of gallows birds, murderers and cavemen."[34] "What will posterity think that a harmless man, who, as Lucan says, did manage to travel safely among the untamed people on the shores of the Rhone river, and though the deserts of the province of Arles . . . was struck down in full daylight in Florentine territory?"[35] Petrarch describes Mainardo Accursio as "sacred," "similar to God," and "a sheep destined for ungodly sacrifice." He exhorts the Florentines to purge the Apennines of the criminals, to wage war against the Ubaldini. His rhetoric is aggressive. Petrarch wants to "punish" the Ubaldini. Failure to do so, he wrote,

---

[29] The letter is seven pages long (in Bernardo) and has no date. Petrarch, *Familiares* VIII, 4, vol. 1, pp. 401–408.

[30] Gur Zak, *Petrarch's Humanism and the Care of the Self* (Cambridge: Cambridge University Press, 2010), pp. 102–104.

[31] Giuseppe Mazzotta, *The Worlds of Petrarch* (Durham, NC: Duke University Press, 1993), p. 90.

[32] Hans Baron, "Franciscan Poverty and Civic Wealth in the Shaping of 'Trecento' Thought: The Role of Petrarch," in *In Search of Civic Humanism*, vol. 1 (Princeton, NJ: Princeton University Press, 1988), p. 172, and "The Evolution of Petrarch's Thought: Reflections on the State of Petrarch Studies," in *From Petrarch to Leonardo Bruni in Studies in Humanistic and Political Literature* (Chicago, IL: University of Chicago Press, 1968), pp. 7–50; Craig Kallendorf, "The Historical Petrarch," *American Historical Review*, 101 no. 1 (February 1996), pp. 130–141.

[33] Petrarch, *Familiares* VIII, 10, vol. 1, pp. 429–435; on the confirmation of the date of the letter, see Roberta Antognini, *Il progetto autobiografico delle Familiares di Petrarca* (Milan: Edizioni Universitarie di lettere economica diritto, 2008), p. 331.

[34] Petrarch, *Familiares* VIII, 10, vol. 1, p. 433.

[35] Petrarch, *Familiares* VIII, 10, vol. 1, p. 431.

"will destroy the foundation from which you [Florence] have sprung high as the stars" and leave the city with the stain of "eternal infamy."[36]

Petrarch's stance is noteworthy for the poet, who, when confronted by violence in his previous sojourn in Italy in 1344, wrote the famous patriotic poem "Italia mia." Petrarch condemned warfare as cruel ("crudel guerra," line 11) and made a threefold call for peace ("pace, pace, pace," line 122) throughout the peninsula.[37] In book XI, letter 8 of *Familiares*, written only a year after the attack on his friends, Petrarch strongly denounces the war between Genoa and Venice (1350).[38] He demands that Andrea Dandolo, the young doge of Venice, refrain from battle and admonishes him for displaying the sins of youth: "Gentleness befits men while wrath befits beasts."[39] Petrarch adds that he saw himself as "an emissary of peace," whose "sole weapon" was his pen.[40]

Petrarch's contradictory attitude may be taken as evidence of his variable nature, a trait noted by the poet himself in his dedicatory letter to *Familiares* addressed to Kempen. Petrarch wrote that he "seemed to be in constant contradiction" throughout the work.[41] Mazzotta has observed a basic analogue between Petrarch's rhetoric and warfare. He argued that Petrarch conceived of himself as a lonely, beleaguered hero in a "war" waged on many fronts.[42] War served as a metaphor for life. Indeed, in the first letter of book VIII, written to a military man, Stefano Colonna the elder, patriarch of an influential Roman family of church dignitaries, Petrarch equates war with the life cycle of man: "Man's life on earth is not only like military service, but like actual warfare."[43] He cites Colonna's concern with accusations that he was involved in more battles than he "ought to have been" and defends his legacy on the grounds that he undertook wars for the "love of peace."[44]

Nevertheless, Petrarch's statements elsewhere in *Familiares* render his call for war against the Ubaldini surprising. The letters to the Genoese and Venetians specifically condemned war as ruinous to the peninsula

---

[36] Petrarch, *Familiares* VIII, 10, vol. 1, p. 433.   [37] *Petrarch's Lyric Poems*, pp. 256–263.

[38] This was the so-called third Genoese-Venetian War, August 1350. On the war, see Frederic C Lane, *Venice: A Maritime Republic* (Baltimore, MD: Johns Hopkins Press, 1973), pp. 175–176; Mario Brunetti, "La Battaglia di Castro, 1350," *Rivista marittima* 43 (1910), 269–282, and "Contributo alla storia delle relazioni veneto-genovesi 1348–50," *Miscellanea di storia veneta*, 3rd series IX (Venice: Viella, 1916).

[39] Petrarch, *Familiares* XI, 8, edited and trans. by Aldo S. Bernardo, vol. 2 (Baltimore, MD: Johns Hopkins University Press, 1982), p. 108.

[40] Petrarch, *Familiares* XI, 8, vol. 2, pp. 14, 15, 105.

[41] Petrarch, *Familiares* I, 1, vol. 2, p. 9.

[42] Giuseppe Mazzotta, "Petrarch's Epistolary Epic: The Letters on Familiar Matters" in *Petrarch: A Critical Guide to the Complete Works*, edited by Victoria Kirkham and Armando Maggi (Chicago, IL: University of Chicago Press, 2009), p. 312.

[43] Petrarch, *Familiares* I, vol. 2, pp. 8–9.   [44] Petrarch, *Familiares* I, vol. 1, p. 9.

and urged the two states to fight external foes, such as Byzantium and Islam. Moreover, Petrarch's letter urging action against the Ubaldini is singularly emotional and aggressive. Petrarch himself appears to have been startled by the tone. He admits that "inflaming Florence to bloody revenge" does not befit "his profession or station." He excuses himself on the grounds that his bellicosity reflects the degree of his grief.[45]

Most important for our purposes, however, Florentine officials responded to Petrarch's plea. Several days after receiving his letter, the Florentine *camera del comune*, the premier fiscal organ of the state, appropriated money for the "army *newly* sent against the Ubaldini" (italics are mine).[46] The city sent numerous ambassadors to the region. Within a week, Florence's twenty-five envoys were in the Mugello and Romagna, near where the crime occurred.[47]

Petrarch's letter clearly fell on receptive ears and stirred the city to action. It reinvigorated the military effort against the clan, in effect turning what appears to have a very limited action into a more thorough going one.[48] In July 1349, officials passed formal legislation condemning the Ubaldini as "outlaws." The decree made their lands and possessions subject to confiscation, including all movable and immovable goods ("beni mobile et immobili").[49] The city offered the cancellation of debts and ten years' freedom from taxation to subjects of the Ubaldini who abjured their loyalty to the family and settled in Florentine lands. Florence forbade its own citizens (under penalty of 500 florins) to give aid or assistance to the clan. It offered 1,000 florins for the capture and 500 florins for the murder of any member, "leggitimo o naturale," of the Ubaldini. In addition, no one from Florence, its *contado* or *distretto*, was allowed to contract "parentado o affinita" with a man or woman descended directly from the male line of the Ubaldini clan or anyone living in Ubaldini lands. Florence appointed a committee of eight good men, popolari and Guelfs ("buoni uomini, popolari e Guelfi") to oversee the reappropriation of Ubaldini wealth and that of the inhabitants of their lands.[50]

---

[45] Petrarch, *Familiares* VIII, 10, vol. 1, p. 434.

[46] "esercito *nuovamente* mandato contro i Ubaldini." ASF, Camera del comune, Scrivano di camera uscita 6 fol. 4v; ASF, Camera del comune, Scrivano di camera entrata, 8 fols. 50r–50v.

[47] ASF, Camera del comune, Camarlenghi di uscita 56 fol. 548r; Scrivano di camera uscita 7 fol. 3v.

[48] Petrarch, *Familiares* VIII, 10, vol. 1, p. 435, also hints at an initial partial action: "Go quickly, go happily back to what you began, and with the assistance of heaven destroy the foul hiding places of the criminals"; Rossi, *Le familiari*, p. 193, lines 33–35.

[49] *I Capitoli del Comune di Firenze, inventario e regesto*, edited by C. Guasti and A. Gherardi, vol. 1 (Florence: Cellini, 1866–1893), pp. 88–89; ASF, Provvisioni, registri 36 fol. 151r.

[50] ASF, Provvisioni, registri 36 fols. 141r–141v.

The chronicler Matteo Villani reinforced the direct connection between the war and Petrarch. He gave a pointed and unusually specific rendering of the *casus belli*: "Returning from Avignon with 2000 florins, a Maghinardo [that is, Mainardo Accursio] of Florence was followed and killed by the Ubaldini, who robbed him in the Florentine contado. And not wishing to make amends to the request of the commune, the Florentines sent to the Alps their soldiers on foot and on horseback."[51]

Villani reported a brief and successful offensive. The Florentine army proceeded "senza contrasto" against the Ubaldini and inflicted a "battitura" on them, returning home triumphantly a few days later.[52] The documents show, however, that the fighting continued until December 1349, when the sides made an uncertain truce.[53] Indeed, Villani himself conceded that the Ubaldini persisted in their violent deeds ("latrocinia superba"). The chronicler Stefani wrote that having first robbed "gli strani" (foreigners), Ubaldini now made amends by robbing "sottoposti" (i.e., locals).

The second campaign followed necessarily from the first. The act condemning the Ubaldini in July 1349 called for the city to make war on the clan every year from January to June until the family was "exterminated." The plan was suggested by Donato Velluti in the meetings of the priors.[54] Florentine officials abided Velluti's advice. In late January 1350 (new style), Florence dutifully enacted a *balia*, a committee consisting of eight men, to manage the renewed effort against the continued "superbia et temeritate" of the clan. The city also issued anew the legislation condemning the Ubaldini.[55]

The second campaign was broader in scope than the first. The war against the Ubaldini was now caught up in a broader crisis in the Romagna, where revolt against the authority of the papacy was spreading. By the winter of 1349–1350, much of the Romagna was in open rebellion from the Church.[56] Florence sent Velluti, the forceful advocate for the war, on embassy to Bologna in March 1350 to seek Bologna's help against the Ubaldini.[57] Pressed by military exigencies of their own, the Bolognese refused to grant assistance.

---

[51] Villani, *Nuova Cronica*, p. 40. An ambassadorial letter (June 1350) shows that "Maghinardo" was a variant of "Mainardo." Demetrio Marzi, *La Cancelleria della Repubblica Fiorentina* (Rocca San Casciano: Cappelli, 1909), p. 681.

[52] Villani, *Nuova Cronica*, p. 40.

[53] ASF, CP 1 fols. 9r–9v; Signori, Missive I Cancelleria 10 #111.   [54] ASF, CP 1 fol. 3r.

[55] ASF, Provvisioni, registri 37 fol. 81r.

[56] Albano Sorbelli, *La Signoria di Giovanni Visconti a Bologna e le sue relazioni con la Toscana* (Bologna: Forni, 1902), p. 4.

[57] *La cronica domestica di Messer Donato Velluti*, pp. 193–196.

The war nevertheless went well for Florence. The army captured key Ubaldini castles in the high mountains along the Santerno and the Senio rivers. The city was unable, however, to take the family headquarters at Susinana. By 28 September, the last date recorded in the *balìa* records, the war with the Ubaldini was over. The violence and armed aggression in the Romagna nevertheless continued. In October, the Pepoli brothers, rulers of Bologna, sold the city to Milan, igniting a still larger conflict. Florence and the Church now opposed Milan. The Ubaldini joined Milan against Florence.

Petrarch's War, Boccaccio, and the University

Petrarch may have called for the war, but why would Florentine officials listen to the poet? Petrarch was a famous and powerful man, but he had little to do with Florence since the exile of his father when Petrarch was a boy. In a metrical letter ("Dulce iter") sent to a Florentine friend, Zanobi della Strada, in 1348, Petrarch complained bitterly that he was welcome everywhere, except in Florence.[58]

Florence's interests nevertheless coincided closely with those of Petrarch. Ubaldini misdeeds were already, as the *consulte e pratiche* records show, the subject of extensive discussions among the Florentine priors, who were so preoccupied by them that they failed to mention the plague or any other contemporary event. In addition, Petrarch had ties within the city. He had corresponded with several local admirers, including two relatives: Giovanni dell'Incisa and Franceschino degli Albizzi. The latter had stayed with Petrarch in France just before the poet had set out for Italy and was a casualty of the plague in 1348.[59] There was, according to Ernest Wilkins, expectation among Petrarch's friends that when he returned to Italy, he would go to Florence.[60] In *Familiares* VII, 10, dated 7 April 1348 and addressed to Incisa, Petrarch says that he had

---

[58] *Francisci Petrarchae Poemata minora quae extant Omnia*, or *Poesia minori del Petrarca*, edited by D. Rossetti (Milan: Societas Tipografica, 1831–4), vol. 3 (letter III, 9 to Zanobi), pp. 72–73. See also Ernest H. Wilkins, *The "epistolae metricae" of Petrarch* (Rome: Edizioni di Storia e Letteratura, 1956).

[59] Petrarch wrote three letters (*Familiares* VII, 10–12, vol. 1) to Incisa and one (undated) to Bruno Casini (*Familiares* VII, 14, vol. 1). Petrarch, *Familiares*, vol. 1, pp. 356–366, 373–374. *Familiares* VII, 10, vol. 1 was a response to a letter written to Petrarch by Incisa on 24 March 1348. Petrarch also received *epistolae metricae* from Casini and Zanobi da Stada. See Ugo Dotti, *Vita di Petrarca* (Bari: Laterza, 1987), pp. 194–202, 222; Daniele Piccini, "Franceschino degli Albizzi, uno e due," *Studi petrarcheschi*, 15 (2002) in *La rassegna della Letteratura Italiana* 108 (2004), n. 1, p. 150.

[60] Wilkins, *Life of Petrarch*, pp. 74–76; Billanovich, *Petrarca Letterato*, p. 98; On book VII, see Antognini, *Il progetto autobiografico delle Familiares*, pp. 159–167. Wilkins, *The "epistolae metricae" of Petrarch*, pp. 9–17; Dotti, *Vita*, p. 134.

considered crossing the "Alps of Bologna" and presenting himself in Florence, but cited ongoing legal disputes there. He apologized for disappointing "the expectations and desires of many people who were awaiting me."[61]

The leading role among Petrarch's friends in Florence was, however, taken by Giovanni Boccaccio. Boccaccio was in the city writing the *Decameron*. He had not yet met Petrarch, but he had admired him since his days in Naples and had written an early biography of Petrarch (1342–1343).[62] Giuseppe Billanovich has called Boccaccio "il discepolo più grande" of Petrarch and asserts that Boccaccio had "acquired the faith of the executives of the city" and was receiving his first governmental posts after returning to the city from Forlì (1346–1347), where he stayed briefly at the court of the local lord Francesco Ordelaffi.[63] Vittore Branca has stressed Boccaccio's involvement in foreign affairs, in the Romagna and in Naples, where Boccaccio had previously lived and which he knew well.[64]

In his public capacity, Boccaccio intervened directly in favor of Petrarch. He obtained a copy of Petrarch's letter (*Familiares* VIII, 10) demanding war against the Ubaldini from the Florentine chancellery and transcribed it.[65] The transcription of Petrarch's letter turned Boccaccio, in Ugo Dotti's words, from a "simple admirer" of Petrarch to "l'animatore" of Petrarch's Florentine advocates.[66] Boccaccio wrote a *carme* to Petrarch in response, his first correspondence with the poet, which is now lost.[67] Branca claims that Boccaccio himself had befriended Mainardo Accursio, the victim of Ubaldini aggression, when Boccaccio had been in Florence in 1341–1342.[68] This may have added extra motivation.

---

[61] Petrarch, *Familiares* VII, 10, vol. 1, p. 357.

[62] A discussion of the nature of the correspondence between Boccaccio and Petrarch, and the dating of the letters is in Gabriella Albanese, "La corrispondenza fra Petrarca e Boccaccio" in *Motivi e forme delle 'Familiari' di Francesco Petrarca*, edited by Claudia Berra (Milan: Cisalpino, 2003), pp. 39–99.

[63] "aquistato la fiduccia dei maggiorenti di Firenze." Billanovich, *Petrarca Letterato*, p. 92; Vittore Branca, *Giovanni Boccaccio: profilo biografico* (Florence: Sansoni, 1997), pp. 82–91. Kristina Olson notes how Boccaccio cultivated his interest in Dante at the court of Francesco Ordelaffi. Kristina M. Olson, *Courtesy Lost: Dante, Boccaccio and the Literature of History* (Toronto: University of Toronto Press, 2014), p. 19.

[64] Branca, *Profilo*, p. 83.

[65] According to Billanovich, Boccaccio also transcribed Petrarch's letter to Cristiani that outlined the plan for a life together with his friends. Billanovich, *Petrarca Letterato*, pp. 91–92.

[66] Dotti, *Vita*, p. 222.   [67] Dotti, *Vita*, p. 221; Wilkins, *Life of Petrarch*, p. 93.

[68] Branca, *Profilo*, pp. 64, 67; Roberto Mercuri, "Genesi della tradizione letteraria italiana in Dante, Petrarca e Boccaccio." In *Letteratura italiana. Storia e geografia*. Vol 1: *L'Età medievale*, edited by Roberto Antonelli, Angelo Cicchetti, and Giorgio Inglese (Turin: Einaudi, 1987), pp. 229–455.

In any case, Boccaccio advocated war and, with it, Petrarch's return to his native Florence. Boccaccio's efforts were linked to the establishment of Florence's university and the hope that Petrarch would take up a professorship there. City officials first sought to establish the university ("studio") in August 1348. The pope approved the plan on 31 May 1349, days before Petrarch sent his letter *Familiares* VIII, 10 to the city.[69] Florence hoped both to improve the quality of human capital in the aftermath of the plague and to attract students and their money to the city.[70] The first appropriation of revenue for the university (to pay professors' salaries) was made on the same day as the first allotment of money for the war against the Ubaldini.[71]

Boccaccio spearheaded the effort to persuade Petrarch to accept a professorship at the studio. According to Ugo Dotti, Boccaccio moved immediately after the pope conceded to Florence the right to a university in order to convince Petrarch.[72] The formal invitation to Petrarch did not, however, arrive until 1351, delayed most likely by the war itself, which ultimately siphoned money away from the university (Chapter 3). Boccaccio himself is believed to have written the invitation ("Movit iam diu," March 1351), which he delivered personally to Petrarch in the spring of 1351.[73] It contains high praise for Petrarch, urging him to cease his wanderings and return to his native town. Boccaccio made clear that the success of the Florentine studio would be assured by Petrarch's participation in it.[74] The statement was not hyperbole. The fate of the studio was hardly certain in the face of demographic contraction and competition from other institutions, notably the famed university of Bologna and the new studio founded at this time in neighboring Siena.

The Ubaldini war and Boccaccio's appeal to Petrarch to return to Florence to take up a professorship were thus connected. Boccaccio's invitation ("Movit iam diu") has in fact been described as a "mosaic" of

---

[69] Florence first moved to establish the university at the end of August 1348. Alessandro Gherardi, ed., *Statuti dell'Università e Studio fiorentino dell'anno MCCCLXXXVII* (Florence: Forni, 1881), pp. 111–113, 116–118.

[70] Jonathan Davies, *Florence and Its University during the Early Renaissance* (Leiden: Brill, 1998), p. 10; Falsini, "Firenze dopo il 1348," pp. 484–485.

[71] ASF, Camera del comune, Scrivano di camera uscita 7 fol. 2v. An additional allotment for the university was made on 19 August for 700 florins. ASF, Camera del comune, Scrivano di camera uscita 7 fol. 7v. See also Billanovich, *Petrarca Letterato*, p. 93 and Dotti, *Vita*, p. 221.

[72] Dotti, *Vita*, p. 232.

[73] Wilkins says that Boccaccio "certainly composed the invitation in March 1351." Wilkins, *Life of Petrarch*, p. 99.

[74] Wilkins, *Life of Petrarch*, pp. 99–100. Boccaccio's letter is reproduced in Gherardi, ed., *Statuti*, part II, appendix X, pp. 283–285.

Petrarchan texts, intended to appeal to the poet by means of imitation.[75] But the invitation also bears the imprint of *Familiares* VIII, 10, which Bocccaccio had transcribed. It shares many common references such that the similarities between the invitation and *Familiares* VIII, 10 stand at the root of scholarly efforts to establish Boccaccio as the invitation's author. If we allow that war with the Ubaldini was a response to Petrarch's call, then we may perhaps view this as the most ever done by a university (and city) to attract scholarly talent!

The archival evidence reinforces the literary material and links the Ubaldini war firmly to both Petrarch and Boccaccio. The *Consulte e Pratiche* records expose the political connections of the men with regard to the Ubaldini.[76] Among the Florentine leaders who called for war in executive meetings was Boccaccio's friend Pino dei Rossi, who was one of the captains of the Guelf party in June 1349. Rossi denounced the Ubaldini and declared that the army should "in the name of God" proceed forcefully against them.[77] Boccaccio wrote the *Epistola consolatoria* (1360) for Rossi and also makes reference in that work to Francesco del Bennino, a prominent Florentine merchant and patron of Boccaccio, who, as we shall see in Chapter 3, played a leading role in the physical prosecution of the war.[78] Bennino helped organize supplies for the army in the field with Jacopo di Donato Acciaiuoli, brother of Niccolò Acciaiuoli of Naples, whose relationship with both Petrarch and Boccaccio is well known.[79] He served as an ambassador in the Mugello at the outset of the war. His name also appears as a seller of silk to the commune in June 1349, for the *palio* held that month to celebrate the feast of the city's patron saint, John the Baptist.[80]

The documents reveal the activities of others in the circle of the poets. Niccolò di Bartolo del Buono, to whom Boccaccio dedicated the *Comedia delle Ninfe fiorentine* (1341–1342), was sent as an ambassador to the Romagna just after officials received Petrarch's letter. He was already on embassy in the war region when the attack on Accursio and Cristiani occurred.[81] The precise nature of Del Buono's diplomatic dealings is

[75] G. Auzzas, "Studi sulle epistole: l'invito della signoria fiorentina al Petrarca," *Studi sul Boccaccio* 4 (1967), pp. 203–240.

[76] Dotti, *Vita*, p. 92.   [77] ASF, CP 1 fols. 2r, 4r–4v.

[78] ASF, CP 1 fols. 3r, 4v. Pier Giorgio Ricci, "Studi sulle opera latine e volgari del Boccaccio," *Rinascimento* 10 (1959), pp. 29–32; Branca, *Profilo*, p. 83.

[79] ASF, balie 6 fol. 58v.

[80] ASF, Camera del comune, Scrivano di camera uscita 6 fol. 9r.

[81] Boccaccio also wrote a letter, epistle 5, to del Buono. See Branca, *Profilo*, pp. 60, 121. Del Buono was in the Mugello in May 1349. ASF, Camera del comune, camarlenghi uscita 53 fol. 119. He was in the Romagna in June. ASF, Camera del comune, camarlenghi uscita 56 fol. 548r. At the same time, Florence also sent Bernardo Ardinghelli

unknown, but he was deeply involved in Florentine finance at the time and is listed in budgets as purchaser of the salt gabelle, a major source of city revenue.[82] He was an associate (*socio*) of the Uzzano bank, one of the largest firms of the day, which helped pay for the war by advancing money to the city to hire mercenary cavalrymen.[83]

Meanwhile, Francesco Bruni, Petrarch's famous correspondent and a friend to both poets, worked in 1349 as a notary for the office of the condotta, which hired and paid soldiers. Bruni personally drew up the terms of a 7,500 florin loan raised by Florence in the early stages of the war to cover expenses.[84] The first official notice of Bruni's career in the secondary sources is not until 1352, when he is identified as a friend both of Boccaccio and Petrarch. The documents show, however, that Bruni worked for the city as a notary of the condotta until the summer of 1351, when Florence waged war with Milan.[85] Petrarch subsequently wrote numerous letters to Bruni, who became secretary to Pope Urban V in the 1360s. Unlike Petrarch, Bruni went on teach at the Florentine studio as a professor of rhetoric.[86]

A less certain figure is Francesco Nelli, another of Petrarch's close friends. Nelli's name appears on Florentine budgets in May/June 1349 as chamberlain of the *camera del commune*, the city's main fiscal office. Nelli's service coincides with the arrival of Petrarch's letter advocating war and the city's decision to send out its army.[87] Petrarch called Nelli "Simonides" and dedicated the epistolary collection *Seniles* in 1361 to him. The identity of our Nelli is not, however, entirely certain. The chief source of biographical information on Petrarch's Nelli is Henri Cochin's dated and flawed introductory essay to Nelli's letters to Petrarch, written in the late nineteenth century.[88] Our documents describe Nelli as being

---

(13 June 1349) to the Mugello. Ardinghelli later accompanied Donato Velluti on his mission to Bologna in March 1350 relating to the war.

[82] ASF, Camera del comune, camarlinghi entrata 34 fols. 198r–202r; Camera del comune, entrata 35 fols. 220r–220v.

[83] ASF, Camera del comune, Scrivano di camera entrata 6 fol. 33r.

[84] ASF, Camera del comune, Scrivano di camera uscita 5 fol. 19v; Camera del comune, camarlinghi uscita 64 fol. 507v. Bruni went on several embassies for the city during the conflict, including to Pisa (19 June 1349). ASF, Camera del comune Scrivano di camera uscita 6 fol. 7r; Camera di comune camarlinghi uscita 56 fol. 550r.

[85] Petrarch wrote to Bruni in *Familiares* XXIII, 20 and *Seniles* I, 6; XI, 2, 6. ASF, Camera del comune, Scrivano di camera uscita 8 fol. 7r; Scrivano di camera uscita duplicato 6 fol. 8r.

[86] On Bruni's early career, see G. Brucker, "An Unpublished Source on the Avignonese Papacy: The Letters of Francesco Bruni," *Traditio* 19 (1963), pp. 351–370.

[87] ASF, Camera del comune, Scrivano di camera uscita 5 fol. 40v.

[88] Henri Cochin, *Un amico del Petrarca: lettere del Nelli al Petrarca* (Florence: Le Monnier, 1901, originally published in French in 1896), p. xii. See also Paolo Garbini, "Francesco Nelli" in *Dizionario Biografico degli Italiani* (Milan: Treccani, 2013), pp. 173–183.

from the *quartiere* of San Giovanni, the part of the city also identified by Cochin for Petrarch's Nelli. But our documents cite Nelli's profession as a mercer (*mercario*), where Petrarch's Nelli is identified as a cleric.[89] Indeed, Petrarch's nickname Simonide evoked the clerical status of Nelli, who comes into sharp view only after he went to work for Niccolò Acciaiuoli in Naples in 1361.

The ambiguity of Nelli notwithstanding, there is a close connection between the committee in charge of setting up the new university and the war with the Ubaldini.[90] One member of the committee, Filippo di Duccio Magalotti, was, along with Rossi and Bennino, part of the executive council that advocated for the war against the clan. He served during the conflict as a chamberlain of the condotta that hired troops.[91] Another committee member, Albertaccio Ricasoli, was the brother-in-law of Petrarch's friend Niccolò Acciaiuoli. Albertaccio served as a consultant (*consigliare*) to the captain of war who led the Florentine army into battle in 1350. Another committee member, Tommaso Corsini, who became the first professor of law at the studio, was likewise part of the circle of Acciaiuoli – a close personal friend.

The most conspicuous member of the university committee from the perspective of the war with the Ubaldini was Giovanni Conte de Medici. There is no evidence that he was part of the circles of the poets or Acciaiuoli, but Giovanni played a leading role in the actual fighting of the war. He was captain of a contingent of soldiers that advanced on the Ubaldini from the north, joining with the main army at the fortress at Montegemoli.[92] Giovanni purportedly hated the Ubaldini, as did the Medici family more generally. The discord is in fact the subject of one of Franco Sacchetti's *novelle* (#180). Sacchetti tells of how Giovanni mocked Ottaviano Ubaldini, leader of the clan, when the latter moved to the city in 1360, performing the unlikely job of escorting the priors to their executive meetings. Sacchetti notes that "between the Medici and the Ubaldini there had never been either peace or good will."[93]

---

[89] ASF, Camera del comune, Scrivano di camera uscita 5 fol. 40v; Camera del comune, Scrivano di camera entrata 8 fol. 2r.

[90] Gherardi, ed., *Statuti*, pp. 111–112.

[91] ASF, CP 1 fol. 14v; Camera del comune, Scrivano di camera uscita 8 fol. 7r.

[92] The committee included Giovanni Conte de Medici, Tommaso Corsini, Bindo di Altoviti, Jacopo Alberti, Nero Lippi, Nicola Lapi, and Filippo Magalotti. Gherardi, ed., *Statuti*, pp. 111–112.

[93] Franco Sacchetti, *Novelle* (Turin: Einaudi, 1970), p. 206 (#180).

"Le tre corone": Petrarch, Boccaccio, and Dante

It is important to stress that the Ubaldini war was not only a response to Petrarch, but also a fundamental part of the historical context of the incipient friendship between him and Boccaccio.[94] Literary scholars have written extensively about the subject without mentioning the war. Ugo Dotti's detailed life of Petrarch emphasizes the poet's pain and loss ("anni di dolore") owing to the Black Death. Ernest Wilkins highlights in successive chapters the role of the plague in Petrarch's life, his residence in Parma and Padua, and then his pilgrimage to Rome, during which he stopped in Florence and first met Boccaccio.[95] Petrarch's personal meeting with Boccaccio in Florence in October 1350 has been viewed as the point of departure in their friendship and the plague served as the motivating force.[96]

Nevertheless, the significance of the attack on Petrarch's friends that preceded his meeting with Boccaccio is manifest. It is evident from the attention Petrarch gave to the letters. Book VIII of *Familiares* is the most reedited and reworked of Petrarch's entire epistolary. It originally consisted of only five letters in the so-called Gamma (γ) version, the closest to the original.[97] The letters to the victim Luca Cristiani (now numbers 2 to 5) were originally a single long letter, and epistles 7 to 9, to Ludwig van Kempen, were also one long letter.[98] Letter 7, Petrarch's famous description of the Black Death, was, as noted earlier, originally part of a single letter that included a description of the attack on Petrarch's two friends. The poet did not separate the two events the way modern scholars have. Indeed, Petrarch's account of the plague lacks a certain passion in comparison to the tone of indignation and

---

[94] William Caferro, "'*Le tre* corone fiorentine' and War with the Ubaldini, 1349–50," in *Boccaccio, 1313–2013*, edited by Francesco Ciabattoni, Elsa Filosa, and Kristina Olson (Ravenna: Longo Editore, 2014), pp. 43–55.

[95] The chapter sequence is "Years of Black Death," "Parma, Padua, Mantua 1349–1350," and "Roman Pilgrimage."

[96] Jason Houston emphasizes the meeting of the two men in Florence in October 1350 as the point of departure of their relationship. Houston, *Boccaccio at Play*, S47–S53.

[97] According to Rossi, the modern editor of the work, *redazione* γ is the closest to original, with the letters in the form sent to the people to whom they were addressed. *Redazione* β contains the first eight books (1356), and *redazione* α is the definitive edition. Rossi, *Le familiari*, vol. 1, p. xiii; Aldo S. Bernardo, "Letter-Splitting in Petrarch's Familiares," *Speculum* 33, no. 2 (April 1958), pp. 236–241.

[98] The original letter to Luca Cristiani was ten pages long, then broken up into four letters and extensively reworked, with paragraphs dropped, added, and edited. Rossi, *Le familiari*, vol. 1, p. xiii; vol. 2, pp. 194–209. See Bernardo, "Letter-Splitting," pp. 236–241.

grief he expressed with regard to his friends. Petrarch's call to war, which ends book VIII, strikes the strongest tone of all.[99]

The historian Hans Baron claimed that the alterations in book VIII involved so many changes that "hardly a single sentence of the originals remained unmodified. Petrarch omitted about one-fifth of the original wording and added twice as much new material.[100] Aldo Bernardo saw the "split letters" of *Familiares* VIII as "one of the most dramatic points of the entire collection."[101] Roberta Antognini noted how book VIII functioned as a "fundamental turning point" in the author's life, as both an end and a prelude to a new era.[102]

In any case, the Ubaldini war neatly frames the actions of the poets. Florence went to war directly after receiving Petrarch's letter. Petrarch then traveled to Florence immediately after the war was over, whereupon he met Boccaccio, who had himself just returned to the city from a brief embassy to Dante's daughter, Beatrice, at the convent of St. Stefano degli Ulivi in Ravenna.[103] Petrarch then went to Rome to participate in the papal jubilee.

The literary and archival evidence converge. They make clear that the Ubaldini war was not only part of the first direct dialogue between Petrarch and Boccaccio, but part of the dialogue between the men with regard to Florence's greatest poet, Dante. The exchange between Petrarch and Boccaccio about Dante is well known. Petrarch was critical of Dante's use of the vernacular and his vocation as a poet. Boccaccio tried to convince Petrarch of Dante's greater merits. Scholars stress the importance of the meeting of the two men in 1351 in Padua, when Boccaccio brought the invitation to the university to Petrarch. This is

---

[99] Rossi published *Familiares* book VIII with ten letters in the *Edizione nazionale delle opere di Francesco Petrarca* (1933–1942) and added the original "unsplit" letters in an appendix. Letter 10 was published earlier by Giuseppe Fracassetti in the appendix of his edition (1859–1863) of the *Familiares* as *varie* #53. *Francisci Petrarcae epistolae de rebus familiares et varie*, edited by Giuseppe Fracassetti (Florence: Le Monnier, 1859–1863). The Italian version of the letters appeared as Fracassetti, *Lettere di Francesco Petrarca delle cose familiari* (Florence: le Monnier, 1863–1867). See Ernest H. Wilkins, *The Prose Letters of Petrarch: A Manual* (New York, NY: S. F. Vanni, 1951), p. 6.

[100] Baron, "The Evolution of Petrarch's Thought," p. 10.

[101] Bernardo, "Letter-Splitting," pp. 237, 238.

[102] Antognini, *Il progetto autobiografico*, p. 169.

[103] For the embassy to Dante's daughter, which was on behalf of the confraternity of Orsanmichele, see Saverio La Sorsa, *La Compagnia d'or San Michele, ovvero una pagina della beneficenza in Toscana nel secolo XIV* (Trani: Vecchi, 1902), p. 90. The original document relating to the embassy is, La Sorsa notes, lost. Giuseppe Pelli states that the "entrata and uscita" books of the captains of Orsanmichele contained the original citation on p. 30. Giuseppe Pelli, *Memorie per servire alla vita di Dante Aligheri* (Florence: Guglielmo Piatti, 1823), p. 30.

regarded as the point at which the two men first discussed Dante directly, whose writings Boccaccio had transcribed and collected since his days in Naples.[104]

But a close reading of *Familiares* VIII, 10 suggests that the dialogue between Petrarch and Boccaccio about Dante began earlier. In urging Florence to undertake war against the Ubaldini, Petrarch referred to the ancient Greek jurist Solon, "the wise legislator," who taught that the basis of a true republic was "reward and punishment," which functioned like two feet. Without one of them, the state would "limp along." The reference was unique to Petrarch, taken from Cicero's letter to Brutus found by Petrarch himself at the Biblioteca Capitolare at Verona (1345).[105] Petrarch stressed the importance of punishment, specifically the need for Florence to seek retribution from the Ubaldini: "If you leave this crime unpunished it will mean the end of your universal reputation, of your justice and ultimately of your safety, of your liberty and your glory."[106]

Boccaccio employed the very same reference to Solon and the republic with two feet at the beginning of his biography of Dante, the *Trattatello in laude di Dante*, written in its first version most likely between 1351 and 1355. "Solon, whose breast was said to be a human temple of divine wisdom ... was in the habit of saying sometimes that every republic, like ourselves, walks and stands on two feet."[107] Boccaccio turns Petrarch's image around. Rather than

---

[104] There are three extant manuscripts of the *Commedia* copied in Boccaccio's hand from early 1350s to early 1370s. Boccaccio attempted to create a collection of Dante's work, copying texts into his *Zibaldone Laurenziano* 29, 8, which includes Dante's Latin eclogues and letters iii, xi, xii of Dante's epistolary. Dotti, *Vita*, p. 232; Simon Gilson, *Dante and Renaissance Florence* (Cambridge: Cambridge University Press, 2005), pp. 26–32.

[105] It is from *Ad brutum* 1:15:3, "ut Solonis dictum usurpem, qui et sapientissimus fuit ex septem et legume scriptor solus ex septem:is rem publicam contineri duabus rebus dixit, praemio et poena." Cicero, *Epistulae ad Quintum Fratrem et M. Brutum*, edited by D. R. Schackleton-Bailey (Cambridge: Cambridge University Press, 2004), p. 105.

[106] Petrarch, *Familiares* VIII, 10, vol. 1, p. 433.

[107] "Solone, il cui petto uno umano tempio di divina sapienza fu reputato, ... era, ... spesse volte usato di dire ogni repubblica, sì come noi, andare e stare sopra due piedi." For the original text in Italian, see G. Boccaccio, *Trattatello in laude di Dante*, edited by Pier Giorgio Ricci, in *Tutte le opere di Giovanni Boccaccio*, edited by Vittore Branca, vol. 3 (Milan, Mondadori, 1974) (first redaction, *Trattatello*, pp. 437–496; second redaction or *Compendio*, pp. 497–538). For the translation in English, see G. Boccaccio, *The Life of Dante*, translated by Vincenzo Zin Bollettino (New York, NY: Garland, 1990). See also M. Eisner, *Boccaccio, and the Invention of Italian Literature: Dante, Petrarch, Cavalcanti and the Authority of the Vernacular* (Cambridge: Cambridge University Press, 2013), pp. 31–35; Elsa Filosa, "To Praise Dante, To Please Petrarch ('Trattatello in laude di Dante')" in *Boccaccio: A Critical Guide to the Complete Works*, edited by Victoria Kirkham, Michael Sherberg, and Janet Smarr (Chicago, IL: University of Chicago Press, 2013), pp. 213–220.

punishment, Boccaccio emphasizes the importance of reward, specifically the need for Florence to reward valorous citizens such as Dante. For Petrarch, Florence risked falling short of the example of Rome by ignoring punishment of the Ubaldini. For Boccaccio, Florence fell short of the example of Rome (and other ancient civilizations, including Assyria, Macedonia, and Greece) by ignoring to reward for Dante. "The footprints which were left by such lofty examples," Boccaccio wrote, "have ... been poorly followed by their successors in the present day, most of all the Florentines."[108]

The mutual citation of Solon and a limping republic connects Boccaccio and his *Trattatello* to Petrarch, and links both to the Ubaldini war. The tie has been lost owing to dim knowledge of the historical context and scholarly disinterest in the study of warfare more generally. The evidence nevertheless fits well with the studies of Todd Boli and Simon Gilson, who emphasize the ways that Boccaccio "accommodated" the *Trattatello* to "Petrarchan standards," seeking to render Dante more "agreeable" to Petrarch.[109] Boli stresses echoes in the *Trattatello* of *Familiares* X, 4 (dated 2 December 1349), Petrarch's letter to his brother Gherardo detailing how poetry can be reconciled with theology. *Familiares* VIII, 10 was written seven months earlier and known to Boccaccio before the letter to Gherardo.

The image of the limping republic appears prominently also in Boccaccio's invitation to Petrarch for a professorship in Florence. Boccaccio equated the lack of a university and the study of liberal arts in Florence with lameness, portraying the city as "limping on its right foot."[110] Petrarch's participation in the studio would not only assure the success of liberal arts, but it would allow Florence, like Rome, to be "the parent of all Italy."[111]

It is clear then that if Boccaccio's evolving friendship with Petrarch was mediated through Dante, it is fair to assert that the Ubaldini war was part of that discussion.[112] Indeed *Familiares* VIII, 10 contains echoes of

---

[108] "Le vestigie de' quali in così alti esempli, non solamente da' successori presenti, ma massimamente da' miei Fiorentini, sono male seguite." Boccaccio, *Trattatello in laude di Dante*, p. 437.

[109] Todd Boli, "Boccaccio's 'Trattatello in laude di Dante,' Or Dante Resartus," *Renaissance Quarterly* 41 (1988), pp. 395–398, 410; Gilson, *Dante and Renaissance Florence*, pp. 26–32.

[110] "cum nuper civitatem nostrum velut dextro pede claudicantem liberis carere studiis videremus." Gherardi, ed., *Statuti*, p. 284. Eisner speaks of a metaphorical shift, from limping as a sign of civic weakness to one of moral weakness. Eisner, *Boccaccio, and the Invention of Italian Literature*, p. 33.

[111] "... ut Res nostra pubblica fulta consilio inter alias, ut Roma parens, omnis Ausonie sedes sibi principatum accipiat ... " Gherardi, ed., *Statuti*, p. 284.

[112] Gilson, *Dante and Renaissance Florence*, p. 27.

Dante, most notably the *Commedia*, even though Petrarch did not yet, as
he claimed in his correspondence with Boccaccio, own a copy of the
work.[113] The echoes are such that *Familiares* VIII, 10 may in fact be
read as a critique of Dante, with inversions of basic notions in the
Commedia.

The central theme of *Familiares* VIII, 10 is the importance of justice
and how Florence needs to act in accordance with it. Petrarch explains
how justice derives from heaven, how it found its earthly incarnation in
the ancient Romans, allowing them to gain dominion over the world.
The equation of justice, heaven, Rome, and worldly dominion is familiar
to readers of the *Commedia*, as a major political theme of the work, most
evident in Justinian's speech in *Paradiso* VI and throughout Dante's
Monarchia. As in *Paradiso* VI, the term "justice" is repeated throughout
Petrarch's letter to add rhetorical emphasis to the theme. But in
Familiares VIII, 10 Petrarch calls Florence "the mistress of justice" and
uses the words "justice," "heaven," and "Florence" together in the same
sentence, a concurrence that would have appalled Dante.[114] Petrarch
specifically attributes Florence's rise to greatness as a city, despite its
lack of geographical advantage and natural resources, to its "fondness for
justice."[115] He goes so far as to say that "even as a child" he had heard
about Florence's "outstanding justice."[116]

The statement is not only pointedly *contra* Dante, but absurd, given
that Petrarch's own father was, along with Dante, exiled from Florence
(Arezzo) when Petrarch was a child, an exile about which Petrarch
himself bitterly and frequently complained. Petrarch references this
"inexhaustible and ancient complaint" in a metrical letter to Zanobi da
Strada in 1348, and again in *Familiares* VII, 10, written just prior to the
Ubaldini war (April 1348), to his Florentine friend Giovanni
dell'Incisa.[117] He mentions it also in *Familiares* XI, 5, his response to
Florence's offer to him of a professorship in 1351.[118]

The contrast with Dante and the *Commedia* is evident. In *Familiares*
VIII, 10, Petrarch specifically lauds Florence for its physical and

---

[113] Gilson, *Dante and Renaissance Florence*, pp. 38–40.

[114] Petrarch, *Familiares* VIII, 10, vol. 1, pp. 431–432.

[115] Petrarch, *Familiares* VIII, 10, vol. 1, p. 432.

[116] "Ego quidem puer audiebam maiores natu narrare solitos populi illius virtutes omnimodas eximiamque iustitiam." Rossi, *Le familiari*, vol. 2, p. 15.

[117] Petrarch, *Familiares* VII, 10, vol. 1, p. 356: "would that our city had more of them whom it would not send into exile" ("quales utinam multos haberet civitas nostra, si tamen non esset in exilium missura").

[118] Petrarch, *Familiares* XI, 5, vol. 2, pp. 94–95. Houston argues that Petrarch's disaffection with Florence for having exiled his father "bleeds through the letter." Houston, *Boccaccio at Play*, S49.

demographic expansion and its accommodation of outsiders. He compares the city to a nurturing "mother" who fills "every corner of the earth with its subjects."[119] Dante famously denounces Florence's growth and its "mixing" of persons in *Paradiso* in the guise of Dante's distant relative, Cacciaguida (*Par.* XV, 109–111; *Par.* XVI, 46–154). Dante compares Florence not to a nurturing mother, but to a "sick woman," tossing and turning (*Purg.* VI, 147–151). Dante complains in *Purgatorio* VI that although many in Florence "have justice in their hearts" and "ready on their lips," (vv. 130–132) the city lacked resolve. As a result, officials were continually "changing laws, coins, offices and customs" (vv. 145–146).[120]

Petrarch's inversion of *Purgatorio* VI is especially noteworthy because Dante's unflattering depiction of Florence was current among Petrarch's contemporaries. The Florentine chronicler Giovanni Villani, predecessor and brother of Matteo, directly quotes *Purgatorio* VI twice in his description of events in the city just prior to the Ubaldini war, for the years 1347 and 1348. Villani pointedly condemns Florence's lack of resolve and frequent changes in policy.[121]

Petrarch's engagement with Dante is in any case clear, even if he had not yet received a copy of the *Commedia* from Boccaccio. The echoes in *Familiares* VIII, 10 are forceful and confirm a pattern noted by literary critics with regard to Petrarch's other works, including his *Trionfi*, written in 1352. The evidence from *Familiares* VIII, 10 is singular in that it predates Petrarch's meeting with Boccaccio in Florence and the era that scholars have traditionally associated with the discourse of the men about Dante.[122]

Boccaccio undoubtedly noticed these echoes when he transcribed *Familiares* VIII, 10, as well as Petrarch's sense of identification with the victim of Ubaldini aggression. For all his bellicosity, Petrarch seems to be speaking of himself when he laments in the letter that his friend Mainardo Accursio was returning to Florence "as an aged person having departed as a boy back to the land that frightened you as

---

[119] Petrarch, *Familiares* VIII, 10, vol. 1, p. 432 "et ipsa etiam felix prole virum et in hoc quoque matri similis ac tante sobolis iam non capax, disseminatis toto orbe civibus, omne mundi latus impleverit."

[120] "Molti han giustizia in cuore" (v. 128); "il popol tuo l'ha in sommo de la bocca" (v. 132); "legge, moneta, officio e costume / hai tu mutato" (vv. 146–147); "quella inferma" (v. 149). Dante Alighieri, *La Divina Commedia: Purgatorio*, edited by Tommaso di Salvo (Bologna: Zanichelli, 1985). John Najemy, "Dante and Florence" in *The Cambridge Companion to Dante*, edited by Rachel Jacoff (Cambridge: Cambridge University Press, 2nd edn. 2007), pp. 245–253.

[121] Giovanni Villani, *Nuova Cronica*, edited by G. Porta (Parma: Fondazione Pietro Bembo, 1991), vol. 2, pp. 508–510, 559.

[122] Gilson, *Dante and Renaissance Florence*, pp. 24, 38–39.

a child."[123] The sentiments – weariness, travel, and age – are familiar to readers of the *Familiares* and appear throughout Petrarch's work. They are evident in Petrarch's response to Florence's invitation to return (*Familiares* XI, 5, April 1351), in which he wrote, "[N]ow thanks to your initiative, you offer me the nest of my youth to which I may fly back, weary at length of my long wanderings."[124]

Familiares VIII, 10 gave Boccaccio tangible hope of bringing Petrarch "home" to Florence. In this manner, the Ubaldini war served a dual function. It was a means of ridding Florence of a persistent enemy, but it was also a way of accommodating Petrarch, a precursor to luring him back to the city for a professorship at the new university. The depiction makes Boccaccio appear as a "uomo potente" in the world of Florentine politics. But Petrarch was useful for Florence. His presence on the faculty of the university would, as Boccaccio noted in the invitation, establish its reputation, which would bring students and their money to Florence, a basic aim of the studio. Petrarch likely understood the self-serving and economic nature of the invitation, which gave added incentive to decline the offer.

The Ubaldini war clearly deserves a place in discussions of Boccaccio's accommodation of Petrarch to Dante. The accommodation coincided with a growing cult of Dante in the city of Florence. Scholars have noted that the poet was acquiring an "imposing status" and becoming increasingly popular with mercantile audiences.[125] The *Commedia* was appropriated in the work of novelist Sacchetti and vernacular poet Antonio Pucci.[126]

The Ubaldini war of 1349–1350 may itself be viewed as an echo and inversion of Dante's own experience. Petrarch called for war against the same clan with whom Dante had allied himself, along with the White Guelfs, immediately after his expulsion from Florence in 1302.[127] The war in 1302 was waged in the same places as in 1349–1350: in the upper Mugello, above the towns of Borgo San Lorenzo and Scarperia.

---

[123] Petrarch, *Familiares* VIII, 10, vol. 1, p. 430.

[124] Petrarch, *Familiares* XI, 5, vol. 2, p. 96.

[125] Gilson, *Dante and Renaissance Florence*, pp. 4, 27; Gianfranco Folena, "La tradizione delle opera di Dante Alighieri" in *Atti del Congresso Internazionale di Studi Danteschi* 1 (1965), pp. 54–56.

[126] Antonio Lanza, *Polemiche e berte* (Rome: Bulzoni, 1989), pp. 267–320; Vittorio Rossi, "Dante nel Trecento e nel Quattrocento" in *Scritti di critica letteraria, Saggi e discorsi su Dante* vol. 1 (Florence: G. C. Sansoni, 1930), pp. 198–227; Aldo Rossi, "Dante nelle Prospettiva del Boccaccio," *Studi Danteschi* 39 (1960), pp. 63–139. See Pucci, *Centiloquio*, lines 289–294.

[127] John A. Scott, *Dante's Political Purgatory* (Philadelphia, PA: University of Pennsylvania Press, 1996), p. 21; Robert Hollander, *Dante: A Life in Works* (New Haven, CT: Yale University Press, 2001), p. xiii.

The decisive battle in 1350 at Montegemoli lay close to the famed castle of Montaccianico, the focal point of fighting in the earlier contest, destroyed by Florence in 1306.[128] The principal enemy in 1349–1350 was, however, Maginardo Ubaldini, the grandson of Ugolino da Senna Ubaldini, who had in fact sided against Dante, the White Guelfs, and the rest of the Ubaldini clan in 1302.[129] This same Maginardo had opposed Henry VII, Dante's Henry, when he came to Italy in 1311.

The complicated politics of Florence in 1349–1350 still need to be sorted out. Cameral budgets and *provvisioni* records show, for example, that the papal legate, Astorgio Durafort, in charge of restoring order to the Romagna, came to Florence on 13 June 1349, soon after the arrival of Petrarch's letter and the mobilization of the Florentine army against the Ubaldini. Durafort's visit is not mentioned in the chronicles or secondary literature.[130] The archival sources are not sufficiently detailed to make clear the purpose of the visit: whether it was in support of Florentine policy toward the Ubaldini or related to the Romagna more generally or something else. The visit appears nevertheless to have been a lavish public affair, which cost the city the considerable sum of 250 florins.[131]

Meanwhile, if Boccaccio stood as advocate for Petrarch and war against the Ubaldini, he did so even though his former patron, Francesco II (*il grande*) degli Ordelaffi (1300–1374), lord of Forlì, was married into the Ubaldini family. Francesco was husband of Marzia ("*Cia*") Ubaldini, the daughter of Vanni Ubaldini of Susinana, who was allied with Maginardo against Florence. Ordelaffi himself became involved in conflict in the Apennines, against the Church in 1350. He attacked the town of Bertinoro in May, at the same time that Florence was fighting the Ubaldini at Montegemoli.[132] When Milan took Bologna in the spring of 1351, Ordelaffi allied with the Milanese, along with the Manfredi lords of Faenza and the Ubaldini.

The circumstances undoubtedly added to Boccaccio's personal sense of disappointment when Petrarch not only refused Florence's offer of a professorship, but chose to live also in Visconti lands when he

---

[128] Robert Davidsohn, *Storia di Firenze: Le ultime lotte contro l'impero*, vol. 3 (Florence: Sansoni, 1960), pp. 322–324.

[129] The branch of Ugolino Feliccione Ubaldini fought with Dante and the White Guelfs.

[130] Brucker stresses in general terms the importance of the papacy to Florentine foreign policy. Gene Brucker, *Florentine Politics and Society, 1343–1378* (Princeton, NJ: Princeton University Press, 1962), pp. 141–142.

[131] ASF, Camera del commune, Camarlinghi di camera uscita 56 fol. 549r (16 June 1349); Provvisioni, registri 36 fol. 107v (13 June 1349).

[132] Sorbelli, *La Signoria di Giovanni Visconti*, p. 4.

returned to Italy in 1353.[133] Boccaccio condemned Petrarch in a letter (*Epistle* 10), written to the poet on 18 July 1353. Jason Houston has described the epistle as "a critical satire of Petrarch's politics and poetics" and groups it with other such texts by Boccaccio including the *Trattatello*.[134]

It is possible to go still further. Boccaccio's angry letter contains echoes also of *Familiares* VIII, 10 and the Ubaldini war. The key point of coincidence is the mutual citation of Virgil's famous line from *Aeneid* III, 56–57: "quid non mortalia pectora cogis | auri sacra fames?" ("to what do you drive human breasts o' cursed hunger for gold?"). Petrarch paraphrases the line in *Famigliares* VIII, 10 in connection with the Ubaldini attack on his friends Mainardo and Cristiani: "If hunger for gold is the true cause of your evil deed. Once your abominable desire has been fulfilled return with your booty to the caves and workshops of your crimes and go visit your hosts who eagerly await you there?"[135] Boccaccio quotes the line directly in *Epistle* 10, in the guise of Simonide, his pseudonym for Petrarch's friend Nelli, to condemn Petrarch's decision to live among the Visconti. Simonide/Nelli denounces Petrarch's hypocrisy, wondering how "a lover of solitude," who exalted "honest poverty," could allow himself to become adorned with "dishonest riches" from the Visconti. Nothing remains for Petrarch, says Boccaccio, than "to blush" and "sing openly to himself Virgil's *carme*: 'to what do you drive human breasts o' cursed hunger for gold.'"[136]

The reference once again connects both poets to Dante, who cites the famous passage from Virgil in *Purgatorio* XX in Statius' discussion of his prodigality ("perché non reggi tuo sacra fame / de l'oro l'appetito de' mortali," vv. 82–83) and in *Purgatorio* XXII in Hugh Capet's discussion of the crimes of his family, who ruled France and whom Dante despised: "O avarizia, che puoi tu piu farne" (vv. 40–41).

---

[133] E. H. Wilkins, *Petrarch's Eight Years in Milan* (Cambridge, MA: Medieval Academy of America), 1958, pp. 9–15.

[134] Houston, *Boccaccio at Play*, S48–S50.

[135] "si auri fames vera sceleris causa est, redite iam nefarii voti compotes, ac pred graves, speluncas criminum officinas et, qui illic avide vos extpectant, hospites vestros inviste." Petrarch, *Familiares* VIII, 10, p. 430; Rossi, lines 44–46, pp. 187–188.

[136] "Hic solitudinum commendator egregius atque cultor, quid multitudine circumseptus aget? quid tam sublimi preconio liberam vitam atque paupertatem honestam extollere consuetus, iugo alieno subditus et inhonestis ornatus divitiis faciet? quid virtutum exortator clarissimus, vitiorum sectator effectus, decantabit ulterius? Ego nil aliud nosco quam erubescere et opus suum dampnare, et virgilianum illud aut coram aut secus cantare carmen: 'Quid non mortalia pectora cogis | auri sacra fames?' (*Epistola*, 10, 27–28). See G. Boccaccio, *Epistole*, edited by Ginetta Auzzas in *Tutte le opere di Giovanni Boccaccio*, edited by Vittore Branca vol. 5/1 (Milan: Mondadori, 1965).

Petrarch in Context and the Meeting in Florence

Familiares VIII, 10 clearly deserves closer scrutiny from literary critics, as does the historical context of Boccaccio's first meeting with Petrarch. The aim of the chapter has been to show that in these years, synonymous with the plague, war mattered– even a minor infrastate one. There was a connection, insufficiently appreciated but undeniably real, between the "tre corone fiorentine" and the Ubaldini conflict.

The evidence helps historicize Petrarch. Indeed, for all its inversions of Dante, *Familiares* VIII, 10 also reflects contemporary influences. It shares Donato Velluti's depiction of the Ubaldini war as a species of "vendetta" and repeats Velluti's call, made in executive councils, that Florence needed to "defend its honor" in order to "avoid infamy."[137] The binary opposition of honor and infamy was typical of representations of warfare at this time.[138] Petrarch implored Florence in *Familiares* VIII, 10 to maintain its honor because "if nothing is done, the city will be tainted with eternal infamy."[139] Meanwhile, Petrarch's portrayal of Florence as a "child of Rome" parallels a contemporary statement in the chronicle of Matteo Villani. Villani describes Florence as the child of Rome during his account of the war with Milan in 1351. But Villani applied the notion to Tuscany more generally. Rome's progeny included also the cities of Perugia and Siena, who were then allied with Florence against Milan. All were "children of Rome," whose "liberty" derived from their Roman heritage.[140]

The need to contextualize Petrarch is all the more necessary given the substantial efforts he appears to have made to decontextualize himself. Albert Ascoli and Unn Falkreid have made clear the degree to which Petrarch left hidden issues of time and place in his work.[141] The poet reveals striking little about his political contacts and connections to Italian civic affairs in 1349–1350. Close reading of book VIII of the *Familiares* exposes how willful Petrarch was in obscuring his political/civic side.

---

[137] The instructions to Velluti from Florence for his embassy are in Marzi, *Cancelleria*, p. 674; ASF, CP fols. 1r–3v.

[138] William Caferro, "Honor and Insult: Military Rituals in Late Medieval Tuscany" in *Ritual and Symbol in Late Medieval and Early Modern Italy*, edited by Samuel K. Cohn Jr., Marcello Fantoni, and Franco Franceschi (Turnhout: Brepols, 2013), pp. 125–143.

[139] Petrarch, *Familiares* VIII, 10, pp. 434, 435.

[140] Matteo Villani, *Nuova Cronica* (book 3 chapter 1), p. 205. Matteo applies Roman liberty to Tuscany (libertá del popolo romano) also in book 4, chapter 77, p. 380. See also Nicolai Rubinstein, "Florence and the Despots: Some Aspects of Florentine Diplomacy in the Fourteenth Century." *Transactions of the Royal Historical Society* 2 (1952), p. 32.

[141] Albert Russell Ascoli and Unn Falkeid, "Introduction" in *The Cambridge Companion to Petrarch* (Cambridge: Cambridge University Press, 2015), pp. 1–2.

Aldo Bernardo and Hans Baron argued that Petrarch edited the letters in book VIII in order to enhance their artistic quality and philosophical bearing.[142] Petrarch himself said that he edited with the intention of making the work more cohesive.[143] Both points are undoubtedly true. But Petrarch went much further.

In the original version of *Familiares* VIII, 9, which survives and has been published by Vittorio Rossi, Petrarch provides additional details about his friends' fateful journey and his frantic attempts to find out what happened to them. The biggest alterations in the letter relate to Petrarch's network of friends and contacts from whom he sought information. In the original, Petrarch tells of messengers he sent to Piacenza, Florence, and Rome to find out about his friends. He tells of a conversation he had with a "noble citizen" from Florence, whom he knew from Avignon, and who now came to meet Petrarch in person in Parma. Petrarch recounts speaking also with a Milanese merchant, whom Petrarch says he already knew well and who had been in Florence during the time of the attack on his friends.[144] The merchant confirmed the hazards of the Apennine roads, complaining that he had to proceed through the woods and forests to avoid danger. Petrarch mentions also an old priest, who was his servant, who found out from another messenger in Tuscany that Mainardo was indeed dead, among several people killed by the Ubaldini ambush. Petrarch ends the original letter 9 by expressing worry that he had not heard from Socrates (van Kempen), to whom the letter is addressed. Petrarch adds a lengthy postscript telling Socrates to say hello to his friends in France.[145]

None of this appears in the final version of *Familiares* VIII, 9. Petrarch excluded the real names of his friends, as well as references to specific locations, notably the papal curia at Avignon, from where his friends started their journey, and to Parma, where Petrarch lived.[146] The changes, as Baron suggests, made the final product more abstract and timeless. But they also abstracted Petrarch from his environment, removing him from Italian politics, of which his advocacy of war with the Ubaldini is the most egregious example. The omission of the papal curia in Avignon corresponds with Ascoli's contention that Petrarch sought to minimize that troublesome relationship. The original letter conveys a real

---

[142] Bernardo, "Letter-Splitting," pp. 237–238; Baron, "The Evolution of Petrarch's Thought," p. 10.

[143] Lynn Lara Westwater, "The Uncollected Poet" in Victoria Kirkham and Armando Maggi, eds., *Petrarch: A Critical Guide to the Complete Works* (Chicago, IL: University of Chicago Press, 2009), pp. 302–303.

[144] Rossi, *Le familiari*, vol. 2, p. 207.   [145] Dotti, *Vita*, pp. 209–210.

[146] Rossi, *Le familiari*, vol. 2, p. 187 (line 19).

sense of time and space, such that it is possible to imagine that the "noble" Florentine citizen with whom Petrarch met after the attack on his friends could have been someone well known, perhaps even Boccaccio's friend Niccolò di Bartolo del Buono, who was on embassy in the region at exactly this time.

In any case, the evidence suggests that Petrarch lived a *vita activa* while advocating the *vita contemplativa* and portraying himself as a rustic recluse. Both he and Boccaccio were political forces. When the campaign against the Ubaldini ended in late September 1350, Petrarch traveled to Florence, for the first time since his family was exiled. He arrived in the city on 1 October 1350, which Vittore Branca describes as a cold day. He was met by Boccaccio, who had just returned to Florence from Ravenna on embassy to Dante's sister. With Boccaccio were Zanobi da Strada, Nelli, and Lapo da Castiglionchio.[147] Petrarch read some poems; Lapo gave Petrarch a copy of *Istituzioni oratorie* of Quintillian and three orations of Cicero. Boccaccio gave Petrarch a ring.[148] On that same day, Florence allocated 300 florins for the "salaries and other expenses" for the university.[149] Petrarch continued on to Rome to join the papal jubilee. On his way, he was kicked by his horse, injuring his left leg below the knee.[150] The painful wound left Petrarch limping – his metaphor with regard to Florence and the Ubaldini war converted now into a painful physical reality.

Days later, the Pepoli brothers of Bologna sold their city to the Archbishop of Milan, Giovanni Visconti. The act touched off war between Milan and Florence, which lasted until 1353.[151] Boccaccio was appointed chamberlain of the *camera del commune*, the chief fiscal organ of the city. Petrarch retreated to France, returning to Italy in 1353 to live in Milan, much to Boccaccio's displeasure.

---

[147] Branca, *Profilo*; Billanovich, *Petrarca Letterato*, p. 99.   [148] Dotti, *Vita*, p. 223.

[149] ASF, Camera del comune, Scrivano di camera uscita 8 fol. 6v.

[150] Petrarch, *Familiares* XI, 1, 2 (November 1350) letter 5 (6 April 1351), vol. 2, pp. 94–96.

[151] ASF, balie 7 bis fol. 1r.

2   The Practice of War and the Florentine Army

First of all then, I state that Italy is divided into two, a left hand and right
hand side. If anyone should ask where the dividing line is drawn, I reply
briefly that it is the range of the Apennines ... These irrigate the whole
country through long conduits, on one side and the other, as far as the
two opposite shores.

Dante, *De Vulgari Eloquentia* book 1, x[1]

The Apennine roads through Ubaldini territory were notoriously difficult
to negotiate. Petrarch described them in his letter to Florence as "rough
and demanding" and had implored his friends not to travel there.[2]
The sixteenth-century Venetian ambassador Marco Foscari complained
that the passages moved along "the harshest mountains and narrowest
and most difficult vales,"[3] and Michel Montaigne in his *Journal de voyage*
(1580) said that he found the stretch through the Apennines the most
"incommode et farouche" of his entire trip in Italy.[4]

The war against the Ubaldini in 1349–1350 was fought in this region, in
the upper Mugello, above the towns of Scarperia and Borgo San Lorenzo.
The Florentine army proceeded along two routes leading toward the
Romagna: through the Santerno river valley, the "orto degli Ubaldini,"
as the chronicler Dino Compagni called it, to Firenzuola (following the
modern day "strada montanara imolese" to Imola), and, further east,

---

[1] Dante, *De Vulgari Eloquentia*, edited and translated by Steven Botterill (Cambridge:
University Press, 1996), p. 25.
[2] Petrarch, *Familiares* VIII, 10, vol. 1, p. 435.
[3] John Larner, "Crossing the Romagnol Appenines in the Renaissance" in *City and
Countryside in Late Medieval and Renaissance Italy: Essays Presented to Philip Jones*, edited
by Trevor Dean and Chris Wickham (London: Hambleton Press, 1990), p. 147;
Paolo Pirillo, *Costruzione di un contado: I fiorentini e il loro territorio nel Basso Medioevo*
(Florence: Casa Editrice le Lettere, 2001); Daniele Sterpos, "Evoluzione delle comunicazioni transappenniniche attraverso tre passi del Mugello" in *Percorsi e valichi
dell'Appenino fra storia e leggenda* (Florence: Arti grafiche Giorgi & Gambi, 1985).
[4] Daniele Sterpos, *Comunicazioni stradali attraverso i tempi: Bologna-Firenze* (Novara: De
Agostini, 1961), p. 110; Michel Montaigne, *Journal de voyage*, edited by Louis Lautrey
(Paris: Publisher, 1906), pp. 184–185. Samuel K. Cohn, *Creating the Florentine State*
(Cambridge: Cambridge University Press, 1999), pp. 21–23.

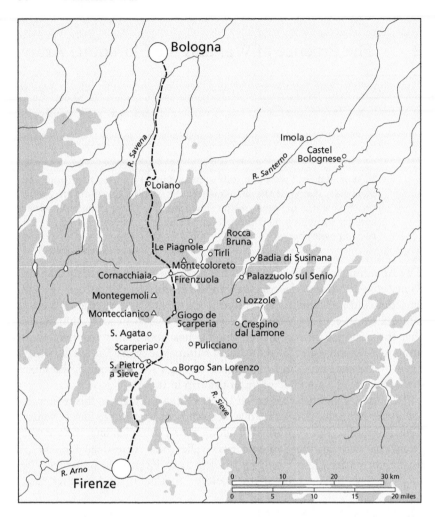

Map 2.1 Site of conflict

following the Senio river to Palazzuolo sul Senio, Badia di Susinana, and Castel Bologenese at the Bolognese border (Map 2.1).[5] Florence assaulted the formidable Ubaldini fortresses at Lozzole (796 meters above sea level), north of Borgo San Lorenzo; le Piagnole (548 meters) on a high ridge overlooking the left bank of the Santerno river northeast of Firenzuola; and Tirlì (361 meters), overlooking the right bank of the Santerno river. The focal point of the campaigns in both 1349 and 1350 was, however,

[5] The Santerno river flows through the towns of Cornachiaia, near Montegemoli, and through Firenzuola to the east and continues north and to Piagnole and Tirlì.

Montegemoli (606 meters), the Ubaldini castle north of Scarperia, just beyond the monastery of Sant'Agata and below the town of Cornacchiaia. The castle was home to Maghinardo Ubaldini, whose crimes initiated the conflict. Florence's ultimate aim was to take the castle at Badia di Susinana (370 meters), the long-time headquarters of the family, where Maghinardo's son Ottaviano and his grandson Carnello lived.[6]

The extant documents shed special light on the organization and execution of war, subjects about which surprisingly little is known for Florence at this time. The Florentine priors discussed strategy in consultation with members of various communal offices, including the condotta, which oversaw the hiring of troops, the *camera del arme*, which oversaw weapons and supplies, and with the captain of the army and his advisors (*consiglieri*) in the field. Officials assembled a fighting force, acquired and distributed supplies, and hired numerous noncombatants, the most faceless sector of the Florentine workforce, but who nevertheless were essential to maintaining the army in the field.

The sources give an unprecedented look at the details, which is strikingly at odds with the general scholarly consensus. Rather than an ad hoc and "backward" force, dismissed after each campaign and lacking a native component, the Florentine army contained a core of trusted, battle-tested soldiers, including mercenary cavalrymen, who had worked long-term for the city and infantrymen employed for similarly extended periods, who, in some cases, even had a financial stake in the city.[7] Contra Machiavelli and prevailing historical opinion, the infantry was more professionalized than expected and included accomplished native captains such as "Ser Mestola" or "half-wit" (Jacobo Chesis from Passignano, site of the famous abbey of Valambrosa), the sobriquet that Boccaccio used for the woman ("donna Mestola") who slept with the Angel Gabriel in the second story on the fourth day of the *Decameron*.[8] Above all, our evidence makes clear that the lines between pacific and

---

[6] The towns of Lozzole, Piagnole, and Tirlì are explicitly mentioned as targets. ASF, CP 1 fols. 4r–4v, 9r. The budgets show that cavalrymen lost horses in these places. ASF, Camera del commune, Scrivano di camera uscita 7 fols. 48r, 56v.

[7] On the ad hoc and "backward" nature of the Florentine army with respect to other contemporary armies, see Michael Mallett, *Mercenaries and Their Masters* (Totowa, NJ: Rowman and Littlefield, 1974), pp. 82–83; Giuseppe Canestrini, "Documenti per servire della milizia italiana del secolo XIII al XVI," *Archivio Storico Italiano*, ser. 1, 15 (1851), p. cvii. The scholarly terms of discussion are in William Caferro, *Mercenary Companies and the Decline of Siena* (Baltimore, MD: Johns Hopkins University Press, 1998), xiv–xv, 1–14, and "Continuity, Long-Term Service and Permanent Forces," *The Journal of Modern History* 80 no. 2 (June 2008), pp. 303–322. See also Jean-Claude Maire Vigueur, *Comuni e Signorie in Umbria, Marche e Lazio* (Turin: UTET, 1987), pp. 175–226.

[8] ASF, Camera del Comune, Scrivano di camera uscita 7 fol. 47r; Giovanni Boccaccio, *Decameron*, edited by Vittore Branca (Turin: UTET, 1956), p. 336. Boccaccio uses the term "Ser Mestola" in *il Corbaccio*.

military sectors of Florentine society were blurred. The distinction is artificial and anachronistic, and has important implications for understanding the overall Florentine public workforce.

War in the Apennines

In his address to the priors of the city in 1349, Donato Velluti called for the Florentine army to proceed against the Ubaldini in a "manly fashion," to use "arson and all means available" to root them out.[9] The precise itinerary of the army in 1349 is difficult to trace. Matteo Villani says little of the initial fighting, other than it lasted for several days, after which the army returned "senza contrasto" to the city. The documents reveal a more stubborn resistance by the Ubaldini and a more sustained and less successful effort by Florence. Florence began by laying siege to the castle of Lozzole, building a tower (*bastita*) and placing near the imposing fortress.[10] The Ubaldini countered by destroying roads and conducting raids against the town of Scarperia, stealing animals, and setting fires.[11]

Florence failed to deliver a decisive blow. But in late July 1349, Florentine forces achieved a notable victory at Crespino del Lamone, south of Palazzuolo sul Senio (536 meters high), near the town of Marradi.[12] They seized the fortress with help from within. Ambrogio Iambonelli, a Florentine exile, opened the gates to the enemy. He was rewarded by Florence with the cancellation of his sentence and was allowed to return to the city. Ubaldini counterraids, however, took a toll on Scarperia. In October 1349 Florence was constrained to offer tax breaks to "persons who settled and built homes" in the town. The stated aim was to replenish the city that had been greatly diminished by plague and "the arrogance and audacity of the Ubaldini."[13]

The second campaign was more extensive than the first. It coincided with the growing rebellion against the Church authority in nearby Romagna in the winter of 1349/1350.[14] In February 1350, Giovanni Manfredi, captain of the people of Imola, seized the town of Faenza from the Church. In spring, Francesco degli Ordelaffi of Forlì, Boccaccio's former patron, attacked Bertinoro (May 1350), another

---

[9] ASF, CP 1 fols. 1r–v.
[10] ASF, CP 1 fol. 3r. On the use of *bastite*, see William Caferro, *John Hawkwood, An English Mercenary in Fourteenth Century Italy* (Baltimore, MD: Johns Hopkins University Press, 2006), pp. 83–84.
[11] ASF, CP 1 fol. 9r; Signoria, Missive Cancelleria 10 #148.
[12] ASF, Provvisioni, registri 36 fol. 144r; Cohn, *Florentine State*, p. 43.
[13] ASF, Provvisioni, registri 37 fol. 12r.
[14] Albano Sorbelli, *La Signoria di Giovanni Visconti a Bologna e le sue relazioni con la Toscana* (Bologna: Forni, 1902), p. 4.

Church possession.[15] The unrest, just beyond the Florentine border, gave a renewed sense of urgency to Florence's campaign against the Ubaldini. Florence sent Donato Velutti, among others, on embassy (March 1350) to seek support from Bologna against the continued "criminal deeds" of the Ubaldini.[16]

The objectives of the second campaign were the same as the first. Florence sought to drive out Maghinardo and his family from their fortresses along the Santerno and Senio rivers. Florence appointed a special ad hoc committee, a *balia*, consisting of eight men, to oversee the war effort. The town of Scarperia – below the famous monastery of Sant'Agata and on the road north to Giogo and the mountain pass (25 kilometers northeast of Florence) to Ubaldini territory – served as headquarters for the Florentine army. The city collected supplies and built trebuchets and siege towers there.[17]

Florence again attacked Lozzole in the high mountains above the Senio river and then moved against the fortresses at le Piagnole and Tirlì.[18] Matteo Villani focuses his account on the castle of Montegemoli, where the two sides fought a bitter battle. The stronghold, which no longer exists today, lay close to the town of Cornacchiaia, northeast of Scarperia and west of the Giogo pass through the high mountains to Firenzuola, off the old main road toward Bologna. It was the gateway to the heart of the Ubaldini patrimony. It stood north of where the famous Ubaldini castle of Monteaccianico had been, the site of the battle between the city and Dante, the White Guelfs, and Ubaldini in 1302. The fortress was destroyed by Florence in 1306.[19]

Villani described Montegemoli as a "montuosità quasi inespugnabile" located at the top of the hill.[20] Maghinardo Ubaldini defended the fort with "valenti masnadieri" of fighters. He had erected a tower, "strong and well-armed," that oversaw the road leading to the castle, with a ditch in front of it, supported by a barricade manned by soldiers.[21] The Florentines

---

[15] Sorbelli, *La Signoria*, pp. 2–11.

[16] Demetrio Marzi, *La cancelleria della repubblica fiorentina* (Rocca San Casciano: Cappelli, 1910), pp. 673–674.

[17] Scarperia is on the road from Vaglia to San Piero a Sieve and then across the Giogo to Firenzuola and ultimately Imola.

[18] The concern for le Piagnole is in ASF, CP 1 fols. 14r–14v.

[19] David Friedman, *Florentine New Towns: Urban Design in the Late Middle Ages* (Cambridge, MA: Harvard University Press, 1989), p. 45; Emanuele Repetti, *Dizionario Geografico Fisico e Storico della Toscana*, vol. 3 (Florence: Firenze libri, 1839), pp. 395–396; Paolo Pirillo, *Forme e strutture del popolamento nel contado fiorentino: gli insedimenti fortificati* (1280–1380), vol. 2 (Florence: Olschki, 2005), pp. 131–132.

[20] Matteo Villani, *Nuova Cronica*, edited by Giuseppe Porta, vol. 1 (Parma: Fondazione Pietro Bembo, 1995), pp. 50–53.

[21] Matteo Villani, *Nuova Cronica*, pp. 51–52.

intended to lay siege to the fortress and brought trebuchets and artillery devices (*dificii*). The army attempted to draw out the Ubaldini by conducting raids on the surrounding area.[22] The ploy worked. Ubaldini *masnadieri*, on account of "too much boldness" according to Villani, strayed from their defensive positions, crossed the ditch, and engaged the Florentines directly. The Florentine cavalry descended from their mounts and went forward on foot, joined by infantrymen.

The dismount of the cavalry from their horses brings to mind the famous battle of Crécy in France fought three years earlier. But the decision was likely made on account of the narrow constraints of the territory around the Ubaldini castle, which did not allow much maneuvering. The fighting was intense. The Florentines forced Ubaldini soldiers to retreat amid a hail of bolts from crossbowmen. The army then advanced toward the fortress, which was defended vigorously. There was, according to Villani, sufficient food for the besieged to hold out for a prolonged period of time. But alarmed at the encirclement and on uncertain terms with other members of the family, Maghinardo Ubaldini sought an accord. He gave the fort to Florence and in return received citizenship and a generous contract for military service against the rest of his clan.[23]

The documents provide a sense of the strategy involved. Just prior to the attack on Montegemoli, Florence had arranged with Count Tano degli Alberti, lord of Montecarelli, just north of Barberino, to allow Giovanni Conte de Medici and a contingent of troops (forty to sixty men) to fortify the town of Monte Vivagni (between Montecarelli and the Futa pass), protecting Florence's northwest flank.[24] From there, Giovanni joined the main army in its attack on Montegemoli.

The sources also show that the siege tower Florence placed at Montegemoli was manned by both cavalrymen and infantrymen. The former included the German captains Johann Dornich and Arrighetto Degan; the latter included the infantry captains Santi Chiarucci, from nearby Tirlì, and Francesco Barufaldi, from nearby Montecarelli.[25] It is not clear what role the tower played in the victory, but the men in it had important roles in both campaigns and were, perhaps, chosen for this service because of their military valor. Meanwhile, ribalds or *barattieri* were sent out into the field to commit

---

[22] Matteo Villani, *Nuova Cronica*, pp. 51–52.

[23] Negotiations were already underway on 29 May. Marzi, *La cancelleria*, pp. 678–679; ASF Provvisioni, registri 38 fol. 69v.

[24] ASF, Provvisioni, registri 38 fol. 36v. This was arranged on 28 February 1350. ASF, balie 6 fol. 78r; Signori Missive I Cancelleria 10 #145.

[25] ASF, balie 7 fol. 32v.

acts of "infamia" to mock the enemy, a basic feature of contemporary warfare.[26] The men also burned houses and picked up stray crossbow bolts, which were then sent back to craftsmen for reworking.[27] Weapons were recycled in fourteenth-century Florence.

The capture of Montegemoli gave impetus to the Florentine army. On 3 June 1350, the city finalized the accord with Maghinardo and eleven other members of the Ubaldini clan. Maghinardo formally ceded Montegemoli to Florence, as well as several other fortresses and possessions along the border with Bologna and Imola.[28] Florentine officials then wrote a letter to the army, instructing the captain to "do all that is necessary" to move the army aggressively and successfully forward. The plan was to seize the fortress of Susinana, the headquarters of the family and thus, in the words of the epistle, "exterminate" the Ubaldini clan.[29] Florence received logistical support from a local lord, Giovanni di Albergettino Manfredi and from the papal legate, the Count of Romagna, who was technically neutral.[30]

Matteo Villani gives an impressionistic, but generally accurate account of what followed. He says that the Florentine army took the fortresses of Montecolereto (970 meters) and Rocca Bruna (765 meters) by siege, and captured Lozzole and Vigiano (just outside of Borgo San Lorenzo) by "trattato." The army did not, however, succeed at taking Susinana or the nearby town of Palazzuolo sul Senio.[31]

Villani's description suggests an orderly north/east itinerary for the Florentine army. But the documents show that the army did not proceed in straight lines, but fanned out, conducting raids, and responding to counterattacks by the Ubaldini. The assault on Montegemoli took place between 23 and 28 May. The capture of the castles at Rocca Bruna and Lozzole occurred on 31 May and 2 June.[32] Lozzole capitulated by means of treason; two men on the inside, identified as Calvo and Bernardo di Nucci, received a 150 florin reward for the deed.[33] By 3 June Florentine forces, or at least a portion of them, reached Montecoloreto and the castle

---

[26] William Caferro, "Honor and Insult: Military Rituals in Late Medieval Tuscany" in *Ritual and Symbol in Late Medieval and Early Modern Italy*, edited by Samuel K. Cohn Jr., Marcello Fantoni, and Franco Franceschi (Turnhout: Brepols, 2013), pp. 125–143.

[27] ASF, balie 7 fols. 29r–30v.

[28] ASF, Provvisioni, registri 38 fols. 69v–70r (3 June 1350).

[29] Marzi, *La cancelleria*, p. 682.

[30] ASF, balie 7 fols. 34r, 35v. See the Florentine ambassadorial dispatch in Marzi, *La cancelleria*, p. 679. The letter said that if the army needed food it could ask the Conte di Romagna and Giovanni di Albergettino.

[31] ASF, Signori Missive I Cancelleria 10 #159.

[32] ASF, balie 7 fols. 29v, 34r–36v, 64r; Camera del comune, Scrivano di camera uscita 10, fols. 51v–53r; Paolo Pirillo, *Forme e strutture*, pp. 146–147.

[33] ASF, balie 6 fol. 84v.

at Susinana, burning nearby fields.[34] The Florentine cavalry appear to have sustained heavy losses at Susinana and also at Scarperia, defending against Ubaldini reprisals.[35] Siege towers were placed at the fortress of Montecoloreto, and at le Piagnole and Tirlì, northwest of Firenzuola, on the road to Palazzuolo[36] In mid-June Montecoloreto surrendered. Its formidable walls, purportedly 14 1/2 meters high, were knocked down by rocks thrown by Florentine trebuchets.[37] Nearby le Piagnole held out, as did Tirlì.[38]

Holdouts notwithstanding, Florence was by mid-June 1350 optimistic. After the capture of Montecoloreto, Florence held a big celebration for the now "happy army" (*felicie esercito*) in the field.[39] The city sent musicians, town criers, and other civic officials to participate in the festivities. Meanwhile, the priors in Florence met three times in executive councils (12 June, 19 June, and 22 June) to arrange for the "final defeat" of the Ubaldini.[40] Filippo Magalotti urged at the 12 June meeting that the city continue its efforts against le Piagnole and Tirlì and try anew at Susinana.[41] Giovanni Gheri suggested that the city negotiate with Ottaviano Ubaldini and his son (Cavarnello), who held Susinana. The city disbursed large sums of money for the war (Chapter 3) to keep the army moving forward.[42] The appropriations (from 4 to 24 June) went to salaries and supplies, but also to refurnish the fortresses taken by the city. Florence sent its own castellans to take charge of Montegemoli and Rocca Bruna.[43]

In early July, Florence finally succeeded in taking le Piagnole. It sent a team of stonemasons to destroy the castle walls.[44] Meanwhile, officials negotiated with Ottaviano Ubaldini and his son. By late July the sides came to a tentative agreement.[45] Ottaviano and Cavarnello, like Maghinardo before them, agreed to cease fighting in return for employment in the Florentine army on generous contractual terms.[46]

---

[34] ASF, balie 7 fols. 29v–30v, 34r; Marzi, *La cancelleria*, p. 679.

[35] ASF, Camera del comune, camerlinghi uscita 70 fol. 34r; Scrivano di camera uscita 10 fols. 51v, 53r.

[36] ASF, CP 1 fols. 14v, 19r; balie 7 fol. 33r.

[37] Paolo Pirillo, "Tra Signori e città: I castelli dell'Appenino alla fine del Medio Evo" in *Castelli dell'Apennino nel medioevo*, edited by P. Fosci, E. Penoncini, and R. Zagnoni (Pistoia: Società Pistoiese, 2000), pp. 26–28.

[38] Pirillo, *Forme e strutture*, pp. 123–129, 160.

[39] ASF, Camera del comune, Scrivano di camera uscita 9 fols. 3v–4v.

[40] ASF, CP 1 fols. 14r–19r.   [41] ASF, CP 1 fol. 14r.   [42] ASF, balie 6 fols. 81v–83v.

[43] ASF, Signori Missive Cancelleria 10 #161.   [44] ASF, balie 6 fols. 24r, 74v.

[45] On 19 June, Uguccione de Ricci suggested, concerning an agreement with Ottaviano, that the city do whatever was most useful. ASF, CP fol. 19r.

[46] The men appear on the city payroll for military service on 28 July. ASF, Camera del comune, Scrivano di camera uscita 10 fol. 35v.

Florentine officials now felt sufficiently successful to change the name of the upper Mugello from "alpi Ubaldini" (Ubaldini Alps) as it had been known for centuries, to "alpi Fiorentine" (Florentine Alps).[47] But the impetus of Florence's army was in fact slowing. The sources show that movement in the high mountains was hampered by lack of pack animals. Susinana proved too well defended to capture.[48] The arrangement between the city and Ottaviano was also contentious. The discussion among the executives show that Ottaviano did not do as he promised and complained about the acts of *infamia* and taunting done by the Florentine *barattieri*. On 11 September, Florentine officials held a banquet on behalf of Ottaviano, and eleven days later the city released two Ubaldini captives, who were perhaps part of the dispute.[49] Meanwhile, the situation in the nearby Romagna continued to deteriorate, complicating matters still further. Florence made a push in September 1350 to hire more troops.[50] But by the last week of that month (27 September), the *balìa* disbanded and the conflict was effectively over.[51]

Matteo Villani claimed victory. He reported that the Florentine army returned "salvi e sani" to Florence. The city had captured the important fortresses of Montegemoli, Lozzole, Rocca Bruna, and le Piagnole in the upper Mugello, and had gained, by agreement with Maghinardo, "ius" and "iurisdictionem" over Ubaldini tolls and taxes in nineteen small towns along the border with Bologna, including Caburaccio, Camaiore, Bordignano, and Rapezzo.[52]

But Florentine armies were unable to "exterminate" the Ubaldini, if indeed that had been a realistic goal. The chronicler Marchionne Stefani gave a more cautious and perhaps realistic assessment of the war. He spoke of a temporary victory, asserting that while some members of the Ubaldini swore obedience to the city, others turned to Milan, which was now deeply involved in affairs in Bologna and would soon purchase that city (October 1350). The purchase of Bologna led to war between Milan and Florence and the papacy. The Ubaldini fought alongside the Milanese and recaptured most of the forts they had lost.

The Florentine Army

The war was ultimately inconclusive. But mobilization for the conflict posed a great challenge for the city. Florentine officials expressed

---

[47] *I Capitoli del Comune di Firenze*, edited by C. Guasti, I, p. 91.
[48] ASF, CP 1 fol. 4r; balie 7 fol. 34r.   [49] ASF, balie 6 fols. 107v, 117r.
[50] ASF, balie 6 fols. 105r–106v.
[51] The last date mentioned in the document is 28 September 1350. ASF, balie 6 fol. 2r.
[52] ASF, Provvisioni, registri 38 fols. 69v–70r.

concerns about procuring men and supplies in the face of the ongoing effects of the Black Death. They complained of a lack of revenue (Chapter 3) and of political discord within the city (Chapter 1).[53] The outbreak of hostilities in 1349 coincided also with a "carestia" of grain and "other necessities" in the city.[54] Logistics in the mountains were always difficult.

The burdens of war fell hard on a Florentine bureaucracy that was more confused and impermanent than centralized (Chapter 3). The *camera del commune*, the "preeminent organ of political finance" of the city, collected and disbursed communal revenue.[55] But its responsibilities overlapped with those of the *camera del arme*, in charge of the city arsenal, and the office of the condotta, which hired soldiers. The *balia* appointed by Florentine officials at the start of 1350 had special powers to circumvent the ponderous bureaucratic machinery of the city to allow more rapid response in the face of the emergencies.[56] But the precise relationship between this and the other war-related offices is unclear.[57] The *balia*, like the condotta, hired soldiers and, like the *camera del arme*, purchased supplies. It received much of its money from the *camera del comune*, but as we will see in Chapter 3, not all came from that source.

In the face of the challenges, Florence moved first to assemble an army against the Ubaldini. The exact size of the force is unknown. As Michael Mallett pointed out, it is impossible to translate paper armies into those that were actually in the field.[58] In discussions in the executive councils just prior to the campaign in 1349, Filippo Machiavelli suggested that Florence would need at least 150 horsemen and 400 infantrymen to

[53] ASF, Provvisioni, registri 36 fol. 82v; Provvisioni, registri 36 fol. 145v, July 31 1349; CP 1 fols. 4v, 6r; Provvisioni, registri 36 fol. 105r. The complaints continued throughout the war. ASF, Provvisioni, registri 36 fol. 132r; balie 7 fol. 32v; CP 1 fols. 4v, 6r–June; Provvisioni, registri 36 fol. 105r.

[54] ASF, Provvisioni, registri 36 fols. 82v, 145v (July 31 1349).

[55] Guidi called the *camera* "il organo preeminente nella politica finanziaria." Guidubaldo Guidi, *Il governo della città-repubblica di Firenze del primo Quattrocento*, vol. 2 (Florence: Leo S. Olschki, 1981), p. 277. See also A Gherardi, "L'Antica camera del comune di Firenze," *Archivio Storico Italiano* 43 (1885), pp. 313–361.

[56] ASF, Provvisioni, registri 36 fols. 141v–142r; balie 6 fols. 2v–119v. The *balia* itself runs from 28 January 1350 (balie 6 fols. 2r, 17r) to 27 September 1350 (balie 6 fol. 34r). The first page is 2r and the document starts anew on 17r and again on 19r and 34r. The dates are not consecutive. The notary for the first part of the volume is Ser Simone Landi di Leccio (2r) and Ser Puccini Ser Lapi (34r) for the later part. On the use of balie at this time, See William Caferro, *Mercenary Companies and the Decline of Siena* (Baltimore, MD: Johns Hopkins University Press, 1998), pp. xviii, 186.

[57] ASF, Provvisioni, registri 37 fol. 81r.

[58] Michael Mallett, *Mercenaries and Their Masters* (Totowa, NJ: Rowman and Littlefield, 1974), pp. 115–116. On the size of contemporary armies, see also Caferro, *John Hawkwood*, pp. 88–91.

besiege the single fortress of Montegemoli. His estimate was based on an acknowledgment that the market in soldiers was severely constricted as a result of the plague and that adding more men would be difficult.[59] The *balia* records of 1350 provide more precise figures. They show that just prior to the offensive against Montegemoli in that year, Florence hired 185 German cavalrymen and 909 infantrymen (February to April). The city continued to recruit men throughout the campaign, adding another 400 cavalrymen and 790 infantrymen from June to September. In all, Florence hired 2,284 men during the second campaign.[60]

This did not, however, constitute the entire army. Florence built upon existing forces. A surviving troop list among the scattered and damaged documents in the *Miscellanea repubblicana* registers shows that Florence already had 400 horsemen and 600 infantrymen on the payroll in late 1348, despite the plague.[61] In addition, Florence appointed Niccolò di Rinuccio della Serra of Gubbio in 1349 as commander of the army, with 25 horsemen and 100 infantrymen.[62] For the second campaign in 1350, the city hired Cecco di Ranieri Farnese as captain, with 50 cavalrymen and 100 infantrymen.[63] In addition, the city deployed contingents of native crossbowmen known as the *balestrieri della ghiera* during the second campaign. The special corps of men was created in the thirteenth century. They were recruited from the city and the contado, and consisted of 474 men in 1350.[64] This brought the number of soldiers in Florentine service in 1350 to more than 3,000 men. The total is large with respect to the rest of Florence's workforce in this period of demographic contraction.

A proper understanding of the Florentine army in the fourteenth century has been limited by prevailing assumptions and lack of adequate research.[65] Scholars have depicted the fourteenth century as a time of

---

[59] ASF, CP 1 fol. 3v.

[60] ASF, balie 6 fols. 38v–39r, 45v, 52v–55r, 60v–62v, 83r, 97v–98r, 105r–106v, 118r, 119r.

[61] ASF, Miscellanea repubblicana 120.

[62] ASF, Provvisioni, registri 36 fols. 66r–66v; Camera del comune, Scrivano di camera uscita 6 fols. 2v–9v. Serra appears to have been made senator in Rome during his service there. ASF, Provvisioni, registri 36 fol. 70r.

[63] ASF, balie 6 fols. 63r–63v.

[64] ASF, balie 6 fols. 69r, 82r–v, 89r. On the *balestrieri*, see Giuseppe Canestrini, "Documenti per servire alla storia della milizia Italiana dal XIII secolo al XVI," *Archivio Storico Italiano*, ser. 1, 15 (1851), pp. xxii–xiii. There is ASF, balie 6 fol. 41r. They appear also on the budget of 1350, Camera del comune, Scrivano di camera uscita 10 fol. 41r.

[65] For the earlier period see Daniel Waley, "The Army of the Florentine Republic from the Twelfth to the Fourteenth Century" in *Florentine Studies*, edited by Nicolai Rubinstein (Evanston, IL: Northwestern University Press, 1968) and "Condotte and Condottieri in the Thirteenth Century," *Proceedings of the British Academy* 61 (1975), pp. 337–371.

"military crisis" that resulted in the disappearance of civic militias and the advent of "the superior organization and technique of the mercenary companies."[66] The "rise of the mercenary system" is inextricably linked in the literature with the "decline of the commune." Daniel Waley dated the formalization of mercenary service in Florence to the wars against Castruccio Castracane in the 1320s.[67] C. C. Bayley pointed to the Florentine military code of 1337 as evidence of the decisive shift to non-native, impermanent armies.[68] Michael Mallett depicted the Florentine army as "backward" and out of touch with respect to those of contemporary states such as Venice and Milan.[69]

Meanwhile, basic issues such as the actual makeup of Florentine forces still require close study. The Florentine army in 1349–1350 consisted of cavalry and infantry units. The infantry was subdivided into shield bearer (*pavesari*) units, crossbowmen (*balestrieri*) units, and "mixed units," which contained both shield bearers and crossbowmen. Each was led by its own captain (*conestabile*).

During the first campaign, the size of individual units was generally smaller than those in the second campaign, reflecting the more limited scope of the first war and most likely the smaller size of the army. The conclusion finds support in the use during the first campaign of Niccolò di Rinuccio della Serra as overall commander of the army. He was at this time also a regular civic official, the *capitano della guardia e conservatore dello stato pacifico* with peacetime juridical duties that involved, among other things, keeping watch over the nobility. The captain of war in 1350 was, by contrast, appointed specifically to lead the army.

Close examination of communal (cameral) budgets shows that in June 1349, cavalry bands in Florentine employ ranged from thirteen to twenty men. Shield bearer units consisted primarily of four to twelve men, with a few of larger size. Mixed bands (shield bearers and crossbowmen) consisted of between ten and twenty-three men. The largest

[66] Ercole Ricotti, *Storia dell compagnie di ventura in Italia*, vol. 1 (Turin: Pomba, 1893), p. 92; Waley, "The Army of the Florentine Republic," p. 70; Vigueur, *Comuni e Signorie in Umbria*, pp. 175–226.

[67] Waley, "The Army of the Florentine Republic," p. 106; Paolo Grillo, *Cavalieri e popoli in armi: Le istituzioni military nell'Italia medievale* (Bari: Editori Laterza, 2008), p. 150. Paoli's old but still useful essay about the communal army in 1302 shows that it was still then largely Florentine in composition. Cesare Paoli, "Rendiconto e approvazioni di spese occorse nell'esercito fiorentino contro Pistoia nel Maggio 1302," *Archivio Storico Italiano*, ser. 3, vol. 6 (1867), pp. 3–16.

[68] C. C. Bayley, *War and Society in Renaissance Florence: The De Militia of Leonardo Bruni* (Toronto: University of Toronto Press, 1961), p. 9; Waley, "The Army of the Florentine Republic," p. 97.

[69] Mallett, *Mercenaries and Their Masters*, pp. 82–83.

infantry unit in the army in 1349 had fifty shield bearers led by two captains from the town of San Godenzo in the Casentino mountains.[70] In the second campaign, Florence employed mostly "banner" units of cavalry and infantrymen – that is, bands consisting of twenty to twenty-five men. This was a standard unit used in much of Italy at the time. Extant ambassadorial dispatches and *balie* records of 1350 show that Florence specifically recruited banner units.[71] The budgets, however, show that there was nevertheless variation. Some bands were smaller than twenty men; some were larger.[72]

Petrarch's disdain for them notwithstanding, Florence's cavalry was made up wholly of mercenaries. For the most part they were Germans, the same "rabbia tedesca" that Petrarch railed against in his famous poem "Italia mia." The Florentine sources, however, refer to them respectfully as "probos viros teotonicos." The city also employed Italian mercenary horsemen, identified as "true Guelfs," an apparent requisite for fighting the Ghibelline Ubaldini family. Among the Italian Guelfs employed by Florence were Nino degli Obizzi and Andrea Salmoncelli, prominent exiles from Lucca.[73] During the second campaign Florence hired the Guelf lords from the nearby towns of Castro Focognano and Borgo San Sepolcro.[74] Florence used German mercenary captains to recruit directly other German captains.[75]

City officials arranged the cavalry explicitly according to "lingua" or language. German mercenaries fought in German units; Italian mercenaries fought in Italian units.[76] The identification of Germans by language – "lingua teotonica" in the documents – is somewhat perplexing given that medieval German was not yet a standardized language and varied widely from region to region.[77] The captains in Florentine employ appear to have come from various parts of the Holy Roman Empire, as did the rank and file of their bands, where such information is available.

The evidence of the provenience of cavalrymen is fragmentary, but instructive. The German captain Johann von Strassburgh (nicknamed

[70] ASF, Camera del comune, Scrivano di camera uscita 7 fol. 59v.
[71] In a letter dated 3 April 1350, the city specifically sought "banners" of twenty-five men. ASF, Signori Missive I Cancelleria 10 #145. Florence's first recruits on 26–27 February 1350 included seven units of shield bearers consisting of between twenty-three and twenty-six men. ASF, balie 6 fols. 36r, 38v, 39v, 60v, 98r.
[72] ASF, Camera del comune, Scrivano di camera uscita 9 fol. 19r; balie 6 fol. 97v.
[73] On Obizzi and Salmoncelli, see Christine Meek, *Lucca 1369–1400: Politics and Society in the Early Renaissance State* (Oxford: Oxford University Press, 1978), pp. 183–184. ASF, balie 6 fol. 91r.
[74] ASF, balie 6 fol. 62r; Cancellaria Missive 10 #117.   [75] ASF, balie 6 fols. 52r, 55v.
[76] ASF, balie 6 fol. 118r.
[77] Lorenz Böninger, *Die Deutsche Einwanderung Nach Florenz Im Spatmittelalter* (Leiden: Brill, 2006).

"Strozza') likely took his name from his city of origin, Strassbourg. But two of the men who served in his band (identified in budgets only because of infractions they committed) were "Rodlich of Cologne" and "Rulschino of Vienna."[78] The men were from entirely different parts of the Holy Roman Empire, not from Johann's home base. Another German captain, Gottfried Roher, is cited as being from Brabant in modern day Belgium, and several members of his band appear in the budgets and were from the same place. Burckhard di Toro, whose native town is unknown, had in his band a soldier from the city of Metz and another from Cologne.[79] The makeup of the German component of the Florentine army was thus varied.

While Florence's cavalry consisted of mercenaries from elsewhere, shield bearer captains came primarily from within the Florentine state (Table 2.1).[80] The evidence is important, as the infantry has remained the most misunderstood part of the Florentine army. Cameral budgets give the provenience of the captains, but not the rank-and-file soldiers in their units. The captains came from throughout the entire Florentine state – north, south, east, and west. Many are identified as being from Florence itself or identified by a parish in the city or a district or simply "from Florence." Others came from the immediate outskirts of city, from Galuzzo, Legnaia, and Peretola. There was in short a native infantry element in Florentine armies, no matter how forcefully Machiavelli and the modern scholarly literature argue against this.[81]

The majority of the shield bearer captains came from the mountainous regions of the Florentine state: near Pistoia (Cutigliano, Carmignano, Petiglio, Larciano) and Pescia (Pontito, Medicina, Villa Basilica, Collodi), from the Casentino (Dicomano, Cietica, Garliano, Poppi, San Godenzo, Romena, Pratovecchio, Stia, Gressa, Ortignano) and, most of all, from the upper Mugello (Firenzuola, Tirlì, Vicchio, Lozzole, Montecarelli, Covigiliao, Barberino). Florence also recruited men from the rugged Garfagnana near Lucca (Barga, Castiglione, Montegarullo).

Florence appears to have consciously sought men adapted to the type of warfare needed against the Ubaldini in the Apennine mountains. The recruitment of soldiers from the Mugello was also likely intended

---

[78] ASF, Camera del comune, camerlenghi uscita 66 fol. 619r; Camera del comune, camerlenghi entrata 37 fol. 26r.

[79] ASF, Camera del comune, camerlenghi uscita 70 fol. 42r–42v; Camera del comune, camerlenghi uscita 54 fol. 701v; Scrivano di camer uscita 8 fol. 25r Camera del comune, camerlenghi uscita 37 fol. 25r.

[80] ASF, balie 6 fols. 14v–15v; Camera del comune, Scrivano di camera uscita 10 fols. 24v, 58v.

[81] William Caferro, "Continuity, Long-Term Service and Permanent Forces: A Reassessment of the Florentine Army in the Fourteenth Century," *Journal of Modern History* 80 (2008), pp. 303–322.

Table 2.1 *Provenience of Shield Bearer Captains, 1349–1350 (in alphabetical order)*

Arezzo	Lucignano
Barberino	Medicina
Barga	Migliaccio di Grosseto
Borgo San Lorenzo	Montecarelli
Borgo San Sepolcro	Montecatini
Buggiano	Montegarullo
Camaiore da Lucca	Montevarchi
Caprese	Montificalli
Careggi	Montopoli
Carmignano	Ortignano
Carmignano	Passignano
Castiglione di Garfagnana	Pelago
Cerruglio	Peretola
Chiusi	Pescia
Cietica	Petiglio
Città di Castello	Pistoia
Collodi	Poppi
Covigliao	Prato
Cutigliano	Pratovecchio
Dicomano	Romena
Empoli	San Casciano
Filattiera di Lunigiana	San Godenzo
Filetto	San Lorenzo di Firenze
Firenzuola	San Miniato al Tedescho
Florence	San Piero a Scheraggio di Firenze
Fuccecchio	San Piero a Sieve
Galuzzo	San Piero in Campo
Garfagnana	Santa Maria Maggiore di Firenze
Garliano	Stia
Gressa	Torriglia
Imola	Tirlì
Larciano di Pistoia	Uzzano
Legnaia	Vicchio
Lozzole	Villa Basilica

Sources: ASF, Camera del comune, Scrivano di camera di uscita 6 fols. 17r–41v; Scrivano di uscita 7 fols. 26v–45v; Scrivano di camera uscita 9 fols. 17r–45r; Scrivano di camera uscita 10 fols. 19r–37r.

to deny the Ubaldini its own source of manpower. The evidence lends support to Chris Wickham's assertions that the mountains were integrated into the larger socio-political world of Tuscan towns. In the case here, they formed part of a military-economic sector of Florence.[82]

---

[82] Chris Wickham, *The Mountains and the City: The Tuscan Apennines in the Early Middle Ages* (Oxford: Clarendon Press, 1988), pp. 4–6.

The sources also show that Florence recruited captains from the environs of the cities of Lucca and Arezzo, raising questions whether the men were professional soldiers, who sold their services not only to Florence, but perhaps to other communes as well. We shall discuss this important point later in this chapter.

The crossbow captains in Florentine service came from both inside and outside of the Florentine state. City officials hired men from the town of Bibbiena in the Casentino, where, according to Andrea Barlucchi's recent study, there was a vibrant metalworking sector that produced materials for war.[83] Officials also recruited bowmen from Modena, just north of the Florentine state, and Casteldurante to the east in the Marche, and Arezzo to the southeast. Florence showed a strong preference, however, for crossbowmen from Liguria (Genoa, Sarzana, Spezia) and Lunigiana (Filetto, Pontremoli, Carrara).[84] The soldiers had a reputation for their skill, and Florence recruited them in much the same manner that it did mercenary cavalrymen. The city sent out intermediaries directly to hire the men, bringing advance pay. One official, Paolo del Nero, identified in the documents as a "Florentine citizen," worked continuously throughout the second campaign prospecting for crossbowmen in the region.[85]

There is no evidence that Florence carefully integrated its bowmen and its shield bearers in the field, as was done at the famous battle of Campaldino a half century earlier (1289). "Mixed" bands in Florentine employ consisted of both crossbowmen and shield bearers, but there does not appear to have been any fixed ratio between the two. The mixed contingent of Nanni di Giovanni from Città di Castello, for example, had seven shield bearers and four crossbowmen in 1349; the band of Agnolo Vanni of Bibbiena had eight shield bearers and two crossbowmen.[86]

Moreover, mixed units routinely changed in shape and size. Santi Chiarucci of Tirlì, who manned the siege tower at Montegemoli in 1350, served as captain of a mixed band of twelve shield bearers and three crossbowmen during the first campaign in 1349.[87] At the start of the second campaign, however, Chiarucci captained a band with twelve shield bearers and no crossbowmen. By the summer of 1350, Chiarucci

---

[83] Andrea Barlucchi, "I centri minori delle conche Appenniniche (Casentino e Alta Valtinertina)" in *I centri minori della Toscana nel medioevo*, edited by Giuliano Pinto and Paolo Pirillo (Florence: Leo S. Olschki 2013), pp. 67–74.

[84] ASF, Camera del comune, Scrivano di camera uscita 8 fols. 27v, 33r.

[85] ASF, balie 6 fols. 40v, 59r, 76r.

[86] ASF, Camera del comune, Scrivano di camera uscita 6 fol. 22v.

[87] ASF, Camera del comune, Scrivano di camera uscita 6 fol. 37r.

was again at the head of a mixed band, now with eighteen men overall, six of whom were crossbowmen.[88]

Chiarucci himself appears to have been a shield bearer who took crossbowmen into his bands. Conversely, the captain Iacomino Buralli was a crossbowman who took shield bearers into his band. During the first campaign in 1349, Buralli headed a crossbow contingent of fifteen men. A year later, in 1350, his band was "mixed" with two shield bearers and fourteen crossbowmen.

Continuity, Professional Army, and Soldiers as Investors

A unique view of the Florentine army as it actually appeared in the field against the Ubaldini is from the second campaign, just prior to the offensive against the castle of Montegemoli in May 1350.[89]

The *balie* records relay the details of preparation and organization. Florentine officials placed German mercenaries at the vanguard of the army, with the *feditori* or "wounders," the striking force, intended to bear the brunt of the battle. This prestigious position was, in the thirteenth century, reserved for native soldiers, among them purportedly Dante at Campaldino.[90] The use of Germans as *feditori* is further proof of the importance of foreign mercenaries to the Florentine army. Indeed, the *balia* adds an interesting aside: that the *feditori* had been, since the war with Pisa in 1341, under the command of a Burgundian captain Giovanni della Vallina.[91]

The German captain Burckhard di Toro was placed in command of the *feditori* in 1350 and given the banner of the lily (*banderia del giglio*), the symbol of the city.[92] The German captain Jakob da Fiore was appointed *marescallo* or marshall of the army (13 May), a post that involved supervising horses.

The *balia* records show that the army had a separate contingent of "spalatores and marraiouli," whose job it was to repair and break up roads.[93] It had a contingent of so-called destroyers (under the *banderia del guasto*, banner of destruction) composed of stonemasons, who serviced trebuchets used to throw stones at Ubaldini fortifications.[94] The size of the two units is not given. The army had, as noted earlier,

---

[88] ASF, Camera del comune, Scrivano di camera uscita 7 fol. 27v; Scrivano di camera uscita 10 fol. 39v.

[89] ASF, balie 6 fols. 68v–69v.

[90] ASF, balie 6 fols. 68v, 97v. Caferro, "Continuity, Long-Term Service and Permanent Forces," pp. 230, 303–322. Waley discusses the use *feditori* as native troops. Waley, "The Army of the Florentine Republic," p. 105.

[91] ASF, balie 6 fol. 68v.   [92] ASF, balie 6 fols. 68v, 97v.

[93] ASF, balie 6 fol. 5v; balie 6 fol. 74r.   [94] ASF, balie 6 fol. 69r.

a contingent of native bowmen, the *balestrieri della ghiera*, consisting of 474 men. It employed fifty *barattieri*, or ribalds, who perpetrated acts of *infamia* and ritual humiliation against the enemy. Robert Davidsohn has described *barattieri* as the poorest element of Florentine society, who owned bordellos and cleaned latrines. Alessandro Gherardi has pointed out that at the start of the *trecento* the term applied more broadly to Florentine employees who inflicted corporal punishment and took plunder.[95]

The army was commanded by the captain of war, Cecco di Ranieri Farnese, who was elected to the office on 31 March 1350.[96] Farnese was assisted by three civilian *consigliares*, appointed in April, who consulted with him on strategy and facilitated communication between the army and the *balia* and priors at home.[97] The three *consigliares* were Albertaccio di Messer Bindaccio Ricasoli, Paolo Bardi de Altoviti, and Giovanni Massai Raffacani – all from prominent Florentine families with political connections. Ricasoli was a member of the committee in charge of establishing the Florentine university (that hoped to recruit Petrarch). He served also as a captain of the Guelf party in July 1349 and was praised by the novelist Franco Sacchetti as "un cavaliere valoroso e morale."[98] Giovanni Raffacani had also been a captain of the Guelf party in 1349 and held several important government positions, including *conservatore* of the town of San Gimignano. Altoviti served as a vicar of Valdinievole.[99]

It is important to note that Florence hired most of its cavalry and infantry *before* appointing its captain of war in 1350. Thus, the captain had little say in the composition of the overall army. His role was more like the modern-day baseball manager, restricted to supervising the personnel he was given.

Moreover, Florence appointed the leader of the various contingents of the army in 1350 just prior to mobilization. The city retained direct control over these officers and over the composition of infantry units, whose rank and file it fired for poor performance.[100] Cavalry captains, however, maintained direct control of the members of their bands.

---

[95] Robert Davidsohn, *Storia di Firenze IV I Primordi della civilta fiorentina, part 1 impulsi interni, influssi esterni e cultura politica Florence* (Florence: G. C. Sansoni, 1977), p. 326; Gherardi, "L'Antica camera," pp. 347–348.

[96] ASF, balie 6 fols. 63r–63v.

[97] The election of Ricasoli, Altoviti, and Raffacani was on 22 April 1350. ASF, balie 6 fol. 65r.

[98] ASF, Camera del commune, camarlenghi entrata #34 fol. 201v. Ricasoli, a magnate, appears to have been made a "popolano" as a result of his service in the war in 1349. ASF, Provvisioni, registri 37 fol. 106r. Ricasoli is mentioned in Sacchetti's fragmentary novella CCLV.

[99] ASF, Camera del comune, Scrivano di camera entrata 8 fol. 14r; Marzi, *La cancelleria*. p. 680. Camera del comune, camarlenghi entrata 34 fol. 201v.

[100] ASF, balie 6 fols. 5v–15v.

Just prior to mobilization Florence fired the leader of the *spalatores*, Bartuccio degli Obizzi, and replaced him with Lancialotto Caccianemici from Bologna. Later in the war, the city replaced the captain of the *barattieri*, Johannes de Loiano, with Passero Venture. This may have been because of the misdeeds of the *barattieri*, whom sources indicate were overly zealous in their taunts against the enemy.[101]

The documents allow a still closer look at the army. Although the size and shape of Florentine forces changed from 1349 to 1350, there was a surprising degree of continuity in personnel despite the plague and demographic crisis. Florence maintained a core of battle-trained captains around which it built its army.[102] Many of the same mercenary cavalry captains fought in both campaigns in 1349 and 1350, including stalwarts such as the Germans Burckhard di Toro, commander of the *feditores*; Jakob da Fiore, the marshal of the army; Johann Dornich, who manned the siege tower at Montegemoli; and the "Guelf" captains Nino degli Obizzi and Andrea Salmoncelli from Lucca (Table 2.2).

Rather than dismiss soldiers at the end of the campaign, as scholars allege, Florence often relied on the same men, adjusting the size of their bands from one campaign to the other. Johann Strassburgh's contingent consisted of fourteen horsemen in 1349 and was increased to twenty men, a full banner, in 1350.[103] Burckhard di Toro captained seventeen horses in 1349 and then a banner of twenty men in 1350; Umberto Moresta had fourteen men and then twenty-five men; Gherard Quartaro had thirteen and then twenty men.[104] The bands of Jakob da Fiore, Gottfried Roher, William Belmont, and Astinicho Mostinbruch remained at twenty horses during both wars, as did those of the Lucchese captains Obizzi and Salmoncelli.[105]

The pattern is the same with infantry captains, supposedly the most ephemeral element of the army (Table 2.3). The Ligurian crossbow captains Bartolomeo Gherarducci, Anichino Andreotti, and Francarello Pucci – all from the town of Sarzana – fought in both campaigns. So did the crossbow captains Iacomino da Buralli of Modena, Piero Berardi of Bibbiena, and others. The shield bearer captains Santi Chiarucci of Tirlì, Jacobo "Ser Mestola" Chesis of Passignano, Francesco "Malamamma" Bartoli of Florence, "Prete" Fortini of Pistoia, Sandro del Corso of

---

[101] ASF, CP 1 fol. 17r; balie 6 fol. 74r.

[102] Caferro "Continuity, Long-Term Service and Permanent Forces," pp. 303–322.

[103] ASF, Camera del comune, Scrivano di camera uscita 6 fols. 19r, 22r, 24r; Scrivano di camera uscita 7 fols. 26v–45v; Scrivano di camera uscita 10 fols. 19r–37r.

[104] ASF, Camera del comune, Scrivano di camera uscita 7 fol. 29r.

[105] ASF, Camera del comune, Scrivano di camera uscita 6 fols. 17v, 19r, 25v, 26r; Scrivano di camera uscita 7 fols. 24r–v; Scrivano di camera uscita 8 fols. 17r, 18r, 23v, 18r.

Table 2.2 *Cavalry Captains Who Fought in Both Campaigns,*
1349–1350

Soldier	Type of Unit
Jakob da Fiore	German mercenary
Gottfried Roher	German mercenary
Burckhard di Toro	German mercenary
Johann Strassburgh	German mercenary
Johann Dornich	German mercenary
William Belmont	German mercenary
Lambercione Dester	German mercenary
Edward Bingher	German mercenary
Hermann Vesternich	German mercenary
Uberto Moresta	German mercenary
Luigi Busci	German mercenary
Nicholetto Grande	German mercenary
Astinicho Mostinbruch (knight)	German mercenary
Goschino d'Avisach	German mercenary
Corrado Inghilspur	German mercenary
Gherard Quartaro	German mercenary
Nino degli Obizzi	Italian mercenary
Andrea Salmoncelli	Italian mercenary

Source: ASF, Camera del comune, Scrivano di camera di uscita 6 fols. 17r–41v;
Scrivano di uscita 7 fols. 26v–45v; Scrivano di camera uscita 9 fols. 17r–45r;
Scrivano di camera uscita 10 fols. 19r–37r.

Florence, Francesco Scale of Gressa, Francesco Barufaldi of Montecarelli,
Filippo Corsini of Pistoia, Vanni Nacchi of Legnaia, and Tone Lemmi of
the Garfagnana, among others, fought in both campaigns.

As with the cavalry, the size of the captains' bands fluctuated from one
campaign to the other. Alpinuccio Nuti of Bibbiena's crossbow unit
consisted of fifteen crossbowmen in 1349 and then twenty-four crossbowmen in 1350. Tone Lemmi of Castiglione's shield bearer unit was
made up of seven men in 1349 and ten in 1350.[106]

A long-term study of the Florentine army is beyond the scope of
this book. But there is ample evidence that the continuity of service
among the captains extended well beyond the two years in question.[107]
Mercenary cavalry captains in Florentine service in 1349–1350 have

---

[106] ASF, Camera del comune, Scrivano di camera uscita 6 fols. 17v, 25v, 26r; Scrivano di
camera uscita 7 fol. 24r–v; Scrivano di camera uscita 8 fol. 17r; Scrivano di camera uscita
10 fol. 30v.

[107] For continuity in fourteenth-century Florentine armies, see Caferro "Continuity, Long-
Term Service and Permanent Forces," pp. 303–322.

Table 2.3 *Infantry Captains Who Fought in Both Campaigns, 1349–1350*

Soldier/Provenience	Type of Unit
Alpinuccio Nuti of Bibbiena	crossbow
Bartolomeo Gherarducci of Sarzana	crossbow
Anichino Andreotti of Sarzana	crossbow
Francarello Pucci of Sarzana	crossbow
Iacomino da Buralli of Modena	crossbow
Mazetto Gherardini of Modena	crossbow
Francesco "Malamamma" Bartoli of Florence	shield bearer
Piero Berardi of Arezzo	shield bearer
Tone Lemmi of Castiglione di Garfagnana	shield bearer
Filippo Corsini of Pistoia	shield bearer
Vanni Nacchi of Legnaia	shield bearer
Francesco Scale of Gressa	shield bearer
Francescho Barufaldi of Montecarelli	shield bearer
Sandro del Corso of Florence	shield bearer
Lando Guasconi of Pratovecchio	shield bearer
Bartolomeo Cennis of Florence	shield bearer
Paganuccio Pecconi of Lucca	shield bearer
Balduccio Gucci of Collodi	shield bearer
Coluccio Gualteri of Camaiore	shield bearer
Bondo Orsucci of Pelago	shield bearer
Santi Chiarucci of Tirlì	shield bearer/mixed
Francesco "Prete" Fortini of Pistoia	mixed

Source: See Table 2.2.

been identified as having had long careers with the city. Burckhard di Toro, commander of the *feditori* in the vanguard of the army in 1350, first worked for Florence in 1341 and continued in Florentine employ for at least eleven years. In 1351 he served as captain general of the Florentine army during the war with Milan.[108] Jakob da Fiore, the marshall of the army in 1350, likewise began in Florentine service in 1341, as did Johann Dornich, Gottfried Roher, and Edward Bingher. They all fought for Florence against Milan in 1351. Jakob da Fiore remained on the Florentine payroll for fourteen years (1341, 1345–1357); Gottfried Roher for eighteen years (1334–1351); and Dornich and Bingher for at least a decade (1341–1351). The Italian captain Nino degli Obizzi fought for Florence for at least twelve years (1347–1358), and the German Hermann Vesternich worked for the

[108] ASF, Signori Missive I Cancelleria 10 #2, 3.

city for more than twenty years – his service extending all the way to 1380.[109]

The same is true of shield bearer and crossbow captains. Francesco "Malamamma" Bartoli worked for Florence for at least fifteen years (1348–1369), during which he fought in the wars against Milan (1351), Pisa (1362–1364), and Milan again in 1369.[110] The captains Alpinuccio Nuti of Bibbiena, Santi Chiarucci of Tirlì, Francesco Scale of Gressa, Paganuccio Pecconi of Lucca, Balduccio Guccio of Collodi, Iacomino Buralli of Modena, and Vanni Nacchi of Legnaia all appear on the *Miscellanea Repubblicana* #120 budgets as being in Florentine service in 1348, prior to the Ubaldini war.[111] It is likely that the men served both earlier and later in Florentine service.[112]

There was, to be sure, a significant ebb and flow of soldiers in the Florentine army. Communal budgets do not list personnel below the level of the captain, perhaps disguising significant fluctuations among the rank-and-file soldiers. But it is clear that Florence did not start anew after each campaign – a notion that despite its currency in the popular sphere (where military history has too long resided) never made sense. Florence relied on a core – perhaps relatively small, but nevertheless significant – of professional captains that it had confidence in, who worked for the city over the long run.

Indeed, the martial skill of the infantry captains is made plain by the chronicler Stefani, who gave a forceful and much neglected description of the men during the war with Milan in 1351. Stefani praised the Florentine infantry for its heroic defense of Scarperia, then, as in 1349/1350, a focal point of military activity. Stefani described the infantry as "some of best ... in the world" and pointed out how they were "prized and honored ... just as today horsemen are honored with golden spurs."[113] He singled out the infantry captains by name, a list that includes Francesco "Malamamma" Bartoli, Martino "Boschereggio" Dandi, "Prete" Fortini and Sandro del Corso – all of whom served as captains against the Ubaldini.[114]

It is important to stress the skill of the infantry. The scholarly literature has treated them as little more than "a mass of men," a phrase often used in Italian chronicle accounts. But "Bad Mamma" Bartoli, a hero in 1351,

---

[109] Caferro "Continuity, Long-Term Service and Permanent Forces," pp. 229–230.
[110] Caferro, "Continuity, Long-Term Service and Permanent Forces," pp. 233–236.
[111] ASF, Miscellenea repubblicana 120 #2, 3.
[112] ASF, Miscellenea repubblicana 120 #3.
[113] Marchionne di Coppo Stefani, *Cronaca Fiorentina*, edited by N. Rodolico, in *Rerum Italicarum scriptores: Raccolta di Storici Italiani dal cinquecento al millecinquecento*, edited by L. A. Muratori (Città di Castello: S. Lapi, 1910), pp. 238–239.
[114] Stefani, *Cronaca Fiorentina*, p. 239.

was employed in the same fighting unit as Martino Dandi, another of Stefani's heroes, and with "Ser Mestola" ("Half-wit") Chesis, against the Ubaldini in 1350.[115] The *balia* records make clear that the men were specifically recruited together, to form a fighting unit, along with three others captains: Bartolomeo Cennis, Piero of Collodi, and Guidalotto Rigucci. The band comported itself so well in 1350 that it earned bonus pay.[116] And apart from fighting skill, there would appear little to link the men. The captains were from different parts of the Florentine state – "Bad mamma" from Florence, "Half-wit" from Passignano, Dondi from San Casciano (south of the city), Bartolomeo Cennis from Montecarelli (north of the city in the Mugello), Piero da Collodi from Pescia (west of the city in the Valdinievole), and Guidalotto Rigucci from Montificalli (southeast of Florence near Greve, in the Chianti region toward Siena).[117]

The most reasonable conclusion is that the captains were professionals and, judging from Stefani's description, *well-known* professionals. Indeed, it may be this fame that caught the attention of Boccaccio, who used the term "Ser Mestola" in the *Decameron* and *Corbaccio*.

But Florence's relationship with its infantry is more striking still. Captains also appear in the documents as holders of shares (*azioni*) of the Florentine public debt (*monte*), acting as investors in the Florentine state, a tie that runs contrary to any portrait of the profession.[118] The evidence is fragmentary, but the holders of shares in the public debt in 1345 (the year of its founding) include the crossbow captains Alpinuccio Nuti of Bibbiena, Iacomino Buralli of Modena, and Francarello Pucci of Sarzana as well as the shield bearer captains Vanni Nacchi of Legnaia, Coluccio Gualtieri of Camaiore, and Filippo Corsini of Pistoia.[119] The men all fought for Florence against the Ubaldini.

The financial tie may explain the willingness of the men to serve over extended periods of time. They were linked to the economic fortunes of the city. And their investments appear, where visible, to have been substantial. Vanni Nacchi, captain of a small "mixed" band of seven shield

---

[115] ASF, Camera del comune, Scrivano di camera uscita 7 fol. 47r.

[116] ASF, Camera del commune, Scrivano di camera uscita 10 fol. 28r.

[117] ASF, balie 6 fols. 8r, 14v–15v, 36r 39v; Camera del comune, Scrivano di camera uscita 10 fols. 24v, 58v.

[118] Roberto Barducci, "Politica e speculazione finanziaria a Firenze dopo la crisi del primo Trecento (1343–1358)," *Archivio Storico Italiano* 137, no 2 (1979), pp. 202–203. Barducci cites Notarile Antecosmiano 570 #56–69, which is now Notarile antecosmiano 5473 #56–70. The list of investors in the Monte also includes three *trombadori*, Niccolo Aiuti, Nicholo vocatus profeta olim magister Merlini, and Pagno Bertini. ASF, Notarile antecosmiano 5473 #56–69.

[119] ASF, Notarile antecosmiano 5473 #56, #63, #64; Camera del comune, Scrivano di camera entrata 8 fols. 28v, 27r, 30r.

bearers and eleven shield bearers in 1349 and 1350, held *azioni* worth 787 lire in 1345.[120] The sum is striking, given his ostensibly minor role in the war, modest pay, and meager professional status. Similarly, the crossbow captain Alpinuccio Nuti from Bibbiena held *azioni* worth 747 lire and Francarello Pucci, the crossbow captain from Sarzana, was owed 663 lire by the city.[121]

Such investment was likely more widespread and deserves careful, detailed study by scholars. The *monte* registers of 1345 list still more soldiers who did not fight for Florence in 1349–1350, but who held shares of the public debt. They included Francesco di Giovanni, a crossbow captain from Genoa, Berto Belezze, a shield bearer captain from Monte San Savino, and Simonelli Giovanni, a crossbow captain from Panicale.[122]

What is abundantly clear is that the Florentine infantry was far different from the scholarly perception of it. Giuseppe Canestrini described *trecento* infantrymen as an "unorganized" mass who "served for several days at a time." F. L. Taylor spoke of them as "universally despised," and Philippe Contamine asserted, for Europe more generally, that they had "little rational organization."[123] This was not true of Florence, even during the confusion of the immediate aftermath of the plague. The native element was not lacking, and the *balia* of 1350 that hired infantrymen described them as "probos viros in armis expertis" (upright men expert in arms), the same respectful language used to describe cavalrymen.[124] This may have been formula, but upon inspection of the deeds of the soldiers, the description does not seem at all inappropriate.[125]

That Florence recruited some shield bearer captains, as we have seen, from outside of the state, raises the question of whether there was a market in professional infantrymen alongside the well-known one in mercenary cavalrymen. Paganuccio Pecconi, who is listed as a shield bearer captain from Lucca, is a particularly intriguing figure. He served during the first campaign in 1349 at the head of nine men. But during the second campaign, Florentine officials elevated him to *istrutore* of the army, the same title given to the Italian cavalry captains Andrea

---

[120] ASF, Notarile antecosmiano 5473 #64.
[121] ASF, Notarile antecosmiano 5473 #63, 64.
[122] ASF, Notarile antecosmiano 5473 #63, 60.
[123] Canestrini, "Documenti," p. cvii; F. L. Taylor, *The Art of War in Italy, 1494–1529* (Westport, CT: Greenwood Press, 1921), p. 5; Philippe Contamine, *War in the Middle Ages*, trans. Michael Jones (Oxford: Blackwell Publishing, 1980), p. 170.
[124] ASF, balie 6 fols. 36r, 38v, 39v.
[125] ASF, Camera del comune, Scrivano di camera uscita 10 fols. 17r–18r; Scrivano di camera uscita 9 fol. 31v.

Salmoncelli and Giovanni Conte de Medici.[126] Pecconi's responsibilities in that post are unclear, but his role was likely a supervisory one and, as the documents show, allowed Paganuccio higher pay. Paganuccio was now something more than a shield bearer, and his example suggests at the very least that there was movement within the infantry hierarchy, room for advancement for more skilled and trusted soldiers.[127]

The point should not be overstated. The number of shield bearers from outside the Florentine state appears to have been relatively small. And it needs to be remembered that Florentine budgets do not give the provenience of the rank-and-file soldiers. And despite the similarities with the cavalry, Florence retained direct control over the personnel of infantry bands, while ceding the same to the captains of cavalry units.[128] In addition, infantry bands contained *ragazzini* (apprentices) in them; cavalry bands did not. And during the last months of the campaign in 1350, Florentine officials hired infantry captains who do not appear to have been professional fighters. The cameral budgets show that men included Jacopo di Naddo, identified as a *fornaio* (baker); Bartolomeo Ghuadagni, identified as a *mugnaio* (miller); Guido Pezzini, a *chalderaio* (metalworker); and Ghuido di Giovanni, *pescaioulo* (fisherman). Each commanded shield bearer units of ten men.[129]

Organization of War: Logistics, Supplies, and Personnel

In addition to its army, Florence devoted a great deal of attention to supplying and maintaining its army in the field. The opening lines of the *balia* of 1350 make it clear that its raison d'etre was to provide an "abundance of supplies and all things necessary" for the army.[130] This involved not only the procurement of food, supplies, and weapons, but also the assembling of a workforce of noncombatants, including spies, artisans, messengers, transporters, troop inspectors, and paymasters to support the army in the field. The workforce was large and the interplay of offices complex. The movement of supplies to the army was rendered all the more difficult by the fact that, according to the documents, it was often done at night, to escape detection by the enemy.

---

[126] ASF, Camera del comune, Scrivano di camera uscita 7 fols. 28v–29r; Scrivano di camera uscita 10 fol. 26r.
[127] He earned a florin a day for the job. ASF, balie 8 fol. 2v.
[128] ASF, balie 6 fols. 5v, 15v.
[129] ASF, Camera del comune, Scrivano di camera entrata 7 fols. 25r–27r.
[130] ASF, balie 6 fol. 2r. For a preliminary discussion of logistics and supplies, see William Caferro, "Military Enterprise in Florence at the Time of the Black Death, 1349–50." In *War, Entrepreneurs, and the State in Europe and the Mediterranean, 1300–1800*, edited by Jeff Fynn-Paul (Leiden: Brill, 2014), pp. 15–31.

The *balia* records allow a close look at Florence's organization of war.[131] The first act (after apportioning money to recruit troops and repay the bankers who advanced money for them) was to hire four "consultants"/"expert *popolares*" from each of the *quartiere* of the city to oversee the procurement of supplies.[132] The consultants were each important merchants and included Boccaccio's friend Francesco del Bennino and Jacopo di Donato Acciaiuoli, the brother of Petrarch's ally Niccolò Acciaiuoli of Naples. The men worked "in consiglio" with the office of *camera del arme*, which paid them a daily salary and reimbursed their expenses. It is not clear if the consultants sold supplies directly to the *camera* or arranged for their purchase from other merchants. The city added more consultants as the war continued, including Bernardo Ardinghelli, a prominent merchant with prior experience in the war region. Ardinghelli helped oversee the construction of a fortress at Firenzuola in 1332.[133]

Florentine officials also appointed two men, Cionetto di Giovenco Bastari and Silvestro di Adovardi Bellfredi, specifically to be in charge of supplies at the town of Scarperia, the headquarters of the war effort. They were each assisted in the task by two *sargenti*, whose precise duties are unclear.[134] Florence also appointed a "custodian" (Francesco di Pieri di Ricci) to oversee the food supply in the town, which was stored in a house belonging to "Tessa, wife of Tano." A notary (Ser Lippo de Grezzano) was hired to keep record of all inflow and outflow of goods.[135]

Just before the army set out for Montegemoli (7 May 1350), Florence appointed Christofano Boninstrade and Domenico di Sandro Donnini to ride along with the army to oversee supplies.[136] The appointments are noteworthy because the financial accounts of the men have survived (*balie* 7). They show that from late May to July 1350 the men distributed sacks of bread, barley, and orzo to the army.[137] They also paid the *barattieri*, who committed acts of arson and retrieved crossbow bolts from the battlefield.

The critical job of physically transporting supplies was entrusted to *vetturali* and *mulattieri*. The workforce, as yet unstudied, appears to have been large, consisting of at least twenty-eight men, identified either by first name or nickname. Their missions lasted from several days to several

---

[131] ASF, balie 7 fol. 33r.   [132] ASF, balie 6 fol. 58v.
[133] ASF, balie 6 fols. 6v, 70r, 75r.
[134] The *sargenti* in turn each had two *servitori*. ASF, balie 6 fols. 7r, 71v; balie 7 fols. 32v, 75v, 88r.
[135] ASF, balie 6 fols. 24r, 89v.   [136] ASF, balie 6 fols. 4v, 68r.
[137] ASF, balie 7 fols. 1r–3v, 29r–30v, 32r–36v, 64r–64v.

weeks.[138] They received daily wages, which depended on the type of animal they used. Transport by mule (*mulattieri*) cost 19 soldi a day; transport by donkey cost 10 soldi a day, nearly half as much. *Vetturali* usually had a combination of animals. One, identified only as "Paolo," used five mules and one donkey to move supplies on 2 July 1350. Another *vetturale* known as "Francesco" employed two mules and one donkey. Nicolaio and Piero employed six mules and a horse. The cost of transport by horse is unclear, but appears to have been more expensive. The proveniences of the *vetturali* are cited, and several came from outside of Florence, most typically from Bologna, particularly those employed along the border.[139]

The movement of supplies was coordinated with the activities at Scarperia, where the city assembled a workforce of artisans to build trebuchets and siege towers.[140] The artisans at Scarperia were, like the "consultants" in the field, hired at the very outset of the campaign. Their basic importance in war was stated forcefully by Machiavelli, who placed "those skilled in the arts (smiths, carpenters, farriers and stone-cutters)" at the very top of the hierarchy of military men in his *Art of War*, just below the all-important citizen infantrymen.[141] On 6 April 1350 Florence hired twenty-seven stonemasons, four of whom were *capomaestri*, with a helper or *discepolo*.[142] Four days later, the city added six sawyers (*segatori*)," six carpenters, and two black-smiths, raising the total number of *maestri* at Scarperia to forty-four men.[143] The number fluctuated, however, as workers, notably the *capomaestri* stonemasons, joined the army in the field and serviced the same machines they built.[144]

The workforce at Scarperia was carefully organized. Officials maintained a separate notary, Ser Luce Pucci, who enrolled all workers, and a foreman, Rustico Lemmi, who coordinated their activities. The four *capomaestri* stonemasons worked specifically on machines "that threw stones" (*ad prohiciendi lapides*). Two *maestri*, Ruffo Gherardi and Francesco Neri, made wooden wheels to move the trebuchets and field

---

[138] ASF, balie 6 fols. 95r–96r.   [139] ASF, balie 6 fol. 95r, 96v.

[140] ASF, balie 7 fol. 32v; balie 6 fols. 4r–11v.

[141] Machiavelli, *The Art of War*, translated by Christopher Lynch (Chicago, IL: University of Chicago Press, 2003), p. 26.

[142] ASF, balie 6 fols. 9r, 51r–51v. The workers are all identified as *maestri di lapide e legname*. Following Goldthwaite, I refer to them as stonemasons. Richard A. Goldthwaite, *The Building of Renaissance Florence* (Baltimore, MD: Johns Hopkins University Press, 1980), pp. 436, 437. See also Sergio Tognetti, "Prezzi e salari nella Firenze tardo medievale: un profile," *Archivio storico italiano* 153 (1995), pp. 302–304.

[143] ASF, balie 6 fols. 8v; 56v–57r, 58r.

[144] ASF, balie 6 fol. 70v. For 14 May, the *balia* lists thirty-nine artisans (two of whom are blacksmiths with *discepoli*) at Scarperia. ASF, balie fols. 6r–8v, 21r–23r.

Table 2.4 *Suppliers of War Material, 1350*

Name (*Craft*)	Goods
Michele Nardi (*mercario*)	crossbows
Bartolo Lapi (*stradario*)	crossbows
Giovanni Nuti (*funaiolo*)	hemp
Giudotto Cenni (*funaiolo*)	hemp
Azzino Gualberti (*fabbro*)	tools
Tollino Dini (*fabbro*)	wire
Bartolomeo Giovanni (*ferraiolo*)	iron, wire, steel
Francesco Corsini (*speziale*)	sinopie/wire
Frasinello Corsini (*fabbro*)	coal, wax
Lottino Lotti	nails, wire
Donato (*fabbro*)	nails
Francesco Becci	lanterns
Giovanni Guascoli (*fabbro*)	wood
Dominie Calie	coal
Filippo Vanni (*maestro legnami*)	wood/lanterns

Source: ASF, balie 6 fols. 4r, 8v, 9r, 23r, 58r, 90v, 93r, 108v.

fortifications into place in the field.[145] A separate blacksmith, Michele Vanni, sharpened tools used for the building of the trebuchets.[146] A notary, Ser Guelfo di Francesco, recorded all the materials used by the *maestri*.[147] And just prior to mobilization against Montegemoli, Florence added two more foremen to expedite work on the siege towers and trebuchets.[148]

There was steady movement of men and material between Scarperia and the battlefield. Ristoro di Cione, a *capomaestro* who made trebuchets, went with the army to serve as captain of the *guastatori* unit in the field in May. He participated in the battle at Montegemoli. The *capomaestri* Stefano Pucci and Iusto Bartoli rode with the army in early July to oversee the destruction of the wall of the castle at le Piagnole.[149] They were joined there by two additional masons, Niccolo Pagni and Tone Corsi, who also had worked at Scarperia.

The *balia* records provide an inventory of supplies at Scarperia used for war (Chapter 3). The city purchased *sinopie* (violet) to sketch designs for its war machines and large quantities of hemp and iron to build them.[150] It purchased wood, steel, coal, wax, locks, nails, keys, bells, shovels, lanterns, axes, awls, scalpels, and scissors.[151] The materials were bought from merchants and artisans, who are named in the sources (Table 2.4).

[145] ASF, balie 6 fols. 23r, 61r.   [146] ASF, balie 6 fol. 8v.   [147] ASF, balie 6 fol. 66r.
[148] ASF, balie 6 fol. 74v.   [149] ASF, balie 6 fols. 22r, 74v.   [150] ASF, balie 6 fol. 4r.
[151] ASF, balie 6 fols. 4r, 11v, 93r.

A spice dealer (*speziale*), Francesco Corsini, sold carbon and *sinopie* to the city; a cord maker (*funaiolo*), Giovanni Nuti, supplied hemp; blacksmiths (*fabbri*) Tollino Dini, Bartolomeo Giovanni, Azzino Gualberti, and Michele Vanni sold nails, iron wire, bells, tools, and scissors.[152] Frasinello Corsini, a *fabbro*, sold coal and wax.

The suppliers were mostly local men, from the environs of Scarperia and the Mugello (Chapter 3). Some were, at the same time, artisans at Scarperia. Frasinello Corsini, a blacksmith working at Scarperia, also sold coal and wax to the city, in addition to his labor.[153] Azzino Gualberti, another blacksmith at Scarperia, sold tools.[154] Filippo Vanni, a *capomaestro* stonemason working on the trebuchets at Scaperia, sold wood and iron lanterns.[155]

Florence's workforce included many additional workers. The city employed messengers (*cursori*) to carry letters to and from the field, spies and explorers to seek out enemy secrets, musicians to coordinate the army in the field and play at celebrations, troop inspectors to evaluate the personnel in the army and fortresses, paymasters to disburse funds to soldiers, and at least one doctor, Andrea Bartoli, who traveled with the army and used oil to help salve wounds.[156] The workforce numbered well over 100 men.

Troop inspectors (*rassegnatori*) performed the important task of reviewing all communal troops and castellans. They ensured that the men were properly armed and ordered, and that their equipment was up to the standards agreed upon when they were hired. The inspectors assessed penalties for *difetti* (i.e., for inferior equipment) and fines for the use of inferior-quality horses (*cavalli scritti a mezzana stima*) as well as other transgressions. The inspections (*mostre*) were carried out once a month under the supervision of the condotta office. *Mostre* lasted for several days and sometimes, as in the case of the review of the army just prior to mobilization in June 1349, a full week.[157] The total number of *rassegnatori* active at any given time is difficult to determine given the ad hoc nature of the job. The budgets show that in July 1349, Florence employed six pairs of men, one of whom was a notary charged with writing down the details of horses and all equipment. The *rassegnatori* were sent throughout the Florentine state to inspect soldiers and castellans in all communal forts.[158]

Paymasters were a more nebulous group. Their services were crucial, but their activities rarely appear in the sources. Indeed, the whole

---

[152] ASF, balie 6 fols. 9r, 108v, 114r.   [153] ASF, balie 6 fol. 22r.
[154] ASF, balie 6 108r, 114r.   [155] ASF, balie 6 fols. 4r, 10v, 23r, 71r.
[156] ASF, balie 6 fol. 109v.   [157] ASF, balie 6 fol. 17r.
[158] ASF, Camera del comune, Scrivano di camera uscita 10 fols. 20v, 35v, 56v.

mechanism of payment of soldiers is an aspect of war about which surprisingly little is known. The budgets make clear that there was no specific employee responsible for the task. Every mercenary cavalry captain had a *procuratore* assigned to him. The *procuratore* appears to have served as intermediary between the captain and the state, a duty that most likely involved physically paying the soldiers. Ser Bonaiuto Sensi, a notary, served as *procuratore*, as did Andree Giovanni, whose name occurs frequently in budgets in connection with German and Italian cavalrymen.[159] Giovanni traveled in June 1349 to the "high Alps" in the Mugello to pay soldiers.[160] The *balia* records mention several additional men – citizens of substance, with experience handling money – who served as paymaster to soldiers and noncombatants. In August 1350 the men included Niccolò di Messer Bencivenni, a chamberlain of the office of the condotta, and Manetto Ser Ricciardi, a banker, who went in person to the Mugello to pay a wide range of workers. In addition, two officials of the *balia* itself, Simone Landi di Leccio and Ser Puccini Ser Lapi, paid soldiers, as did Silvestro Advardi de Bellfredi and Cionetto Giovenchi de Bastari, two of the "consultants" in charge of supplies at Scarperia.[161] Meanwhile, an official of the *camera del arme* (Uguccione Bonisegne Gherardi) traveled to Scarperia in May 1350 specifically to pay the salaries of *vetturali* there.[162] Two accountants of the *camera del comune*, Simone Lapi Schutiggi and Spinello di Luca Alberti, paid soldiers at various times during the summer of 1350.[163]

The largest part of the workforce of noncombatants was that which was involved in the flow of information. Florence derived news (*novelle*) from a variety of sources.[164] It employed messengers (*cursori*), whose task it was to bring letters from city officials to the army and vice versa. The *balia* records contain 111 separate entries for messengers during the brief period from May to September 1350![165] The entries give a sense of the rhythms of the campaign. Florence sent out twenty-nine messengers just prior to the offensive against Montegemoli in May 1350 and then thirteen messengers to Scarperia and Florence just after the capture of the fortress.[166] The majority of men were employed in June, a critical time when the army moved forward.

---

[159] ASF, balie 6 fols. 75v, 88r, 91r–91v, 104v.

[160] ASF, Camera del comune, camarlenghi uscita 55 fol. 574r.

[161] ASF, balie 6 fols. 2r, 34r.   [162] ASF, balie 6 fol. 77r.

[163] ASF, balie 6 fols. 84v, 107r, 114v.

[164] On spies and informants, see Gherardi, "L'antica camera," pp. 329–330; Caferro, *John Hawkwood*, pp. 81–82.

[165] There are thirty-two citations for *cursori* on 30 June and another thirty-seven for 22 September 1350. ASF, balie 6 fols. 85v–86r, 113r.

[166] ASF, balie 7 fol. 33v; balie 6 fol. 43r.

The *cursori* were, like the *vetturali*, identified in the documents by first name or nickname. Their labor appears to have been specialized. The messenger known as "Tigna," for example, brought letters specifically to the captain of war. Another, named "Campolino," carried letters from the members of the *balia* to Maghinardo Ubaldini. Unlike *vetturali*, the messengers did not receive a daily wage, but were paid separately for each mission they undertook. As we will discuss more in Chapter 5, the fee took into account the difficulty and danger of the mission.[167]

More covert, but no less important, was the work of spies and informants who sought out the secrets of the enemy. Florence had a well-articulated network.[168] A proper understanding of the network is, however, impeded by confused terminology. The men are listed alternately in the sources as *nuntio, messo, esploratore,* and *spia.* The terms are often used interchangeably. Jacopino da Pinerolo, hired by Florence at the outset of Ubaldini war in 1349, is described in one place as *messo e spia,* and in another as *nuntio e esploratore.*[169] Stefano Arrighi is listed first as *nuntio* and later as *spia.*[170]

The documents nevertheless suggest a basic distinction. *Esploratori* (explorers) appear to have been hired primarily for short-term missions and were paid by the day; their activities were overseen by the office of the *camera del comune. Spie* (spies) were hired for longer periods and paid monthly wages; their activities were overseen by the office of the condotta.[171] Spies covered a broad arc of territory. Jacopino da Pinerolo's first service in May 1349 as *messo e spia* was in Puglia, Rome, Schiavonia, and Lombardy. His later service in 1350 as *nuntio and esploratore* was local, in Florence and the Romagna.[172] Francesco di Giovanni went to Puglia and Naples in 1350 to "*spiare novelle*" arising from the ongoing war between the Angevins, and Giovanni Petri went at the same time to Milan and Lombardy to find out information there.[173] The diversity of terms for those who sought *novelle* suggests that spying in medieval Florence was done by numerous officials, both formally and informally. The risks attendant upon the task are evident. Stefano Arrighi was captured in the Romagna by members of the Ubertini

---

[167] ASF, balie 7 fols. 33r–33v.
[168] Davidsohn, *Storia di Firenze,* vol. 1, part V, pp. 207–210.
[169] ASF, Camera del comune, Scrivano di camera uscita 6 fol. 26r; Camera del comune, camarlenghi uscita 54 fol. 716r.
[170] ASF, Camera del comune, camarlenghi uscita 52 fol. 264r.
[171] ASF, Camera del commune, Scrivano di camera uscita 7 fol. 55r; balie 6 fols. 74r, 80v.
[172] ASF, Camera del commune, Scrivano di camera uscita 6 fol. 26r.
[173] ASF, Camera del comune, Scrivano di camera uscita 7 fol. 55r; Camera del comune, camarlenghi entrata 34 fol. 197r; Scrivano di camera uscita 5 fol. 35v.

clan, then at odds with Florence, who tortured him by slowly extracting his teeth.[174]

Finally, it is necessary to include as part of Florence's military work-force musicians who accompanied the armies into the field. Dante gives an evocative image at the beginning of *Inferno XXII* of "knights setting forth … with trumpets, with bells, with drums" (*Inferno* XXII, 1–7). Machiavelli stressed the utility of music for coordination of the move-ments of the army and to aid the fighting spirit. "For just as he who dances proceeds with the time of the music … so an army, while obeying the music, does not get disordered."[175] A Parisian writer, Johannes de Grocheio, stressed the emotional impact of trumpets and drums in war as instruments that "move the souls of men."[176]

The commanders of the Florentine army had musicians in their indi-vidual units. Niccolò della Serra, who led Florentine forces in the first campaign, had a *trombatore* (musician with a long straight trumpet, 41/2 to 5 feet in length), a *trombetta* (smaller trumpet), and *nacherino* (kettle drum) in his band. At the outset of the offensive in June 1349, Florence sent five additional musicians to Niccolò, including three *trombatori*, a *cenamellaio* (double reed wind instrument player), and *tamburino* (tam-bourine player).[177] Prior to an attack on the castle at Montegemoli in May 1350, city officials sent two *trombatori* (Ghettino Ture and Francesco Andree) and a *nacherino* (Betto Vanucci) to the captain of war, whose band already contained a *trombatore*, a *trombetta*, and a *nacherino*. In early July 1350, the city sent three more musicians to the army.[178] By August, all nine of Florence's civic musicians, employed in the first instance to perform at communal festivities and ceremonies, were in the Mugello with the captain of war.[179]

The sources do not say how the musicians were deployed, what signals they used, or how these affected the movement of the army. It is likely that whatever role the musicians had in the field, they also served as part of the psychological aspect of warfare, performing below Ubaldini fortifications, perhaps in conjunction with the acts of *infamia* done by the *barattieri*. This was a basic technique of *trecento* warfare, used by Florence most notably during its campaign against Pisa in 1362–1364. Trumpeters tormented

---

[174] Cohn, *Florentine State*, pp. 176–177.   [175] Machiavelli, *Art of War*, p. 57.

[176] Timothy McGee, *The Ceremonial Musicians of Late Medieval Florence* (Bloomington, IN: Indiana University Press, 2009), p. 45.

[177] ASF, Camera del comune, Scrivano di camera uscita 6 fols. 2r–2v; Timothy McGee, "Dinner Music for the Florentine Signoria, 1350–1450," *Speculum* 74 (1999), pp. 95–114 and *Ceremonial Musicians of Late Medieval Florence*, pp. 44–62.

[178] ASF, Camera del comune, Scrivano di camera uscita 6 fol. 2v; ASF, balie 6 fols. 74v, 93r.

[179] ASF, Camera del comune, Scrivano di camera uscita 10 fol. 4r.

the enemy by playing loudly at the city gates throughout the night.[180] After taking Montecoloreto and Lozzole from the Ubaldini in June 1350, Florence sent *trombatori* and a *nacherino* to the army for what appears to have been a big celebration. The musicians were met at Montecoloreto by numerous government officials, including the chamberlain of the *camera del arme*, the *sindaco* of the city, two of the "custodians" of the *camera del comune* (Francesco Talenti and Micho Bonanni), and two members of the *balìa* (Bernardo Nerozzo Alberti and Niccolo di Bencivenni).[181] In the peculiar practice of war of the day, celebration by one side meant shaming the other.[182]

"Military" and "Pacific" Spheres

The last example emphasizes both the highly mobile nature of the Florentine bureaucracy and the blurred lines between the city's military and pacific spheres. Florence's bureaucracy was not a modern, sedentary one. Chamberlains and important communal officials traveled to the field to participate directly in military affairs. They then returned to the city to meet in person with priors and join in executive councils. Niccolò Malagonelle, a chamberlain of the condotta, rode with the army for two weeks, from 1 to 15 June 1350, accompanied by the cleric/chamberlain of the *camera del arme*, Filippo Dini.[183] In July 1350, as the army proceeded deeper into Ubaldini territory, two members of the *balìa*, Francesco Brunelleschi and Arnaldo Altoviti (the latter also a captain of the Guelf party in July 1349) went to the army to look after affairs.[184] Brunelleschi and Altoviti then returned to Florence to discuss the circumstances in the executive councils that met later that month.

Drawing too narrow a distinction between military and pacific spheres is similarly anachronistic for post-plague Florence. Florence possessed no military industrial complex as understood today. There was a fluidity of movement between "military" and "pacific" labor. Along with this, there existed no clear division between Florence's "temporary" day workers and its more "permanent" monthly, semester, and yearly workers. Most of all, our evidence makes clear that a substantial part of Florence's post-plague workforce was involved in the war with the Ubaldini, even though the conflict was limited in scope. The personnel, apart from the army, consisted not of "professionals," but of short-term employees, who had

---

[180] Caferro, *John Hawkwood*, pp. 99–100.
[181] ASF, Camera del comune, Scrivano di camera uscita 9 fols. 3v–4v.
[182] Davidsohn, *Storia di Firenze*, vol. 5, p. 462.
[183] ASF, balie 6 fol. 39r; Camera del comune, Scrivano di camera uscita 9 fol. 3v.
[184] ASF, balie 6 fols 87r–v; Camera del comune, camarlenghi entrata 34 fol. 202v.

other pacific "occupations." Paymasters and troop inspectors of the army are listed in the city budgets as accountants, notaries, and chamberlains. Simone Schutiggi served as both paymaster and troop inspector during the second campaign. But he appears in budgets as an accountant for the *camera del comune*.[185] The same is true of Spinello di Luca Alberti, who was likewise an accountant of the *camera del comune* in 1350, but served as a paymaster and troop inspector.[186] Men identified as town criers (*banditori*) traveled with the army in June and July 1349.[187] Procurators of cavalrymen worked also as messengers for the officials in charge of provisions. Officials in charge of provisions held other government posts.[188]

The documents give many more examples that will be discussed in greater detail in Chapter 4. The concurrence reinforces the portrait of an overall post-plague shortage of labor. Florence clearly sought workers from outside of the city, employing *cursori*, *vetturali*, and even spies from elsewhere, often neighboring cities and towns.[189] Meanwhile, the workforce of skilled laborers – particularly artisans – was greatly reduced. The *capomaestro* stonemason Ristoro di Cione, who built trebuchets at Scarperia and served as captain of the *guastatori*, was originally appointed to the committee to oversee the building in Florence of the church of Sant'Anna, dedicated to the memory of the victims of the plague.[190] Another *capomaestro* employed at Scarperia, Stefano Pucci, was likewise selected for the building project. It is a testament to the importance of war that both Ristoro di Cione and Stefano Pucci were taken off the project to allow them to work at Scarperia and with the army so that the operations against the Ubaldini could proceed.

The degree of the shortage of labor and simultaneous obligations of workers is most apparent with respect to the office of condotta, responsible for hiring soldiers for war. A careful reading of the extant budgets shows that the condotta was strikingly different from the governmental institution carefully outlined in the extant military code of 1337.[191] Its setup was the same in 1349–1350, but the personnel consisted not of workers specific to that office, but men who simultaneously held other

---

[185] ASF, Camera del comune, Scrivano di camera uscita 9 fol. 9r; Scrivano di camera uscita 7 fols. 11r, 56v, ASF, balie 6 fol. 84v.

[186] ASF, Camera del comune, Scrivano di camera uscita 10 fol. 2v; balie 6 fol. 107v.

[187] ASF, Camera del comune, Scrivano di camera uscita 6 fol. 8r; Scrivano di camera uscita 7 fol. 9r.

[188] ASF, balie 6 fols. 75v, 88r, 91r–91v, 104v 119v.

[189] ASF, Camera del comune, Scrivano di camera uscita 10 fol. 26r; Scrivano di camera uscita 7 fol. 55r.

[190] Saverio La Sorsa, *La Compagnia d'or San Michele, ovvero una pagina della beneficenza in Toscana nel secolo XIV* (Trani: V. Vecchi, 1902), pp. 110–111, 240.

[191] This is reproduced in Canestrini, "Documenti," pp. 497 ff. See also Bayley, *War and Society in Renaissance Florence*, pp. 9–11.

public jobs in the city. The condotta was, in short, a separate office only in name. In June/July 1349, at the start of the Ubaldini war, the condotta office had eighteen employees (six chamberlains, two accountants, two notaries, a *scrittore*, two judges, and five *messi*).[192] The accountants of the condotta were the same men who were accountants of the *camera del comune*. The notaries and judges concurrently held the same job with the *camera del comune*.[193] The *scrittore* of the condotta was Ser Niccholaio di Ser Venture Monache, who was the chancellor of the commune.[194] One chamberlain served also on the committee of eight men charged with finding new sources of revenue for the commune. Two other chamberlains served as troop inspectors in the field to review soldiers. Little is known of the remaining condotta officials, but it is likely they too worked other jobs.[195]

The point is nevertheless clear. The inclusion of war in our portrait of post-plague Florence raises basic questions about the overall nature of the Florentine workforce, the bureaucratic and institutional structure of the government, and our understanding of occupation. These issues will be investigated at greater length in Chapters 4 and 5.

---

[192] ASF, Camera del comune, Scrivano di camera uscita 7 fols. 10v, 21r.
[193] ASF, Camera del comune, Scrivano di camera uscita 7 fols. 10v, 49r.
[194] ASF, Camera del comune, camarlenghi uscita 66 fol. 590r.
[195] ASF, Camera del comune, camarlenghi uscita 54 fols. 707r–709r.

3   Economy of War at a Time of Plague

> The Florentines, seeing that their haughty larceny was not diminished by a beating, passed a decree that every year the city would ride against the Ubaldini until they were deprived of their Alpine caves.
>
> Matteo Villani, *Nuova Cronica*[1]

> All inhabitants of lands of Ubaldini ... may freely and without penalty come with their families to settle in the Florentine contado and they will receive ten-years immunity from taxes.
>
> ASF, Provvisione, registri 36 fol. 141r (July 1349)

> And I beg even more firmly that at least your public road ... since we are about to celebrate the Jubilee, be purged of bandits and be open to pilgrims.
>
> Petrarch, *Familiares* VIII, 10[2]

In the less bellicose passages of *Familiares* VIII, 10, Petrarch spoke of the economic importance of taking on the Ubaldini. He argued for the need, nay obligation, of the city to keep its public roads safe for merchants and pilgrims, particularly in light of the upcoming papal jubilee in Rome. In a letter (*Familiares* XI, 8) written in 1351 to Andrea Dandolo, the Venetian doge, Petrarch reiterated the point, but from the opposite point of view. He warned the young ruler of the harmful effects of war on trade routes, complaining that the internecine battle with Genoa would lose for Italy its commercial supremacy on the seas.[3]

In both instances, Petrarch articulated a basic truth about contemporary warfare: it was strongly economic in nature. For all the fraternal bitterness that the Florentines expressed toward the Ubaldini, at the

---

[1] Matteo Villani, *Nuova Cronica*, edited by Giuseppe Porta, vol. 1 (Parma: Fondazione Pietro Bembo, 1995), p. 37.

[2] Francesco Petrarch, *Rerum familiarum libri, I–VIII*, translated and edited by Aldo S. Bernardo, vol. 1 (Albany, NY: State University of New York Press, 1975), pp. 434–435 (cited hereafter as Petrarch, *Familiares*).

[3] Francesco Petrarch, *Rerum familiarum libri, IX–XVI*, vol. 2, translated and edited by Aldo S. Bernardo (Ithaca, NY: Italica Press, 2005), pp. 102–108.

core of the contest lay the desire of the republic to control trade routes and keep open its access to markets.[4]

The chronicler Matteo Villani made explicit the financial goals of the campaign. Florence sought to divest the Ubaldini of "the profits from their caves" (i.e., the tolls they imposed on merchants and travelers who passed through their land).[5] The decree formally condemning the Ubaldini in July 1349 made their lands and possessions subject to confiscation by Florence, and offered ten years of remission from taxes to those inhabitants of the Ubaldini territory who settled in the Florentine state.[6] The decree must be understood in terms of the plague, as it aimed to repopulate the much-depleted Florentine state, as well as reduce the Ubaldini state.[7] With this objective in mind, Florentine officials offered tax breaks in October 1349 to those who settled in the town of Scarperia, which, according to the legislation, was "greatly diminished" on account of both "the arrogance and audacity of the Ubaldini" and the plague.[8] In the peace settlement of 1350, Florence gained jurisdiction over Ubaldini tolls in their strongholds along the border with Bologna and possession of nineteen small towns.[9]

The economic angle was in short writ large, and we should include under that rubric the offer to Francesco Petrarch to work at the new university. The establishment of the university was a fundamentally economic act.[10] It was intended to bring students and their money to the city and improve human capital in the face of the plague. There was no better way to do this than to hire Petrarch, a famous man whose reputation, as Boccaccio noted in his invitation, would put the new institution on a firm foundation. Florence's additional offer to restore Petrarch's family

---

[4] Giovanni Villani stressed the importance of Romagna and routes through the Mugello for the Florentine grain supply. Giovanni Villani, *Nuova Cronica*, vol. 3, edited by Giuseppe Porta (Parma: Fondazione Pietro Bembo, 1991), p. 558. Petrarch's statements about the economic effects of war mirror those made by modern economists such as Douglass North and John Munro. See Douglass C. North and Robert Paul Thomas, *Rise of the Western World: A New Economic History* (Cambridge: Cambridge University Press, 1973), pp. 78–89; John Munro, "Industrial Transformations in the North-West European Textile Trades, c. 1290–1340: Economic Progress or Economic Crisis?" in *Before the Black Death: Studies in the "Crisis" of the Early Fourteenth Century*, edited by Bruce M. S. Campbell (New York, NY: St. Martin's Press, 1991), pp. 120–130.

[5] Matteo Villani, *Nuova Cronica*, vol. 1, edited by Giuseppe Porta (Parma: Fondazione Pietro Bembo, 1995), p. 37.

[6] ASF, Provvisioni, registri 36 fols.141r–141v; *I Capitoli del Comune di Firenze*, vol. 1, edited by C. Guasti and A. Gherardi (Florence: Cellini, 1866), pp. 88–89.

[7] ASF, Provvisioni, registri 36 fol. 81r.   [8] ASF, Provvisioni, registri 37 fol. 12r.

[9] ASF Provvisioni, registri 38 fols. 69v–70r.

[10] Alessandro Gherardi, ed., *Statuti della Università e Studio fiorentino dell'anno MCCCLXXXVII* (Florence: Forni, 1881), p. 111.

patrimony may be read as an economic investment with an aim toward a still greater return.

War, Plague, and Public Finance

Waging war at a time of plague placed great pressure on public finances. Florence, like all Italian states, had difficulty raising money even in the best of times. War required the rapid collection and disbursement of large sums of money, a requisite inherently ill suited to the ponderous administrative apparatus of the state.[11] As we saw in Chapter 2, there were numerous offices involved in handling money for the Ubaldini war, with overlapping and unclear jurisdictions, that furthered confusion. The appointment of a *balia* intended to streamline the apparatus to handle the short-term emergency only added to the confusion.

In this context, the war helps fill out the portrait of the Florentine economy during the plague years. For all the literature devoted to the impact of the Black Death in the city, little is known about its effect on public finance and warfare.[12] The lacuna stands as tribute to the compartmentalization of scholarly study and the marginalization of war as a serious topic of inquiry. Our sources allow a close look at the ways the city managed the fisc and apportioned its resources, and how these resources were affected by war. They tell a tale of fiscal and bureaucratic confusion and, most strikingly, of the direct conversion of plague-related

---

[11] William Caferro, *Mercenary Companies and the Decline of Siena* (Baltimore, MD: Johns Hopkins University Press, 1998), p. 142.

[12] William Caferro, "Petrarch's War: Florentine Wages and the Black Death," *Speculum* 88 (2013), pp. 145–146; see also Caferro, "Warfare and Economy of Renaissance Italy, 1350–1450," *Journal of Interdisciplinary History* 39 (2008), pp. 169, 171–172. On Florentine public finance at this general time, see Marvin Becker, "Economic Change and the Emerging Florentine Territorial State," *Studies in the Renaissance* 13 (1966), pp. 7–39 and *Florence in Transition*, 2 vols. (Baltimore, MD: Johns Hopkins University Press, 1967–1968); Anthony Molho, "Città-stato e i loro debiti pubblici: Quesiti e ipotesi sulla storia di Firenze, Genova e Venezia" in *Italia 1350–1450: Tra crisi, trasformazione, sviluppo. Tredicesimo convegno di studi, Pistoia, 10–13 maggio 1991* (Pistoia: Centro Italiano di Studi di Storia e d'Arte, 1993), pp. 185–215. For public finance elsewhere, see William Caferro, *Mercenary Companies and the Decline of Siena* (Baltimore, MD: Johns Hopkins University Press, 1998); Luciano Pezzolo, "Government Debt and State in Italy, 1300–1700." Working paper, 2007, University of Venice "Ca' Foscari," Department of Economics. www.dse.unive.it/en/pubblicazioni and William M. Bowsky, *The Finance of the Commune of Siena, 1287–1355* (Oxford: The Clarendon Press, 1970); Christine Meek, *The Commune of Lucca under Pisan Rule, 1342–1369* (Cambridge, MA: Medieval Academy of America, 1980); Michael Knapton, "City Wealth and State Wealth in North East Italy, 14th–17th Centuries" in *La ville, la bourgeoisie et la genèse de l'État moderne*, edited by Neithard Bulst and J.-Ph. Genet (Paris: Éd. du CNRS, 1985), p. 199; Patrizia Mainoni, *Le radici della discordia: Ricerche sulla fiscalità a Bergamo tra XIII e XV secolo* (Milan: Edizioni Unicopli, 1997).

money into warfare. Florence relied on funds from the confraternity of Orsanmichele, the city's chief institution for social assistance to the poor and indigent, made rich by bequests from plague victims. It raised money also from fines on a fractious and unsettled urban population and from loans from soldiers who fought in the campaigns. The complicated economic portrait includes consideration of the effects of rises in gabelle rates, taxes on the countryside, recycling of money through the *dirittura* (unstudied) tax, and more generally the profits and losses from the war itself.

It needs to be said from the outset that Florentine finances were in bad shape even before the plague. Chronicler Giovanni Villani described the city as in "desperate straits" in 1347, a judgment confirmed by the modern studies of Carlo M. Cipolla and Gene Brucker.[13] The plague of 1348 reduced the population, which in turn reduced revenue and rendered the physical collection of funds problematic.[14] On the same day that Donato Velluti first called for action against the Ubaldini (24 April 1349), the Florentine city council complained that the city had "no money" to pay soldiers and state stipendiaries, whose salaries were already in arrears and who were owed large sums. The council expressed little hope that circumstances would improve in the future.[15]

The situation is similar to that which has been outlined by scholars for contemporary France and England, which likewise endured a reduction of revenue alongside difficulty collecting taxes. John B. Henneman depicts the fiscal crisis in France during the two years after the plague as the "most acute" of the entire fourteenth century.[16] G. L. Harriss highlights widespread resistance to levies in England.[17] Christine Meek in her seminal studies on the city of Lucca demonstrates declining revenues and difficulty collecting the sums after the Black Death in 1348.[18]

---

[13] Carlo M. Cipolla, *Monetary Policy of Fourteenth Century Florence* (Berkeley, CA: University of California Press, 1982), p. 43; Gene Brucker, *Florentine Politics and Society 1343–1378* (Princeton, NJ: Princeton University Press, 1962), p. 9.

[14] ASF, Provvisioni, registri 36 fol. 20r; A. B. Falsini, "Firenze dopo il 1348: Le consequenze della peste nera," *Archivio storico italiano* 129 (1971), p. 438.

[15] ASF, Provvisioni, registri 36 fol. 81r.

[16] John B. Henneman, "The Black Death and Royal Taxation, 1347–1351," *Speculum* 43 (1968), pp. 413–420 and *Royal Taxation in Fourteenth Century France: The Development of War Financing, 1322–1356* (Princeton, NJ: Princeton University Press, 1971).

[17] G. L. Harriss, *King, Parliament, and Public Finance in Medieval England to 1369* (Oxford: Clarendon Press, 1975), p. 313. See also W. Mark Ormrod, "The Crown and the English Economy, 1290–1348" in *Before the Black Death: Studies in the "Crisis" of the Early Fourteenth Century*, edited by Bruce M. S. Campbell (Manchester: Manchester University Press, 1992), pp. 149–183 and *Edward III* (New Haven, CT: Yale University Press, 2011).

[18] Christine Meek, *The Commune of Lucca under Pisan Rule, 1342–1369* (Cambridge, MA: Medieval Academy of America, 1980), pp. 65–66.

Table 3.1 *Florentine Military Expenditure from* Scrivano *Budgets*

Year	Month	Military Expenditure*	Overall Expenditures*	Percentage
1349	May/June	75,989	95,596	79.5
	July/Aug	73,942	94,434	78.3
	Sept/Oct	34,200	47,948	71.3
1350	May/June	90,338 (condotta)		
		10,681 (castellan)		
		101,019 (total)	125,019	80.8
	July/August	97,650 (condotta)		
		4,083 (castellan)		
		101,733 (total)	121,735	83.6

* Sums are rounded to the nearest lire.
Sources: ASF, Camera del comune, Scrivano di camera uscita 6 fols. 2r–10v, 17r–41r; Scrivano di camera uscita 7 fols. 2r–11r, 17r–60r; Scrivano di camera uscita 8 fols. 2r–7v, 17r–36r; Scrivano di camera uscita 9 fols. 2r–9v, 17r–45v; Scrivano di camera uscita 10 fols. 17r–59r.

War was first and foremost expensive. The extant Florentine sources are fragmentary, but sufficient to give a general portrait. *Scrivano* "uscita" budgets – vernacular redactions of the original Latin budgets of the *camera del commune* – provide summaries of overall expenditure for the period from May to August 1349 and May to August 1350 – the height of both campaigns (Table 3.1, Figure 3.1). The budgets represent communal expenditures figured bimonthly.[19]

The financial documents show that war was by far the most expensive undertaking by the state. From May to June 1349, Florence spent a total of 95,596 lire (29,874 florins at 64 soldi per florin); 75,989 lire (23,747 florins) of the sum, or 79.5 percent, went to the office of the condotta to pay the salaries of soldiers in the field and castellans who guarded forts.[20] In July/August 1349 the city spent roughly the same amount, 94,434 lire, of which 73,942 lire, or 78.3 percent, went to soldiers and castellans.[21] The end of the formal military campaign in September/October reduced

---

[19] In 1349, Florentine budgets were divided into two basic rubrics: "general" income/expenditure and "condotta" income/expenditure. In 1350, the budgets became divided into three rubrics, with a separate entry for expenditure/income for castellans (*castellani*).

[20] It may be noted that Florentine expenditure increased nearly two and half times (234 percent) at the onset of hostilities in May/June 1349 from that of January/February 1349, for which we have another extant scrivano budget. Florence spent 31,989 lire. ASF, Camera del comune, Scrivano di camera uscita 5 fols. 17r–40r.

[21] ASF, Camera del commune, Scrivano di camera uscita 7 fols. 2r–11r, 17r–60r .

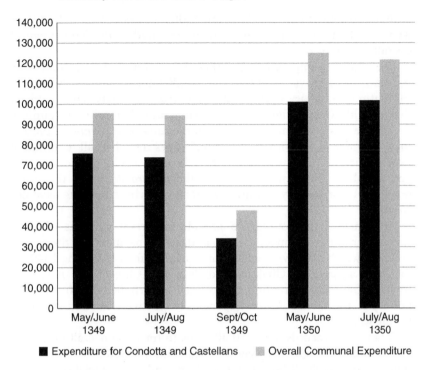

Figure 3.1 Military expenditure/overall expenditures

communal expenditures by half, to 47,948 lire. But it is notable that
expenditures for the wages of soldiers and castellans remained high (47,
948, lire), representing 71.3 percent of overall expenses.[22] Florence
clearly did not dismiss its army after its offensive, and military expenditure remained the largest part of public expenditures.

The second campaign against the Ubaldini was more expensive than
the first, affirming the broader nature of the offensive. The extant
scrivano uscita budget of May/June 1350 shows that Florence spent
125,019 lire in these months, with 101,019 lire, or 80.8 percent,
going to pay soldiers and castellans.[23] The budgets indicate, however,
that Florence changed accounting procedure. The expenditure for
castellans (10,681 lire) is now listed separately from condotta expenditure (90,338 lire). In July/August 1350, the city spent 121,735 lire, with

---

[22] ASF, Camera del comune, Scrivano di camera uscita 8 fols. 2r–7v, 17r–36r; Camera del
comune, Scrivano di camera uscita 3 fol. 6r.
[23] ASF, Camera del comune, Scrivano di camera uscita 9 fols. 2r–9v, 17r–45v.

97,650 lire going to the condotta and 4,083 for castellans; 101,733 lire
went to soldiers and castellans. This represented a full 83.6 percent of
overall expenditure.[24]

The sums are impressive, but they do not represent all the money
Florence spent on war. The Ubaldini conflict does not fit neatly into the
Florentine budgetary cycle, and few *scrivano* budgets have survived
that provide overall figures. In addition, the Florentine accounting
procedure was often inconsistent, and the *camera del comune*, although
the "premier fiscal organ of state," does not list all communal
expenditure.[25] Our figures do not include payments for noncombatants
and supplies. These were made by the *camera del arme*, the office
responsible for the city's military arsenal, but whose budgets have not
survived.

Nevertheless, the sources do provide important glimpses of these
expenditures. For example, *scrivano* budgets list payments by the *camera
del arme* (which oversaw the communal arsenal) for 14–23 June 1349 for
the "war against the Ubaldini," totaling 5,200 lire (1,650 florins).[26]
In July 1349, the Florentine city council apportioned 1,920 lire (600
florins) to the *camera del arme* specifically for "weapons and supplies"
for the war.[27]

Extant *balia* records for 1350 allow us to trace the overall outlay for
the second campaign. They give a precise and integrated economic portrait, showing daily disbursements of funds and the financial rhythms of
war. The first payment by Arnaldo Manelli, the chamberlain of the *balia*,
in March 1350 went to repay bankers, who had lent sums to the city to
help recruit soldiers.[28] In April, Manelli hired and paid the salaries
of artisans assembled at Scarperia to make war machines, purchased
supplies, and paid the merchants, who supervised the distribution of
materials in the field.[29]

---

[24] In his famous description of Florence in 1338, Giovanni Villani claimed that the pay of
"castellani e guardie di rocche" amounted to 4,000 florins a year. Villani, *Nuova Cronica*,
vol. 3, p. 196. The figure appears small in comparison to expenses for four months in
1350, which amount to 14,764 lire or 4,614 florins, more than Villani gives for all of
1338. ASF, Camera del comune, Scrivano di camera uscita 10 fols. 17r–59r.

[25] The limits of the *camera del comune* as a source has been pointed out by Anthony Molho
and Charles M. de La Roncière. See also Anthony Molho, *Florentine Public Finance in the
Early Renaissance, 1400–1433* (Cambridge, MA: Harvard University Press, 1971), pp.
2–3; Charles M. de La Roncière, "Indirect Taxes or 'Gabelles' at Florence in the
Fourteenth Century: The Evolution of Tariffs and the Problems of Collection" in
Florentine Studies: Politics and Society in Renaissance Florence (London: Faber and Faber,
1968), p. 163.

[26] ASF, Camera del comune, Scrivano di camera uscita 7 fol. 3r.

[27] ASF, Provvisioni, registri 36 fol. 132v.   [28] ASF, balie 6 fol. 41r.

[29] ASF, balie 6 fols. 64r–v.

The week of 11–17 May was particularly busy. The city made final preparations to mobilize its army for the battle at the castle of Montegemoli. Manelli bought supplies and paid the salaries of *vetturali*, messengers, spies, and explorers.[30] He also provided advance wages for twenty days (14 May 1350) to the captains of the army and to those in charge of supplies in the field.[31] It is evident that in order for the army to proceed forward, Florence had to compensate key personnel *prior* to battle.

June 1350 was the most active month of the campaign. After the initial success at Montegemoli, Florence made a push for "the final extermination of the Ubaldini."[32] In the span of three days (4–6 June 1350), Manelli spent the considerable sum of 9,779 lire (3,056 florins) on personnel and supplies and for restocking the fortresses taken from the Ubaldini.[33] A detailed list of the goods purchased for Montegemoli includes 580 *sestari* of grain, 17 *sestari* of farina, 230 pounds of *prosciutto*, a portable bed (*lettiga*) with a *baldacchino* that perhaps served as a stretcher, crossbows, iron, wood, a *bombarda* or cannon that shot "iron balls," and *corde pisane* (a strong ropelike wire used for torture).[34] Florence also sent artisans to the captured fortress at Montecoloreto to help rebuild its walls.[35]

It is important to point out, however, that the precise relationship among the *balia*, the *camera del commune*, and other communal offices involved in disbursing war money is not entirely clear. The *balia* theoretically received its funds from the *camera del comune*, but close examination of the documents reveals that the chamberlain Manelli actually spent more money than he received from that office. The budgets of the *camera del comune* for the month of February 1350, for example, list two payments to the *balia* of 200 florins and 300 florins.[36] But the *balia* itself shows that Manelli spent 900 florins during that month.[37] Similarly, for 4–6 June 1350, the *camera* paid 2,556 florins to the *balia* for the war, yet Manelli spent 3,056 florins. The *balia* therefore received money from sources other than the *camera*, but it is unclear from where.

---

[30] ASF, balie 6 fols. 4v–11r, 19v–23r, 70r–74r.   [31] ASF, balie 6 fols. 6v–10v, 21r–23v.
[32] ASF, balie 6 fol. 80v.
[33] ASF, balie 6 fols. 80v–82v. Overall, Manelli spent 22,067 lire (6,896 florins) that month. ASF, balie 6 fols. 11r, 23v, 80v–92v.
[34] The cost for outfitting the fort was 512 lire (160 florins). ASF, balie 6 fols. 11v, 93r; balie 7 fol. 32r. The refurbishing of the fort continued until the middle of June (17 June 1350); ASF, Ufficiali delle Castella 5 fol. 1v.
[35] ASF, balie 6 fol. 14r.
[36] ASF, Camera del comune, camarlenghi uscita 64 fols. 420r–420v.
[37] ASF, balie 6 fols. 35v–37r.

Table 3.2 *Price of Supplies Purchased by the* Balia *in 1350*

Item	Quantity	Stated Price
Crossbow bolts	1,000	21.6 lire–17.1 lire
Hemp	100 pounds	18 lire–13.3 lire
Wire	100 pounds	6 lire
Wood	1 piece	1.5 lire
Lanterns (iron candle holder)	1	15 soldi
Carbon	1 sack	12 soldi
Steel	1 pound	2 soldi/6 denari
Iron nails	1 pound	1 soldo/7 denari
Iron	1 pound	1 soldo/2 denari
Bread	1 sack	4–2 denari

Exchange rate: 1 florin = 64 soldi
             1 lira = 20 soldi = 240 denari
             1 soldo = 12 denari
Source: ASF, balie 6, 7.

What is nevertheless abundantly clear is that the *balia* had direct responsibility for the workforce and supplies at the town of Scarperia, the headquarters of the second campaign. As we saw in the Chapter 2, it bought a wide array of goods, including raw materials and finished products.[38] It paid the salaries of artisans as well as the wages of a large number of noncombatants involved in the war effort in the field (Tables 3.2, 3.3, 3.4).

The detailed source material provides a sense of the parameters of military expenditure, about which little is known for the entire *trecento*. Iron and wire were relatively inexpensive items. Wood, carbon, hemp, and steel were, on the other hand, costly (Tables 3.2, 3.3).[39] Wire and hemp were sold by the hundreds of pounds and were likely used to build trebuchets and service crossbows. From April to September 1350 the city purchased 1,934 pounds of hemp and 631 pounds of wire.[40] It bought crossbow bolts by the thousands, including 40,000 on a single day, 4 June.[41] The price of hemp and crossbows varied according to supplier; the prices of other goods remained constant (Table 3.2).

---

[38] ASF, balie 6 fol. 108r.
[39] For further details, see William Caferro, "Military Enterprise in Florence at the Time of the Black Death, 1349–50" in *War, Entrepreneurs, and the State in Europe and the Mediterranean, 1300–1800*, edited by Jeff Fynn-Paul (Leiden: Brill, 2014), pp. 15–31.
[40] ASF, balie 6 fols. 4r–v, 20r.   [41] ASF, balie 6 fol. 81r.

The city purchased only a small amount of steel (25 pounds), thirteen pieces of wood, and a few sacks of carbon. A pound of steel cost twice as much as the same amount of iron. A single sack of carbon cost ten times more than a pound of iron. Wood was the most expensive item. A single piece cost two and half times more than a sack of carbon and twice the price of a lantern, a finished good (Table 3.2).

The least expensive item was a sack of bread. The surviving accounts of Cristofano Bonistradi and Domenico Donnini, who oversaw supplies to the army, show that the price fluctuated from 2 to 4 denari from May to June 1350.[42] The price was about the same as a single crossbow bolt. It is unclear how much bread a sack represented and how many men it fed. The price of a bushel (*staio*) of grain at this time was about twice the price of the sacks (average) distributed at Montegemoli.

The cost of the materials of war may be compared also with nonwar-related expenditure in city budgets at this time. Florence, for example, spent 23 lire for two months' (May/June 1350) worth of writing materials (paper, sheepskin, and ink) for officials of Signoria (purchased from a *cartolaio* named Taddeo di Gieri).[43] The outlay was roughly the same as that for the steel, wood, and sacks of carbon used at Scarperia. Meanwhile, Florence spent about half as much (12 lire) for the ceremonial civic race (*palio*) dedicated to San Barnabas, run in May 1350. The *palio* dedicated to the city's patron Saint John the Baptist, run in June 1350, however, cost the city 380 lire, more than 30 times more than the one for Barnabas and more than Florence's total expenditure for wire and hemp for the Ubaldini war in 1350.[44] The city spent still greater sums for "food and drink" to feed members of the Signoria, which cost 496 lire a month, among the greatest expenditures of the city. In the face of all the difficulties, Florentine public officials clearly ate well.

Table 3.3 compares the cost of war items with the price of "basic necessities" of daily Florentine life, in particular wine and wheat.[45] The cost of wood again stands out against the others. A single piece used at Scarperia was worth more than a whole bushel (*staio*) of wheat (23.75 soldi per *staio*) and a whole barrel (*barile*) of wine (26.9 soldi per *barile*). A single sack of carbon was worth about a half a bushel of wheat.

---

[42] ASF, balie 7 fol. 64v.

[43] ASF, Camera del comune, Scrivano di camera uscita 10 fol. 9v.

[44] ASF, Camera del comune, Scrivano di camera uscita 9 fol. 8r.

[45] Tognetti points to wine and wheat as the most basic of commodities. Sergio Tognetti, "Prezzi e salari nella Firenze tardo medievale: un profile," *Archivio storico italiano* 153 (1995), p. 276. Pinto includes items such as vitella and oil. Giuliano Pinto, "I livelli di vita dei salariati fiorentini, 1380–1430" in *Toscana medievale: Paesaggi e realtà sociali* (Florence: Le lettere, 1993), p. 113.

Table 3.3 *Price of Supplies in Terms of "Basic" Necessities for 1350*

Item	Amount	Price*
Wood	1 piece	30
Lantern	1	15
Carbon	1 sack	12
Hemp	1 pound	3.6–2.6
Steel	1 pound	2.5
Iron nails	1 pound	1.6
Iron	1 pound	1.2
Wire	1 pound	1.2
Wine	**1 liter**	**.66 (1 gallon = 2.5 soldi)**
Wheat	**1 pound**	**.61**
Crossbow bolt	1	.38–.32
Bread	**1 sack**	**.33–.25**

Note: The basic necessities are in bold. A *barile* (40.7 liters = 10.75 gallons) of wine cost 26.9 soldi. A *staio* of grain (24 liters = 18 kg = 38.7 pounds) cost 23.75 soldi.

** Prices are in *soldi di piccioli*. All prices are converted to soldi for comparison. *Sources*: ASF, balie 6, 7; Sergio Tognetti, "Prezzi e salari," pp. 317, 319, 321, 323, 325.

A pound of iron, on the other hand, was double the same amount of wheat. A single crossbow bolt was relatively inexpensive.

The *balia* records also contain detailed data on the payment of workers involved in the war in 1350 (Chapter 2). Table 3.4 lists their wages, which were all paid daily. The evidence sheds light on this most hidden part of the Florentine workforce.

The civilian advisors (*consiglieri*) of the captain of war received the highest salaries, 220 soldi a day, more than double that of the next highest paid worker – paymasters of soldiers, who earned 90 soldi a day. The paymasters earned the same wage as those in charge of the food supply at Scarperia. Interestingly, those paymasters who compensated food transporters (*vetturali*) earned significantly less (30 soldi a day) than those responsible for soldiers.

The chamberlain of the *balia* itself, Arnaldo Manelli, was paid 70 soldi a day, the same salary as the officials who supervised distribution of food and supplies in the field and the same rate as those sent to recruit crossbowmen from Liguria and Lunigiana. One of the recruiters, Paolo del Nero, spent more than two months prospecting for crossbowmen in Genoa and its environs.[46]

---

[46] ASF, balie 6 fol. 76r.

Table 3.4 *Nominal Daily Wages of Artisans and Noncombatants, 1350*

Job	Salary
Consigliares/advisors to captain of war	220 soldi
Paymasters for soldiers	90 soldi
Custodians of food supply at Scarperia	90 soldi
Foreman of artisans at Scarperia	80 soldi
Chamberlains of *balia* of war	70 soldi
Overseers of supplies in the field	70 soldi
Capomaestro/blacksmith (with *discepolo*)	50 soldi
Capomaestro/stonemason (with *discepolo*)	40 soldi
Doctor	30 soldi
Paymasters for *vetturali*	30 soldi
Captain of *Marraioli, Spalatores*	25 soldi
Musicians	20 soldi
Vetturale with mule	19 soldi
Stonemasons	18–12 soldi
Sawyers	18 soldi
Sargenti/famuli of overseers of supplies	15 soldi
Procurators for mercenary cavalrymen	15 soldi
Messengers of the *balia*	10 soldi
Explorers	10 soldi
Vetturale with donkey	10 soldi

Source: ASF, balie 6 fols. 2v–119v.

Stonemasons and blacksmiths (*maestri di lapide e legname*) at Scarperia stood at the middle of the pay scale. *Capomaestri* stonemasons, with their own helper (*discepolo*), earned 40 soldi a day. *Capomaestri* blacksmiths, with a *discepolo*, earned 50 soldi a day.[47] Ordinary stonemasons received between 18 soldi and 12 soldi a day (most typically the former). Florence employed forty-four stonemasons at Scarperia, but only two blacksmiths, both of whom were *capomaestri*. The wages of the stonemasons were consistent with the average pay calculated for the profession in 1350 by Richard Goldthwaite (16.8 soldi a day).[48] A doctor who rode with the army earned 30 soldi a day, less than a *capomaestro*.[49]

---

[47] ASF, balie 6 fols. 9r, 51r. The stonemasons were all identified as *maestri di lapide e legname*. For a full description of the professions, see Richard A. Goldthwaite, *The Building of Renaissance Florence* (Baltimore, MD: Johns Hopkins University Press, 1980), pp. 436, 437; Tognetti, "Prezzi e salari," pp. 302–304.

[48] Goldthwaite, *The Building of Renaissance Florence*, pp. 436, 437.

[49] ASF, balie 6 fols. 24r, 109v.

The lowest paid workers were explorers (10 soldi a day), who sought out information about the enemy. Meanwhile, the pay of *vetturali* varied according to the animal they used in transport. A transporter with a mule received 19 soldi a day; a transporter with a donkey earned 10 soldi a day. The pay appears to have been based, at least in part, on the cost of maintenance of the animal.

No figures have survived for 1349, so the effect on salaries of the Black Death over the two years cannot be judged. Nevertheless, the evidence from the *balia* records makes clear the relative high cost of the labor with respect to supplies. On the "busy" day of preparations for battle on 14 May 1350, the sources show that Florence spent 395 lire for the salaries of masons at Scarperia (for fifteen days of labor), 910 lire in advance pay to the captains of army, but only 31 lire for supplies.[50] Similarly on 4 June 1350 (another busy day), the city spent 4,363 lire (1,254 florins) for salaries of personnel, but 1,067 lire (333.5 florins) for crossbows, hemp, and wire.[51]

Soldiers' salaries dwarfed all other expenses (see Chapter 4). The wage for a single German captain and his band for one month in 1350 was 1,226 lire (383 florins), more than the total expenditure for all supplies at Scarperia from May to June.[52]

Death and Taxes

How did the commune raise the money for war? The surviving budgets for income (*entrata*) are unfortunately more fragmentary than those for expenditure. There are only two extant *scrivano* budgets (May/June 1349 and May/June 1350) for the period of the war with comprehensive figures.[53] These may, however, be augmented by non-*scrivano* Latin originals, which provide scattered but useful data.[54]

The general outlines are clear. For the first campaign in 1349, Florence relied on loans from the confraternity of Orsanmichele,

---

[50] ASF, balie 6 fols. 8v–10v, 21v–23v.   [51] ASF, balie 6 fols. 81r–81v.

[52] This is the pay for Jakob da Fiore and his band. ASF, Camera del comune, Scrivano di camera uscita fol. 9v.

[53] ASF, Camera del comune, Scrivano di camera entrata 8 (May/June 1349), fols. 2r–52v; Scrivano di camera entrata 9 (May/June 1350), fols. 2r–36v. The Scrivano budgets for income are out of order. Scrivano di camera entrata 7 fols. 2r–37v is for March/April 1350, that is after Scrivano di camera uscita entrata 8.

[54] The fragmentary Latin originals used here are ASF, Camera del comune, camerlenghi entrata 32 (March/April 1349) fols. 203r–219r, 220r–221v; camerlenghi entrata 34 (July/August 1349) fols. 124r–198r, 200r–202r; camerlenghi entrata 35 (September/October 1349) fols. 203r–219r, 220r–221v; camerlenghi entrata 38 (March/April 1350) fols. 39r–89r; camerlenghi entrata 40 (July/August 1350) fols. 126r–186v; camerlenghi entrata 41 (September/October 1350) fols. 187r–223r.

which had, as noted previously, become wealthy in the immediate aftermath of the plague from the bequests of victims of the contagion. Florence also garnered revenue from fines on its own citizens, and from loans from soldiers and other persons directly involved in the war. For the second campaign in 1350, the city relied more on gabelle revenue and on the rural *estimo*, a direct tax imposed on inhabitants of the countryside.

The role of the gabelles needs to be underlined in both instances. They were, as David Herlihy has asserted, the foundation of urban finance in medieval Italy.[55] They consisted of a wide array of direct and indirect taxes, and were used to pay back interest on loans from citizens. The most important of the gabelles were those on retail wine sold in the city, contado and *distretto* (*vino venduto a minuto*), on goods passing through the city gates (*porte*), and on salt (*sale e saline*). Giovanni Villani highlighted these in his famous description of Florence in 1338, as the most remunerative of public taxes.[56] The salt gabelle was a state monopoly (*dogana*), which required individuals to buy a given quantity at a set price.

The budgets show that the city assigned specific gabelles to specific expenditures. In 1349/1350 "general" expenses (i.e., nonwar related) were paid for primarily by "minor" gabelles. These included the gabelle on livestock sold in the city (*gabella del mercato delle bestie vive che si vendono in città*), the gabelle on fresh vegetables and fruits (*gabella del trecche e trecconi*), and the gabelle on revenue from mills and fishing in the city and in the contado (*gabella di muline e gualchiere*).[57] The revenue from the "major" gabelles – those on wine, gates, and salt – was assigned directly to the condotta office to pay soldiers' wages.

---

[55] David Herlihy, "Direct and Indirect Taxation in Tuscan Urban Finance, c. 1200–1400" in *Finances et comptabilité urbaines du 13e au 16e siècle* (Bruxelles: Centre pro civitate, 1964), pp. 385–405. See also Bernardino Barbadoro, *Le finanze della Repubblica fiorentina: imposta diretta e debito pubblico fino all'istituzione del Monte* (Firenze: Leo S. Olschki, 1929). La Roncière, "Indirect Taxes," p. 143; Molho, *Florentine Public Finances*, pp. 22–59; E. Fiumi, "Fioritura e decadenza dell' economia fiorentina," *Archivio storico italiano* 115 (1957), pp. 385–439. For relative information on public finance elsewhere in Italy, see William Bowsky, *The Finance of the Commune of Siena, 1287–1355* (Oxford: Clarendon Press, 1970).

[56] Giovanni Villani, *Nuova Cronica*, pp. 1347–1348.

[57] The preceding taxes appear in all the budgets. Florence also assigned (if inconsistently) to general expenses the proceeds of the gabelles on silver and black money (*gabella di moneta dell' ariento e nero*), on towers (*gabella delle torre*), and on baked bread (*gabella di pane cotto in citta e contado*). ASF, Camera del comune, Scrivano di camera entrata 9 fols. 2r–31r; Camera del comune, camarlenghi entrata 34 fols. 124r–184r; Scrivano di camera entrata 7 fols. 2r–37v; Camera del comune, camarlenghi entrata 35 fols. 203r–219r (204r); Camera del comune, camarlenghi entrata 40 fols. 126v–182v.

The gabelle on contracts (*contratte*) was used to pay the salaries of castellans.

Like other Italian cities, Florence usually responded to armed conflict by raising gabelle rates. The practice throughout the peninsula was to double rates across the board at the start of hostilities.[58] Florence did this during its wars with Milan (1351) and Pisa (1362–1364). Charles de La Roncière called 1349 "a conspicuous year" for rises in gabelle rates, citing significant increases, which he attributed to the plague. The increases owed, however, to both the plague and war.[59] Florence doubled the tax on wine, gates, and salt and those on flour, meat, and bread at the outbreak of the Ubaldini war. According to Matteo Villani, the salt gabelle rose from 60 soldi per *staio* (bushel) in 1348 to 108 soldi per *staio* in 1349.[60] But Florentine officials adjusted rates up and down without noting the reason for the change, particularly when the change was in the downward direction.[61]

Whatever the actual rates, the budgets make clear the difficulty the city had collecting gabelle money.[62] This was, as noted earlier, true throughout Italy and in Europe more generally.[63] In Florence, the plague killed tax farmers who purchased gabelles in advance in installments. Death interrupted the payments and the flow of money to the fisc. The cameral budget of May 1349 notes that Ser Paolo Mori and "compagni," purchaser of the gate gabelle in 1348, "died of the plague," and his *compagni* were unable to pay the rest of the money they owed the city. The responsibility fell to a guarantor (*mallevadore*), Bardo d'Arrighi Giandonati, who also failed to pay. Florence never received its due.[64]

---

[58] Caferro, "Warfare and Economy"; Bowsky notes this practice for Siena. William M. Bowsky, *The Finance of the Commune of Siena, 1287–1355* (Oxford: Clarendon Press, 1970), p. 131. See also La Roncière, "Indirect Taxes," p. 150; Enrico Fiumi, " Fioritura e decadenza dell'economia fiorentina," *Archivio storico italiano* 115 (1957), p. 449.

[59] La Roncière, "Indirect Taxes, p. 150. Barducci also notes increases in gabelle rates at this time. Roberto Barducci, "Politica e speculazione finanziaria a Firenze dopo la crisi del primo Trecento (1343–1358)," *Archivio Storico Italiano* 137, no. 2 (1979), p. 197.

[60] Matteo Villani, *Nuova Cronica*, vol. 1, p. 57; La Roncière, "Indirect Taxes," pp. 150, 158.

[61] Bowsky, *The Finance of the Commune of Siena*, pp. 132–137.

[62] La Roncière makes clear that this was a fundamental problem throughout the fourteenth century. La Roncière, "Indirect Taxes," pp. 176–185.

[63] Bowsky's classic study of Siena dissents from this general view. He sees little direct effect of the plague on gabelle revenue in that city. Bowsky points to a lowering of the public debt and increases in gabelle income that in 1349–1350 "slightly surpassed that of any comparable earlier period." The income from the wine gabelle was 11 percent of budget in 1349, comparable to the late 1320s and early 1330s. Bowsky, *The Finance of the Commune of Siena*, pp. 250, 274–275.

[64] ASF, Camera del comune, Scrivano di camera entrata 8 fol. 49v.

Florence turned to loans (*preste*) to make up for the shortfall and raise money to fight the Ubaldini. In April 1349, just prior to the start of the war, Florence enacted a *presta* of 8,000 florins (25,600 lire) on citizens "to pay all soldiers' salaries that were in arrears."[65] The city offered lenders an interest rate of 15 percent, backed by the proceeds of the gabelle on retail wine. The revenue from the loan went directly to the office of the condotta. In June 1349, as the city mobilized its forces, officials sought help from the confraternity of Orsanmichele. The city borrowed 15,000 gold florins and pledged repayment again from the proceeds of the gabelle on wine sold at retail. The revenue again went directly to the condotta office to pay the salaries of soldiers. But no interest rate was mentioned.

The role of Orsanmichele in Florentine public finance in the immediate aftermath of the plague is well known.[66] Matteo Villani reported that it inherited a "grande tesoro" from bequests (*lasciti*) of those who died from the disease.[67] The modern scholar John Henderson has shown how the state, short of cash, used the charitable institution as a source of revenue for its everyday business. The extant *entrata* budgets show that in June 1349, 24,000 lire (7,500 florins) from Orsanmichele was deposited directly into the condotta office to pay for soldiers. The payments were made in five installments.[68] In November 1349 the condotta received another 7,500 florins from Orsanmichele, recorded in a notarial deed drawn up by Petrarch's friend Francesco Bruni.[69]

Table 3.5 lists the leading sources of revenue of the condotta (May/June 1349) for the first campaign. The proceeds from the salt and gate gabelles amounted to only 7,532 lire, less than a third of the sum borrowed from Orsanmichele. The returns reflect the dislocation and demographic contraction resulting from the plague. Revenue from the

---

[65] ASF, Provvisioni, registri 36 fol. 81r.

[66] Goldthwaite, *The Building of Renaissance Florence*, pp. 338–389. On Orsanmichele as an institution, see John Henderson, *Piety and Charity in Late Medieval Florence* (Oxford: Clarendon Press, 1994), pp. 175–190.

[67] Matteo Villani estimated Orsanmichele's fortune at 350,000 florins. Villani accused the captains of Orsanmichele of keeping much of the money for their own personal purposes. Henderson is skeptical of Villani's claims, but does not discount the possibility. Henderson, *Piety and Charity in Late Medieval Florence*, p. 180. Falsini suggests that several confraternities and pious institutions gained money from "lasciti" as a result of the plague. Falsini, "Firenze dopo il 1348," pp. 453–456. The account books of the confraternity are not sufficiently complete to make a definitive statement about the degree to which the state relied on the institution. Henderson shows that the city borrowed 9,635 florins against the gabelle on wine from the summer of 1349 to summer of 1351. Henderson, *Piety and Charity in Late Medieval Florence*, pp. 175–190.

[68] ASF, Camera del comune, Scrivano di camera entrata 8 fols. 50r–50v; Camera del comune, camerlinghi uscita 66 fol. 587v.

[69] ASF, Camera del comune, camarlenghi uscita 64 fol. 507r.

Table 3.5 *Main Sources of Revenue for the Condotta
(May/June 1349)*

Source	Amount*
Loans from Orsanmichele	24,000 lire
Gabelle on retail wine	12,990 lire
Fines/condemnations	8,000 lire
Gabelle on salt	4,305 lire
Gabelle on gates	3,227 lire
Payment from town of Mangona**	313 lire

* Sums are rounded to the nearest lira.
** Mangona in the Val di Sieve had been recently purchased by
   Florence.
Source: ASF, Camera del comune, Scrivano di camera entrata 8
fols. 49r–52v.

wine gabelle was higher than the others, but only about half of the sum
received from Orsanmichele. Much of the wine gabelle was assigned to
repayment of loans.

Revenue from the gabelles on salt and gates remained low in subsequent months. The tax on salt brought in only 872 lire to the condotta
office in July/August 1349 and 3,665 lire in September/October 1349.[70]
The gate gabelle produced 4,100 lire and 3,065 lire, respectively,
in these months.[71] The revenue from the gabelle on retail wine was
stronger, reaching as high as 20,000 lire in September/October.[72]
The relative buoyancy may reflect quality-of-life issues – perhaps it
suggests some truth to the notion that citizens drank much after the
contagion. Communal business through the city gates slowed, however, and fewer people remained to purchase salt.

The use of fines as a source of revenue in 1349 must be underlined.
Florentine officials raised 8,000 lire in May/June from assessments on its
inhabitants, more than from the gabelles on salt and gates combined.[73]
The evidence reinforces chronicle accounts that tell of upheaval in the city
in the immediate aftermath of the plague, and the appointment of
a special committee to arrange peace among citizens.[74] The fines were
imposed by the city's chief judicial officials – the podestà, the *conservatore/*

---

[70] ASF, Camera del comune camarlenghi entrata 34 fols. 200r–202r; Camera del comune,
   camarlenghi entrata 35 fols. 220r–221v.
[71] ASF, Camera del comune, Scrivano di camera entrata 7 fol. 49v.
[72] ASF, Camera del comune, camarlenghi entrata 35 fols. 220r–221v.
[73] ASF, Camera del comune, Scrivano di camera entrata 8 fol. 49v.
[74] Civil strife is noted in the legislation of 13 June 1349. The city elected men "circa paces
   treguas et concodias" in the city. ASF, Provvisioni, registri 36 fol. 105v.

capitano della guardia, and the executor of justice.[75] The *conservatore* Niccolò della Serra, who also led Florentine forces in the field against the Ubaldini, handed out the largest penalties. He fined Sandro di Ser Ricoveri 6,000 florins, of which 1,000 florins (3,129 lire) were paid in June 1349.[76] The sentence was apparently tied to an earlier condemnation of Tommaso di Vanni Agolanti, a Ghibelline magnate, who was exiled from the city soon after the plague.[77] Niccolò della Serra also assessed a fine of 5,000 florins on Agnolo di Lapo Davizzani, a judgment likely related to the war. The Davizzani were allies of the Ubaldini.[78] Agnolo paid 1,500 florins (3,447 lire) of the sum in June.[79]

The revenue went directly to the condotta office to pay the salaries of soldiers. The fines assessed by the other judges were generally smaller and related to specific crimes committed in the city. The podestà, for example, sentenced Andrea Falchini in July 1349 to pay 80 lire "for striking Meo Lippi in the face with a rock," and Uguccione di Piero Sacchetti was required to pay 100 lire in August 1349 for stabbing Lotto Ser Ghani.[80] The executor of justice meanwhile fined Mona Agata, wife of Ser Gino da Calenzano, 10 lire for wearing ermine, in violation of the sumptuary laws.[81]

Meanwhile, Florentine officials continued to seek loans to augment income. In June 1349, the wealthy banker Giovanni di Alberto Alberti (of the Alberti nuovi firm), who served also as the chamberlain of the wine gabelle, lent the city 1,000 florins to pay the salaries of soldiers.[82] The loan was contracted covertly; there is no mention of it in city legislation. It appears only in an *entrata* budget, which gives no interest rate. Alberti received instead a fee of 19 florins, which represented about 2 percent of his payment. Similarly, the *entrata* budgets show that the city received, in August 1349, a loan of 400 florins for the condotta from the captains of the Guelf party, whose membership included Giovanni

---

[75] ASF, Camera del comune, camarlenghi entrata 34 fol. 124v. On condemnations by the executor of justice assessed on magnate families, see Christiane Klapisch-Zuber, *Ritorno alla politica: I magnati fiorentini, 1340–1440* (Rome: Viella, 2009), pp. 114–117. ASF, Camera del comune, camarlighi entrata 34 fol. 124v.

[76] ASF, Camera del comune, Scrivano di camera entrata 8 fol. 51r.

[77] ASF, Camera del comune, camarlenghi entrata 32 fols. 40v–41r, 48v, 61r. On the Agolanti and their Ghibelline affiliation and problems with the city, see Klapisch-Zuber, *Ritorno alla politica*, pp. 33–34.

[78] ASF, Provvisione, registri 36 fol. 151r.

[79] ASF, Camera del comune, Scrivano di camera entrata 8 fol. 50r.

[80] ASF, Camera del comune, Scrivano di camera entrata 8 fol. 52r; Camera del comune, carmarlinghi entrata 34 fol. 124r.

[81] ASF, Camera del comune, Scrivano di camera entrata 8 fol. 51v; Camera del comune, carmarlinghi entrata 35 fol. 203r.

[82] ASF, Camera del comune, Scrivano di camera entrata 8 fol. 49v; Camera del comune, camarlenghi entrata 32 fol. 65r.

Massai Raffacani, one the advisors to the captain of war in 1350, and Francesco de Brunelleschi, a member of the *balia* in 1350.[83] This loan also states no interest rate.

In August 1349 city officials imposed a more straightforward loan of 4,830 florins on citizens to pay both soldiers and other public officials.[84] Repayment was backed by the gabelles on wine and gates. The loan is noteworthy because it gives the names of the creditors and the amounts owed to them by the city. The list includes soldiers who fought in the war and others linked directly to the campaign. The Italian cavalry captain Nino degli Obizzi of Lucca was owed 280 florins by the city. Ser Bonaiuto Sensi, a procurator of cavalrymen and paymaster of troops, was owed 45 florins. Cherico Geri da Sommaria, listed as a creditor of soldiers who had "died from the plague," maintained an impressive debt of 1,117 florins with the commune.[85] The largest creditor, Mazzuoli di Vanuccio Mazzuoli (owed 1,618 florins) does not appear to have been directly connected to the war. His surname is nevertheless the same as Petrarch's famous friend, Zanobi da Strada (Zanobi di Giovanni Mazzuoli da Strada), who was the father of Boccaccio's first grammar teacher.

The financing of the second campaign differed from the first in that Florence no longer relied on loans from Orsanmichele. Revenue from fines decreased, while gabelle returns increased. The change likely owed much to the legislation of January 1350 specifically aimed at "increasing revenue" from the gabelles. Florence appointed a committee of eight exactors, headed by Niccolò di Messer Bencivenni, who was also a chamberlain of the condotta, to seek ways to augment communal income ("crescere le rendite del comune a fare venire denari in comune").[86] In March 1350, the city passed a law requiring that all "unsold" gabelles be collected directly by the state rather than by tax farmers.[87]

The measures were successful, at least initially. In March/April 1350, on the eve of the second campaign, Florence collected 81, 282 lire from the gabelle on retail wine, a more than sixfold increase from the start of the previous campaign.[88] Interestingly, the chamberlain responsible for the collection of the wine gabelle, Tommaso di Francesco Davizzi, was a direct relation to the Ubaldini family – from a branch of "faithful

---

[83] ASF, Camera del comune, camarlenghi entrata 34 fol. 201v. For Florence's use of loans from the Guelf party in earlier years, see Barbadoro, *Le finanze della Repubblica fiorentina*, pp. 479, 480, 488–491, 496, 561–563.

[84] ASF, Provvisioni, registri 37 fols. 86r–86v. Camera del comune, camarlenghi entrata 34 fol. 202r.

[85] ASF, Camera del comune, Scrivano di camera uscita 7 fols. 44r, 44v.

[86] ASF, Provvisioni, registri 37 fols. 67v–68v, 79v–81v.

[87] ASF, Provvisioni, registri 38 fol. 4v; La Roncière, "Indirect Taxes," p. 183.

[88] ASF, Camera del comune, Scrivano di camera entrata 7 fols. 48r–53r.

Table 3.6 *Main Sources of Revenue for the Condotta (May/June 1350)*

Source	Amount*
Eight officials to increase revenue	34,250 lire
Gabelle on retail wine	29,660 lire
Estimo	14,196 lire
Gabelle on salt	5,275 lire
Gabelle on gates	1,597 lire

* Sums are rounded to the nearest lira.
Source: ASF, Scrivano di camera entrata 9 fols. 33r–36v.

Guelfs" who were specifically exempted from overall condemnation of the clan in 1349.[89] The money went to the office of the condotta to pay soldiers.

Rather than borrow from Orsanmichele, the city began repaying its loans from the institution. In February 1350 the city sent 1,600 lire (500 florins) back to Orsanmichele, disbursed directly from the condotta office. It continued to do so in monthly installments. The repayment schedule makes clear that the city did not pay interest on the original loans.[90]

The proceeds from the wine gabelle fluctuated. It declined to 29,660 lire in May/June 1350 and to 19,220 in July/August 1350, before rising again to 29,022 lire in September/October 1350. Meanwhile, the revenue from the gabelles on gates and salt remained steadfastly low. The former produced only 1,579 lire, 3,156 lire, and 1,600 lire in May/June, July/August, and September/October, respectively. The latter returned 5,275 lire, 640 lire, and 7,886 lire in those months.[91] It is unclear whether the meager returns reflect the continued effects of plague and war or the assignment of proceeds to repayment of loans or all of the above.

The most lucrative source of revenue in May/June 1350 according to our lone surviving *scrivano entrata* budget was from the committee of exactors (Table 3.6).[92] It is unclear what sources of revenue the money

[89] They were descendents of Octaviano de Galliano de Ubaldini, who remained Guelf. ASF, Scrivano di camera entrata 7 (March/April 1350) fols. 48r–53r.
[90] ASF, Camera del comune, camarlenghi uscita 64 fol. 507v; Camera del comune, camarlenghi uscita 66 fol. 587v.
[91] ASF, Camera del comune, camarlenghi entrata 37 fols. 32v–34r; Camera del comune, camarlenghi entrata 40 fols. 183r–186r; Camera del comune, camarlenghi entrata 41 fols. 220v–223r.
[92] ASF, Camera del comune, Scrivano di camera entrata 9 fols. 33r–36v.

represented. The committee paid 49,398 lire (15,437 florins) directly into the condotta, which constituted nearly half of the proceeds of that office. City officials sought no new loans. They imposed instead a direct tax, the *estimo*, on the countryside.[93] The tax returned 14,196 lire in May/June, more than from the gabelles on gates and salt combined, and an additional 27,976 lire in July/August and 10,388 lire in September/October.[94] Castellan salaries in Florence were, in 1350, paid for from the proceeds of the gabelle on contracts, which produced 10,681 lire in May/June 1350.[95]

The imposition of the rural *estimo* in 1350 (the urban *estimo* had been eliminated in 1315) may be taken as evidence that there was wealth in that sector, or, perhaps, that Florentine officials sought to press harder on the countryside. G. L. Harriss has shown that in England, officials placed a greater burden on the rural classes after the plague.[96]

God, Justice, and Public Finance

A consistent source of revenue in all *entrata* budgets is from a tax called *dirittura*. The impost, long in use by the city, has been largely – and curiously – overlooked in the scholarship on public finance. Bernardino Barbadoro's seminal study of Florentine public finance in the thirteenth and early fourteenth centuries says little of it; as does La Roncière in his assessment of Florentine gabelles.[97] In 1349/1350 the tax consisted of a deduction of 12 denari (1 soldo) per lira (8.3 percent) on all financial transactions, including payment of salaries and transfers of money, even from one communal office to another, as well as on money spent to feed members of the Signoria and on the clothes the city gave to communal musicians.[98] The returns from the tax were therefore intrinsically linked to the overall amount of public expenditure, which was, as we have seen, linked closely to war, the most costly undertaking by the city.

---

[93] ASF, Camera del comune, Scrivano di camera entrata 10 fol. 34v.

[94] ASF, Camera del comune, Scrivano di camera entrata 9 fols. 33r–36v.

[95] ASF, Camera del comune, Scrivano di camera entrata 9 fols. 37r–37v.

[96] Harriss, pp. 333–334. W. M. Ormrod sees a shift after the death from direct taxation to indirect taxation. Ormrod, *Edward III*, p. 375.

[97] Gherardi in his essay on the *camera del comune* in 1303 notes the imposition of *dirittura* back then. Alessandro Gherardi, "L'antica camera del comune di Firenze e un quarderno d'uscita de suoi camarlenghi del anno 1303," *Archivio Storico Italiano* 43 (1885), pp. 320–321.

[98] ASF, Camera del comune, Scrivano di camera uscita 6 fol. 41r; balie 6 fols. 5r–11r; Camera del comune, camarlenghi entrata 32 fols. 31r–31v, 35r, 39r; Camera del comune, camarlenghi entrata 34 fol. 197r; Scrivano di camera entrata 9 fol. 25v.

The rationale behind the tax is not explicitly stated. Dante used the term *dirittura* in *Convivio* 4 17 6 to signify justice, honesty, and moral rectitude. "Giustizia ordina noi ad amare e operare *dirittura* in tutte cose" ("Justice is the virtue which disposes us to love rectitude"). Boccaccio used the term in the *Decameron* for day 1, story 2, with regard to Gianotto da Civigni and his Jewish friend Abraham. Boccaccio juxtaposes the term *dirittura* with *lealtà*, qualities both men share, translated by modern scholars as "uprightness" and "honesty/fidelity," respectively.[99] Gianotto is described elsewhere in the story as "lealissimo e diritto" and Abraham as "leale e diritto."

Close examination of the Florentine documents suggests that the *dirittura* tax was similarly related to moral rectitude. Revenue from the tax appears both in cameral budgets and the *balia* registers, and is specifically aimed at recycling money back to the state for the purpose of the betterment of the city. There was a set formula. Of the 12 denari per lira assessed for *dirittura*, 10 denari went to the new university to pay "for salaries to hire professors" and 2 denari went to the wool cloth guild for the upkeep and beautification of the cathedral. The proceeds of the *dirittura* went directly to the chamberlains in charge of those offices. The *scrivano entrata* budget shows that on 14 July 1349 the city paid 1,788 lire from the tax to Arrigho Bellondi, head of committee that oversaw the establishment of the university, and 388 lire from the tax to Neri Pitti, chamberlain of the wool cloth guild.[100] On 14 August 1349, the city paid 2,240 lire to Bollondi and 277 lire to Pitti.[101] During the height of the second campaign against the Ubaldini in June 1350, the studio received 2,518 lire from *dirittura* and the wool cloth guild 1,005 lire.[102] The existence of only a few *scrivano* budgets makes it difficult to trace the overall outlay by the city, which was undoubtedly much greater.[103]

In any case, the *dirittura* reveals a logic, or ethos, imbedded in Florentine public finance that needs to be acknowledged. The tax constituted a conscious effort on the part of the commune to make good from bad, to use money spent on war and violence – the most expensive of the city's financial dealings – to improve human capital

---

[99] The words recur in the story. Boccaccio says later of Abraham that "la cui *dirittura* e la cui lealtà veggendo Giannotto, gl'incominciò forte ad increscere." Giovanni Boccaccio, *The Decameron*, translated by Mark Musa and Peter E. Bondanella (New York, NY: Norton, 1977), pp. 28–29.

[100] ASF, Camera del comune, Scrivano di camera uscita 6 fol. 41r.

[101] ASF, Camera del comune, Scrivano di camera entrata 7 fol. 7v.

[102] ASF, Camera del comune, Scrivano di camera entrata 9 fol. 6v.

[103] In April 1350, the city disbursed another 1,280 lire (400 florins) for the studio and 250 lire for the Duomo. ASF, Camera del comune, Scrivano di camera entrata 7 fol. 2v.

(via the university) and honor God. Indeed, the tax transformed all manner of fiscal transactions into the public good. For our purpose here, the *dirittura* tax directly linked the Ubaldini war to the establishment of the university. It provides a kind of fiscal and moral symmetry. As Florence spent large sums of money on war to gain the services of Petrarch for its university, its spending helped establish the studio itself.[104]

In this regard, the *diriturra* may perhaps be seen as a precursor to the *onoranza* of the fifteenth century. The tax, described by Michael Mallett, was a flat rate imposed by Venice and Milan on soldiers' salaries on behalf of the Church.[105] Scholars have treated the *onoranza* with cynicism, seeing it as little more than a nod and wink at religion. But the Florentine *dirittura* was a fundamental part of Florence's overall fiscal policy. The desire on the part of city officials to make financial transactions useful, in effect to sanctify them, reflects a very real Christian civic pride.

Indeed, it is notable that the fines imposed on soldiers for failure to pass inspection (*difetti*) were assigned to "general expenses" rather than to the condotta office.[106] City officials appear not to have sought to recycle military wages back into war, but to use for the revenue for the everyday business of the city. The aim was, as with *diriturra*, to convert war money into civic purposes.

The Christian civic element in public finance matches well the basic involvement of the Church in Florentine fiscal affairs. However strong the temptation may be, it is impossible to separate religion from Florentine economic affairs and warfare. As we have already seen, two of the four chamberlains in charge of the *camera del commune*, which handled the city's money, were monks from the abbey of San Salvatore in Settimo. The chamberlains in charge of the *camera del arme*, which maintained the city's supply of armaments, were monks. The loan money paid by the confraternity of Orsanmichele to the city in June 1349 to pay for soldiers against the Ubaldini was transferred from monk to monk: from those in charge of Orsanmichele directly to the those in charge of the *camera del arme*.[107] The *camera del arme* then turned the money over to the lay chamberlains of the condotta, who in turn paid the troops. The frequency

---

[104] William Caferro, "Le Tre Corone Fiorentine and War with the Ubaldini," in *Boccaccio 1313–2013*, edited Francesco Ciabattoni, Elsa Filosa, and Kristina Olson (Ravenna: Longo editore, 2015), p. 53.

[105] Michael Mallett, *Mercenaries and Their Masters* (Totowa, NJ: Rowman and Littlefield, 1974), pp. 137–138; Caferro, "Warfare and Economy," p. 193; Peter Blastenbrei, *Die Sforza und ihr Heer* (Heidelberg: Winter Universitätsverlag, 1987), p. 205.

[106] The fines touched all soldiers and were often substantial. See for example ASF, Camera del comune, Scrivano di camera entrata 8 fol. 19r.

[107] ASF, Camera del comune, Scrivano di camera entrata 8 fols. 50r–50v.

of such transfers is unknown, but churchmen clearly added an additional sense of security in financial affairs. When Florence could not collect taxes from the newly captured town of Lozzole in 1350, it sent a monk as its principal financial officer in the explicit hope that he would "lessen frauds and gain the confidence" of the locals.[108]

Toward an Economy of War

For all the detail relayed in the documents, it remains difficult, as Jay M. Winter said about warfare in general, to create a balance sheet of profits and losses for the Ubaldini campaigns.[109] Although limited in scope, the war was clearly expensive and placed great pressure on a fisc that was already reeling from the plague. The conflict rendered still more difficult the movement of merchants and merchandise through important roads, creating short-term dislocations. The burning of houses and the stealing of livestock struck hard at both sides. The effort to repopulate Scarperia in October 1349 on account of the twin effects "of enemy raids and the plague" is stark evidence of this.[110] At the same time, however, the Ubaldini, unlike interstate opponents such as Pisa or Milan, did not bring the war to the gates of Florence. Florence brought the war to them. Thus, Ubaldini territory suffered more damage; it was their castles and tolls that were ultimately appropriated by the Florentines, who sought to stifle the enemy from the outset by offering tax breaks to the adherents of the Ubaldini to induce them to switch sides. The defeat of the clan in 1350 opened the Apennine roads, allowing Petrarch and pilgrims to travel to Rome for the jubilee. The repair and refurbishing of captured fortresses provided Florentine merchants with opportunities for investment and artisans opportunities for work.

The importance of recycled money stands out in our discussion. While Florence's population decreased sharply as a result of the plague, its money remained. The confraternity of Orsanmichele, long dedicated to social assistance, became transformed into a source of funds for destruction and military matters. Fines on a fractious urban citizenry and magnates augmented communal income. The *balia* records of 1350 show that the artisans employed at Scarperia were largely from the environs of that town, as were the men who supplied materials

---

[108] Demetrio Marzi, *La cancelleria della Repubblica Fiorentina* (Rocca San Casciano: Cappelli, 1909), p. 679.

[109] Jay M. Winter, ed., *War and Economic Development: Essays in Memory of David Joslin* (Cambridge: Cambridge University Press, 1975), p. 2.

[110] ASF, CP 1 fol. 9r; Signoria Missive Cancelleria 10 #148. The letter indicates that the Ubaldini stole 117 sheep and goats and 45 cows in April 1350.

there. The *capomaestro* blacksmith, Frasinello Corsini, was from Pulicciano, a small town just east and south, not far from Vicchio in the Mugello. Giovanni Guascoli, who sold wood, was from Scarperia, as was Francesco Corsini, a spice dealer, and Guidotto Cennis, who sold hemp, and Lottino Lotti, who sold nails, and Azzino Gualberti, another *capomaestro* blacksmith.[111]

The money earned by the men presumably went back to the local economy, helping to offset the losses in the region from Ubaldini attacks. The return was augmented by the fact that Florence appears not to have imposed taxes on the workers at Scarperia and on artisan/suppliers who sold goods there. The city specifically exempted the men from the *dirittura*.[112] The profits of the suppliers, where we are able to get a glimpse of them, were significant. Azzino Gualberti, who was both a blacksmith and supplier of goods at Scarperia, earned 840 lire (250 florins) during the second campaign.[113] Bartolo Lapi, a seller of crossbows, earned 1,160 lire (350 florins) in sales, free of tax.[114]

The war-related profits of the men likely exceeded pacific sales, which were in fact taxed. The differing policies were perhaps intended by Florence as incentive for artisans to sell goods to the state rather than privately. Given the demographic crisis, it seems unlikely, however, that there was strong countervailing demand on the pacific side. Florence exempted still others from taxes on account of war service, including Ser Piero Mazzetti, the notary of the priors, who paid no gabelle on the income he received for letters he drew up specifically for the war. The extent to which Florence made such exceptions is, however, not clear (Chapter 5).[115]

The provenience of the soldiers was likewise an important factor in the recycling of money. Shield bearer captains, as we have seen (Chapter 2), came primarily from within the Florentine state, most often from mountain communities. The money they earned returned to those communities. The evidence supports Samuel K. Cohn's startling conclusion that there was significant wealth in the Florentine mountain communities (notably the upper Mugello) in the years after the plague.[116] It may also help explain why Florence decided in 1350 to impose the rural *estimo*,

---

[111] ASF, balìe 6 fol. 22r.

[112] The salaries of all of the artisans at Scarperia – stonemasons, carpenters, and sawyers – were exempt from taxes ("sine retention alicuis gabelle et diritture"). ASF, balìe 6 fols. 51r, 64r–v.

[113] ASF, balìe 6 fols. 108r, 114r.   [114] ASF, balìe 6 fol. 20r.

[115] The exemption also included messengers, *vetturali*, and troops inspectors. ASF, balìe 6 fol. 51r, 64r–v.

[116] Samuel K. Cohn, *Creating the Florentine State: Peasants and Rebellion* (Cambridge: Cambridge University Press, 1999).

perhaps seeking to appropriate money that had been recycled into the countryside.

Recycling was further enhanced by the investment of infantrymen in the communal *monte* (Chapter 2). Captains of both shield bearer and crossbow units in 1349/1350 held shares in the public debt (*azioni*). The Italian cavalry captain Nino degli Obizzi from Lucca invested both in the *monte* and lent money to the war effort itself (August 1349). The examples raise the intriguing possibility – which I have raised elsewhere – that war itself was seen as an investment for those who fought it, a prospect for which there is notable evidence for later in the *trecento*.[117]

We must take care, however, not to press the argument too far. Many of the crossbow captains in Florentine service came, as we have seen, from outside of the Florentine state. Studies of German mercenaries suggest that the men sent money home, to build estates for families in their native lands.[118] Moreover, if war stimulated business for artisans in the war region, it did not serve as an overall stimulus to the Florentine "munitions" industry. Florence possessed no military-industrial complex. Artisans who sold materials for war did so alongside their usual pacific trade. Demand for weapons was limited. The documents show that Florence recycled crossbow bolts. *Barattieri* picked them up from the field to be reworked and then reused.[119] There is no evidence of purchases by soldiers of expensive items such as armor. Florence kept armor as part of its communal arsenal, but the sources are silent with regard to sales to soldiers.[120] Meanwhile, Florentine officials provided soldiers with supplies and provisions free of charge. The detailed accounts of the overseers of supplies, Cristofano Boninstrade and Domenico di Sandro Donnini, for the army in 1350 show that while the city sold bread to the army, it also gave much of it away. The accounts give an explicit rationale behind the latter policy: "so that the army would not stop but give continuous battle."[121] Bread was distributed free of charge prior to the offensive at Montegemoli in late May and on 14 June, 24 June, and 27 June, as the army passed through difficult terrain.[122] An ambassadorial letter from June 1350 indicates that Florence even sent food and provisions to crossbow contingents recruited in Liguria in anticipation of their service.[123]

---

[117] Caferro, "Warfare and Economy," p. 205.

[118] Eduard A. Gessler, "Huglin von Shoenegg. Ein Basler Reiterführer des 14. Jahrhunderts in Italien: Ein Beitrag zur damaligen Bewaffnung," *Basler Zeitschrift fur Geschichte und Altertumskunde*, XXI (1923), pp. 75–126; Stephan Selzer, *Deutsche Söldner im Italien des Trecento* (Tubingen: Niemeyer, 2001), pp. 176–177.

[119] ASF, balie 7 fols. 33r, 33v, 34r.   [120] ASF, Provvisioni, registri 36 fol. 132v.

[121] "nullam denari exigerent a dictis stipendiaries." ASF, balie 7 fol. 32r.

[122] ASF, balie 7 fols. 29r–30v, 64r–64v.

[123] ASF, Signori, Missive I Cancelleria 10 #159.

War was, in short, too important a matter to be left wholly to the vagaries of the marketplace. There is no evidence of "self-sustaining markets" composed of soldiers and merchants, as envisioned by the historian William McNeill.[124] Supplies for the army in the high mountains were purchased not from within the Florentine state, but from across the Apennines in the Romagna.[125] The choice made logistical sense. In June 1350, Florence bought bread, notebooks, and ink from the town of Massa dei Alidosi, when the army was near Tirli.[126] A letter sent to the army by Florentine officials in June 1350 instructed the captain to seek supplies from the papal legate Conte di Romagna and Giovanni di Giovanni di Albergettino Manfredi, local lord in the Romagna.[127]

The limits of the financial returns from the war are most evident with respect to prominent merchants. Florence employed bankers to advance money to hire troops and pay for personnel and supplies (Chapter 2).[128] The bankers represent some of the most important firms of the day and advanced large sums of money. Francesco Rinuccini, one of Florence's richest men, lent, along with his "sotii mercatores," 500 florins for the hire of crossbowmen from Liguria.[129] Galeazzo Lapi da Uzzano, a partner in a bank with branches in Pisa, Bologna, Genoa, Rome, and Naples, gave 1,400 florins to pay for stipendiaries.[130]

Florentine officials made repayment of the advances a top priority and paid the salaries and expenses of the factors of the bankers, who did the actual recruiting. But the financial reward for the merchant was meager.[131] The banker received a fee of 5 denari per florin on each advance, which represented less than 1 percent (.06 percent) of the

---

[124] William H. McNeill, *The Pursuit of Power* (Chicago, IL: University of Chicago Press, 1982), p. 74. A fuller discussion of this issue is in Caferro, "Warfare and Economy," pp. 191–198.

[125] ASF, Provvisioni, registri 36 fols. 82v, 150r–150v; balie 7 fols. 33r, 33v.

[126] ASF, balie 7 fols. 35r, 64v.

[127] Marzi, *La cancelleria*, p. 679. ASF, balie 7 fols. 34r, 35v.

[128] The role of bankers in war deserves greater scholarly attention. See Caferro, "Warfare and Economy," pp. 167–209. The involvement of Florentine bankers in hiring troops in the fourteenth century appears in the account books of the Alberti bank. Richard A Goldthwaite, Enzo Settesoldi, and Marco Spallanzani, eds., *Due libri mastri degli Alberti: una grande compagnia di Calimala, 1348–1358*, vol. 1 (Florence: Cassa di Risparmio, 1995), pp. ciii–cix, 9, 33, 37, 40, 190. See also Richard A. Goldthwaite, *The Economy of Renaissance Florence* (Baltimore, MD: Johns Hopkins University Press, 2009), p. 47.

[129] ASF, balie 6 fols. 40v; Brucker, *Florentine Politics and Society*, p. 21.

[130] ASF, balie 6 fols. 40v, 110v. For the Da Uzzano bank, see Victor I. Rutenburg, "La compagnia di Uzzano" in *Studi in onore di Armando Sapori*, vol. 1 (Milan: Instituto editoriale cisalpino, 1957), pp. 689–706.

[131] ASF, balie 6 fol. 57r.

outlay.[132] For the 1,400 florins the da Uzzano bank loaned to the city, it received only 29 lire (roughly 9 florins) in return.[133] Meanwhile, the risks were substantial. The banker Manetto ser Ricciardi lost the entirety of the 900 florins he advanced for German mercenary cavalrymen.[134] Paolo del Nero, an intermediary in hiring bowmen from Sarzana, lost the advance he gave to soldiers, which included his own personal funds.[135]

The participation of bankers appears to have been more of a service to the state than a chance for profits. The same is true of those merchants who oversaw the purchase and distribution of supplies in field.[136] As we have seen (Chapter 2), they included important businessmen such as Jacopo di Donato Acciaiuoli and Petrarch's patron Francesco del Bennino. The precise relationship between the men and the *camera del arme*, with whom they "consulted" about war materials, is not clear. We do not know if they sold supplies to the *camera* or merely acted as agents in the field. But the risks outweighed the rewards. The documents show that the men were required to give surety for the job, in effect putting their own wealth on the line for the state and making them personally responsible for shortfalls. The *balie* records reveal that few of the merchants remained on the job for more than a few days or weeks, suggesting that the job was not desirable.[137] And unlike the artisans/suppliers at Scarperia, the merchants in charge of supplies in the field paid taxes on their salaries and on their sales.[138]

The evidence is reinforced by the example of Giovanni di Alberto Alberti, the wealthy merchant/banker, who, as we have seen, secretly lent the city 1,000 florins (3,200 lire) during the first campaign in return for only a 2 percent fee. But Alberti's example also demonstrates the difficulty of assessing the overall financial portfolios of prominent merchants. Extant registers from the Vatican archives reproduced by Karl Heinrich Schäfer show that Alberti was, at the same time he lent money to Florence, the papal treasurer in charge of financing the ongoing war in the Romagna. The opportunities for profit (and loss) were not restricted to Florence.[139] And it is impossible to say whether he and other wealthy merchants received from Florentine officials under the

---

[132] ASF, balie 6 fol. 40v.   [133] ASF, balie 6 fols. 110v, 108r.
[134] ASF, balie 6 fols. 57r, 108r.   [135] ASF, balie 6 fol. 108r.   [136] ASF, balie 6 fol. 58v.
[137] ASF, balie 6 fol. 67r.
[138] ASF, Camera del comune, Scrivano di camera entrata 8 fol. 19r.
[139] Alberti advanced 10,000 florins to the pope in 1350. Karl Heinrich Schäfer, *Die Ausgaben der Apostolischen Kamera (1335–1362)* (Paderborn: F. Schöningh, 1914), pp. 417, 436.

table emoluments or political considerations that are not easily quantified.

In any case, individual financial gains from the war must be judged against raises in gabelle rates, which cut into profits. John U. Nef, in his rejoinder to Werner Sombart's famous "war as economic stimulus" thesis, stressed the many factors needed to make an accurate assessment of the impact of war, including the possibility that war funds could have been more profitably invested elsewhere.[140] It is perhaps here that the Ubaldini campaign allows a most definitive statement.

The employment of so many men for the war effort at a time when the labor force was severely constricted had palpable consequences. The documents show clearly that city officials were forced to postpone the plan in July 1349 to build the church of Sant'Anna in honor of plague victims. The project, overseen and paid for by the confraternity of Orsanmichele, ceased due to a shortage of capable stonemasons. The captains of the confraternity of Orsanmichele explicitly blamed the war against the Ubaldini for making it "impossible to find *capomaestri*."[141] The two men appointed by Orsanmichele in July 1349 to direct the project were in fact Ristoro di Cione and Stefano Pucci, the same two who went to Scarperia to oversee the building of war machines for the Ubaldini war.

The church of Sant'Anna was never built. And the *dirittura* revenue used to finance the university ultimately, and predictably, became siphoned off by the Ubaldini war. In July 1350, Florentine officials were constrained to divert 6,400 lire (2,000 florins) intended for the studio to pay for the wages of soldiers.[142] The diversion of funds slowed the launch of the new university, which was not firmly established until years later.

---

[140] John U. Nef, "War and Economic Progress, 1540–1640," *Economic History Review* 12 (1942), p. 231 and *War and Human Progress* (Cambridge, MA: Harvard University Press, 1950), p. 65.

[141] Saverio La Sorsa, *La Compagnia d'or San Michele, ovvero una pagina della beneficenza in Toscana nel secolo XIV* (Trani: V. Vecchi, 1902), pp. 110–111, 240–250.

[142] ASF, Provvisioni, registri 36 fol. 38v.

4   Plague, Soldiers' Wages, and the Florentine Public Workforce

> We should subdue our natural proneness to follow the proclivities of our fathers ... The outstanding discovery of recent historical and anthropological research is that man's economy, as a rule, is submerged in his social relationships. He does not act so as to safeguard his individual interest in the possession of material goods; he acts so as to safeguard his social standing, his social claims, his social assets.
>
> Karl Polanyi, *The Great Transformation*[1]

> Classical theory is applicable to a special case only ... the special case assumed by classical theory happens not to be those of the economic society we actually live in.
>
> John Maynard Keynes, *The General Theory of Employment*[2]

> Sticky wages ... are a glaringly obvious feature of the real world.
>
> Paul Krugman, *The New York Times* (July 2012)[3]

No aspect of the plague has received more attention than its effect on wages. The years immediately following the contagion are treated as ones of "panic and compulsion" in markets, when "demand for labor was at its height."[4] Florentinists depict the years as ones of dramatic change. Charles de La Roncière spoke of a "spectaculaire montée salariale" in nominal and real wages from 1349 to 1350.[5] Richard Goldthwaite cited

---

Some of the material in this chapter appears in "Petrarch's War." The data and argument have been expanded and updated.

[1] Karl Polanyi, *The Great Transformation* (Boston: Beacon Press, 2nd paperback edn., 2001), pp. 44, 74.

[2] John Maynard Keynes, *The General Theory of Employment, Interest and Money* (New York, NY: Harcourt Brace, 1936), p. 3.

[3] Paul Krugman, "Sticky Wages and the Macro Story," *New York Times* (July 22, 2012).

[4] James E. Thorold Rogers, *A History of Agriculture and Prices in England from the Year after the Oxford Parliament (1259) to the Commencement of the Continental War (1793)*, vol. 1 (Oxford: Clarendon Press, 1866), p. 265.

[5] Charles M. de La Roncière, *Prix et salaires à Florence au XIVe siècle, 1280–1380* (Rome: École française de Rome, 1982), p. 457. See also Charles M. de La Roncière, "La condition des salaries a XIVe Florence au siècle" in *Tumulto dei Ciompi: un momento di storia fiorentina ed Europea*, edited by Atti del Convegno internazionale (Florence: Leo S. Olschki, 1981), p. 19.

a "sharp rise" and Sergio Tognetti a "forte ascesa" in salaries.[6] Carlo Cipolla, extrapolating from La Roncière's data, argued that the increases in 1349–1350 set the stage for an era of "fat cattle," a golden age for the Florentine laboring classes, from 1350 to 1369.[7] Paolo Malanima extended the conclusions to all of Italy, finding "rapid growth" in salaries throughout the peninsula.[8]

The conclusions are based on consideration of the wages of day laborers, notably from the building sector, taken from account books of large private institutions for which there are available figures.[9] To the extent that there has been scholarly discussion, it has focused on real wages, standards of living, and the "basket of goods" used to determine them.[10]

What is conspicuously absent from the current scholarship is consideration of soldiers' wages. The lacuna reflects the general disinterest in warfare and the anachronistic distinction made by modern scholars between the pacific and military spheres. It is unfortunate because, as we have seen, soldiers constituted a significant part of the workforce in Florence.[11] Our sample size is larger than that for the building industry,

---

[6] Richard A. Goldthwaite, *The Building of Renaissance Florence* (Baltimore, MD: Johns Hopkins University Press, 1980), p. 317; Sergio Tognetti, "Prezzi e salari nella Firenze tardomedievale: un profilo," *Archivio Storico Italiano* 153 (1995), pp. 305, 310.

[7] Carlo M. Cipolla, *The Monetary Policy of Fourteenth Century Florence* (Berkeley, CA: University of California Press, 1982), pp. 48–49, 54; La Roncière, *Prix et salaires*, pp. 494–496.

[8] Paolo Malanima, *L'economia italiana dalla crescita medievale alla crescita contemporanea* (Bologna: Il Mulino, 2012), p. 239.

[9] La Roncière deals with the period from 1280 to 1380. Pinto treated the years 1380–1430. Goldthwaite focused on the fourteenth and fifteenth centuries. Tognetti brought together the work of the other scholars and extended it to 1500. The wage data is taken from account books of the hospitals of Santa Maria Nuova and San Gallo and the monasteries of Santissima Annunziata and Carmine. Pinto has stressed the richness of these sources. Giuliano Pinto, *Toscana medievale: Paesaggi e realtà sociali* (Florence: Le lettere, 1993), p. 114. La Roncière, *Prix et salaires*; Richard A. Goldthwaite, *The Building of Renaissance Florence*; Tognetti, "Prezzi e salari nella Firenze tardomedievale." See also Franco Franceschi, *Oltre il 'Tumulto': I lavatori fiorentini del Arte della lana fra tre e quattrocento* (Florence: Leo S. Olschki, 1993)and Cipolla, *Monetary Policy*; Gene Brucker, *Florentine Politics and Society, 1343–1378* (Princeton, NJ: Princeton University Press, 1962), pp. 9–27. On the economic conditions of workers, see John M. Najemy, *A History of Florence, 1200–1575* (Oxford: Blackwell Press, 2006), pp. 157–160. Tognetti notes "una certa parzialita" for study of the salaries of day laborers in Florence and for the whole preindustrial age. Tognetti, "Prezzi e salari," p. 264.

[10] An assessment of the factors that go into the establishment of real wages and cost of living is in Goldthwaite, *The Building of Renaissance Florence*, pp. 342–350; La Roncière, *Prix et salaires*, pp. 381–396, 423–450; Pinto, *Toscana medievale*, pp. 129–130; and Tognetti, "Prezzi e salari," pp. 298–300.

[11] This is reflected in budgets in which military expenditure is the largest part of state expenditure, even in times of peace. William Caferro, "Continuity, Long-Term Service and Permanent Forces: A Reassessment of the Florentine Army in the Fourteenth

for which there are relatively few surviving figures. La Roncière found salaries for only 130 laborers at the Hospital of Santa Maria Nuova from 1350 to 1380. The oldest Florentine guild register from 1358 lists 434 men.[12] Christopher Dyer noted the "inevitability" of studying building wages for medieval England, but pointed out that the data for many years was "few."[13]

The data for the army does not, however, correspond to current wage models and raises questions about the scholarly consensus.[14] It challenges our understanding of nominal wages and, examined alongside the wages of other public employees, exposes the dangers of extrapolating broad conclusions from a single set of data. Florence maintained various workforces that behaved differently in these dynamic years.

Infantry and Cavalry, 1349–1350

The course of the wages of the Florentine army 1349–1350 may be simply stated. The nominal pay of infantrymen rose from 1349 to 1350, consistent with the general pattern outlined by scholars for day laborers. Cavalry wages, however, remained the same for both years. The rigidity is notable not only for its contrariness to the scholarly status quo, but also for its variance with our basic understanding of mercenaries, who were theoretically the most mobile part of the Florentine workforce and their profession synonymous with greed. As Machiavelli famously stated in *The Prince*, the men lacked "fear of God and fidelity toward men" and had no reason for keeping the field except for their stipend.[15]

In the absence of scholarly studies of the Florentine army, it is necessary first to examine the structure of wages in it. Florentines soldiers were hired on contracts ranging from four to six months in duration. They were paid monthly, the money going directly to the captain (*conestabile*) in charge of the unit, who then distributed it to his men according to a rate set by Florentine officials and stated explicitly in budgets. The point

---

Century," *Journal of Modern History* 80 (2008), pp. 303–322 and *Mercenary Companies and the Decline of Siena* (Baltimore, MD: Johns Hopkins University Press, 1998).

[12] A 1391 register lists 915 *maestri*. Goldthwaite, *The Building of Renaissance Florence*, p. 252. La Roncière, *Prix et salaires*, p. 322. Thorold Rogers called the number of artisans in medieval England "very small." Thorold Rogers, *Six Centuries of Work and Wages*, pp. 179, 180–183.

[13] Christopher Dyer, *Standards of Living in Later Middle Ages: Social Change in England, 1200–1320* (Cambridge: Cambridge University Press, 1989), pp. 220–223.

[14] A preliminary treatment of the data is in William Caferro, "Petrarch's War: Florentine Wages at the Time of the Black Death," *Speculum* 88, no. 1 (January 2013), pp. 144–165. The present chapter extends and revises the prior evidence and conclusions.

[15] Machiavelli, *The Prince*, translated and edited by David Wootton (Indianapolis, IN: Hackett Publishing Co., 1995), p. 43.

needs emphasis against a scholarly tradition that has assumed that the captains alone were responsible for paying their men, according to rates set by themselves. Military captains, in fact, had less discretion in this regard than other Florentine employees such as the podestà, who paid his entourage/family (*comitiva*) as he saw fit, according to rates not fixed by the state and thus unknown.

Table 4.1 lists the nominal wages of Florentine soldiers for the first campaign against the Ubaldini in 1349. Mercenary cavalrymen earned the highest wage, and the German cavalry captain was the highest paid soldier of all. His wage was sixteen times greater than that of a shield bearer, at the bottom end of the pay scale. The next highest salary was that of the Italian mercenary cavalry captain, who earned about half what was earned by his German counterpart. The Italian cavalry captain received 25 percent more if he were a knight, a distinction that did not apply to the German captain, whose wage was the same whether or not he had been knighted. The ordinary German cavalryman came next, followed by crossbow captains from Liguria and Lunigiana, Italian mercenary cavalrymen and crossbow captains from Bibbiena and Modena, who earned

Table 4.1 *Nominal Monthly Wages (in Rank Order, Highest to Lowest) of Florentine Soldiers in 1349*

Job (Unit Size)	Nominal Wage*
German mercenary cavalry captain (13–20 men)	1,920
Italian mercenary cavalry captain (15 men)	1,000–800
German mercenary cavalryman	522
Captain crossbow unit from Liguria/Lunigiana (23–25 men)	448
Italian mercenary cavalryman	400
Crossbowman in units from Liguria/Lunigiana	207
Captain crossbow unit from Bibbiena/Modena (10–26 men)	202
Captain mixed infantry unit (10–23 men)	202–150
Captain shield bearer unit (20–25 men)	200
Captain shield bearer unit (4–12 men)	150
Crossbowman in units from Bibbiena/Modena, mixed units	136
Shield bearer	120
Apprentice (*Ragazzino*) in a shield bearer unit	100

Notes: Communal budgets were kept in money of account, figured at 1 lira = 20 soldi = 240 denari. An exchange existed between the gold and silver currency. In 1349 one florin equaled 64 soldi. This is an average of rates from April to August 1349.

* Wages are in *soldi di piccoli*.

Sources: ASF, Camera del comune, Scrivano di camera uscita 6 fols. 17r–41r; Scrivano di camera uscita 7 fols. 17r–60r; Scrivano di camera uscita 8 fols. 17r–36r.

half as much as their counterparts from Liguria and Lunigiana and only slightly more (15 percent) than shield bearers. The wages of shield bearers were the same whether they served in their own contingents or mixed ones. The lowest pay of all went to apprentices (*ragazzini*), who were in shield bearer units.

That Florence's pay scale favored cavalry over infantry is perhaps predictable in this "age of the horse," as Philippe Contamine has famously called it. Contamine argued that the infantry had lost both "its quantitative and qualitative" importance at this time – an opinion widely accepted.[16] Our data nevertheless show that crossbowmen from Liguria and Lunigiana were well compensated. A captain earned more than an Italian mercenary cavalryman and twice the salary of his non-Ligurian/Lunigiana crossbow counterpart.

The evidence confirms the considerable status and reputation of the men, who, as we saw in Chapter 2, were recruited in a manner similar to that of mercenary cavalrymen. As with cavalrymen, merchant bankers served as intermediaries in their hire, advancing funds to the soldiers in anticipation of their service.[17]

Unlike much studied craft wages, the soldiers' pay rates were fixed. There is no seasonal variation, no difference depending on the length of employment, and thus no need to take an average or "typical" figures.[18] It is thus possible to avoid the methodological challenges faced by scholars of craft wages (Thorold Rogers, Phelps-Brown and Hopkins, Goldthwaite, Tognetti, and La Roncière).[19] The greatest variation in our data is with respect to the pay of captains of mixed units. Their wage depended on whether they were themselves a crossbowman or a shield bearer. The former earned more than the latter. When mixed

---

[16] Philippe Contamine, *War in the Middle Ages*, translated by Michael Jones (Oxford: Oxford University Press, 1984), p. 126.

[17] ASF, balie 6 fols. 40v, 59r.

[18] Goldthwaite discusses the issues involved in taking data for building wages. The entries themselves are not uniform. He notes changes in rates for different seasons and diverse types of labor. Rates were also affected by length of service – small-term or long-term projects. Goldthwaite, *The Building of Renaissance Florence*, pp. 317–320, 435–436. La Roncière discusses similar issues with regard to his data. La Roncière, *Prix et salaires*, pp. 263–268. For a discussion relating to England, see Dyer, *Standard of Living*, pp. 211–233. A general statement on the variable nature of medieval wages is in Steven A. Epstein, "The Theory and Practice of the Just Wage," *Journal of Medieval History* 17 (1991), p. 65.

[19] E. H. Phelps Brown and Sheila V. Hopkins, "Seven Centuries of Building Wages," *Economica* 22 (1955), p. 196. Tognetti provides the minimum and maximum wages and then takes an average. Tognetti, "Prezzi e salari," pp. 302–304. La Roncière notes specific variations such as for a *maestro* named Tommaso, whose salary from March to June 1349 varied from 14 soldi/6 denari a day to 8 soldi (May 9). La Roncière, *Prix et salaires*, p. 274.

units morphed into shield bearer and crossbow units, the captains' pay remained the same. Thus, the now familiar shield bearer captains Santi Chiarucci of Tirlì, who played an important role at the battle of Montegemoli, earned the same wage when he led a unit of twelve shield bearers in June 1349 as he did when he led a mixed unit of fifteen men, including three crossbowmen, in July 1349.[20]

As in present-day corporate America, the pay scale within military contingents was top heavy. The captaincy of a mercenary unit had substantial financial meaning. A German cavalry captain earned three times as much as a member of his band. An Italian cavalry captain earned twice as much as his men, as did a crossbow captain from Liguria and Lunigiana. Crossbow captains from Modena and Bibbiena earned 50 percent more than their men. The captaincy of a shield bearer and mixed unit, on the other hand, offered relatively little advantage. A shield bearer captain received a lira and a half (20 percent) more than a member of bands in units of four to twelve men. But pay shifted higher in larger bands, so a shield bearer captain of a banner unit of twenty to twenty-five men was paid twice that of his men. There were, however, few bands of that size in the army of 1349.

It is unclear whether the ratios were officially set by the city. It is also not clear what precise coins were used to pay the troops, a problem that, as Goldthwaite has pointed out, applies to Florentine wages more generally.[21] For the sake of comparison in this chapter, the salaries in Table 4.1 have been rendered in *soldi di piccioli*, based on money of account (1 lire = 20 soldi = 240 denari), linked to the silver currency, cited in the budgets.[22] Money of account was, however, "ghost money" (as Cipolla called it) and did not correspond to actual physical payments.[23] Florence's monetary system was bimetallic, consisting of gold coins (florins) and silver coins (grossi, quattrini, denari).

---

[20] ASF, Camera del comune, Scrivano di camera uscita 6 fol. 29v.

[21] Richard A. Goldthwaite, *The Economy of Renaissance Florence* (Baltimore, MD: Johns Hopkins University Press, 2009), p. 611.

[22] On the Florentine monetary system and monies of account, see Raymond de Roover, *The Rise and Decline of the Medici Bank, 1397–1494* (Cambridge, MA: Harvard University Press, 1963), pp. 31–34; Anthony Molho, *Florentine Public Finances* (Cambridge, MA: Harvard University Press, 1971), p. xiv; Goldthwaite, *The Building of Renaissance Florence*, pp. 301–317, and *The Economy of Renaissance Florence*, pp. 609–614; Richard Goldthwaite and Giulio Mandich, *Studi sulla moneta fiorentina (secoli XIII–XVI)* (Florence: Leo S. Olschki, 1994). For wage studies that use silver, see William Beveridge, "Wages in the Winchester Manors," *Economic History Review* 7 (1936), pp. 22–43; Wilhelm Abel, *Agrarian Fluctuations in Europe from the Thirteenth to the Twentieth Century*, translated by Olive Ordish (New York, NY: Columbia University Press, 1966). I follow here Goldthwaite, who advocated using lire/soldi. Goldthwaite, *The Economy of Renaissance Florence*, pp. xvi–xvii.

[23] Cipolla, *Monetary Policy*, pp. 20–29.

The soldiers, like other employees, were paid in both currencies, as we shall discuss in more detail in Chapter 5. The choice of currency had economic and social implications. The gold florin – stable in value and widely accepted throughout Italy and Europe – was the more desirable coin. It escaped the debasement suffered by lesser silver coins used in the marketplace.

Table 4.2 lists soldiers' wages in 1350 during the second phase of Petrarch's war. The effect of the Black Death is apparent (Figure 4.1). The pay of all infantrymen increased. The wages of shield bearer captains of banner units rose a full 170 percent from 1349, while those of their men 42 percent. The nominal wage of a crossbow captain and his men in banner units from Bibbiena and Modena increased 39 percent and 30 percent, respectively. Crossbowmen from Liguria and Lunigiana saw more modest gains of 14 percent for captains and 24 percent for their men. The increases vaulted infantrymen into the upper ranks of the military pay scale (Table 4.2). It was a particularly good time to be a foot soldier!

Changes in unit size also affected pay increases of captains. The broader scope of the second campaign required Florence to hire larger bands. The wages of crossbow captains from Moderna and Bibbiena rose by 14 percent in bands that consisted of ten to eighteen men, while the salaries of the rank-and-file crossbowmen increased by 30 percent. Shield bearer units that grew from four to twelve men (common in 1349) to twenty to twenty-five men in 1350 saw gains for captains of 227 percent. The relatively smaller percentage increase in the wages of crossbowmen from Lunigiana and Liguria may be the result of the stability of the size of their units, which remained at between twenty-three and twenty-five men in both campaigns.

What is in any case clear is that during the immediate aftermath of the plague, the nominal wages of infantrymen rose across the board. The wages of apprentices in shield bearer bands increased by 70 percent, reaching the same level as shield bearers themselves and surpassing that of the captains of small shield bearer units. Florence employed a broader range of crossbowmen during the second campaign, including units now from the town of Casteldurante and bowmen of the *balestrieri della ghiera* from the city and contado. The pay of the banner units of crossbowmen from Casteldurante was the same as for those from Lunigiana and Liguria. The native bowmen of the *ghiera* earned slightly less, but still more than their counterparts from Bibbiena and Modena (Table 4.2). They were made up of thirty units, ranging in size from three to ten men. Apprentices now appear in these and other crossbow units.

Table 4.2 *Rank Order and Comparison of Monthly Wages of Florentine Soldiers, 1349–1350*

Job (Unit Size in 1350)	Wage 1349*	Wage 1350*	Increase since 1349 (%)
German mercenary cavalry captain (20–25 men)	1,920	1,920	0
Italian mercenary cavalry captain (20 men)	1,000–800	1,000–800	0
German mercenary cavalryman	522	522	0
Captain crossbow unit from Liguria, Lunigiana, Casteldurante (23–25 men)	448	512	14
Italian mercenary cavalryman	400	400	0
** **Captain shield bearer unit (20–31 men)**	**200**	**340**	**170**
** **Captain crossbow, Bibbiena/ Modena (20–25 men)**	**202**	**280**	**39**
Captain crossbow, Bibbiena/Modena (10–18 men)	202	230	14
Crossbowman in units from Liguria, Lunigiana	207	256	24
Captain mixed infantry unit (8–25 men)	150–202	170–230	13/14
Crossbowman of the *ghiera* (3–10 men)	—	192	—
Crossbowman in units from Bibbiena, Modena	138	180	30
Captain shield bearer unit (4–12 men)	150	170	13
** **Shield bearer (20–31 men)**	**120**	**170**	**42**
Shield bearer (4–12 men)	120	140	13
Apprentice in shield bearer unit	100	170	70

Notes: Rank order change in bold.
1 florin = 64 soldi
* Wages are in *soldi di piccoli*.
** Increased unit size from 1349.
Sources: ASF, Camera del comune, Scrivano di camera uscita 6 fols. 17r–41r; Scrivano di camera uscita 7 fols. 17r–60r; Scrivano di camera uscita 8 fols. 17r–36r; Camera del comune, Scrivano di camera uscita 9 fols. 17r–45r; Scrivano di camera uscita 10 fols. 17r–59r.

The change in rates altered the structure of infantry wages. By 1350, the difference between the wage of a shield bearer captain and his men in a banner unit resembled that of a captain and his men in Italian cavalry units. In both instances the captain earned exactly twice the salary of his men. Conversely, the gap in pay between a captain and his men in crossbow units from Bibbiena/Modena narrowed. The pay structure of units from Liguria and Lunigiana stayed the same, as did the size of their units.

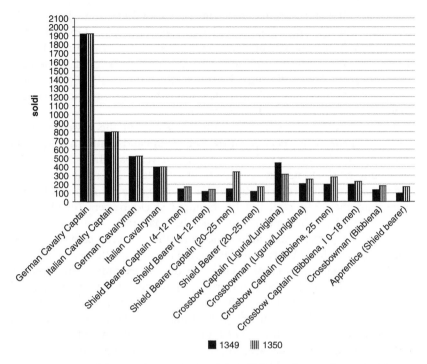

Figure 4.1 Nominal monthly wages of Florentine soldiers, 1349–1350

The most striking pattern from our data, however, is with regard to the cavalry. The nominal wages of these soldiers did not change from 1349 to 1350 (Table 4.2/Figure 4.1). They stayed the same.

This is true despite the fact that, as with shield bearers, the size of units grew larger in the second campaign. German cavalry bands increased from between thirteen and twenty men in 1349 to full banners units of twenty to twenty-five men in 1350. Italian mercenary units, which consisted of fifteen men in 1349, grew to twenty men in 1350. Changes in the size of units did not affect cavalry wages.

The trend is unexpected and difficult to explain. All studies of Florence argue for substantial increases in nominal wages for workers immediately after the plague. La Roncière called the evidence "incontestable" and cited rises of 160 percent in the nominal wages of masons and 354 percent for unskilled laborers in the three years after the plague at Santa Maria Nuova and increases of 200 percent and higher for gardeners from 1350 to 1356.[24] Tognetti argued that the wages of Florentine laborers in general were 2.3 times higher in 1350 than in 1348.[25] Goldthwaite's precise yearly figures for construction workers show raises for 1349 and 1350 in nominal wages of masons and unskilled workers of 25 percent (13.4 soldi to 16.8 soldi) and 19 percent (8.4 soldi to 10 soldi), respectively. The patterns resemble in basic outline those of Florentine infantrymen (Figure 4.2),[26] but not cavalrymen.

The contrasting patterns are readily apparent in the cavalry/infantry bands of Gianello Baldocci of Castro Focognano and Canto di Borgo San Sepolcro hired by the city in 1350. Cavalrymen were paid the same rate as in 1349, but the shield bearers received the 1350 rate.[27] The same was true of the captain of war Cecco di Ranieri Farnese's band. His fifty cavalrymen were paid the 1349 rate, but his hundred shield bearers (divided into banners of twenty-five men) were paid the 1350 rate. The *balia* records reinforce the portrait and show that while the city progressively offered higher rates to shield bearers, it always paid cavalrymen the same wage.[28]

The discrepancy is still more curious when we examine contemporary legislation. Unlike elsewhere in Europe, Florence did not enact a general law seeking to control wages in the aftermath of the plague.[29] There is no Florentine equivalent of the English Statute of Laborers or the French *Grande Ordonnance*. In July 1349 Florentine officials passed a law explicitly allowing wage increases for infantrymen, citing "*inopiam personarum*" (lack of men). The law, which explicitly mentions the Ubaldini war, does not include cavalrymen.[30]

Florentine budgets, however, show that officials had already begun de facto increasing infantry wages in June 1349. They offered a special *accrescimento* (increase) to soldiers in apparent response to the rapidly changing market conditions.[31] On 27 June 1349 the crossbow captain Alpinuccio da Bibbiena received an *accrescimento* of 1 lira for himself and each of the infantrymen in his band of twelve men.[32] The shield bearer captain Tone

---

[24] La Roncière, *Prix et salaries*, pp. 275, 348, 457. The wages of gardeners, "journaliers agricoles," went up 237 percent. La Roncière, *Prix et salaries*, pp. 343–357.

[25] Tognetti, "Prezzi e salari," pp. 301–305.

[26] Goldthwaite, *The Building of Renaissance Florence*, pp. 436–437.

[27] ASF, balie 6 fol. 62r.   [28] ASF, balie 6 fols. 52v–55r; 119r.

[29] Samuel K. Cohn, "After the Black Death: Labour Legislation and Attitudes towards Labour in Late-Medieval Western Europe," *Economic History Review* 60 no. 3 (2007), pp. 457–485.

[30] ASF, Provvisioni, registri 36 fol. 47r; balie 6 fol. 38v; A. B. Falsini, "'Firenze dopo il 1348: Le consequenza della peste nera," *Archivio storico italiano* 129 (1971), pp. 439–440; Cohn, "After the Black Death," pp. 457–485.

[31] ASF, Camera del comune, Scrivano di uscita 6 fols. 23r, 30v, 33r–v, 37r; Scrivano di uscita 7 fols. 17r–17v, 19r, 26r, 28v.

[32] ASF, Camera del comune, Scrivano di uscita 6 fol. 37r.

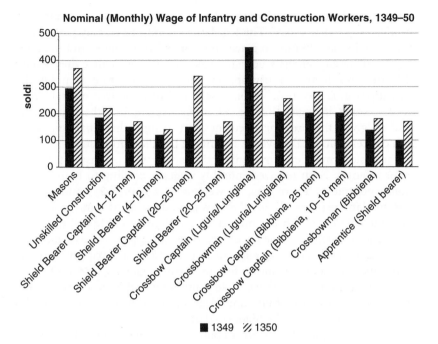

Nominal (Monthly) Wage of Infantry and Construction Workers, 1349–50

■ 1349 ⫽ 1350

Figure 4.2 Nominal monthly wages of infantry and construction workers, 1349–1350
Note: Daily wages of construction workers have been converted to monthly wages, based on twenty-two days of labor according to tradition.

Lemmi likewise received an additional lira for himself and his men.[33] The city did this despite the fact that the soldiers were bound by four- to six-month contracts. The *balia* that managed the war in 1350 stated explicitly the rationale: "for smaller pay we do not believe that we can have men."[34]

But city officials took no action to increase cavalry wages, nor do they appear to have imposed restrictions on their wages. The sources are silent on the issue.

Plague, War, and Market Forces

The preferential treatment afforded the infantry is unusual. Samuel Cohn in a recent study argued that Florence treated its rural workforce harshly

---

[33] ASF, Camera del comune, Scrivano di uscita 7 fol. 17v.   [34] ASF, balie 6 fol. 38v.

in the immediate aftermath of the plague, seeking in that sector alone to prohibit wage increases.[35] The legislation of July 1349 may perhaps be interpreted as an attempt to place limits on infantry wages. But the rates suggested by city officials actually exceeded the level that they would ultimately reach and clearly appear aimed at attracting men (as the legislations in fact states).[36] Conversely, it is possible that officials froze cavalry wages in legislation as yet undiscovered, but the prospect is unlikely given the pressing need for men to fight the Ubaldini, along with concerns about the overall security of the Florentine state.[37]

The basic terms of employment for the cavalry were ostensibly the same as for infantry. Both received monthly wages according to four- to six-month contracts. There was, as we saw in Chapter 2, continuity of personnel in the ranks of both. There was no shortage of wars throughout the peninsula for which the mercenary cavalrymen could sell their services, and the plague, as we have seen, does not appear to have inhibited their movement. The ongoing conflict between the papacy and the Romagna offered opportunities for employment close by. Bruno Dini in his study of the Florentine wool cloth industry at this time stressed the connection between mobility and wage rates, with those workers who moved about garnering the highest salaries.[38]

How do we explain the divergent patterns? We may begin with classical economic notions of supply and demand and hypothesize that the differences between cavalry and infantry wages reflect differences in the sizes of the respective labor forces. Was there a shortage of infantrymen and a glut of cavalrymen in the immediate aftermath of the plague?

The prospect is prima facie plausible. Despite the lack of precise figures for the size of the Florentine army, we have seen that the city recruited for the Ubaldini campaign more infantrymen than cavalrymen. Florence also drew its cavalry from a wider pool, from elsewhere in Italy and also from beyond the Alps. Medieval cavalrymen were by standard definition aristocrats and landholders, the class that suffered most from the demographic contraction attendant the plague. The contagion lowered the value of land, decreased rents, and increased the price of labor. The stability of cavalry wages may perhaps be read as evidence that in the face of economic challenge, landholders sold their labor as soldiers to

[35] Cohn, "After the Black Death," pp. 457–485.

[36] ASF, Provvisioni, registri 36 fols. 132r–v.

[37] ASF, Provvisioni, registri 36 fol. 47r; Falsini, "'Firenze dopo il 1348: Le consequenza della peste nera," pp. 439–440; Cohn, "After the Black Death," pp. 457–485.

[38] Bruno Dini, "I lavoratori dell'Arte della Lana a Firenze nel XIV e XV secolo" in *Artigiani e salariati. Il mondo del lavoro nell'Italia dei secoli XII–XV, Pistoia, 9–13 ottobre 1981* (Bologna: Centro Italiano di Studi di Storia e d'Art, 1984), p. 49.

make up their losses, thus increasing the number of available cavalrymen seeking employment in communal armies. Infantrymen, on the other hand, were recruited locally, from the much-depleted Florentine state, and from nearby regions. The pool was smaller, which allowed the infantry to demand higher wages – so high, in fact, that service as a shield bearer may be said to have become a good way to make a living in difficult times. The presence of apprentices in shield bearer contingents but not in cavalry units may perhaps be read as evidence that the shortage of men for the former was greater than the latter.

The thesis has a neat cause-and-effect appeal. Both cavalry and infantry were drawn to war: in the first case to preserve profits otherwise lost, in the second to gain profits previously unavailable. Extended further, the interpretation connects the cycle of plague to the increased incidence of warfare that historians have long observed for the second half of the fourteenth century. Men willing and eager to earn profits gave impetus to war. The thesis minimizes the role of political and diplomatic factors, but it has obvious appeal.

Cause and effect notwithstanding, the interpretation is difficult to prove based on the available evidence. Although mercenaries did not represent the "dregs of society," as scholars once claimed, and many of the Germans and Italian cavalry captains were indeed from the aristocracy, it remains unknown what the social backgrounds of most of the men were, especially those below the rank of captain. In addition, the Florentine documents indicate that rather than a glut of cavalrymen there was a decided lack of them. In the debates of the Florentine executive councils just prior to the war in 1349, Donato Velluti complained specifically about a lack of cavalrymen and suggested that the city seek them from the papal legate Astorgio Duraforte.[39] At the beginning of the second campaign, Velluti himself went on embassy to Bologna to ask for troops, a request that was denied. Meanwhile, extant Florentine diplomatic dispatches show that throughout the war, the city actively sought to recruit cavalrymen from allies.[40] City officials wrote to the Malatesta rulers of Rimini in October 1349 for men, but they refused, citing their own lack of troops. In May 1350, Florence refused Duraforte's request for cavalrymen on the same grounds, claiming that it needed men for its own armies.[41] There may well have been other diplomatic and political motives at play, but the most reasonable

---

[39] ASF, CP 1 fol. 2r.   [40] ASF, Signori Missive Cancelleria 10 #143.
[41] Demetrio Marzi, *La cancelleria della repubblica fiorentina* (Rocca S. Casciano: Capelli, 1910), pp. 656–657.

conclusion is that the market for cavalrymen was, as with soldiers more generally, tight.

Contextualizing Soldiers' Wages

The same budgets that contain the wages of soldiers also contain the salaries of a range of communal stipendiaries that provide important perspective on the issue. They allow us to contextualize soldiers' wages in terms of other public employees.[42] The employees were all paid by the *camera del comune*, which, as we have seen, was the main financial organ of the city. It was established in 1289 just after the institution of the office of the priors. Along with paying city workers, it handled expenses including rent for houses and *botteghe* (shops) used by the commune; ink and wax needed to write and seal public documents; the *pasto* (food) for the communal lion, the symbol of the city; and the costs of public festivals. The *camera* was headed by four chamberlains (*camarlinghi*), who were in charge of communal monies, each possessing a key to the strong box (*cassa*) that held the cash.[43]

The Florentine public workforce has not been the subject of comprehensive study. City statutes relating to public employees survive for 1322, 1325, and 1355, but not for the years under consideration here.[44] The overall number of workers employed by the state in 1349/1350 is not known. The budgets do not contain the salaries of the priors and the twelve *buonomini* who ran the city. However, they do include many judges and notaries, confirming Luigi Chiappelli's opinion that such men constituted their own "corpo d'arte" and a disproportionately large part of

---

[42] For the various offices of the Florentine state, see G. Guidi, *Il governo della città-repubblica di Firenze del primo quattrocento*, 3 vols. (Florence: Leo S. Olschki, 1981); Gene Brucker, "Bureaucracy and Social Welfare in the Renaissance: A Florentine Case Study," *Journal of Modern History* 55 (1983), pp. 1–21; Timothy McGee, "Dinner Music for the Florentine Signoria, 1350–1450," *Speculum* 74 (1999), pp. 95–114 and *The Ceremonial Musicians of Late Medieval Florence* (Bloomington, IN: Indiana University Press, 2009).

[43] For the workings of the Florentine *camera del comune*, Robert Davidsohn, *Storia di Firenze: I primordi della civiltà fiorentina. Impulsi interni, influssi esterni e cultura politica*, vol. 4 (Florence: Sansoni, 1977), 147–148, 160–163; 200–204. Gherardi examines the structure of the office in 1303. Alessandro Gherardi, "L'antica camera del comune di Firenze e un quaderno d'uscita de' suoi camarlinghi dell'anno 1303," *Archivio storico italiano* 26 (1885), pp. 313–361; Guidi, *Il governo della città-repubblica di Firenze del primo Quattrocento*, vol. 2, pp. 275–279; Brucker, "Bureaucracy and Social Welfare in the Renaissance"; Timothy McGee, "Dinner Music," pp. 95–114 and *The Ceremonial Musicians of Late Medieval Florence*.

[44] See *Statuti della Repubblica fiorentina, Statuto del Capitano del Popolo: 1322–25*, edited by Giuliano Pinto, Francesco Salvestrini and Andrea Zorzi (Florence: Leo S. Olschki, 1999) and *Statuti e legislazione a Firenze dal 1355 al 1415, Lo Statuto cittadino del 1409*, edited by Lorenzo Tanzini (Florence: Leo S Olschki, 2004).

the Florentine workforce.[45] Gene Brucker called the notaries "a veritable city hall clique" within the Florentine bureaucracy. Giovanni Boccaccio made fun of Florence's bloated juridical sector in the *Decameron* (day 8, story 5), chiding Florentine judges ("rettori marchigiani" as he called them) as "uomini di povero cuore e di vita strema e tanto miseria," who brought with them their many associates who seemed like they came "straight off the farm" rather than from schools of law.[46]

The budgets also list numerous chamberlains, who headed civic offices. They contain the salaries of castellans, who manned forts throughout the Florentine state; of accountants, ambassadors, policemen, communal musicians, town criers and members of the "famiglia," the "petty officials" as Brucker called them, who performed the basic services of the Signoria, including "acting as ushers for guests and servants to the priors."[47] Florence had two police forces (*berrovieri*): one consisting of a hundred men, who protected the palace of the priors (now the Palazzo Vecchio), and another consisting of eighty men, who protected the palace of the podestà (now the Bargello).

Table 4.3 lists the nominal monthly wages of Florentine employees that appear on budgets. The table represents forty-four public jobs and approximately 450 people. The salaries have been converted to monthly wages and money of account (soldi) to facilitate comparison.

What is immediately clear is that Florence maintained diverse schedules of pay with its employees. Some workers received daily wages, others were paid by the month, semester (six months), and year. Daily labor, the focus of current wage studies, represented just *one* type of employment. The most common arrangement for Florentine state workers was monthly pay. The meaning of this in terms of actual disbursement of wages is unclear. Florentine budgets were compiled bimonthly and show that employees, no matter what the schedule, received regular sums within that time span. The key point, however, is that Florence conceptualized jobs in diverse ways. Florentine soldiers, on four- to six-month contracts, most nearly resemble foreign judges – the podestà, executor of justice, and judge of appeals, who were hired by semester (six months).

---

[45] Chiappelli saw the judges as forming their own "corpo d'arte." Luigi Chiappelli, "L'amministrazione della giustizia in Firenze durante gli ultimi secoli del medioevo e il periodo del Risorgimento, secondo le testimonianze degli antichi scrittori," *Archivio storico italiano* 15 (1885), pp. 42–43; Brucker described the notaries "a veritable city hall clique" within the Florentine bureaucracy.

[46] Brucker, *Florentine Politics and Society*, p. 60.

[47] On the *famiglia*, see Brucker "Bureaucracy and Social Welfare in the Renaissance," p. 4, and Guidi, *Il governo della città-repubblica di Firenze del primo Quattrocento*, vol. 2, pp. 38–39.

Table 4.3 *Monthly Salaries (in Rank Order, Highest to Lowest) of Florentine Stipendiaries, 1349–1350*

Job (Terms of Service)	Wage* 1349	Wage* 1350
Podestà (semester)	26,666.7	26,666.7
Executor of the Ordinances of Justice (semester)	6,666.7	6,666.7
Judge of appeals (semester)	1,833.2	1,833.2
Ambassadors (day)	1,760–880	1,760–880
Compagno of executor of justice (semester)	1,333	1,333
Troop inspectors (day)	1,320–880	1,320–880
Chancellor of commune (year)	533.33	533.33
Castellans (month)	440	440
Notary of *Riformagione* (year)	416.6	416.6
Captain of *Berrovieri* of palace of priors (month)	400	400
Notary for expenditure of *camera* (month)	400	400
Notary of priors (semester)	400	400
Accountant/*anoveratore* of *camera* (month)	384	384
Superintendants of *Stinche* prison (semester)	333.3	333.3
Notary/*scrittore* of condotta (month)	300	300
Gonfalonieri del popolo (month)	280	280
Notary/*aiutatore* of chancellor (year)	266.62	266.62
Accountant of the *camera* (month)	200	200
Public doctor, to medicate poor (month)	200	200
Notary for income of the *camera* (month)	200	200
Notary of condotta (month)	200	200
Notary of judges/*savi* (month)	200	200
Spy (month)	200	200
Sindaco (month)	—	200
Cleric/chamberlains of *camera* (semester)	166.7	166.7
Notary of condotta (month)	160	160
Famigliare of notary of *Riformagione* (year)	166.7	166.7
Berrovieri of Palace of Priors (month)	**150**	**170**
Lay chamberlains of *camera* (month)	160	160
Town criers (*banditori/approvatori*) (month)	122	122
Chamberlains of condotta (month)	120	120
Notary of supervisors of prison (month)	120	120
Messi of the condotta (month)	90	90
Berrovieri of palace of podestà (month)	90	90
Musicians (month)	**80**	**100**
Custodians/guards of the *camera* (month)	80	80
Bell ringers, palace of podestà (month)	80	80
Bell ringers, palace of priors (month)	80	80
Cook (month)	80	80
Servants (*donzelli, servitori*) of the priors (month)	80	80
Massai of the *camera* (month)	80	80

Table 4.3 (*cont.*)

Job (Terms of Service)	Wage 1349	Wage 1350
Judges e *Savi* of the *camera* (month)	60	60
Notaries of *massai* (month)	60	60
Pages of the cook (month)	60	60

Notes: Daily wages are converted to monthly wages using 22 days, according to tradition.
1 florin = 64 soldi (average)
* Wages are in *soldi di piccioli*. Wages that change are in bold.

The data raise basic questions about the overall structure of communal wages that will be dealt with more fully in the next chapter. The salaries of "foreign" judges soar above those of other government officials.[48] The podestà, an executive entrusted with keeping peace inside the city, was by far the highest paid civic employee.[49] His wage reflects his large entourage or family (*comitiva*) of notaries and judges, whose salaries were paid directly from his stipend. The size of the podestà's entourage for 1349–1350 is not stated. But Guidubaldo Guidi lists the entourage in 1344 as consisting of fifty-eight men: eleven judges, thirty-two notaries, three knights/*compagni*, twelve *donzelli* (servants).[50] The executor of the ordinances of justice (*esecutore dei ordini di giustizia*) was the next highest paid official. The post involved applying antimagnate legislation that protected the *popolo* from the *grandi* and visiting the communal prison once a month. Like the podestà, the executor had a family that was paid from his stipend. The budgets show that this included ten men (judges and notaries) in 1349–1350.[51] The foreign judges, as Boccaccio notes, were, like Italian mercenary cavalrymen in Florentine service, from other

[48] Giovanni Villani highlights the importance of the "foreign" judges (podestà, executor of justice, the judge of appeals) in his famous description of Florence in 1338, who had the power to "punire reale e personale." Giovanni Villani, *Nuova Cronica*, vol. 3, pp. 194–197. See also Chiappelli, "L'amministrazione della giustizia," p. 42; Davidsohn, *Storia di Firenze*, pp. 163–166; Guidi, *Il governo della città-repubblica di Firenze del primo Quattrocento*, vol. 2, pp. 157–158; and Christiane Klapisch-Zuber, *Ritorno alla politica: I magnati fiorentini, 1340–1440* (Rome: Viella, 2009), pp. 109–114.

[49] Daniel Waley, The Italian City Republics, 3rd edn. (London: Longman, 1988), pp. 42–43. On the rules relating to the Florentine podestà, see *Statuti della repubblica fiorentina*, vol. 2, pp. 5–18.

[50] Guidi, *Il governo della città-repubblica di Firenze del primo Quattrocento*, vol. 2, p. 171.

[51] The post of executor of justice (*esecutore dei ordini di giustizia*) was instituted in 1307. The office arose from the ordinances of justice. Guidi, *Il governo della città-repubblica di Firenze del primo Quattrocento*, vol. 2, pp. 183–186.

parts of Italy. The podestà in 1350 was Messer Bonifazio di Messer Cionello from Modena, the executor of justice, Guiglelmo de Piedizochi was from Brescia and the judge of appeals, Nicholaio di Matteo, was from Urbino. Much of Florence's public workforce consisted of non-Florentines.

At the other end of the scale were the wages of the chamberlains in charge of the important communal offices. The chamberlains of the *camera del comune* itself were paid less than the notaries who worked for them. The chamberlains of the *condotta,* which hired troops, earned less than the lowest-paid soldier in the Florentine army. The judges (*savi*) who consulted directly with the priors on important matters were at the very bottom of the hierarchy, their nominal wage less than that of the communal cook, who prepared food for the executives of the Signoria. Meanwhile, the notary who recorded the expenditure of the camera earned twice the salary of the notary who recorded communal income – though they seemingly performed the same service. The wage of the notary for expenditure was the same salary as the public doctor, Niccolò "delle ossa" ("of the bones"), who was employed by the city to "medicate the indigent."[52]

Soldiers' wages compare favorably with those of other state workers, confirming the high cost of war. The salary of a German cavalry captain, the highest paid of the soldiers, resembles that of the judge of appeals (*giudice della ragone e appellagione*), the third highest paid communal official, who, like the other judges, came from outside of the Florentine state and whose stipend paid also his *comitiva.*[53] The wage of an ordinary German cavalryman was about the same as the Florentine chancellor, a prestigious position that involved handling the official correspondence of the commune and would be occupied by famous humanists who helped define Florence as a Renaissance city. Meanwhile, infantry wages compare favorably to those of other Florentine employees. By 1350 an ordinary shield bearer received higher pay than a town crier or a bell ringer at the palace of the priors and at the palace of the podestà. The captain of a shield bearer unit earned higher wages than accountants, spies, and the public doctor in government service. War appears, in short, to have been a good job choice when set against other public wages.

---

[52] According to Katharine Park, Niccolò was preceded in this job by his father Jacopo "delle Ossa," whose employment goes back to 1336. Katharine Park, *Doctors and Medicine in Early Renaissance Florence* (Princeton, NJ: Princeton University Press, 1985), pp. 91–92.

[53] The job of *guidice della appellagione* first appears in Florentine records in 1285. His family usually consisted of three or four lawyers, six policemen, and two *nunzi*. Guidi, *Il governo della città-repubblica di Firenze del primo Quattrocento,* vol. 2, pp. 187–188; Davidsohn, *Storia di Firenze,* pp. 163–166.

For the purposes of the discussion here, however, the most salient fact is that the nominal wages of the majority of Florentine stipendiaries remained the same from 1349 to 1350. There is no steadfast march upward of money wages, no "spectaculaire montée salariale" or "forte ascesa" as predicted by current studies. Instead we find widespread stickiness, a phenomenon in fact noted by Adam Smith and John Maynard Keynes about wages in general and studied most rigorously for the long-term in the Middle Ages by John Munro and Steven Epstein.[54] Keynes cited such patterns as evidence against the tendency of classical economic theorists to minimize anomaly.[55] Paul Krugman, as noted in the quotation at the start of the chapter, called stickiness "a glaringly obvious feature of the real world."[56]

Our evidence involves two years, but it is no less striking. Nominal rates stagnate precisely when scholars speak of the "fullest effect" of plague.[57] These were years, according to La Roncière, of "fort dynamisme" of Florentine wages and when, as Goldthwaite argues, the effects of "the demand/supply mechanism" were sharpest and demand for labor was "intense."[58]

The lack of movement of rates applies to all schedules of pay: daily, monthly, semester, and yearly wages. It applies to those workers – accountants, notaries, and doctors – whose labor was governed by guilds, as well as those workers – spies, cooks, and town criers – whose labor was not governed by guilds. It applies to "foreign" judges, who came from

---

[54] Adam Smith, *An Inquiry into the Nature and Causes of the Wealth of Nation*, edited by Edwin Cannan (New York, NY: Modern Library, 1937), pp. 74–75; John Munro, "Wage-Stickiness, Monetary Changes and Real Incomes in Late-Medieval England and the Low Countries, 1300–1450: Did Money Really Matter?" *Research in Economic History*, edited by Alexander J. Field, Gregory Clark, and William A. Sundstrom, vol. 21 (Amsterdam: JAI, 2003), pp. 185–297. See John Munro, "Urban Wage Structures in Late-Medieval England and the Low Countries: Work Time and Seasonal Wages" in *Labour and Leisure in Historical Perspective, Thirteenth to Twentieth Centuries*, edited by Ian Blanchard (Stuttgart: F. Steiner, 1994), pp. 65–78, and Steven A. Epstein, "The Theory and Practice of the Just Wage," *Journal of Medieval History* 17 (1991), p. 65 and *Wage Labor and Guilds in Medieval Europe* (Chapel Hill, NC: University of North Carolina Press, 1991), p. 65, who said wages tend to be stable over time.

[55] John Maynard Keynes, *The General Theory of Employment, Interest and Money* (New York: Harcourt Brace, 1936), pp. 257–260. Keynes' statements have elicited considerable debate among economists. See Robert M. Solow, "Another Possible Source of Wage Stickiness," *Journal of Macroeconomics* 1 no. 1 (1979), pp. 79–82 and Robert J. Gordon, "A Century of Evidence on Wage and Price Stickiness in the United States, the United Kingdom, and Japan" in *Macroeconomics, Prices, and Quantities*, edited by James Tobin (Washington, DC: Brookings, 1983), pp. 85–133.

[56] Paul Krugman, "Sticky Wages and the Macro Story," *New York Times* (July 22, 2012).

[57] Thorold Rogers, like Florentine scholars, asserts that rates doubled. Thorold Rogers, *Six Centuries of Work and Wages*, vol. 1, p. 265.

[58] La Roncière, "La condition," pp. 21–24; Goldthwaite, *The Building of Renaissance Florence*, pp. 335–338, 342–343.

outside of Florence, and to castellans, who, like soldiers, actively protected the Florentine state. There is no evidence that day labor was more volatile than monthly labor. The daily wages of ambassadors and troops inspectors remain the same.

Taken together with cavalry wages, the data makes clear that a significant portion of Florence's public labor force does not correspond to current models. It renders problematic any simple macroeconomic interpretation of the movement of Florentine wages in the immediate aftermath of the Black Death and highlights the dangers of extrapolating from a single set of data. Florence had numerous wage patterns, and there was an array of factors at play that need to be carefully assayed and analyzed by scholars. To paraphrase the economist Robert Solow's observation for contemporary labor, the medieval Florentine workforce represents an inscrutable "puzzle" to those who try to study it.[59] Medievalists do well to follow the lead of modern labor economists in treating labor forces as representing diverse markets, even for workers of similar skills.[60]

Table 4.3 shows that there were only two jobs that, like infantrymen, saw rises in nominal wage rates from 1349 to 1350. They were musicians, who played at communal ceremonies, and *berrovieri* or policemen, who guarded the palace of the priors (Palazzo Vecchio). The increases in rates are explicitly mentioned in communal legislation. Florence passed a law raising policemen salaries in July 1349 and a law raising musicians' pay in February 1350.[61]

What common forces were operating? Is it fair to group the two sets of workers together along with the infantrymen and craftsmen? The correspondences are not readily apparent. Musicians are treated by scholars as "skilled" labor. Timothy McGee described them as "well educated" and "of considerable talent" and placed them beside town criers, who sounded a silver trumpet when making public announcements.[62] The legislation that raised musician's salaries in

---

[59] Robert M. Solow, "Insiders and Outsiders in Wage Determination," *The Scandinavian Journal of Economics* 87, no. 2, Proceedings of a Conference on Trade Unions, Wage Formation and Macroeconomic Stability (June 1985), p. 411.

[60] George J. Borjas, *Labor Economics* (New York, NY: Irwin/McGraw Hill, 2008), pp. 166, 473–478.

[61] On 31 July 1349, city officials raised the wages of policemen by 1 lira a month. ASF, Provvisioni, registri 36 fol. 145v. In February 1350, the city raised the pay of musicians by 1 lire a month. ASF, Provvisioni, registri 37 fols. 95r–97r. The increase for musicians was likely in response to their petition in February 1350, complaining that they could not afford to live on their salary. ASF, Provvisioni, registri 37 fol. 94r; Falsini, "'Firenze dopo il 1348," p. 471.

[62] McGee called the two "respectable" jobs. McGee, *The Ceremonial Musicians of Late Medieval Florence*, pp. 44–45, 53–55. On town criers, see Stephen Milner, "Fanno

1350 specifically mentions their skill. It states the intention to increase the wages of the men to improve the overall quality of the troupe by "attracting skilled" *tubatores* (*tubadores*), who played large trumpets that were vital to civic events.[63] The men were specifically intended to replace unskilled tambourine players who had, by necessity, been hired right after the plague to fill out the workforce.[64] *Berrovieri*, on the other hand, were a species of soldier, whose "skills" were seemingly quite different from those of *tubatores*. The job involved protecting the palace of the priors, locking the city gates at night, and guarding the doors of the meeting rooms of the Signoria.[65] The extant statute of the podestà in 1325 describes the men as armed with knives and weapons.[66] The movement of *berrovieri* wages resembles that of shield bearers in the Florentine army. Both increase from 120 soldi in 1349 to 170 soldi a month by 1350. And like the shield bearers, the *berrovieri* were paid by the office of the condotta, responsible for soldier's pay.

Generalizations are difficult to make. Although the wages of the *berrovieri* of the palace of the priors increased from 1349 to 1350, the wages of the *berrovieri* who guarded the palace of the podestà remained the same. Florence therefore had two urban police forces whose salaries behaved differently. And while the wages of musicians increased, those of town criers, grouped together by McGee, remained the same. The criteria for comparison are clearly problematic. The statute of 1325 required (not surprisingly) the town criers to be able to read and write to perform their jobs.[67] Robert Davidsohn singled out town criers, bell ringers and *messi*, as men who "knew how to make rhymes"[68] When Florence increased the pay of musicians, it sought also to increase their overall number in 1350. But when city enacted legislation raising the pay of *berrovieri*, it reduced the number of men from 100 to 90 men.[69]

---

bandire: Town criers and the Information Economy of Renaissance Florence." *I Tatti Studies in The Italian Renaissance* 16 (2013), pp. 107–151.

[63] The legislation cites the need to replenish the number of "tubatores," who "sciant sonare tubis longis," whose numbers had declined to just three men. ASF, Provvisioni, registri 37 fols. 95r–97r.

[64] The statute of 1325 refers to the civic musicians collectively as "tubatores." The troupe consisted of six men then. *Statuti della Repubblica fiorentina*, edited by Giuliano Pinto, Francesco Salvestrini, and Andrea Zorzi, vol. 2, p. 46.

[65] Brucker, "Bureaucracy and Social Welfare," p. 4. See Guidi, *Il governo della città-repubblica di Firenze del primo Quattrocento*, vol. 2, p. 36 and *Statuti della Repubblica fiorentina*, vol. 2, pp. 21–23.

[66] *Statuti della Repubblica fiorentina*, vol. 2, pp. 21–23.

[67] *Statuti della Repubblica fiorentina*, vol. 2, p. 37.

[68] "sapeva maneggiare la rima." Davidsohn, *I primordi della civiltà fiorentina, impulsi interni, influssi esterni*, vol. 4, pp. 311–313, 317–318.

[69] ASF, Provvisioni, registri 36 fol. 145v.

A possible connection between musicians and the *berrovieri* is that both participated in civic ceremonies. In a city beset with funerals and public processions on account of the plague, it may be argued that the demand for the men increases and thus inclined their wages upward. *Tubatores* in particular were associated with communal authority. The rich sound of their instrument lent pomp to civic events. The *berrovieri* served as the visible face of the commune, in addition to their more obvious role in defending the palace.

But if ceremony were the key factor in moving wages higher, we would expect that the wages of town criers, who also participated in the public activities, would also increase. They do not. And if defense of the public order in the face of post-plague factionalism was a factor, then presumably the wages of the *berrovieri* who protected the palace of the podestà, would, like their counterparts at the palace of the priors, increase. They do not either.

Indeed, the closer we look, the more complicated the portrait becomes. Although the wages of the *berrovieri* of the palace of the priors go up, the wage of the captain of the force stayed the same! Meanwhile, there is no evidence to suggest that the need for musicians or policeman was greater than the need for mercenary cavalrymen, ambassadors, or public doctors – who stood on the frontline of contagion. The nominal wages of all these employees remained the same.

A telling example in this regard is the wages of castellans, who manned forts in the Florentine countryside. The workforce is most obviously comparable to that of soldiers. Both defended the state. Little, however, is known about Florentine castellans.[70] Paolo Pirillo recently pointed out that it is impossible to draw "a complete and detailed portrait" of them owing to the fragmentary nature of the surviving evidence. Scholars still use Giovanni Villani's estimate from 1338 of forty-six fortresses in the Florentine contado and *distretto* as a guideline.[71] The overall number of men employed at any given fort and at any given time is not clear. The city often sent reinforcements during times of trouble.

---

[70] The limited bibliography includes Paolo Pirillo, *Forme e strutture del popolamento nel contado fiorentino: gli insedimenti fortificati (1280–1380)*, vol. 2 (Florence: Leo S. Olschki, 2005) and *Costruzione di un contado: I Fiorentini e il loro territorio nel Basso Medioevo* (Florence: Casa Editrice, 2001); Riccardo Francovich, *I Castelli del contado fiorentino nei secoli XII e XIII* (Florence: CLUSF, 1976); G. M. Varanini, "Castellani e governo del territorio nei distretti delle città venete (XIII–XV sec.)" in *De part et d'autre des Alpes: Les châtelains des princes à la fin du Moyen Âge*, edited by Guido Castelnuovo and Olivier Mattéo (Paris: Flammarion, 2006), pp. 25–58.

[71] Villani adds also that Florence held nineteen *castelli morate* in the district and *contado* of Lucca in 1338. Giovanni Villani, *Nuova Cronica*, vol. 3, p. 190. See Davidsohn, *I primordi della civiltà fiorentina, impulse interni, influssi esterni*, vol. 4, p. 461; Pirillo, *Costruzione di un contado*, pp. 15, 73.

Table 4.4 *Nominal Monthly Wages of Castellans and Infantry Units, 1349–1350*

Castellans (Unit Size, 1349–1350)	Wage* 1349	Wage* 1350
Castellan Fucecchio	440	440
(20–20 infantrymen)	(120)	(120)
Castellan Buggiano	440	440
(25–25 infantrymen)	(120)	(120)
Castellan Montopoli	440	440
(20–20 infantrymen)	(120)	(120)
Castellan Carmignano	440	440
(16–16 infantrymen)	(120)	(120)
Castellan Rocca del Borro	440	440
(12–12 infantrymen)	(120)	(120)
Castellan Civitella	500	440
(15–20 infantrymen)	(128)	(120)
Castellan Laterina	500	440
(15–15 infantrymen)	(128)	(120)
Castellan Uzzano	340	340
(6–15 infantrymen)	(100)	(100)
Castellan Castel Fiorentino	334	440
(9–25 infantrymen)	(100)	(120)

* Wages are in *soldi di piccioli*.
Sources: ASF, Camera del comune, Scrivano di camera uscita 6 fols. 17r–39r; Scrivano di camera uscita 7 fol. 39r, Scrivano di camera uscita 9 fols. 46r–47v; Scrivano di camera uscita 10 fols. 59v–61v.

Table 4.4 lists the wage rates for castellans and their contingents from the budgets of 1349–1350. The documents list 138 men employed in Florentine forts in 1349 and 168 in 1350. The number likely represents only a part of Florence's overall castellan force.

The contingents of 1349–1350 consisted most often of a captain and twenty infantrymen. In this way, they resemble banner units in the regular army. But the size of the contingents appears also to have depended on the size of the fortress and the importance of its location. The castle at Uzzano in the Chianti region near Greve had only six men in it in June 1349 and fifteen men in June 1350. The fort at Buggiano near the border with Pisa had twenty-five infantrymen in 1349 and 1350. Precisely what type of infantrymen these were – shield bearers or cross-bowmen – is not clear. The budgets are specific in only one case, for

Montopoli (in the Valdarno) in 1350, which had twenty infantrymen, consisting of eight crossbowmen and twelve shield bearers.

Castellans and their men were paid monthly. The standard salary of a castellan was 440 soldi a month (22 lire), slightly more than that of an Italian mercenary captain (400 soldi or 20 lire a month). The typical infantryman was paid 120 soldi a month (6 lire a month) the same as a shield bearer in the regular army in 1349. In both cases, however, wages remained the same from 1349 to 1350. The pattern is the same as mercenary cavalrymen, but different from movement of infantry wages in the regular army.

Wages appear to have increased when a castellan's contingent increased sharply in size, as happened at the fortress at Castel Fiorentino. The band grew from nine to twenty-five men from 1349 to 1350, and the salary of the castellan, which had been lower than the others at 334 soldi, moved up to 440 soldi. More often, however, castellan wages tended to *decline* during our period, even when the size of the contingent stayed the same. The salary of the castellan and his men at forts at Civitella and Laterina decreased from 1349 to 1350, from 500 soldi to 440 soldi (Table 4.4).

The evidence suggests yet another post-plague pattern. And there is no doubt that there was a shortage of men for these jobs in Florence. In January 1349, city officials explicitly complained that they could not find citizens willing "to accept the position" of castellan in the "lands, contado and district" of Florence.[72] At that time, the city raised the salaries of castellans by two lire a month. But the complaint of lack of personnel was repeated in June 1349, at the start of the campaign against the Ubaldini – indeed was occasioned by the campaign.[73] Nevertheless, nominal wages of the men stayed the same and began, in several cases, to decline by 1350.

The Meaning of the Florentine Public Wages

The example of the castellans exposes still further the dangers of extrapolating larger patterns from any single set of wage data. Similarly, it makes clear the limits of market forces in explaining trends and the importance of understanding wage data on its own terms. Florence had numerous labor forces, ringed with their own set of qualifications and logic, the details of which we do not entirely understand. The economic system, as Karl Polanyi argued more generally, was embedded in a social system that remains to be studied more carefully.[74]

[72] ASF, Provvisioni, registri 36 fol. 47r.   [73] ASF, Provvisioni, registri 36 fol. 97r.
[74] Karl Polanyi, *The Great Transformation*, p. 46.

To interpret our data, we do well to consider distinctions within the labor force: whether workers were employed by the state or by local institutions, or by fellow citizens (Chapter 5). It is useful to consider prevailing medieval notions of "just wage" which potentially held salaries down. Steven Epstein has found evidence of this for Genoa, indicating a connection between theory and practice.[75] If, as Raymond de Roover has argued, the implementation of "just wages" relied on "municipal authorities of towns, cities, and boroughs," then where better to find evidence of it than in public wages, which were, as we have seen (Chapter 3) disbursed by chamberlains who were monks.[76] The Florentine *camera del arme*, which oversaw the communal arsenal of arms, was likewise headed by monks.

Conclusions are hampered – as with consideration of all aspects of medieval wages – by lack of evidence about how workers and employers came to terms. Bargaining in the distant past is, as Epstein asserts, "an elusive historical subject."[77] It is necessary to include in our analysis notions of honor and social distinction embedded in public service that may have brought reward apart from money. This translates well to Florentine government jobs of importance but low pay, such as chamberlain of the *camera del comune* and the condotta (Table 4.3). Indeed, the nineteenth-century scholar Demetrio Marzi argued that Florentine state jobs constituted an obligation rather than an economic opportunity for employees. Workers accepted "base pay" (*salari meschanissimi*) for service to the "patria."[78] La Roncière repeated this statement.[79] In his extant *ricordanze*, Niccolò di Ser Ventura Monachi, the chancellor of Florence from 1349 to 1350, complained precisely about this issue. He said that his salary was too low to make the job worthwhile financially.

The notion of obligatory service fits well the job of castellan. The post was clearly not a remunerative one, a fact that supports Brucker's assertion that it was often rejected by appointees, who saw it as an inconvenience.[80] A careful examination of the budgets of 1349–1350 reveals that castellans were from notable Florentine families with important political connections. The castellan at Fucecchio in 1349 was Donnino di Sandro Donnini, whose brother Domenico was in charge of

[75] Steven A. Epstein, "The Theory and Practice of the Just Wage," *Journal of Medieval History* 17 (1991), pp. 63, 65 and *Wage Labor and Guilds in Medieval Europe* (Chapel Hill, NC: University of North Carolina Press, 1991).

[76] Raymond de Roover, "The Concept of the Just Price: Theory and Economic Policy," *The Journal of Economic History* 18 no. 4 (1958), p. 428.

[77] Epstein, "The Theory and Practice of the Just Wage," p. 54.

[78] Marzi, *La cancelleria della repubblica fiorentina*, pp. 95–96. See also Falsini, "'Firenze dopo il 1348," p. 440.

[79] La Roncière, "La condition," p. 14.   [80] Brucker, *Florentine Politics*, p. 79.

supplies for the army in 1350 and became a prior in 1352.[81] Donnino himself was elected to the priorate in 1373. The castellan of Buggiano in 1349 was Piero Falco Rondinelli, who was involved in many aspects of Florentine public life at this time, and the castellan of Civitella was Sandro di Gieri del Bello, whose brother Giovanni was also a prior in 1351. The castellans of other forts included members of the Velluti and Scali families.[82] According to Davidsohn, castellans were required to post surety (*sicurtà*) for the job to ensure their honesty. The obligation undoubtedly restricted the workforce and added to the undesirability of the job.[83]

The need to post surety applied also to other public jobs, but it is not clear which ones. Alessandro Gherardi's study of the *camera del comune* at start of the fourteenth century shows that lay chamberlains of the *camera*, accountants, and some notaries who worked for the city gave surety for their positions.[84] It is unknown how much they paid or whether the practice continued into the middle of the century. The requirement did not, however, apply to clerics, who served as chamberlains. Their religious status made their honesty manifest and absolved them from the obligation. The practice adds still another variable to consider with regard to the Florentine public workforce.

It is in any case incorrect to assert, as Marzi does, that government jobs constituted an obligation that offered only "base salaries."[85] There are simply too many wage patterns to justify such a conclusion. The range of wages for notaries speaks directly to this. The notary of the Riformagione (Ser Grifo da Pratovecchio) whose job involved transcribing the acts of the priors and drafting internal letters, was one of the highest paid communal officials, with a salary of 28.3 lire a month.[86] The notary of the condotta office earned a more modest 15 lire a month. The notary working for the *massai* received only 3 lire a month and stood at the bottom of the communal pay scale.[87]

---

[81] ASF, Camera del comune, Scrivano di camera uscita 6 fol. 28r; Scrivano di camera uscita 7 fol. 39r.

[82] ASF, Camera del comune, Scrivano di camera uscita 7 fols. 39r–40r.

[83] According to Davidsohn, *castellani* paid the substantial sum of 3,000 lire. Davidsohn, *Storia di Firenze*, vol. 4, p. 461. Guidi says little about the policy with respect to castellans for our period. G. Guidi, *Il governo della città-repubblica di Firenze del primo Quattrocento*, vol. 2, p. 213.

[84] Gherardi says they were required to give surety of 1,000 florins. Gherardi, "L'antica camera," pp. 316–317.

[85] ASF, Camera del comune, Scrivano di camera uscita 10 fol. 4v.

[86] G. Guidi, *Il governo della città-repubblica di Firenze del primo Quattrocento*, vol. 2, pp. 44–45. Brucker, *Florentine Politics*, p. 60. When he was in office, none of his male relatives could hold major offices. He worked for two months and lived in the palace.

[87] ASF, Camera del comune, Scrivano di camera uscita 10 fol. 49r.

A critical factor in understanding wages is to avoid equating them with compensation. As Simon Penn and Christopher Dyer warn about plague-era England, nominal rates cast only an indirect light on overall earnings.[88] It is here that our evidence is perhaps most striking of all. As we first saw in Chapter 2, participation in war offered opportunities for additional income for workers. Artisans who built war machines at Scarperia augmented their wages by selling supplies. City officials – the notary of the priors, the chancellor, and others – were paid separate fees for the work they did for the war.[89] Musicians, who played at civic events in the city, rode with the army, for which they received additional pay, as did town criers. The office of the condotta was staffed by the same men who simultaneously held posts with the *camera del comune* (Chapter 2). Meanwhile, day laborers such as paymasters and troop inspectors included men identified in budgets with other "occupations" such as notary, chamberlain, and accountant.

The examples may be multiplied, and they reinforce the importance of including war in our discussion of plague. But the practice was not restricted to war. Ser Luce Pucci of Gubbio, the highly paid *compagno* (1,333 soldi per semester) of the executor of justice also received a monthly wage in 1350 for his service on the committee to increase communal revenue and a daily wage for unspecified missions (as a *nuntio*) he undertook for the city.[90] Guidoriccio Ture, listed in one place as a *nuntio* of the *camera* in 1350, is listed elsewhere as a tax collector for the *estimo* imposed on the countryside in the same year.[91]

The evidence makes clear that Florence's day labor force was not distinct from its monthly or semester or yearly labor force – just as the "military" sphere was not separate from the "pacific" one. The information calls into question not only the reliability of nominal wages, but the very concept of occupation at this time – an issue that will be dealt with more fully in the next chapter.

Meanwhile, the overlapping responsibilities allowed for a considerable gap between nominal wages and actual income. The town crier Martino Lapi's nominal salary for that job was 4 lire (80 soldi) a month. But he earned an additional lira a day for seven days of service to the army in

---

[88] Simon A. C. Penn and Christopher Dyer, "Wages and Earnings in Late Medieval England: Evidence from the Enforcement of the Labour Laws," *Economic History Review* 43 no. 3 (1990), pp. 356–376.

[89] ASF, balìe 6 fols. 4v, 114v.

[90] ASF, balìe 6 fol. 19v. Pucci traveled for twenty-three days and was paid 12 soldi a day. ASF, balìe 6 fol. 80v; Camera del comune, Scrivano di camera uscita 9 fol. 7r.

[91] ASF, balìe 6 fol. 39v; Camera del comune, Scrivano di camera uscita 6 fol. 8r.

June 1349.[92] Another town crier, Salvi Lapi, traveled with the army for twenty-four days in July earning 24 lire, six times his monthly wage. Simon Schutiggi is listed in the budgets as an accountant of the *camera del comune*, for which he was paid 10 lire (200 soldi) a month in 1349. But at the same time he was also accountant for the condotta office, earning 3 lire (60 soldi) a month, and in July and August 1349 he served as paymaster for troops for three days (13 lire) and troop inspector for five days (11 lire) – extra work that more than doubled his income, raising it above that of a German cavalryman![93] In 1350 Schutiggi, still an accountant of the *camera del comune*, worked for twenty-seven days as a troop inspector in the lower Valdarno, adding 67 lire to his pay that year. His name also appears on an extant entrata budgets as purchaser of one of the communal gabelles, bringing him still more income, although it is not certain how much.[94] Ser Guelfo di Ser Francesco's concurrent jobs as notary of the *balia* and overseer of supplies raised his income to 201 lire for May 1350. Meanwhile Niccolò Bencivenni, a lowly paid chamberlain of the condotta in 1350, served as paymaster of troops for sixteen days in high mountains in July 1350 (80 lire), overseer of supplies at Scarperia (14 lire), and remitter of exchanges for thirty-six days (180 lire).[95] His monthly nominal wage was 6 lire, but his income was 1,274 lire.

The case of Niccolò di Ser Ventura Monachi is perhaps the most instructive. Monachi explicitly complained in his *ricordanze* that his pay as chancellor of the city (320 lire a year) was "meager." But in the same *ricordanze* Monachi indicates that he actually earned 912 lire from July 1349 to 1350 or nearly triple his nominal "professional" wage.[96] It is not clear how Monachi made his money. He served, as we have seen, also as *scrittore* of the condotta and appears to have received a substantial bribe from Guido di Chito Gangalandi, who worked for Monachi as his helper (*aiutatore*) as chancellor. The bribe was for Gangalandi's appointment to the committee in July 1350 that oversaw the repair of forts captured during the Ubaldini war in the Apennines.[97] The practice of bribing high government officials in Florence is well

[92] ASF, Camera del comune, Scrivano di camera uscita 7 fol. 5r. According to the statute of the podestà, in 1325 both musicians and town criers received 15 soldi a day for service with the army. *Statuti della Repubblica fiorentina*, vol. 2, pp. 37–39, 46.

[93] ASF, Camera del comune, Scrivano di camera uscita 9 fol. 9r; Scrivano di camera uscita 7 fols. 11r, 56v; balie 6 fol. 84v.

[94] For one year, January 1350 to December 1350. ASF, Camera del comune, camarlenghi entrata 41 fol. 207r.

[95] ASF, Provvisioni, registri 37 fols. 79v–81r; Camera del comune, Scrivano di camera entrata 9 fols. 33v; Scrivano di camera uscita 9 fol. 7r; balie 6 fols. 19v, 80v.

[96] *Sonetti editi ed inediti di Ser Ventura Monachi: Rimatore fiorentino del XIV secolo*, edited by Adolfo Mabellini (Turin: G. B. Paravia e comp, 1903), p. 10.

[97] *I Capitoli del Comune di Firenze*, vol. 1, edited by C. Guasti, pp. 89–90.

documented. The novelist Franco Sacchetti described it as a "golosa consuetudine" in the city. For this reason, Sacchetti hoped that his son would grow up to be a "hunter" rather than a student of law – a profession he saw, from the example of Florentine government officials, as utterly corrupt.[98]

The examples support Bronislaw Geremek's famous observation about the "caractère hétérogène" of medieval wages.[99] And as Geremek pointed out for construction workers at the hospital of Saint-Jacques in Paris, compensation included emoluments such as food, clothes, and gratuities. John Hatcher has shown the often glaring gap between the written sources about the plague and extant financial documents, arguing that in contemporary England the "pursuit of internally consistent wages series" misses the reality that "not everything which counted ... can be covered by historians." He cited "unquantified extras" as an "extremely significant element" of wages.[100]

The same may be said of Florentine public workers. The budgets indicate that the chamberlains of the *camera del comune*, the *camera del arme*, the chancellor, notary of the priors, *gonfalonieri*, *berrovieri* of the palace of the priors, and the eleven members of the *famiglia* of the priors all received lodging and meals.[101] As noted in Chapter 2, food for the Signoria was one of the biggest monthly expenditures in communal budgets.[102] The castellans lived in their fortresses and were presumably fed and equipped at a communal expense.[103] The statute of podestà in 1325 required the *berrovieri* of that official to eat and live only at the podestà's palace.[104] Florence provided uniforms twice a year, at Christmas and the feast of San Giovanni, for civic musicians, town criers,

---

[98] Franco Sacchetti, *Novelle* (Turin: Einaudi, 1970) #77, pp. 196–198. See also Chiappelli, "L'amministrazione della giustizia," p. 44.

[99] Bronislaw Geremek, *Le salariat dans l'artisanat parisien aux XIIIe–XVe siècles* (Paris: La Haye, Mouton, 1968), p. 85. For Spain, see Charles Verlinden, "La grande peste de 1348 en Espagne: Contribution à l'étude de ses conséquences économiques et sociales," *Revue Belge de Philologie et d'Histoire* 17 (1938), pp. 17–25.

[100] John Hatcher, "England in the Aftermath of the Black Death," *Past and Present* 144 (1994), pp. 12–19, 21–25.

[101] According to Guidi, based on evidence from 1415, the chamberlains of the *camera del arme* resided on the first floor of the palazzo dei priori. The chancellor had a room on the second floor of the palazzo priori, where the priors and gonfaloniere di guistizia also stayed. The statutes of the captain of the people in 1355 say that the *famiglia* ate and slept in the palace. Guidi, *Il governo della città-repubblica di Firenze del primo Quattrocento*, vol. 2, pp. 35–36; Davidsohn, *Storia di Firenze*, vol. 4, pp. 98–99. See also Nicolai Rubinstein, *The Palazzo Vecchio, 1298–1532* (Oxford: Oxford University Press, 1995), p. 18.

[102] ASF, Camera del comune, Scrivano di camera uscita 6 fol. 3r. Camera del comune, camarlenghi uscita 60 fol. 464r.

[103] Davidsohn, *I primordi della civiltà fiorentina, impulse interni, influssi esterni*, vol. 4, p. 462.

[104] *Statuti della Repubblica fiorentina*, vol. 2, p. 22.

and members of the *famiglia*. Four times a year the city gave musicians a banner (*pennone*) emblazoned with the Florentine *giglio* to adorn their instruments.[105] The budgets show that the uniforms and banner cost more than the monthly salaries of the men in 1350.[106] The executor of justice was compensated for the ink and paper he used and sometimes given a portion of the fines he levied.[107] And in what may have been a distinctly Florentine tradition, the city held poetic contests among government officials for an award of precious cloth.[108] There were undoubtedly additional emoluments that are not apparent in the extant budgets, as well as differing rules concerning the workforces. The statute of 1325 required that the policemen of the podestà come from the same town, but it required that the entourage of the judge of appeals specifically not be from that official's own city.[109]

Toward a Reassessment of Mercenaries?

The qualifications apply also to soldiers in Florentine service, the issue with which we began this chapter and with which it is well to end it. For all our discussion of cavalry wages, we do not in fact know what their entourages looked like. It is unclear how many horses a captain supported, how many assistants there were, and whether these numbers changed from 1349 to 1350.[110] As we have seen for the Florentine public workforce in general, the size of entourages greatly affected salary.

And if we contextualize wages, we must consider the possibility that soldiers, like other government employees, had access to revenue apart from their nominal wage. Indeed, cavalrymen stood to gain from ransoms and war booty, well-known perquisites of war. But in medieval Italy, mercenary cavalrymen were eligible for bonuses of double pay for victories in the field and for reparation (*menda*) for injured horses. These were spelled out in the contracts (*condotte*) between the city and the cavalrymen and were a well-known point of contention between both

---

[105] McGee, *The Ceremonial Musicians of Late Medieval Florence*, pp. 53–55.

[106] ASF, Camera del comune, camarlenghi uscita 67 fol. 633v.

[107] For paper and writing instruments. ASF, Camera del comune, Scrivano di camera uscita 7 fol. 4r.

[108] William Robins, "Poetic Rivalry: Antonio Pucci, Jacopo Salimbeni and Antonio Beccari da Ferrara" in *Firenze alla vigilia del Rinascimento*, edited by Maria Bendinelli Predelli (Fiesole: Cadmo, 2006), pp. 319–322.

[109] *Statuti della repubblica fiorentina*, vol. 2, pp. 25–32.

[110] The captain of war, for example, had three horses – a *corserio, palafreno, destriere* – and three musicians – a *tubatore, trombetta,* and *nacherino* – as part of his personal entourage, paid by him from his salary. The *conservadore* had three horses – a destrier, *palafreno,* and *ronzino* (pony) – and four musicians as part of his entourage, paid by his salary.

sides.[111] The *condotte* were what today we would call "incentive-laden" contracts. The base salary of a cavalryman thus constituted more of a rough guideline to earnings that were expected to be augmented by the spoils of war.

No *condotte* from 1349 to 1350 have survived. But the budgets and *balìa* records show that German and Italian cavalrymen did receive bonuses for their service. In June 1350 the city paid 3,123 lire to twenty cavalry captains for the capture of the town of Montegemoli. The recipients included the captains Johann Dornich, Burckhard di Toro, Andrea Salmoncelli, and Jakob da Fiore, all of whom, as we have seen in Chapter 2, played a leading role in the army.[112] Meanwhile, a close reading of budgets shows that the city also compensated cavalrymen for horses injured or killed in battle.[113] The budgets regularly list payments for horses, ranging in value from 15 florins to 50 florins, to German and Italian cavalrymen whose horses were killed in skirmishes at Montegemoli, Tirlì, Susinana, Lozzole, and elsewhere.[114]

Bonuses and incentive-laden contracts do not, however, entirely resolve the issue. Monetary rewards were offered widely during the war. Florence set rates for the capture and murder of members of the Ubaldini family at the outset of the campaign. The documents confirm that payments were made for these, by the captain of war of the army, with money provided by city officials. The captain paid the shield bearer (17 September 1350) Santi Chiarucci of Tirlì for the capture of Arrighetto of Tirlì, a "traditore," who was taken in front of the Ubaldini castle at Tirlì.[115] On 26 May 1350, the captain of war gave rewards to two infantrymen for seizing a servant of Maghinardo Ubaldini at Montegemoli.[116] The city even paid bonuses to the *barattieri* for houses they burned. A tambourine player, identified only as Niccolò, received 10 lire for torching a residence near Susinana.[117]

The bonus system was clearly more systematized for cavalrymen. It was a formal part of their contracts.[118] This was not the case for infantry, who

---

[111] On *condotte*, see Daniel P. Waley, "Condotte and Condottieri in the Thirteenth Century," *Proceedings of the British Academy* 61 (1975), pp. 337–371; Michael Mallett, *Mercenaries and Their Masters* (Totowa, NJ: Rowman and Littlefield, 1974), pp. 80–106; William Caferro, *John Hawkwood, an English Mercenary in Fourteenth Century Italy* (Baltimore, MD: Johns Hopkins University Press, 2006), pp. 71–79.

[112] ASF, balìe 6 fols. 91r–92v.

[113] ASF, Camera del comune, Scrivano di camera uscita 7 fols. 48r, 56v; Scrivano di camera uscita 9 fols. 51v–54r.

[114] ASF, Camera del comune, Scrivano di camera uscita 7 fols. 48r, 56v; Scrivano di camera uscita 9 fols. 51v–54r, 55r; Camera del comune, camarlenghi uscita 70 fols. 41r–43r.

[115] The captain paid the men and the city reimbursed him. ASF, balìe 6 fols. 84r–v, 112r.

[116] ASF, balìe 6 fol. 78v.   [117] ASF, balìe 7 fol. 35r; balìe 6 fol. 112r.

[118] Caferro, *John Hawkwood*, pp. 71–79.

also did not maintain costly horses. It is noteworthy in this regard that when Florence formally raised infantry wages in July 1349, the legislation also mentions cavalrymen, but only to affirm their rights to double pay for taking castles – underscoring the importance of rewards for cavalry rather than hikes in wage rates.[119]

Nevertheless, even if we allow for incentive-based contracts for cavalry, it is still justifiable to ask why the nominal wages of mercenary cavalrymen did not increase in the face of the plague? The basic greed of the profession has been well documented and famously emphasized by Machiavelli. The market for the services of mercenary cavalrymen was, as noted earlier, robust, with opportunities throughout the peninsula, including close at hand in the Romagna, which was in open rebellion against the Church.

The best answer, however counterintuitive it may be, is that cavalry captains and their men accepted the incentive-based contracts and with them stagnant nominal wages. In so doing, the cavalrymen willy-nilly accepted the notion embedded in such contracts that "good" service brought its own rewards. The interpretation suggests the possibility that mercenary cavalrymen viewed themselves differently from the way they have been depicted by scholars, and differently from their contemporary infantry counterparts. Horsemen de facto represented an aristocratic element of the military labor force, as opposed to infantry, a distinction that may have conditioned their demand for wages. The nonquantifiable reward of political influence does not apply to mercenaries, who were hired exactly because they were outsiders and therefore disinterested in local affairs. But war was itself an ennobling activity, even if the backgrounds of the men were in some cases dubious. A soldier astride a horse who performed well in battle was a man of honor in an honor-bound profession. Such labor was not to be quantified solely by a nominal wage.

All this muddies the portrait of the mercenary, the most relentlessly misunderstood figure in medieval history. It seems shocking in light of Machiavelli's portrayal of them and Petrarch's well-known slights. But the depiction would have been less surprising to more practically minded contemporaries like Geoffroi de Charny (d. 1356), author of the *Book of Chivalry*, who includes mercenary cavalrymen under the rubric of chivalry. Charny specifically praises foreign men, who, like the Germans in Florentine service, "left their homes and traveled to fight in Lombardy, Tuscany and Puglia."[120]

---

[119] ASF, Provvisioni, registri 36 fol. 132v.
[120] Geoffroi de Charny, *Book of Chivalry*, edited by Richard W Kaeuper and Elspeth Kennedy (Philadelphia, PA: University of Pennsylvania Press), p. 2.

The key term is "cavalry" rather than "mercenary." Many of the cross-bowmen in Florentine service in 1349–1350 were, as we have seen, a species of mercenary, hired from outside of Florence and recruited in a similar manner as mercenary cavalry. But they clearly sought and received higher nominal wages. The cavalrymen did not, lending further support to the thesis that there was something related to that activity – cavalry service – that conditioned demand. The willingness of mercenary cavalrymen to pay the *dirittura* tax to the state (Chapter 3) may be adduced as additional evidence. For all their apparent advantages in the marketplace, the cavalrymen did not seek exemption from Florentine imposts. Mercenary crossbowmen, on the other hand, specifically bargained for this. The crossbowmen recruited from Casteldurante in 1350 refused to take up service until Florence exempted it from the *dirittura* tax.[121] Florentine officials reluctantly agreed. The *dirittura* was, as we have seen, specifically intended for "good works" in the city, for the betterment of the cathedral, and for the establishment of the university. The mercenary cavalry paid the *dirittura* as well as fines from inspections, which were often substantial. The combination made the cavalrymen the most highly taxed of all Florentine employees. The fact that the *dirittura* consciously sought to make "good" from "bad" (Chapter 3) may well have been a factor in the acceptance of it by cavalrymen. The tax may also have been perceived as ennobling.

The lack of "apprentices" (*ragazzini*) in mercenary cavalry units can be read as further proof of an alternate self-definition. The *ragazzini* appeared in increasing numbers in infantry units, which we have argued was reflective of a shortage of men. But there was also a shortage of cavalrymen and undoubtedly newcomers joining the rank and file. Nevertheless, no apprentices are listed in their units. The term, which conjures notions of guild related labor, is used only with respect to infantry – an indication perhaps that infantry was viewed as a "laboring" class while cavalry fell under a nonguild aristocratic rubric. Indeed, it is useful in this regard to compare the mercenary cavalry captain to the podestà of the city. Both came from outside of the city, stood at the head of their own unit and had marketable skills that presumably could have been sold elsewhere. But in both cases their nominal wages remained the same from 1349 to 1350. Daniel Waley has referred to the podestà as a "citizen noble," and our sources refer to the men employed by Florence in 1349–1350 as "knights."[122] The noble bearing

---

[121] ASF, balie 6 fols. 38v, 53r; Signori Missive I Cancelleria 10 #145.
[122] Daniel Waley, *The Italian City Republics*, 3rd edn. (London: Longman, 1988), pp. 42–43; ASF, Camera del comune, Scrivano di camera uscita 8 fol. 2r; Scrivano di camera uscita 10 fol. 2v.

of the job perhaps indicates that it belongs, like cavalry, in a category other than traditional labor.

The revisionist interpretation should not be pushed too far. As we have seen, the term "knight" did have economic significance. Italian mercenary captains with that title received higher pay than those without it. But the economic value of the distinction did not depend on market forces. And its lack of value in terms of German captains suggests that these men were viewed as distinct from Italian mercenary cavalry. Indeed, Italian captains were specifically identified as "faithful Guelfs," a political association all too often ignored in the Anglophone historiography, but which was an important requisite for service in the city, where Guelf-Ghibelline labels still mattered, and Florence's enemy in 1349–1350 was a Ghibelline clan. The Guelf designation would appear to have limited the market in Italian mercenary soldiers and helped drive up wages. That it did not happen indicates that, as with the Germans, the men were bound to their employer by something other than their stipends. "Guelfism" was an ideology that may have inclined the men to take up service and continue at the same wage rates despite the dramatic change in market forces.

There is in any case a great deal going on with respect to the cavalry and much more research is needed. The evidence presented here is difficult to reconcile with the careers of famous mercenary captains such as John Hawkwood, who sought ever-higher stipends and held whole towns for ransom. But such men were unusual, the equivalent of the "rock stars" of the profession. They share common characteristics with the lesser lights but cannot be taken as representative of the whole. It is necessary to admit the likelihood that there were varying paradigms of mercenary cavalry service, just as there were varying labor forces more generally in Florence.

What is clear from the foregoing discussion is that, as Polanyi observed in his "bird's eye view" of economic systems of the distant past in *The Great Transformation*, the "organization of labor" is "embedded in the general organization of society."[123] The example of Florence's mercenary cavalry supports Polanyi's statement that man "does not act so as to safeguard his individual interest in the possession of material goods; he acts so as to safeguard his social standing, his social claims, his social assets."[124]

---

[123] Polanyi, *The Great Transformation*, p. 76.
[124] Polanyi, *The Great Transformation*, p. 76.

5   The Bell Ringer Travels to Avignon, the Cook to Hungary

Toward an Understanding of the Florentine Labor Force, 1349–1350

> The interpretation of wage entries ... is a fascinating exercise in detective logic for the solution of puzzles and the discovery and avoidance of pitfalls.
>
> Beveridge, "Wages in the Winchester Manors"[1]

> Quantitative evidence allows us to convert a metaphysical conundrum into an empirical question.
>
> Fischer, The Great Wave[2]

> I speak about the cook, who, as you know, is considered the most vile of servants.
>
> Petrarch, Familiares VIII, 4[3]

In his pioneering study of medieval English wages from 1208 to 1453, Sir William Beveridge compared his mode of investigation to "driving a car by night, through unfamiliar country." The glare of the headlights would light up only "a narrow strip of road and hedge," obscuring spots around the edges that were undeniably important. He lamented his inability to explore the edges, afraid that his "journey" would never end. He called upon historians to look more closely at the evidence, to further "the fascinating exercise in detective logic."[4]

The present study has helped scatter Beveridge's beam and make clear, as Beveridge himself suspected, that the edges are indeed worthy of inquiry and, perhaps more philosophically, that the journey itself is as worthy as the result. When war is added to the analysis of post-plague Florence, the analysis changes. Petrarch and Boccaccio appear as more steadfastly political figures, and their incipient friendship gains layers of

---

[1] William H. Beveridge, "Wages in the Winchester Manors," *Economic History Review* 7 (1936), p. 23.

[2] David Hackett Fischer, *The Great Wave: Price Revolutions and the Rhythm of History* (Oxford: Oxford University Press, 1996), pp. xv–xvi.

[3] Francesco Petrarch, *Rerum familiarum libri, I–VIII*, vol. 1, translated and edited by Aldo S. Bernardo (Albany, NY: State University of New York Press, 1975), p. 401.

[4] Beveridge, "Winchester," p. 22.

complexity, as does their relation to their forebear Dante. The Florentine army is less ad hoc and more professionalized – a curious constant amid a landscape of change. The mercenary cavalryman looks less "Machiavellian" and more faithful. The "intensified market forces" of supply and demand that purportedly drove up wages missed a substantial part of the Florentine workforce. Meanwhile, the notion of occupation appears variable or, more precisely, distinct from our modern conception of it.

The last points deserve emphasis. It is with respect to wages and the workforce that the assumptions for our period are most stubbornly fixed.[5] The scholarly focus on determining real wages and reconstructing standards of living over the long term has hindered proper study of nominal wages. Scholars too often assume the reliability of the figures and fail to submit them to proper scrutiny.

The status quo is exacerbated by synthetic centuries-long wage series that use nominal wages uncritically for the sake of broad comparative conclusions that situate events in the distant past in terms of the present day. The tradition has involved the study of day labor and craftsmen wages: data deemed most "available" and "usable" for study. But the data is neither copious nor representative. The very recourse to "usable" statistics is teleological and constitutes an obstacle to good history. It has promoted, particularly among economists, a tendency to apply a simplified form of economic analysis to the distant past, befitting, as it were, the simplicity of the period itself. The Harvard economist Claudia Goldin asserts this explicitly when arguing, ironically, in favor of the applicability of historical evidence to economic theory. She states that "empiricists have learned that historical data is often better than current figures." They are ringed with fewer qualifications and reflective of "a less litigious society."[6] Goldin was speaking of early twentieth-century America. But the statement reveals embedded modern suppositions about the study of the past. The problem is still greater with respect to the Middle Ages, which for some modernists functions as an archetypical primitive, for which numbers, however isolated and scarce, are all the more valuable.

Nominal wages provide the connective tissue for such study. They are the most empirical of empirical evidence. The focus here on two years has allowed a more complete view and rendered more visible the array of factors at play and the dangers of placing too much faith in the empirical

---

[5] ASF, balìe 6 fol. 69r.
[6] Claudia Goldin, "Cliometrics and the Nobel," *Journal of Economic Perspectives* 9 no. 2 (Spring 1995), p. 191.

quality of numbers. It gives substance to Marc Bloch's assertion, back in 1934, that short-term study exposes aspects of society obscured in long-term studies.[7] Numbers are contextual and, like texts, represent different narratives.

The point is not new, nor restricted to Bloch. Joseph Schumpeter argued in his *History of Economic Analysis* that an "understanding of historical facts" is fundamentally important to understanding economic phenomena. He evocatively described "historical technique" as a "passenger on the bus we call economic analysis" and concluded that "derivative knowledge is always unsatisfactory."[8]

The small scale renders visible inconsistencies and contradictions that, when carefully assayed rather than discarded, offer important insights into society. On this point Bloch and Schumpeter agree also with John Maynard Keynes. Keynes advised, in his famous critique of classical economic theory, that we should "avoid putting more order into the system than there actually was."[9]

Currency and Taxation

Nowhere is this point more evident than with respect to currency and taxation, two aspects of wages that have not received adequate scholarly attention. The first is usually earmarked for "later discussion" on account of its "complexity" or dismissed for its "lack of utility" for comparative study. Taxation is dealt with in the "wholly separate" field of public finance.[10]

The scholarship misses the larger point. Currency and taxation may be complicated and have little to do with the type of long-term conclusions researchers have sought, but they are historical variables important to understanding societies of the distant past. Most immediately, they tell us

---

[7] Marc Bloch, "Le salaire et les fluctuations économique à longue period." *Revue Historique* 173 (1934), pp. 3–6. See also John Day, "Money, Credit and Capital Formation in Marc Bloch and Ferdinand Braudel" in *Money and Finance in the Ages of Merchant Capitalism* (London: Blackwell, 1999), p. 123.

[8] Joseph Schumpeter, *History of Economic Analysis* (Oxford: Oxford University Press, 1954), pp. 12–14.

[9] "Classical theory are applicable to a special case only ... the special case assumed by classical theory happen not to be those of the economic society we actually live in." John Maynard Keynes, *The General Theory of Employment, Interest and Money* (New York: Harcourt Brace, 1936), p. 3.

[10] Even though Beveridge notes five episodes of debasement in his study of English wages from 1208 to 1453, he ultimately concludes that he "would be surprised if ... currency had much to do with any of the more striking movements of the wage series." Beveridge, "Winchester," p. 24. Tognetti found money of account rather than actual currency suitable for the purpose of comparison over time. Sergio Tognetti, "Prezzi e salari nella Firenze tardo medievale: un profile," *Archivio storico italiano* 153 (1995), pp. 268–270.

much more about the configuration of wages in 1349–1350 and how to better understand the Florentine workforce.

Florentine budgets, as noted in Chapter 4, were figured in money of account. This was "ghost money" that did not correspond to the actual coins the city paid its employees. Economic historians traditionally present wages in grams of silver in their studies. The practice is well suited to medieval England, from whence it derived, and where silver was at this time the most basic means of exchange.[11] But it is ill suited to Florence, where gold payments were common. Gold florins were more stable in value than silver money, particularly petty Florentine coins (quattrini, denari), which were subject to debasement and restricted primarily to small-scale transactions.

The choice of currency in payment of wages had important economic and social implications. Carlo Cipolla called the relation between silver and gold "a question of preeminent general interest" in *trecento* Florence with the potential to cause "widespread social tension and unrest."[12] He asserted that gold florins were reserved for clothiers, bankers, merchant houses, moneylenders, doctors, lawyers, big-landed proprietors, and, more generally, "members of the patriciate and members of the *arti maggiori* (major guilds)." Conversely, silver was paid to craftsmen and lower status workers.[13] Just prior to the plague, in 1345–1347, Florence devalued its silver currency, in

---

[11] Thorold Rogers set the standard, which Beveridge and others followed. Thorold Rogers notes the general lack of gold coined in England in the period. See James E. Thorold Rogers, *A History of Agriculture and Prices in England from the Year after the Oxford Parliament (1259) to the Commencement of the Continental War (1793)* (Oxford: Clarendon Press, 1866), p. 177 and *Six Centuries of Work and Wages: The History of English Labour*, vol. 1 (London: Swan Sonnenschein and Co., 1894), pp. 323–325; Beveridge, "Winchester," pp. 23–24. More recently, van Zanden justifies the use of silver to facilitate comparison across Europe and "allow us to make international comparisons of nominal wages and grain prices." Jan Luiten van Zanden, "Wages and the Standards of Living in Europe, 1500–1800," *European Review of Economic History* 2 (1991), p. 80. See also Robert C. Allen, "The Great Divergence in European Wages and Prices from the Middle Ages to the First World War," *Explorations in Economic History* 38 (2001), pp. 412–415; Özmucur Süleyman and Şevket Pamuk, "Real Wages and Standards of Living in the Ottoman Empire, 1489–1914," *Journal of Economic History* 62 (2002), pp. 292–321. Gregory Clark's recent comparative history does not even mention issues of currency, see *A Farewell to Alms* (Princeton, NJ: Princeton University Press, 2007), pp. 40–43.

[12] Carlo Cipolla, *The Monetary Policy of Fourteenth Century Florence* (Berkeley, CA: University of California Press, 1982), p. 28.

[13] Cipolla, *Monetary Policy*, p. 26. Tognetti has recently restated that gold was handled mostly by wealthy merchants, bankers and well to do artisans. Tognetti, "Prezzi e salari," pp. 268–270. See also Giuliano Pinto, *Toscana medievale: paesaggi e realtà sociali* (Florence: Le Lettere, 1993), p. 115 and Charles M. de La Roncière, *Prix et salaires à Florence au XIVe siècle, 1280–1380* (Rome: Palais Farnese, 1982), pp. 469–518.

response to the falling price of gold. The plague and demographic crisis brought monetary equilibrium.[14]

The profound concern with currency is readily apparent in Florentine budgets, which dutifully list the daily rate of exchange between silver and gold in the margins of wage entries. The rates were also made available to the general public, allowing citizens, as Cipolla noted, to be "acutely aware of the health of the local economy."[15] In both 1349 and 1350 the average yearly exchange rate was 64 soldi per florin.

Florentine cameral budgets unfortunately do not give the precise coins used in payments (Chapter 4), but they do state, if inconsistently, the currency Florence paid to its employees: whether silver or gold or a combination thereof.[16] This is written at the bottom of wage entries, particularly those (*scrivano*) rendered in the vernacular, which use the term "ebbe" or "ebbero" ("he had," "they had"). Close inspection of the budgets shows that officials made distinctions with regard to citation (Table 5.1). All salaries are ultimately configured in money of account (lire) to facilitate adding them together. But some are cited initially in gold florins. There is no explanation for the practice. Florentine officials knew what they were doing, and apparently felt no need to explain it. Giuliano Pinto has argued, based on extant budgets of the Florentine hospital of San Gallo, that citation in florins meant payment to the employee in that currency, while citation in lire/money of account gave officials leeway to use either silver or gold. Pinto interpreted the florin citation as intended to protect employees against the possible devaluation of silver and small money.[17] This appears to be true of Florentine cameral budgets for salaries paid to city employees.

Consideration of currency reveals intriguing patterns for 1349–1350. During the first campaign against the Ubaldini in 1349, the wages of German cavalrymen and Italian crossbowmen in Florentine service were listed in florins, before being converted to money of account (lire) for the purposes of adding them. The wages of Italian mercenary cavalrymen and shield bearer units were, however, listed only in lire. In terms of currency citation, then, cavalry and infantry components of Florence's army were, surprisingly, grouped together. Florence made distinctions within the cavalry, between German and Italian cavalry units, and within the infantry, between crossbow and shield bearer units (Table 5.1). The evidence

---

[14] Cipolla, *Monetary Policy*, p. 48.   [15] Cipolla, *Monetary Policy*, pp. 27–28.

[16] Richard A. Goldthwaite, *The Economy of Renaissance Florence* (Baltimore, MD: Johns Hopkins University Press, 2009), p. 611.

[17] Giuliano Pinto, "Il personale, le balie e I salariati dell'Ospedale di San Gallo di Firenze (1395–1406)" in *Toscana medieval: paesaggi e realtà sociale* (Florence: Le Lettere, 1993), p. 77.

Table 5.1 *Citation of Wages of Florentine Soldiers in Cameral Budgets for the Ubaldini War*

	1349	1350
German cavalry captains	florins	florins
German cavalrymen	florins	florins
Crossbow captains (Liguria/Lunigiana)	florins	florins
Crossbowmen (Liguria/Lunigiana)	florins	florins
Captain crossbow (Bibbiena/Modena)	**florins**	**lire**
Crossbowmen (Bibbiena/Modena, mixed units)	**florins**	**lire**
Italian mercenary cavalry captain	lire	lire
Italian mercenary cavalryman	lire	lire
Captain shield bearers	lire	lire
Shield bearer	lire	lire

Note: Bold denotes change.
Sources: ASF, Camera del comune, Scrivano di camera uscita 6 fols. 17r–41r; Scrivano di camera uscita 7 fols. 17r–60r; Scrivano di camera uscita 8 fols. 2r–7v, 17r–36r; Scrivano di camera uscita 9 fols. 2r–9v, 17r–45v; Scrivano di camera uscita 10 fols. 17r–59r.

lessens still further the distance between cavalry and infantry components of the Florentine army that we saw in Chapters 2 and 4. Inasmuch as gold was the more desirable monetary unit, it may be concluded that German cavalrymen and crossbowmen were the more favored parts of the army in 1349.

The citation of currency for crossbowmen wages changed during the second campaign. The salaries of men from the towns of Bibbiena and Modena, cited in florins in 1349, were cited in lire in 1350. Alpinuccio Nuti of Bibbiena and his crossbowmen, listed as receiving 3½ florins a month and 2 florins a month respectively during the first campaign, were paid 14 lire a month and 9 lire a month respectively during the second campaign.[18] The adjustment constituted an increase in nominal wages of 39 percent for the captain (202 soldi to 280 soldi) and 30 percent for crossbowmen (128 soldi to 180 soldi). But the soldiers now received silver, a less desirable unit, rather than gold. At the same time, however, the citation of the wages of crossbowmen from Liguria and Lunigiana remained in florins from 1349 to 1350, as did the citation of the wages of German mercenaries. Italian mercenaries and shield bearers remained in lire.

[18] Overall Alpinuccio Nuti earned 25 florins and 12 soldi a oro in July 1349. ASF, Camera del comune, Scrivano di camera uscita 6 fol. 40v; Scrivano di camera uscita 7 fol. 17r. Scrivano di camera uscita 9 fol. 35r; Scrivano di camera uscita 10 fols. 23v, 34v.

The evidence thus suggests that Florence was willing to give men from Bibbiena and Modena higher wages, but in a less desirable currency. It also indicates, at the very least, that Florence conceived of the cross-bowmen in its service in different ways.

Budgetary citations notwithstanding, many soldiers in Florentine service during the first campaign appear to have been paid in florins. The salaries of Italian mercenary cavalry captain Nino degli Obizzi and his men are cited in lire, but according to the "ebbero" listing at the bottom of the citation, he received florins during the first campaign.[19] The shield bearer units led by Santi Chiarucci of Tirlì, Jacobo "Ser Mestola" Chesis of Passignano, Francesco "Malamamma" Bartoli of Florence, Tone Lemmi of the Garfagnana, and Balduccio Gucci of Collodi were all paid in florins in July/August 1349.[20] German cavalry-men and crossbow units also received payment in gold that year.

The fragmentary nature of the sources makes comprehensive analysis impossible. But there is intriguing evidence of a shift from payment in gold to silver from the first campaign in 1349 to the second campaign in 1350. Crossbowmen from Bibbiena and Modena were, as we have already seen, shifted to silver during the second campaign. This was also true of the shield bearer units and Italian mercenary cavalrymen.[21] The wages of crossbowmen from Liguria and Lunigiana continued to be both cited and paid in florins. The *balestrieri della ghiera* and crossbow units from Casteldurante, employed only in 1350, were paid in florins, as were German mercenary cavalrymen.[22]

Florence's precise strategy is unclear. We may perhaps interpret the evidence as an attempt on the part of the government to soften the impact of rising wages by paying soldiers, particularly infantrymen, in a less desirable currency. Nevertheless, when currency is added to our analysis, crossbowmen from Liguria and Lunigiana were the most favored of the city's soldiers. Their nominal wages increased and continued to be paid in gold florins. German cavalrymen received gold during both campaigns, but their nominal wages remained the same. Italian mercenaries fared

---

[19] ASF, Camera del comune, Scrivano di camera uscita 6 fols. 29r–v: Scrivano di camera uscita 7 fol. 44r. For others, see ASF, Scrivano di camera uscita 6 fols. 2r–10r.

[20] ASF, Camera del comune, Scrivano di camera uscita 6 fols. 29v, 35r, 37r, 40v; Scrivano di camera uscita 7 fols. 19r, 25r. The evidence corresponds with Florentine city council legislation that lists shield-bearer wages in florins. ASF, Provvisioni registri 36 fols. 132r–v.

[21] ASF, Camera del comune, Scrivano di camera uscita 9 fols. 20r, 35r; Scrivano di camera uscita 10 fols. 18r, 26r, 35r.

[22] ASF, Camera del comune, Scrivano di camera uscita 6 fol. 29r; Scrivano di camera uscita 9 fol. 20r, Scrivano di camera uscita 10 fol. 34r. For others, see Scrivano di camera uscita 9 fols. 31r–31v.

worst. Their wages were stagnant and, during the second campaign, they were paid silver rather than gold.

The trends raise important questions. As in Chapter 4, it is useful to compare soldiers' wages with those of other Florentine public employees in 1349–1350. Table 5.2 shows that the salaries of only a few city workers were cited in florins before being converted to lire. The vast majority were listed in money of account.

But as was the case with wages for soldiers, wages for many Florentine public employee were paid in gold in 1349 during the Ubaldini campaign despite the citation in money of account. These employees include the foreign judges (podestà, executor of justice, judge of appeals), the notary of the Riformagione, castellans, the bell ringers of the palace of the priors, servants (*donzelli*) of the priors, musicians, town criers, troop inspectors, the public doctor, ambassadors, and the communal cook.[23]

The list provides additional proof that, contra Cipolla, gold was not narrowly reserved for the "patriciate and members of the major guilds."[24] The social distinctions are not so simple. The salary of the chancellor, a key government official and man of substantial social standing, was both cited and paid in gold florins. But the chamberlains of other important offices such as the *camera del comune* and the *camera del arme* were listed in lire and paid in silver in 1349, as were the salaries of the judges (*savi*) who advised them, and the notaries who wrote out the income and expenditure accounts of the *camera del comune*.[25] At the same time seemingly lower-level officials such as bell ringers, troop inspectors, and the communal cook were paid in gold. One accountant of the *camera del comune* was paid in gold; the other was paid in silver. Two judges and four notaries of the podestà were singled out for payment in gold, but the rest of the podestà's entourage received silver.

There is evidence, as was the case with soldiers, of a shift from payment in gold to silver from the first campaign against the Ubaldini in 1349 to the second in 1350. But the shift is less pronounced. Town criers, the communal doctor, and cook were paid in florins in 1349, but received silver in 1350.[26] Foreign judges continued to be paid in gold, as were the

---

[23] ASF, Camera del comune, Scrivano di camera uscita 6 fols. 4r–6r, 18r, 21r, 30r; Scrivano di camera uscita 7 fol. 31r.

[24] Cipolla, *Monetary Policy*, p. 26; Bowsky concurs for Siena. William M. Bowsky, *A Medieval Italian Commune: Siena under the Nine, 1287–1355* (Berkeley, CA: University of California Press, 1981), pp. 226–227.

[25] ASF, Camera del comune, Scrivano di camera uscita 6 fols. 6r, 10r; Scrivano di camera uscita 7 fol. 10v.

[26] ASF, Camera del comune, Scrivano di camera uscita 9 fols. 3v, 4v–5v, 8v; Scrivano di camera uscita 10 fol. 6r; Scrivano di camera uscita 10 fol. 39r.

Table 5.2 *Citation of Wages of Florentine Stipendiaries during the Ubaldini War*

	1349	1350
Podestà	lire*	lire*
Executor of the ordinances of justice	lire*	lire*
Judge of appeals	lire*	lire*
Ambassadors	lire*	lire*
Compagno of executor of justice	lire	lire
Two judges/four notaries of the podestà	**florins**	**florins**
Troop inspectors	lire*	lire
Chancellor of commune	**florins**	**florins**
Castellans	lire*	lire*
Notary of *Riformagione*	lire*	lire*
Captain of *Berrovieri* of the palace of the priors	lire*	lire*
Notary for expenditure of the *camera*	lire	lire
Notary of priors	lire	lire
Accountant/*anoveratore* of the *camera*	**florins**	**florins**
Accountant of the *camera*	lire	lire
Superintendants of *stinche*	lire	lire
Notary/*scrittore* of the condotta	lire	lire
Gonfalonieri del popolo	lire	lire
Notary/*aiutatore* of chancellor	**florins**	**florins**
Accountant of the *camera*	lire	lire
Public doctor	lire*	lire
Notary for income of the *camera*	lire	lire
Notary of the condotta	lire	lire
Notary of judges/*savi*	lire	lire
Spy	lire	lire
Sindaco	—	lire
Monk chamberlains of the *camera*	lire	lire
Famigliare of notary of *Riformagione*	lire	lire
Berrovieri of the palace of the priors	lire*	lire*
Lay chamberlains of the *camera*	lire	lire
Town criers (*banditori/approvatori*)	lire	lire
Chamberlains of the condotta	lire	lire
Notary of supervisors of prison	lire	lire
Messi of the condotta	lire	lire
Berrovieri of the palace of the podestà	lire	lire
Musicians	lire*	lire
Custodians/guards of the *camera*	lire	lire
Bell ringers of the palace of the podestà	lire	lire
Bell ringers of the palace of the priors	lire*	lire
Cook	lire*	lire
Servants (*donzelli, servitori*) of the priors	lire*	lire
Massai of the *camera*	lire	lire
Judges/*savi* of the *camera*	lire	lire
Notaries of *Massai*	lire	lire
Pages of the cook	lire	lire

* Citation in lire, but payment in florins.
   Source: ASF, Camera del comune, Scrivano di camera uscita 6, 7, 9, 10.

chancellor and castellans.[27] Ambassadors were paid in gold in both years.[28]

The more limited shift in currency may derive from the fact that the nominal wages of most public employees did not increase from 1349 to 1350. Indeed, only two jobs (Chapter 4), musician and policeman (*berrovieri*) of the palace of the priors, received higher salaries. Both were paid in gold in 1349. Musicians' salaries reverted to silver in 1350.[29] The wages for policemen continued to be paid in gold in that year.

Castellan wages were paid in gold during both years, distinguishing that workforce from Italian mercenary cavalrymen, whom they otherwise resemble in terms of nominal rates. Italian cavalry wages went from gold to silver in 1349–1350. Castellans follow the example of German mercenaries, whose wage rates remained the same, but were always paid in gold. The policemen of the palace of the podestà meanwhile follow the general pattern of crossbowmen from Liguria and Lunigiana, with increases both in nominal rates and continued payment in gold in 1349–1350. Civic musicians' wages resemble those of shield bearers and crossbowmen from Modena and Bibbena. The nominal rates increased, but there was a shift from gold to silver. Italian mercenary cavalrymen again appear to have fared worse. Their nominal wages not only remained the same, but they received silver instead of gold. The wages of the podestà, judge of appeals, and other foreign judges remained stagnant, but were paid in gold in both years.

It is important to emphasize that the currency shifts occurred even though the average yearly exchange rate between gold and silver was, as previously noted, stable from 1349 to 1350.[30] A detailed inspection of daily rates, however, shows that although the general trend was one of stability, there were short-term fluctuations. From April to August 1349, the value of the florin moved gently downward, starting at just above 64 soldi and ending at just above 63 soldi. On 1 May 1349 it reached a peak at 64 soldi/8 denari (64.75 soldi), and at the end of August it reached a low of 62 soldi/10 denari (62.83 soldi). During the second campaign, the value of the gold florin moved in the other direction, increasing slightly with respect to silver from February to September 1350. In February, the exchange rate stood just below 63 soldi, and in September it was slightly above 64 lire. March 1350 was a surprisingly turbulent month. On 8 March, the gold

[27] ASF, Camera del comune, Scrivano di camera uscita 9 fols. 46r–47v.

[28] ASF, Camera del comune, Scrivano di camera uscita 6 fols. 3v, 4r, 4v, 5r, 8v; Scrivano di camera uscita 7 fols. 3v, 4r, 4r.

[29] ASF, Camera del comune; Scrivano di camera uscita 6 fols. 3v, 4r, 4v, 5r, 8v; Scrivano d camera uscita 7 fols. 3v, 4r, 4r; Scrivano d camera uscita 9 fols. 3v, 8v.

[30] Cipolla, *Monetary Policy*, p. 48.

Table 5.3 *Monthly Average Exchange Rates, 1349–1350*

January 1349	64 soldi
February 1349	64 soldi
April 1349	64 soldi
May 1349	64 soldi
June 1349	64 soldi
July 1349	63 soldi
August 1349	63 soldi
September 1349	63 soldi
October 1349	63 soldi
January 1350	63 soldi
February 1350	63 soldi
March 1350	64 soldi
April 1350	64 soldi
May 1350	64 soldi
June 1350	64 soldi
August 1350	64 soldi
September 1350	64 soldi

Note: Rates show the value of 1 florin to the nearest *soldo*.
Sources: The figures are taken from the budgets and differ from the figures given by Carlo M. Cipolla, who asserted that the florin fluctuated from 60 soldi to 63 soldi at this time. ASF, Camera del comune, Scrivano di camera uscita 6–10, camarlenghi uscita, 51–72; Cipolla, *Monetary Policy*, p. 49.

florin was worth 63 soldi/2 denari (63.17 soldi), and in little over a week (17 March 1350) it rose to 65 soldi/5 denari (65.41 soldi).[31] The increase evoked concerns in the city council and proved to be an augur of events of a year later, when the price of gold rose significantly with respect to silver.[32] It is unclear why there was such fluctuation in March 1350. Florentine officials in any case appear to have gotten the situation under control. The price of gold fell and by 1 April 1350 the florin was again worth 64 soldi, and on 10 May 1350, it dipped to 63 soldi/10 denari (63.83 soldi), where it had been the previous summer. Throughout June, August, and September 1350 the florin held firm at about 64 soldi.[33]

Much more work needs to be done on currency, including the effect of war itself on the overall supply of specie. We must look still more closely at

[31] ASF, Camera del comune, camarlenghi uscita 65 fol. 577r; camarlenghi uscita 66 fols. 585r–621r. Cipolla notes that in late March 1350 there was an abundance of silver in Florence. Cipolla, *Monetary Policy*, p. 49.

[32] ASF, Provvisioni, registri 38 fols. 3v–4r. See La Roncière, *Prix et salaries*, pp. 491–493.

[33] Mario Bernocchi, *Le Monete delle Repubblica Fiorentina*, vol. 1 (Florence: Leo S. Olschki, 1974), pp. 118–123, 126; vol. 3, pp. 196–197.

sources, to see whether Florence further alternated payments in silver and gold over the months. From our limited vantage, however, it seems clear that the decline in the relative value of the florin, albeit small during the first campaign in 1349, served as incentive for the city to pay in gold. Conversely, the increase in the value of gold during the second campaign, particularly the "scare" in March 1350, inclined city officials to hold onto gold florins and pay in silver. Given the high level of expenditure by the state at this time, the change to silver was collectively significant. It was financially advantageous for the city to limit the outflow of florins.

Most important from the perspective of this chapter is that currency *mattered* in the configuration of wages. Our evidence does not point to a single pattern, but various patterns and arrangements that Florence had with its employees. The differences are such that ringers of bells cannot be all lumped in the same category. Those who worked at the palace of the podestà in 1350 were paid in silver, while the bell ringers of the palace of the priors received their wages in gold.[34]

The reasons for the distinction are unclear. What is certain, however, is that Florentine officials carefully distinguished the type of currency it used, and payment in gold was a privilege to those who received it. The troop inspectors who reviewed men in the war zone in the Mugello in June 1349 were paid in gold. Troop inspectors who reviewed soldiers outside of the war zone were paid in silver.[35] Gold was a reward for more dangerous work. Similarly, *vetturali* and couriers who undertook hazardous missions such as bringing arms and supplies to Montegemoli during the siege and moving material to and from Scarperia at night were paid in gold.[36] Those who undertook more routine missions were paid in silver. Officials who worked for important government committees like the one that oversaw the imposition of the rural *estimo* in 1350 and attempted to increase revenue from gabelles, were paid in florins.[37] It is, in any case, not possible to explain currency shifts in wages solely by means of "intensified forces of supply and demand" owing to the immediate effects of the plague.

The same is true of taxation, an equally vexing subject of inquiry. Whatever advantages workers had as a result of the plague, it is clear that taxes on wages remained an accepted convention. Florentine

---

[34] ASF, Camera del comune, Scrivano di camera uscita 6 fol. 8v, Scrivano di camera uscita 7 fol. 9v, Scrivano di camera uscita 8 fol. 4v; Scrivano di camera uscita 9 fol. 7r.

[35] ASF, Camera del comune, Scrivano di camera uscita 6 fols. 17r, 17v, 18r, 21r; Scrivano di camera uscita 7 9v; Camera del comune, Scrivano di camera uscita 9 fols. 38v, 35r; Camera del comune, camarlenghi uscita 53 fols. 194r–205v.

[36] ASF, balie 7 fols. 33r–33v.

[37] ASF, Camera del comune, Scrivano di camera uscita 10 fol. 8v.

employees paid them, most notably the soldiers who fought for the city (Chapter 3).

But as with currency, the portrait of taxation needs to be further nuanced. As we have seen, the state granted exemptions to workers involved in the Ubaldini war effort, including artisans and suppliers at Scarperia, as well as messengers and *vetturali* in the field (Chapter 3). The crossbowmen hired in 1350 from Casteldurante bargained specifically, and successfully, for exemption from taxes on their wages by threatening to withhold their services.[38]

But bowmen from Casteldurante were the exception that proves the rule. The salaries of the overwhelming majority of soldiers were not exempt from taxes, including those of Florence's most successful cavalrymen and infantrymen. Indeed, soldiers were often the most heavily taxed of city employees (Chapter 4). They were responsible not only for imposts on their wages, but also for payment of fines (*difetti*) for failure to pass muster and other infractions. The castellans who defended the city forts also paid taxes on their wages, as did spies, troop inspectors, and others directly involved in the war. Ambassadors and musicians paid taxes on their wages, as did all of Florence's highly paid foreign judges.

The cameral budgets show that there was, however, a cadre of public officials whose wages were always exempt from taxes. These were chamberlains of the condotta, the *camera del arme* and *camera del comune*; the chancellor of the city, the two judges/*savi* who advised the chamberlains of the camera, the custodians and guards of the *camera*, the notary of the *Riformagione*, the accountants who balanced budgets, the notaries who wrote them up, and the policemen of the palace of the priors (Table 5.4).

It is not clear why this group of employees was singled out. It would appear incorrect to place the men in the same category as the tax-exempt artisans at Scarperia and others directly involved in the war effort. Perhaps the officials belong under a separate rubric entitled "personnel essential to the functioning of the commune." We may rightfully ask whether the tax break was compensation for low wages and substantial public responsibility, or whether it was related to currency, or given to those who were required to pay surety for their posts.

Generalizations are again elusive. The wages of the previously mentioned chamberlains were low and paid in silver. But the wages of the chancellor and notary of *Riformagione* were high and paid in florins. If exemptions were granted to employees who gave surety for their jobs, then the castellans, who paid large sums for their posts, belong

[38] ASF, balie 6 fol. 51r.

Table 5.4 *Florentine Wages Specifically Exempt from Taxes,*
1349–1350

Accountants of the *camera del comune*
Chamberlains of the *camera del arme*
Chamberlains of the *camera del comune*
Chamberlains of the condotta
Chancellor
Custodians/guards of the *camera del comune*
Judges/*savi* of the *camera del comune*
Notary for income of the *camera del comune*
Notary for expenditure of the *camera del comune*
Notary of the *Riformagione*
Policemen (*Berrovieri*) of the palace of the priors

on the list; they are not there. The chamberlains of the *camera del comune* included two monks, who as members of the church were not required to pay state taxes. But the other two chamberlains were lay officials and thus theoretically subject to them. The police force that protected the *palazzo dei priori* appears on the list of those exempt from tax, but the police force that protected the *palazzo del podestà* is not. Did Florence consider opportunity costs when granting tax exemptions to artisans at Scarperia, who may have had other options for employment (Chapter 3)? The questions are worth asking. In any case, taxation, like the wage rates themselves, cannot be explained entirely by market forces and "intensified forces of supply and demand" owing to the immediate effects of plague in 1349–1350.

When taxation is figured into our overall analysis, the policemen who guarded the palace of the priors emerge as the most fortunate of all city employees. They were the only public workers whose money wages increased from 1349 to 1350, who were paid both years in gold and did not pay taxes. Civic musicians, by contrast, received wage increases, but were paid in silver in 1350 and paid taxes. There was clearly something special about being a policeman at the palace of the priors.

The Florentine Public Workforce Revisited

Consideration of currency and taxation highlights the variety of factors that went into the configuration of salaries and the "numerous narratives" that they represent. William Beveridge was right to call wages "a puzzle" for those who study them, an assessment repeated by the modern economist and Nobel laureate Robert Solow, who spent much of his career trying to unravel present day patterns.[39]

It is important to stress again that our wage data is for *public* workers. The employees examined here all worked for the city of Florence, and thus their wages came from communal revenue. The current scholarly consensus is built on data from private institutions for Florence (hospitals, confraternities) and for Europe (monasteries, manors) more generally. The sources of revenue differed. As we have seen, the confraternity of Orsanmichele in Florence became rich from bequests of victims in the immediate aftermath of the plague, which affected its ability to pay its workers. Katharine Park noted in her study of Florentine doctors that rates of pay varied depending on the type of employer and were less for those who worked for private religious institutions.[40]

State revenue in Florence in 1349–1350 was reduced by the contagion and rendered more difficult to collect (Chapter 3).[41] Bruno Casini's brief but important analysis of Pisa showed that officials in that city had similar difficulties immediately after the Black Death. They were forced to consolidate government offices, eliminating some, suspending others, and even reducing wages. This occurred while city artisans and agricultural workers saw increases in their nominal wages.[42] In his seminal study of the effect of the Black Death on Siena, William Bowsky spoke of rises in wages, but his evidence for public workers (in an appendix) suggested a pattern of stagnation in that sector. The salary of the podestà (5,000 lire a semester) of Siena stayed the same from 1349 to 1350, and the nominal wage of the captain of war actually declined from 11,500 lire to 9,500 lire.[43] And Bowsky made clear that in Siena, as in Florence, private religious institutions fared comparatively well financially and that there was little legislation issued by the state restricting wages.[44]

---

[39] Robert M. Solow, "Insiders and Outsiders in Wage Determination," *Scandinavian Journal of Economics* 87 no. 2, Proceedings of a Conference on Trade Unions, Wage Formation and Macroeconomic Stability (June 1985), p. 411.

[40] Katharine Park, *Doctors and Medicine in Early Renaissance Florence* (Princeton, NJ: Princeton University Press, 1985), p. 99.

[41] Florentine city council legislation from 1349 to 1350 contains ample evidence of the difficulties. ASF, Provvisioni, registri 36 fols. 65r, 133v–134v; Provvisioni, registri 37 fol. 45v. See also Albert Benigno Falsini, "Firenze dopo il 1348: Le consequenze della peste nera," *Archivio storico italiano* 129 (1971), pp. 443–445.

[42] Bruno Casini, "Note sul potere di acquisto dei salari a Pisa nei primi anni della signoria gambacortiana," in *Studi in onore di Leopoldo Sandri*, vol. 1 (Rome: Ministero per i beni culturali e ambientali, 1983), pp. 227–275.

[43] William M. Bowsky, "The Impact of the Black Death upon Sienese Government and Society," *Speculum* 39 (1964), pp. 29, 34.

[44] Bowsky, "The Impact of the Black Death," pp. 16, 30–31.

Such issues are familiar to modern labor economists. In his detailed analysis of contemporary American public sector jobs for the U.S. National Labor Relations board, the economist Richard B. Freeman argued that public wages are determined above all by public revenue, which varies from year to year. Freeman emphasized the role of "budgeting" in the assignment of wages. Public officials allot a specific amount for a specific job. The Florentine budgets suggest that this was also the case in the distant past. The city often apportioned a specific sum directly to a job rather than to the individual performing it. For example, the city assigned 42 lire a month to the job of town crier, to be divided among the seven men in 1349 and 1350. Since the number of town criers stayed the same in both years, the nominal wage of each worker also remained the same. Similarly, city officials assigned 400 lire each semester for the six superintendents (*soprastanti*) of the communal prison (*stinche*) and 100 lire per semester for the two monk/chamberlains of the *camera del comune*.

The importance of the practice for understanding public wages is evident in the case of the now familiar *berrovieri* of the palace of the priors. When the city increased their wages in 1350, it reduced the size of the overall force from one hundred to ninety men. The stated reason in the communal legislation was that it was "necessary for the state" to spend "as little money as possible."[45] Thus, despite the pay raise for individual policemen, Florence actually spent only 15 lire more (750 lire to 765 lire) for the whole force from 1349 to 1350. The same rationale appears in the legislation of 14 July 1349, which raised the salaries of infantrymen in the Florentine army. The city sought to impose a limit on the number of men (150) hired at that rate to minimize overall expenditure.[46]

How frequently the city did this with other jobs remains to be studied. But the last example exposes the limits of the practice. The expedient regarding infantrymen did not, as we have seen, work. Florence continued to hire men at increasingly higher wage rates. As Freeman himself ultimately concluded about the modern day American labor force: budgeting notwithstanding, public wages do indeed respond to economic conditions.[47] In Florence, infantry rates grew dramatically despite severe constraints on public finance.

There are additional factors that went into the configuration of Florentine wages. The Franciscan monk and economic thinker Pierre Olivi (d. 1298) argued that jobs requiring skill and knowledge demanded

---

[45] "utilia est *modico* expedere" ASF, Provvisioni, registri 36 fol. 145v.

[46] ASF, Provvisioni, registri 36 fol. 132r.

[47] Richard B. Freeman, "How Do Public Sector Wages and Employment Respond to Economic Conditions?" in *Public Sector Payrolls*, edited by David A. Wise (Chicago, IL: University of Chicago Press, 1987), pp. 183–184, 202–203.

higher pay, reasoning that high office should be compensated on account of "expertise, lengthy experience and study."[48] This does not appear to have been true of the Florentine public workforce. Chamberlains of important offices routinely received low wages paid in silver, as did the judges/*savi* who advised them.

Skill and expertise, however, may have been a factor in the assessment of wages of notaries, who generally earned well in comparison to other employees. The wage of the notary of the condotta (15 lire a month), for example, was the highest of all the employees of that office and more than 2½ times more than the salary of the chamberlain in charge of it.[49] The wage may reflect opportunities for such men in the private sector, where they also often received compensation for individual transactions in which they participated.

Social status is a similarly uncertain variable. Cavalrymen earned high salaries, befitting their societal rank. But knighthood, a notable distinction, allowed Italian cavalrymen, as we saw in the previous chapter, higher wages, 25 percent higher than for those who were not knights. But the distinction did not apply to German cavalrymen, who received the same pay whether a knight or not. The reason for this is nowhere stated in the sources.

Knightly status was a factor in the wages of Florentine ambassadors. Those listed in budgets as "dominus" or "militus" (knights) received higher pay than those who were not designated as such. Pay in this instance was linked to the number of horses with which the ambassador traveled.[50] The knight/ambassador traveled with four horses whereas it was customary for a non-knightly ambassador to travel with three. Florence assessed salary according to a formula consisting of 1 lira per horse, so the knight/ambassador earned 4 lire per day as opposed to 3 lire a day for the non-knight. The larger entourage added to the pomp and display of the embassy, but it also increased the cost to the ambassador. Interestingly, ambassadors' salaries do not appear to account for the distance the men traveled. The formula for pay generally remained the

---

[48] Odd Langholm, *Economics in Medieval Schools: Wealth, Exchange, Value, Money, and Usury According to the Paris Theological Tradition, 1200–1350* (Leiden: Brill, 1992), p. 363; Diana Wood, *Medieval Economic Thought* (Cambridge: Cambridge University Press, 2002), p. 153.

[49] ASF, Camera del comune, Scrivano di camera uscita 7 fol. 10v.

[50] Alessandro Gherardi, "L'antica camera del comune di Firenze e un quaderno d'uscita de' suoi camarlinghi dell'anno 1303," *Archivio storico italiano* 26 (1885), p. 329. See also the statute of the 1325, which gives the same formula and suggests that ambassadors travel with a notary. *Statuti della Repubblica fiorentina, Statuto del Capitano del Popolo: 1322–25*, vol. 2, edited by Giuliano Pinto, Francesco Salvestrini, and Andrea Zorzi (Florence: Leo S. Olschki, 1999), pp. 57–59.

same whether the embassy was to a neighboring commune or to a foreign country.

The connection between nominal wages and number of horses maintained provides an interesting potential link to status. It may well have been that Italian cavalry captains who were knights maintained more horses than those who were not, and that all German captains had the same number of horses. The wages of *vetturali*, who transported food and provisions, was linked to the *type* of animals they used. Transport by donkey earned the men 19 soldi a day and transport by mule earned them 10 soldi a day.

The size of personal entourages or *comitive* was, as we saw in Chapter 4, another factor in pay. The salaries of Florence's foreign judges – the highest of all Florentine employees – depended directly on number of helpers (people, not animals) in their *comitive*, whom they themselves were responsible for paying. The entourages may themselves have reflected the status of the judges, or perhaps just the realities of the execution of their jobs.

Once again the economic value of knighthood is inconsistent. The judge of appeals, Nicholaio di Matteo of Urbino, in 1350 is listed in the cameral budget as a knight (*Messer*), but his counterpart in 1349 is not.[51] Yet both men earned the same pay. The size of their entourages may have differed, but this is not known. The executor of justice in 1350, Guadagno di Ser Landi Becci of Gubbio, is not listed as a knight, but, curiously, his *compagno*, Bindo di Ser Spoglie, who worked under him at a considerably lower nominal wage, is listed as one.[52] In 1349, the *compagno* of the executor, Biaggio of Città di Castello, was not a knight, but he received the same wage as Bindo, who was a knight. It is again unclear whether the sizes of their respective *comitive* differed. Indeed, we cannot be entirely sure if the changes in designation owed to actual differences in the status of the workers or are the result of omissions on the part of the scribe who wrote out the budgets!

What is undeniably true is that the employees just discussed and designated as knights in the Florentine budgets did *not* see increases in their money wages from 1349 to 1350 and all were paid in gold.[53] The evidence links well to our discussion of mercenary cavalrymen at the end of Chapter 4, who likewise possessed the status and skills to demand higher wages, but did not receive them. The podestà was always a knight and his wage remained stagnant even though he possessed the

---

[51] ASF, Camera del comune, Scrivano di camera uscita 9 fol. 3r; Scrivano di camera uscita 6 fol. 4r.

[52] ASF, Camera del comune, Scrivano di camera uscita 10 fol. 4v.

[53] ASF, Camera del comune, Scrivano di camera uscita 8 fol. 2r; Scrivano di camera uscita 10 fol. 2v.

highly desired skills of policing and meting out civic justice. It may have been that such skills were suited only to public employment, for which there were limited opportunities just after the plague, owing to a lack of public revenue, not only in Florence but throughout Italy. In any case, it appears that Florence's ostensibly most skilled and mobile employees did not receive increased wages after the plague despite dramatically favorable market forces. The evidence directly contradicts A. B. Falsini's view that such workers, in short supply, were particularly favored.[54]

As a final point, it is worth stressing again the heterogeneous nature of the Florentine public workforce. A large number of the employees came from outside the city. These included the major judges, who brought with them substantial *comitive* from their home bases. In 1350, the executor of justice was from Brescia, the podestà from Modena, and the judge of appeals was from Urbino.[55] Meanwhile, the notary of the *Riformagione* was from Pratovecchio (near Arezzo), the captain of the police force of the palace of the priors was from Montalcino (south of Siena), and the public doctor was from Rome, as was the *sindaco*. The "foreign" presence was, in combination with the Florentine army, significant, and notable with regard to understanding wages that are often viewed as dependent on the mobility of workers.

Contradiction, Anomaly, and Occupation

The evidence adds important nuance to our understanding of Florentine wages. It reveals an array of factors such that it is necessary to speak of multiple social and economic systems with regard to Florentine labor markets and of contradiction and anomaly rather than coherence. The diverse arrangements collectively tell their own tale, even if our data is not "usable" for the long term. What emerges is a variety of special conditions that give a more accurate account of what was actually going on.

If we accept anomaly rather than suppress it, our evidence in fact links well to other wage studies for Florence. Bruno Dini and Franco Franceschi have highlighted the diverse arrangements with workers in the wool cloth industry, Florence's biggest business. Franceschi asserted that the "estrema varietà" of conditions of employment required the "work of an alchemist" to sort out its hierarchies.[56] Employees were

---

[54] Falsini, "Firenze dopo il 1348," p. 441.

[55] According to the statute of Podesta in 1325, the *comitiva* of the judge of appeals was not from his own town. *Statuti della Repubblica*, vol. 2, edited by Pinto, Salvestrini, and Zorzi, pp. 25–32.

[56] Franco Franceschi, *Oltre il "tumulto" I lavoratori fiorentini dell'Arte della lana fra Tre e Quattrocento* (Florence: Leo S. Olschki, 1993), p. 199.

paid according to piece rate, by day, by week, and by year.[57] La Roncière in his essay "La condition des salaries à Florence au XIVe siècle" called the wool cloth industry "the heart of the salaried workforce" ("le coeur du salariat") of fourteenth-century Florence, but concluded that the many terms of service and payment of wages were too confusing for useful study.[58] Sergio Tognetti concurred, noting that the complicated nature of wage arrangement for the wool cloth industry did not offer "clear patterns over the long term."[59]

Dini's notion of "two markets" – one for "stable" personnel in the wool business, who worked at the same shop after the plague and received generally low salaries, and a second for "more mobile workers," who moved from one shop (bottega) to another and received higher salaries – does not apply to Florentine public workers in 1349–1350.[60] But the diversity of arrangements and lack of clear pattern resemble the Florentine public workforce. The common element is fragmentation. Indeed, if we remove the discussion of the wool cloth industry from the strictures of the debate about the "proletarianization" of the Florentine workforce and the later Ciompi revolt in 1378, we see important suppor-tive evidence. Both Dini and Franceschi see changes in the conditions of employment of workers' attendant the Black Death more than shifts in remuneration. Franceschi asserted that the most basic change from the first half of the fourteenth century to the second as a "lessening of control by employers" of the workforce, now disinclined to tie themselves to a single shop.[61]

The evidence corresponds with what scholars have found for else-where in Europe. Christopher Dyer has noted that in England after 1349, "work patterns were more fragmented," as men moved around for jobs "and even seeking leisure time."[62] In an essay written together with Simon Penn, Dyer showed how diverse the choices could be. Short-term, seasonal workers in England pursued a variety of occupations, including seemingly radical shifts such as a ploughman who also worked

---

[57] Bruno Dini, "I lavoratori dell'Arte della Lana a Firenze nel XIV e XV secolo" in *Artigiani e salariati. Il mondo del lavoro nell'Italia dei secoli XII–XV, Pistoia, 9–13 ottobre 1981* (Bologna: Centro Italiano di Studi di Storia e d'Arte, 1984), pp. 34–40.

[58] Charles M. de La Roncière, "La condition des salaries à Florence au XIVe siècle" in *Tumulto dei Ciompi: un momento di storia fiorentina ed Europea*, edited by Atti del Convegno internazionale (Florence: Leo S. Olschki, 1981), p. 17. See also La Roncière, *Prix et salaries*, pp. 262–264.

[59] Tognetti, "Prezzi e salari," p. 264.   [60] Dini, "I lavoratori dell'Arte," p. 49.

[61] Franceschi, *Oltre il "tumulto,"* pp. 203–204, 328–330; Dini, "I lavoratori dell'Arte," pp. 49–50.

[62] Christopher Dyer, *Standard of Living in the Later Middle Ages: Social Change in England, 1200–1320* (Cambridge: Cambridge University Press, 1989), p. 224.

as a mariner.[63] The evidence corresponds with French and Spanish legislation of 1351 that sought not only to control wage rates, but to limit short-term employment and the mobility of workers.[64]

The fragmentation calls still further into question the notion of occupation at this time, which cannot so easily be transferred to the modern day. The same plague that affected wages also affected the conditions of employment. Florentine cameral budgets give evidence that the city took this into consideration. Employees who worked for the office of the *condotta*, for example, were paid once every four months. This was, as we saw in Chapter 2, because the men had other jobs.[65] Few Florentine public or private wages were figured by year and there is little evidence that contemporary Florentines conceived of wages in the yearly sense that we do today. The chancellor of the city was among the few public employees whose wage was quoted yearly. The overwhelming evidence suggests that Florence conceived of salaries in the short term. Indeed, the budgets of the *camera del comune* were compiled on a bimonthly basis, not on a yearly one.

The point is vital because the extension of wages to yearly sums is precisely what long-range studies have done. Scholars consciously choose data that can be "translated," to the present day. La Roncière chose the day wages of workers of the hospital of Santa Maria Nuova, which he admitted were "très lacunaire," because he believed they were most suited to a modern apprehension of wages.[66] Scholars use 250 days as the number for conversion into yearly wages, a figure that accounts for religious holidays, when medieval men did not work.[67] They use 22 days, as we have seen, to translate the wages into monthly ones. But the conversions ignore the basic nature of the employment of the men in their historical context.[68] In Florence, for example, the podestà and other foreign judges served for a "semester" or six months, and were paid accordingly (per semester). Communal statute mandated that they be replaced after their term was over. They did not work, and *could* not work, for a full year. *Castellani*, according to the statute of 1322, were not allowed to serve consecutive terms.[69] Thus extension of the wages to fit modern perceptions is prima facie ahistorical.

---

[63] Simon Penn and Christopher Dyer, "Wages and Earnings in Late Medieval England: Evidence from the Enforcement of the Labour," *Economic History Review* 43 (1990), pp. 360–366.

[64] Wood, *Medieval Economic Thought*, p. 145.

[65] ASF, Camera del comune, Scrivano di camera uscita 10 fol. 4r.

[66] La Roncière, "La condition des salaries," pp. 14, 17.

[67] Allen, "Great Divergence," pp. 425–426; Tognetti, "Prezzi e salari," p. 265.

[68] The first step in configuring standard of living, as the economist Robert Allen asserts, is to determine total earnings over a year. Allen, "Great Divergence," p. 413.

[69] *Statuti della Repubblica fiorentina*, vol. 1, pp. 23–24.

This is especially true with respect to war. As we have seen, Florence paid daily wages to the officers of its army, in addition to their monthly rates. The daily wage was used exactly because the service was temporary. It ended when the service work ended. It is thus incorrect to extrapolate yearly pay either from the daily rate or even the monthly rates.

The far more common element with respect to Florentine employees is the stagnant nature of their wages. The coincidence with the wool cloth industry is apparent. Franceschi's carefully culled figures showed a general stability and even decline in wages (daily and piece rate) in the wool cloth industry from the last third of *trecento* to the first third of the *quattrocento*.[70] Phelps Brown and Hopkins in their famous synthetic study of building wages of England found that "stickiness" was a general characteristic for 500 of the 690 years they examined.[71] Even William Beveridge, although he accepted Thorold Rogers' notion of a "panic and compulsion" in markets immediately after the plague, in fact found little increase in wage rates from 1349 to 1350 in his data from Winchester manors."[72]

When the teleological aspect is thus removed from the study of wages, the most basic statement we can make is that occupation and the compensation that went along with it were different then from today. Florentine workers often did more than one thing. The workforce was variable and made more so in the immediate aftermath of the plague.[73]

The point should not be surprising. The evidence for a different concept of occupation in medieval Florence is readily at hand for students of the city. Buonaccorso Pitti's famous fourteenth-century diary depicts a life worthy of a picaresque novel. But it also begs the question: what did Buonaccorso actually do for a living? The answer is a number of things. He traded horses and commodities, gambled at various courts, and fought as a mercenary soldier in the battles of the Hundred Years War. Likewise, Donato Velutti's diary makes clear that the title of "judge" is inadequate. He was also a merchant and a diplomat, and he held numerous governmental posts.

Servants, Bell Ringers, and Cooks

The most striking evidence of the variable nature of occupation is the job of ambassador. In medieval Florence, the post was short-term and

---

[70] Franceschi, "*Oltre il "tumulto*," pp. 246–247.
[71] E. H. Phelps Brown and Sheila V. Hopkins, "Seven Centuries of Building Wages," *Economica* 22 (1955), p. 202.
[72] Beveridge, "Winchester," pp. 26–27.
[73] Dyer, *Standard of Living*, p. 213; Z. Razi, "Family, Land and the Village in Later Medieval England," *Past and Present* 93 (1981), pp. 31–33.

involved the participation of prominent citizens, who, as Richard Trexler has asserted, represented the city's "highest honor and deepest aspirations."[74] As we have seen, Donato Velluti served as ambassador to Bologna just prior to the second campaign against the Ubaldini.

The constriction of the Florentine workforce, however, made the job of ambassador available to a broader range of people. Two of Florence's town criers, Salvi Lapi and Martino Lapi, went on embassy to the town of Montopoli in July 1349. The *capomaestro* stonemason, Stefano Pucci, who worked during the war at Scarperia, served as ambassador in the Mugello in April 1349.[75] Four civic musicians, Pagno Bertini, Ghettino Ture (both *tubatori*), Betto Vanucci (*nacherino*), and Brunello Durante (*trombetta*) went on embassy to Prato for seven days in August 1350.[76]

The practice is easily missed because the documents do not in any way distinguish these embassies from others. Civic musicians, as Timothy McGee has pointed out, occasionally accompanied ambassadors on diplomatic missions.[77] Guidubaldo Guidi has spoken of "mandatari," lower-level informal messengers, who sometimes preceded formal embassies.[78] But our examples are of independent full-scale embassies involving Florentine employees not associated with the job. The sources refer to the men as "honorabiles cives ambaxiatores" and "cives populares Florentinis ambaxiatores pro comuni Florentie." The vernacular term "oratore" is also used.[79] The citations are precisely the same as those used for the embassies of Donato Velluti and Niccolò di Bartolo del Buono, Boccaccio's wealthy friend, who served as ambassador "to parts of the Romagna" just prior to the attack on Petrarch's friends in May 1349.[80]

The use of such men was extensive and included most frequently, and most dramatically, members of the Florentine *famiglia*, the civic employees that Gene Brucker refers to as "petty officials" of the Signoria, and Nicolai Rubinstein describes as "servants," who attended the priors at the

---

[74] Richard Trexler, *Public Life in Renaissance Florence* (New York, NY: Academic Press, 1980), pp. 279–330. See now Isabella Lazzarini, *Communication and Conflict: Italian Diplomacy in the Early Renaissance, 1350–1520* (Oxford: Oxford University Press, 2015).

[75] ASF, Camera del comune, Scrivano di camera uscita 7 fol. 9r; Camera del comune, camarlenghi uscita 53 fol. 200v.

[76] ASF, Camera del comune, Scrivano di camera uscita 10 fol. 8v.

[77] Timothy McGee, *The Ceremonial Musicians of Late Medieval Florence* (Bloomington, IN: Indiana University Press, 2009), p. 51.

[78] Guidubaldo Guidi, *Il governo della città-repubblica di Firenze del primo quattrocento*, vol. 2 (Florence: Leo S. Olschki, 1981), pp. 217–219.

[79] ASF, Camera de comune, camarlenghi uscita 60 fol. 466v.

[80] ASF, Camera del comune, Scrivano di camera uscita 7 fol. 5r. The similarity of the embassies has disguised the practice from scholars. Cipolla cites the embassy of Giovanni Paoli and Piero Alderotti of 18 June 1350 alongside the others with no statement about the jobs of the men. Carlo Cipolla, *Francesco Petrarca e le sue relazioni colla corte Avignonese al tempo di Clemente VI* (Turin: Vincenzo Bona, 1909), p. 41.

dinner table and their bedrooms.[81] The Florentine *famiglia* in 1349 and 1350 consisted of eleven men: six *donzelli*/servants of the priors, two bell ringers of the palace of the priors, and the communal cook and his two assistants.[82] The terms *donzelli, servitori,* and *famigliari* are used interchangeably in budgets.[83]

Florence employed members of the *famiglia* to go on long-distance, long-term embassies to important destinations. In June 1349, at the start of the Ubaldini campaign, Florence sent three *donzelli* (Giovanni Pieri, Fastello Bonaiuti, and Arrigho Mazzei), and the bell ringer of the palace of the priors (Francesco Mini) on embassy to "parts of Germany" ("ad partes Magna") for sixty-eight days.[84] In August 1349, Florence sent the cook Chambino Gianini and the other bell ringer of the palace of the priors Giovanni Paoli, nicknamed "il schocchino" or "little idiot," to Hungary for 104 days.[85] Soon after the end of his embassy to Hungary, "schocchino" was sent on embassy to the papal court at Avignon for forty days, with the *donzello* Piero Alderotti.[86]

A bell ringer in Avignon? A cook in Hungary? There is nothing in the current scholarly literature to prepare us for such embassies.[87]

---

[81] Gene Brucker, "Bureaucracy and Social Welfare in the Renaissance," *Journal of Modern History* 55 (March 1983), p. 4; Nicolai Rubinstein, *The Palazzo Vecchio, 1298–1532* (Oxford: Oxford University Press, 1995), p. 21; Guidi calls them "personale esecutivo del priorato" and, based on 1415, he includes *tavolaccini, messi* (12) *trombetti* (8). Guidi, *Il governo della città-repubblica di Firenze*, vol. 2, pp. 38–39.

[82] There is disagreement about the size of the *famiglia*. Brucker says the group consisted of 140 men, a number that includes the police force. Brucker, "Bureaucracy and Social Welfare," p. 4. I have taken my number from the cameral budgets themselves and those officials specifically identified there as *famiglia*.

[83] ASF, Camera del comune, Scrivano di camera uscita 6 fol. 5v.

[84] The *donzelli* each traveled with three horses at a salary of 3 lire a day; Mini, the bell ringer, traveled with two horses and was paid 2 lire a day. ASF, Camera del comune, Scrivano di camera usciya 6 fol. 8v.

[85] Each traveled with three horses at a salary of 3 lire a day. ASF, Camera del comune, Scrivano di camera uscita 7 fol. 10r.

[86] ASF, Camera del comune, camarlenghi uscita 65 fol. 580r.

[87] See among others Nicolai Rubinstein, "Florence and the Despots: Some Aspects of Florentine Diplomacy in the Fourteenth Century," *Transactions of the Royal Historical Society* 2 (1952), pp. 21–45; Donald Queller, "The Development of Ambassadorial *Relazioni*" in *Renaissance Venice*, edited by J. R. Hale (London: Faber and Faber, 1973), pp. 174–196; *Politics and Diplomacy in Early Modern Italy: The Structure of Diplomatic Practice, 1450–1800*, edited by Daniela Frigo (Cambridge: Cambridge University Press), p. 262; Riccardo Fubini, "L'istituzione diplomatica e la figura dell'ambasciatore nel XV secolo (in particolare riferimento a Firenze)" in *L'Italia alla fine del Medioevo: I caratteri originali nel quadro europeo*, edited by Francesco Salvestrini (Florence: Florence University Press, 2006), pp. 333–354; Michael Mallett, "Ambassadors and Their Audiences in Renaissance Italy," *Renaissance Studies: Journal of the Society for Renaissance Studies* 8 no. 3 (1994), pp. 229–243; Sharon Dale, "Contra damnationis filios: the Visconti in Fourteenth-Century Papal Diplomacy," *Journal of Medieval History* 33 no. 1 (March 2007), pp. 1–32; William M. Bowsky, "Italian Diplomatic History:

The Florentine statute of 1325 speaks of special priority given to ambassadors sent to the "papacy, kings and emperors," allowing higher wages, and disallowing employment for more than six months.[88] Meanwhile, Brucker argued that the members of the Florentine *famiglia* were recruited from the "lower levels" of society.[89] Petrarch in *Familiares* VIII, 4 suggested that cooks were perceived as the "most vile" of servants. The modern scholar Christopher Dyer in his study of standards of living in England called servants in that country "the lowest position of all" in the social hierarchy.[90]

Nevertheless, servants of the Florentine Signoria were the most well-traveled of all communal employees. In October 1349, the two *donzelli* Piero Alderotti and Gherardo Amananti went on embassy to the pope at Avignon for seventy-four days.[91] Alderotti then returned to the city in December, long enough, according to the cameral budget, to perform the domestic task of purchasing food and drink for the meals of the priors and members of the Signoria. Alderotti then left that same day to go to Hungary ("ad partes Hungarie") with another servant Fastello Bonaiuti, where he stayed for 115 days.[92] Alderotti then traveled at the beginning of 1350 to Avignon ("ad partes Vignone") with Giovanni Paoli, the bell ringer.[93] In June 1350, Alderotti and Paoli went to Milan for sixty days.[94] If we include Alderotti's embassy in late May 1349 for sixty-one days to Puglia, then in little over a year – from May 1349 to August 1350 – Alderotti spent 350 days on embassy.[95] He visited in succession Puglia, Avignon, Hungary, Germany, and Milan.

The itinerary is extraordinary! The places to which Alderotti traveled were all critical to Florentine diplomacy – the papacy, the Holy Roman Emperor, the lords of Milan, the king of Hungary, and the warring factions of the Angevin family in Puglia. The journeys of other members of the *famiglia* were similar. The *donzello* Arrigho Mazzei went on embassy to "parts of Germany" for 68 days in June 1349,[96] to Hungary for 105

A Case for the Smaller Commune" in Order and Innovation in the Middle Ages: Essays in Honor of Joseph R. Strayer, edited by William C. Jordan, Bruce McNab, and Teofilo F. Ruiz (Princeton, NJ: Princeton University Press, 1976), pp. 55–74.

[88] *Statuti della Repubblica fiorentina*, vol. 2, pp. 57–59.

[89] Brucker, "Bureaucracy and Social Welfare," p. 4.

[90] Dyer, *Standards of Living*, p. 233.

[91] ASF, Camera del comune, camarlenghi uscita 35 fol. 213v.

[92] ASF, Camera del comune, camarlenghi uscita 60 fol. 464r.

[93] ASF, Camera del comune, camarlenghi uscita 65 fol. 580r.

[94] ASF, Camera del comune, Scrivano di camera uscita 9 fol. 4v.

[95] ASF, Camera del comune, camarlenghi uscita 58 fol. 508v; camarlenghi uscita 60 fol. 404r; Scrivano di camera uscita 6 fol. 4v.

[96] ASF, Camera del comune, Scrivano di camera uscita 6 fol. 5r; camarlenghi uscita 56 fol. 552v.

days, starting in August 1349,[97] and to Avignon for 173 days in December 1349.[98] In the space of a year, Mazzei was ambassador for 346 days! The bell ringer Giovanni Paoli, "il schocchino," traveled to Hungary for 104 days (August 1349),[99] to Germany for 71 days (October 1349), to Avignon for 40 days (April 1350),[100] and Milan for 60 days (June 1350).[101] From August 1349 to August 1350, Paoli was on embassy for 275 days! During the same period, the cook, Chambio Gianini, traveled to Germany, Hungary, and Lombardy on embassies spanning 253 days.[102]

The *famigliari* were thus among the few Florentine employees who actually worked the requisite number of days that scholars have used as the baseline for comparative wage study. Their prolonged service is all the more surprising given Garrett Mattingly's famous assertion that long-term embassies were "a creation of the Italian Renaissance" in the fifteenth and sixteenth centuries and an expression of a "new kind of state, "the Renaissance state," which also coincided with a "new style of classical scholarship."[103]

It would be inaccurate to portray the embassies in 1349–1350 as long term in the sense that Mattingly understood the term. Mattingly's Renaissance diplomat resided full time at a specific court. The members of the Florentine *famiglia* appear to have rotated among several courts, traveling most frequently to Avignon, Germany, and Hungary. From 1349 to 1350, Florence always had a servant, bell ringer, or cook at the papal court in Avignon, Florence's most important and problematic ally. The Florentine budgets leave no doubt that the men were at the "corte di Roma a Avignone," that is, visiting the pope and his entourage.

The service of the *famigliari* highlights again the problematic nature of modern notions of occupation posited into the distant past. It also highlights the discrepancy between nominal wages and actual income outlined in Chapter 4. The members of the *famiglia* stood at the bottom of the Florentine public pay scale, earning only 4 lire a month. But in reality, when their embassies are figured into the equation, they were among Florence's highest paid officials.

[97] ASF, Camera del comune, Scrivano di camera uscita 7 fol. 10r.
[98] ASF, Camera del comune, camarlenghi uscita 60 fol. 464r.
[99] ASF, Camera del comune, Scrivano di camera uscita 5 fol. 3v; Scrivano di camera uscita 7 fol. 10r.
[100] ASF, Camera del comune, camarlenghi uscita 65 fol. 580r.
[101] ASF, Camera del comune, camarlenghi uscita 67 fol. 629r.
[102] ASF, Camera del comune, Scrivano di camera uscita 10r; Camera del comune, camarlenghi uscita 35 fol. 21r; camarlenghi uscita 60 fol. 424v.
[103] Garrett Mattingly, *Renaissance Diplomacy* (New York, NY: Penguin Books, 1955), p. 51.

For his trip to Naples for 74 days the servant Puccino Bartoli earned 222 lire, paid him in florins (69 florins). The bell ringer Giovanni Paoli earned 725 lire, again paid in florins (227 florins), for his 275 days as ambassador. The cook Chambino Gianini earned 655 lire or 205 florins for 253 days of service, and the servant Arrigo Mazzei earned an astounding 1,038 lire (324 florins) for his embassies from August 1349 to August 1350.[104] Mazzei's salary was more than three times greater than the yearly wage of the chancellor of the city (100 florins), and only a little less than the semester wage of the judge of appeals (350 florins), whose salary went also to pay a substantial entourage.[105] And like those men, the ambassadors were paid in florins.

Meanwhile, the protracted service of the men as ambassadors would appear to have left the Signoria without the usual personnel to handle daily chores. In October 1349, nine of the eleven *famigliari* were away on embassy, including the cook Gianni Chambini, who was in Germany, and the two bell ringers, who were in Aquileia and Germany, respectively. We may rightly ask: who then was preparing the food for the Signoria, tucking the priors in bed at night, and ringing the bell at the palace of the priors? In June of 1350, nine of eleven *famigliari* were again on embassy, including both bell ringers.

The questions are important, as bell ringers in particular were critical to the conduct of daily life. The sounding of bells, as Robert Davidsohn notes, convened councils into session and warned against advancing enemies. But more surprisingly, Florence conducted its foreign policy in a completely unexpected manner. It sent *famigliari* to politically sensitive places at important times. The *famigliari* visited the Hungarian king while he was fighting the rival branch of the Angevins for control of the kingdom of Naples. They went to Milan while that city was actively plotting in the Romagna.[106] Piero Alderotti's embassy to Puglia on 3 June 1349 (for 72 days) coincided with the fateful battle of Meleto (6 June 1349), which saw the defeat of the Hungarian Angevins by the French Angevins. The embassy of the cook and bell ringer to Hungary

---

[104] ASF, Camera del comune, Scrivano di camera uscita 5 fol. 3v; Scrivano di camera uscita 7 fol. 10r.

[105] The embassies are among the largest expenditures listed in the budgets. The embassy to Puglia in May 1349 for sixty-one days cost the city 236 florins overall. ASF, Camera del comune, Scrivano di camera uscita 6 fol. 4v. The embassy to Germany in June 1349 cost the city 265 florins. ASF, Camera del comune, Scrivano di camera uscita 6 fol. 8v. The embassy to Aquileia cost 203 florins. ASF, Camera del comune, Scrivano di camera uscita 10 fol. 7v. The embassy to Germany and Hungary at the beginning August 1349 for 105 days cost 400 florins. ASF, Camera del comune, Scrivano di camera uscita 7 fol. 10r.

[106] Gene Brucker, *Florentine Politics and Society, 1343–1378* (Princeton, NJ: Princeton University Press, 1962), pp. 141–142.

in August 1349 coincided with the signing of a truce in the war in Naples. Puccino Bartoli's stay in Naples coincided with the devastating earthquake that hit the region in September 1349.[107] The bell ringer Giovanni Paoli's embassy to Milan in May and June 1350 occurred at the same time that the Florentine army was in the field against the Ubaldini and tensions ran high between Milan and the papacy over issues in the Romagna, near the fighting.[108] Even the embassy of the *donzelli* Fastello Bonaiuti, Giovanni Pieri, Arrigo Mazzei and the bell ringer Francesco Mini to Aquilea in June 1350 is noteworthy.[109] Aquileia was the seat of a powerful patriarchate and a key entry point for Germans into Italy as well the flow of goods to and from the peninsula. When the Florentine embassy arrived (for fifty-four days) the patriarch, Bertrand of St. Genesius, a Gascon, was then at war with the neighboring count of Gorizia.[110]

The evidence contradicts our basic understanding of the Florentine diplomat and communal diplomacy at this time. The chronicler Giovanni Villani devoted one of the lengthiest discussions in his chronicle to Florence's embassy to the king of Hungary in 1347. He described a lavish public spectacle, with ambassadors – all prominent Florentine citizens – dressed in scarlet robes, attending the monarch. Villani lamented that the embassy was in fact not opulent enough because it lacked members of nobility, which would have added still greater luster. The historian Richard Trexler has emphasized the ritual aspects of Florentine diplomacy and the connection to civic identity.[111] More recently, scholars have stressed the stirrings in this period of the employment of the humanist ambassador – and the effect more generally of humanism on diplomatic practice.[112] Boccaccio, as we have seen, began his diplomatic service for Florence at this time, visiting Dante's sister in September 1350 and, most famously, going to Padua to speak with

[107] Paolo Antonio Costantino Galli and José Alfredo Naso, "Unmasking the 1349 Earthquake Source: Paleoseismological and Archaeoseismological Indications from the Aquae Iuliae fault," *Journal of Structural Geology* 31 (2009), pp. 128–149.

[108] ASF, Camera del comune, Scrivano di camera uscita 9 fol. 4v.

[109] ASF, Camera del comune, camarlenghi uscita 58 fol. 507v.

[110] Carlo Cipolla, *Documenti per la Storia delle relazioni diplomatiche* (Venice: A spese della Societa, 1907), pp. 477–478, 483–488.

[111] Trexler, *Public Life in Renaissance Florence*, p. 291.

[112] See Patrick Gilli, "La fonction d'ambassadeurs d'après les textes juridiques italiens du XVe siècle et le traité de Martino Garati da Lodi: une impossible representation," *Mélanges de l'Ecole française de Rome. Moyen Âge* 121 no. 1 (2009), pp. 173–187 and "Il discorso politico fiorentino nel Rinascimento e l' umanesimo civile" in *Firenze e la Toscana. Genesi e trasformazioni di uno stato (XIV–XIX secolo)*, edited by Jean Boutier, Sandro Landi, Olivier Rouchon (Florence: Mandragora, 2010), pp. 255–271; Brian Maxson, *The Humanist World of Renaissance Florence* (Cambridge: Cambridge University Press, 2014), pp. 14, 15, 89, 110–111.

Petrarch in the spring of 1351. Petrarch himself served as ambassador on numerous occasions, including to the Hungarian king (on behalf of the papacy) in 1347.

The Florentine *famigliari* were not humanists. Indeed, it is not at all clear who they were, nor do we know the precise nature of their embassies. Curiously, letters of instructions to ambassadors have survived for these years, including those written to Donato Velluti and Sandro Biliotti relating to the Ubaldini. These are in *Missive I Cancelleria 10*, which was partially transcribed by Demetrio Marzi and Agostino Pepoli in the nineteenth century.[113] But none of the extant instructions in the *Missive* relate to the ambassadorial activities of the members of the *famiglia*. One wonders whether this was intentional; whether the city wanted to keep the embassies secret.

In any case, the reliance on such men may likewise be read as evidence of the undesirability of the job of ambassador. Donato Velluti himself stated this in his diary. Velluti complained about the sacrifice that his embassy to Bologna in 1350 entailed.[114] He lamented the discomfort and inconvenience of travel and the necessity of abandoning his children, house, and goods, while his wife was away on the papal jubilee in Rome. Despite "molte pregherle e scuse," Velutti found "né pietà né misericordia" from Florentine officials, who insisted that he go.[115] The city's hardline stance is surely understandable given, as we have seen, Velutti's critical role as an advocate of the war.

Embassies were undoubtedly a burden, particularly for prominent merchants such as Velluti, who wished to look after their own interests. The undesirability was increased by the plague, which made all manner of movement risky, particularly long-distance travel.

Florentine Politics Reconsidered?

Whatever the precise motivation for the use of members of the *famiglia* of the Signoria as ambassadors, the evidence raises basic questions about the

---

[113] See Demetrio Marzi, *La cancelleria della repubblica fiorentina* (Rocca S. Casciano: Capelli, 1910) and Agostino Pepoli, *Documenti storici del secolo XIV estratti dal R Archivio di Stato Fiorentino* (Firenze: Arnaldi Forni, 1884). Some ambassadorial instructions are also reproduced in Guiseppe Canestrini, "Di alcuni documenti riguardanti le relazioni politiche dei papi di Avignone coi Comuni d'Italia avanti e dopo il tribunato di Cola di Rienzo e la calata di Carlo IV," *Archivio Storico Italiano* 7 (1849), pp. 347–446.

[114] *La cronica domestica di Messer Donato Velluti*, edited by Isidoro del Lungo and Guglielmo Volpi (Florence: G. C. Sansoni, 1914), pp. 193–196.

[115] "né di mia debolezza, né di mio sconcio, né abbandonamento di figliuoli e di case, o masserizia," *La cronica domestica di Messer Donato Velluti*, p. 194.

nature of Florentine government in the immediate aftermath of the plague. Nicolai Rubinstein famously spoke of Florence's conscious self-definition at this time as a "republican" state against growing lordships on the peninsula.[116] He emphasized in particular the use of the "language of liberty" in communal diplomacy, which served as a precursor to Florence's famous stance at the end of the *trecento* as the bastion of republican freedom against the lordly oppression of Milan. Guido Pampaloni pointed precisely to diplomacy as the one sector in which the "Florentine constitution," which he called the "caratteristica particolare" of the city, functioned like a modern democracy. Power in Florence was not concentrated in one office, but carefully spread among various offices.[117]

Our evidence suggests precisely the opposite. In the immediate aftermath of the plague at least, Florence's practice of diplomacy resembled more that of the lordships they condemned than the republic they purported to be. Unelected "petty" officials (to use Brucker's term) with close personal connections to the priors of the city conducted important negotiations at the most notable courts.[118] The absence of letters of instruction to these ambassadors may be an indication that the nature of their business was secret or perhaps instructions were not necessary for emissaries so closely connected to the priors.

In any case, the constriction of Florence's post-plague workforce, read by scholars in terms of real wage and standard of living, had very real and very unexpected political consequences for the city. The extent to which the use of *familiari* continued in future years requires further study. There is nevertheless precocious evidence that the *famiglia* remained key players in Florentine civic affairs. Among the *carte sciolte* in the *Miscellanea Repubblicana* there have survived two undated documents, which, based on internal evidence, indicate they are from 1364 and 1370, when Florence was at war with Pisa and Milan, respectively. Both relate to the activities of Giovanni Paoli, described as "schocco," our bell ringer from 1349 to 1350 – now older and no longer "little idiot" (*schocchino*) but full idiot (*schocco*). The documents show that Paoli was still deeply involved in Florentine affairs. In 1364 he personally oversaw the payment of large sums of money from the *camera del comune* to mercenary soldiers fighting against Pisa. In 1370 he served as an ambassador for Florence in

---

[116] Rubinstein, "Florence and the Despots," p. 22.

[117] Guido Pampaloni, "Gli organi della Repubblica fiorentina per le relazioni," *Rivista di studi politici internazionali* 20 (1953), pp. 265–266.

[118] Brucker, "Bureaucracy and Social Welfare," p. 7.

negotiations in 1370 with Francesco Carrara, lord of Padua, to arrange for hiring troops directly from Germany.[119]

By 1370, Paoli would have been in Florentine employ for at least twenty-one years. The lengthy service recalls that of another bell ringer, Antonio Pucci, the famous vernacular poet, who worked at the palace of the podestà in 1349 and became a town crier in 1350, a job he held for the next seventeen years.[120] The examples provide further proof that "petty" officials in post-plague Florence were indeed not petty. The communal bureaucracy was personal, permeable, and, above all, not readily understandable in modern terms.[121] The priors tightly controlled long-distance diplomacy in the immediate aftermath of the plague, with *famigliari* cast in the role of retainers at court. The whole management of the city appears by necessity to have been in the hands of a small group of trusted men, who performed numerous tasks.

These peculiarities make clear that the immediate effects of the plague on Florence went beyond that of initiating an era of "fat cattle" for the laboring classes. The constriction of the workforce had complex results. The porous and personal nature of bureaucratic and political institutions in the city lends additional support to the depiction of Petrarch and Boccaccio as powerful public figures engaged in personal webs of influence in which a letter calling for war against a lordly clan could be heard, particularly when the motives coincided with those of the state more generally.

---

[119] ASF, Miscellanea Repubblicana 120 #7.
[120] McGee, *The Ceremonial Musicians of Late Medieval Florence*, p. 54.
[121] In examining Florentine *camera del comune*, Brucker spoke of the development of a Weberian bureaucratic rationality by the fifteenth century. Brucker, "Bureaucracy and Social Welfare," p. 7.

Epilogue: Why Two Years Matter (and the Short-Term Is Not Inconsistent with the Long-Term)

The lack of long-term perspective in our culture remains. The disease even has a name – short-termism. Short-termism ... is now so deeply ingrained in our institutions that has become a habit, frequently followed but rarely justified.

Guldi and Armitage, The History Manifesto[1]

And if, on account of such care [with statistics], the reader becomes fatigued at times, we will happily say ... too bad!"

Bloch, "Le salaire et les fluctuations économiques à longue periode"[2]

I anticipate that the facts and comments contained in these volumes will attract few readers. The form of such work is necessarily repulsive and the dry details ... will have but little charm for the general public.

Thorold Rogers, History of Agriculture and Prices in England, vol. 1[3]

Our study of Petrarch's war has helped illuminate the various forces operating in Florence in the immediate aftermath of the plague. As historians call for a return to a *longue durée* approach, with the laudable intention of finding "big ideas" and keeping history relevant, the present study has emphasized that important ideas and relevance may also be found in the small scale.[4] The "crisis of short-termism" has been greatly exaggerated, and its opposition to "long-termism" is an artificial one.[5] Both require the careful reading of data, weaving out the

---

[1] Jo Guldi and David Armitage, *The History Manifesto* (Cambridge: Cambridge University Press, 2014), p. 2.

[2] "Et si, de ce soin même, il resulte, par moments, quelque fatigue pour le lecteur, nous dirons volontiers ... tant pis!" Marc Bloch, "Le salaire et les fluctuations économiques à longue periode," *Revue Historique* 173 (1934), p. 3.

[3] James E. Thorold Rogers, *A History of Agriculture and Prices in England from the Year after the Oxford Parliament (1259) to the Commencement of the Continental War (1793)* (Oxford: Clarendon Press, 1866) vol. 1, p. vi.

[4] Guldi and Armitage, *The History Manifesto*, p. 7.

[5] Guldi and Armitage, *The History Manifesto*, p. 38. For critique of the *Manifesto*, see the exchange in the *American Historical Review* 120 (April 2015), pp. 530–542. On the benefits of micro and long-term approaches, see Francesca Trivellato, "Is There a Future for Italian Microhistory in the Age of Global History?" *California Italian Studies* 2 no. 1 (2011) http://escholarship.org/uc/item/0z9 4n9hq (last accessed 15 February 2017).

"layers superimposed and knotted into one another," as Clifford Geertz would have it. And while, as Marc Bloch argued in the essay cited at the beginning of this epilogue, such detailed study of economic phenomena (Chapter 5) runs the risk of boring the reader, the emphasis on long-term trends can obscure important short-term variables that may alter conclusions. The present volume hopes that the trends uncovered here will indeed help serve as the basis for more considered long-term study.

Florence was "turned upside down" in 1349–1350, as noted by plague studies. But it was upside down in ways different from those depicted by the current consensus. There are, for our years, a set of variables specific to the place and time that connect famous literary figures in unexpected ways and integrate military, political, and economic aspects of Florentine society that are too often segregated. The service of bell ringers, servants, and cooks on long-term important diplomatic missions provides a striking example of the very different realities in mid-*trecento* Florence.

Collectively, the evidence reinforces medievalists' claims to "alterity" for their period – that it cannot be easily apprehended in terms of the present. But it also affirms the more timeless importance of attention to detail, nuance, and contradiction that stands at the core of the historians' craft. Focus on the periphery can lead to better understanding of the core. It is not the followers of "normal science," as Thomas Kuhn has famously argued, who change the paradigm. And it is often the pursuit of "useless satisfactions", in Abraham Flexner's formulation, (see the Introduction), that serve as "the source from which undreamed of utility is derived."[6] There remain still more variables to consider.

As an epilogue, it is important to stress again the problematic nature of long-term wage studies and the potential pitfalls of the Cliometric and *Annales* schools that encourage them. Scholars too often use numbers as an "empirical" device to cut through the layers of the historical past. Even Clifford Geertz, when advocating a careful "weaving out of layers" (a "venture in") and the importance of "thick description," saw the "automized routine of data collection" as more certain. David Landes argued that statistical studies are by their very nature difficult to critique because "there are few men who would care to repeat ten years of work simply to check its accuracy."[7] David Hackett Fischer makes a forceful affirmation of the importance of numbers. Drawing on the *Annales* and Cliometric traditions in his popular book, *The Great Wave*, Fischer asserts

[6] Abraham Flexner, "The Usefulness of Useless Knowledge," *Harper's Magazine* 179 (June 1939), p. 549.
[7] David Landes, "The Statistical Study of French Crises," *Journal of Economic History* 10 no. 2 (November 1950), p. 196.

that "numbers make it possible for us to put the pieces together. They allow us to compare events that are otherwise incomparable. They tell us the way the world is moving. They help us think in general terms about particular events, and then test our generalizations against the evidence of empirical indicators." The "nature of change," Fischer concludes, belongs to "philosophers," but "the growing accessibility of quantitative evidence allows us to convert a metaphysical conundrum into an empirical question."[8] Accordingly, he traces the movement of prices and wages in his book from medieval times all the way to modern America.

The discussion of wages in Chapters 4 and 5 has, by dint of its many qualifications, made clear that numbers are contextual, embedded in a social system, and that understanding them requires the same close inspection of particulars that we apply to written texts. The factors that went into the configuration of Florentine nominal wages included consideration of currency, status, danger, size of entourage, and communal budgeting – in addition to the well-known and much discussed issues of food and lodging embedded in pay. Working one job did not preclude working another, creating an often substantial difference between wage rates and actual compensation. The notion of occupation was understood differently then than it is today, a distinction often lost in long-termism. Indeed, the "anomalous" data for Florentine public labor allow better integration with the extant and (for La Roncière) less "usable" data for the Florentine wool cloth industry, the city's largest private employer. Lengthy diplomatic missions undertaken by servants of the priors, cooks, and bell ringers to distant places raise questions about the nature of Florentine politics and its famous self-definition as a "republic among tyrants" in the aftermath of the Black Death.

The aim has been to replace a derivative synthetic "empiricism" with a more self-reflective and critical alternative. The current long-term methodological construct is as stubborn as it is pernicious. It is exacerbated by the use of the Middle Ages by economists as a measure of the present day or, in the case of the Black Death, as a turning point in the broader economic history of Western Civilization. The pioneer of long-term wage studies, James E. Thorold Rogers, was a member of Parliament and a champion of social causes in Victorian England, who consciously studied wages and labor in the distant past over many centuries to understand his own day. He believed that the English nation had "not been molded into its present shape by its constitution and laws," but by "economical" motivation, which remained essentially the same over

---

[8] David Hackett Fischer, *The Great Wave: Price Revolutions and the Rhythm of History* (Oxford: Oxford University Press, 1996), p. xiii.

time.[9] Wilhelm Abel's highly influential and much cited synthetic study, *Agricultural Fluctuations in Europe: From the Thirteenth to the Twentieth Centuries* (originally published in German in 1935) traces long-term movements of wages and prices in England, France, Italy, Germany, and Austria with the explicit intention of comparing the trajectories of the economies of these countries to the modern day.[10] Slicher van Bath's equally famous *The Agrarian History of Western Europe, 500–1800* extended Abel's investigation further back in time to gain additional perspective on the economic circumstances of Europe prior to industrialization.[11] Important recent studies by the economists Robert Allen, Sevket Pamuk, Jan Luiten van Zanden, and Gregory Clark use wage and price data from the Black Death to help assess standards of living and the "great divergence," when the west, notably northern Europe, emerged industrialized (and triumphant) with respect to the east.[12] Pamuk wrote that "even a cursory look at real wage series makes clear that modern economic growth and the Black Death are the two events that led to the most significant changes in wages and incomes during the last millennium."[13] Paolo Malanima established the "big argument" for Italy, combining numerous regional studies to trace Italian wages, prices, and standards of living from the Middle Ages to the present day, with the sadder intention of explaining why the peninsula did not emerge as a "winner" in the modern era despite its economic head start in the Middle Ages.[14]

The importance of such studies is manifest. They have shaped their field and serve as an important reminder that the past informs the present. But progressively lost in the scholarship has been the qualifications and context relating to the data used. These are, as argued here, significant and constitute the very essence of the historians' task.

[9] Thorold Rogers, *A History of Agriculture and Prices in England*, pp. vii, viii.

[10] Wilhelm Abel, *Agricultural Fluctuations in Europe: From the Thirteenth to the Twentieth Centuries* (London: Metheun, 1980 English edn.).

[11] B. H. Slicher van Bath, *The Agrarian History of Western Europe, 500–1800*, translated by Olive Ordish (London: E. Arnold, 1963).

[12] Robert C. Allen, "The Great Divergence in European Wages and Prices from the Middle Ages to the First World War," *Explorations in Economic History* 38 (2001), pp. 411–447; Jan Luiten van Zanden, "Wages and the Standards of Living in Europe, 1500–1800," *European Review of Economic History* 2 (1991), pp. 75–95; Süleyman Özmucur and Şevket Pamuk, "Real Wages and Standards of Living in the Ottoman Empire, 1489–1914," *The Journal of Economic History* 62 (2002), pp. 292–321; Şevket Pamuk, "The Black Death and the Origins of the 'Great Divergence' across Europe, 1300–1600," *European Review of Economic History* 11 (2007), pp. 289–317; van Zanden, "Wages and the Standards of Living," pp. 79–82.

[13] Pamuk, "The Black Death and the Origins of the 'Great Divergence,'" p. 292.

[14] Paolo Malanima, *L'economia italiana: della crescita medievale alla crescita contemporanea* (Bologna: Il Mulino, 2012).

Thorold Rogers openly admitted the problems with his wage data taken from college and estate accounts of Oxford and Cambridge. He noted that nominal day rates depended on season, the type and duration of a task, and the inclusion of food and drink and various other emoluments, some of which Thorold Rogers did not himself fully understand. He saw the wages of threshers as "the best example of market forces," but focused instead on carpenters and builders because their records were more copious and "continuous," and thus more felicitous for present day models.[15] Thorold Rogers' data for carpenters and builders was projected forward to a new generation of scholars by E. H. Phelps Brown and Sheila Hopkins in their "Seven Centuries of Building Wages" (1955).[16] The authors included Thorold Rogers' reservations about his data and even pointed out his methodological flaws, noting that he took averages of salaries in one place and the highest wage in another place. But they endorsed his evidence on the grounds that carpenters and builders' wages were "most numerous and continuous" and therefore the most useful for comparative purposes, which involved as the necessary next step constructing a price series to determine real wages and standards of living. Like Thorold Rogers, Phelps Brown and Hopkins pointed out the scarcity of the data, which consisted of about fifteen craftsmen a year for much of the 700 years they deal with.[17] William Beveridge expressed similar concerns about his data for laborers at manors and estates in Winchester. He compared the limits of his technique, as we saw in Chapter 5, to the glare of a car's headlights, which necessarily left the fringes in the dark. Beveridge noted that he lacked both the space and wherewithal to deal with the many qualifications and contradictions in his data.[18]

In the process of demonstrating long-term patterns and searching for historical turning points, Allen, in a comparative study of craft wages of twenty European cities from the Middle Ages to World War I, briefly

---

[15] Thorold Rogers, *A History of Agriculture and Prices in England*, pp. 254–275; Thorold Rogers ultimately judged the data important for its availability over a long time, and used it for a separate study on workers. James E. Thorold Rogers, *Six Centuries of Work and Wages: The History of English Labour*, vol. 1 (London: Swan Sonnenschein and Co., 1894), p. 177. For an evaluation of the early English literature on the plague, see John Hatcher, "England in the Aftermath of the Black Death," *Past and Present* 144 (August 1994), pp. 3–6.

[16] E. H. Phelps Brown and Sheila V. Hopkins, "Seven Centuries of Building Wages," *Economica* 22 (1955), p. 200. This was soon followed by a related study of prices. "Seven Centuries of the Prices of Consumables, Compared with Builders' Wage-Rates," *Economica* 23 (1956), pp. 296–314.

[17] Phelps Brown and Hopkins, "Seven Centuries of Building Wages," pp. 195–196, 202.

[18] William Beveridge, "Wages in the Winchester Manors," *Economic History Review* (1936), pp. 22–43.

noted anomalies in his data set, but corrected them by "refining" his "technique of analysis." This entailed establishing a more mathematically nuanced "consumer price index" – a notion that is itself anachronistic as applied to the distant past. It allowed Allen to arrive at the counter-intuitive conclusion that the period from 1500 to 1750, not the Industrial Revolution itself, was responsible for the initiation of the different economic trajectories of countries.[19] The importance of his conclusion masks the reality that his wage data is derivative and ringed with too many qualifications to offer such conclusions. The greater goal of the study, tracing Europe's path toward industrialization, is enough to excuse what Allen calls "minor" statistical flaws. Indeed, Allen very consciously placed his goal before his method, openly articulating a troubling teleology. The data he chose to use was the only material "comprehensive enough to answer our questions."[20] Similarly, Phelps Brown and Hopkins apologized for "piecing and patching with secondary sources when the primary materials are probably there for more detailed and solid work." But they argued that "the results which can be won from what is immediately accessible seem worth setting out for the grand perspective."[21] Slicher van Bath cited many qualifications for his data, but concluded that the wages of "farm hands and carpenters" were useful because they were available for "considerable length of time."[22]

The availability and translatability of wage data have been the key. The selection is contingent on the type of conclusions scholars wish to make. As we have seen for Florence, La Roncière specifically chose craft day wages for Florence from the Hospital of Santa Maria Nuova for his study, despite his belief that the wool cloth industry was "the heart of the salaried workforce." He did so because the former provided "usable" patterns for comparative purposes, even if the data was far more limited.[23] Süleyman Özmucur and Pamuk used craftsmen wages to compare economic conditions in the Ottoman Empire with those in Europe, with the intention, like Allen, of better understanding modern industrialization – in this case how the Ottomans ultimately lost the great competition in the world market.[24] In a separate essay, Sevket Pamuk explicitly

---

[19] Allen, "The Great Divergence in European Wages," pp. 412–413.

[20] Allen, "The Great Divergence in European Wages," pp. 412–414.

[21] Phelps Brown and Hopkins, "Seven Centuries of Building Wages," p. 195.

[22] Slicher van Bath, *The Agrarian History of Western Europe*, pp. 98, 102.

[23] Charles M. de La Roncière, "La condition des salaries à Florence au XIVe siècle" in *Tumulto dei Ciompi: un momento di storia fiorentina ed Europea*, edited by Atti del Convegno internazionale (Florence: Leo S. Olschki, 1981), pp. 14, 17.

[24] Süleyman Özmucur and Şevket Pamuk, "Real Wages and the Standards of Living in the Ottoman Empire, 1469–1914."

lauded craftsmen wages as the "basic tool" for comparative study of Europe and the Eastern Mediterranean."[25]

The teleology is evident. Scholars extend day wages to 250 days in order to represent the modern concept of yearly salaries, and convert them to silver, the presumed currency in which all such workers were paid (Chapter 5). Allen added a "notional medieval family" consisting of a wife and two children for whom the wages were intended, to better get at standards of living. But as noted in Chapter 5, day wages do not translate to yearly wages. Day workers at Scarperia and officers of the Florentine army were paid specifically for the short run, their rates figured with that in mind. Jobs like the podestà, executor of justice, and others had decisive term limits. Even Thorold Rogers, the inspiration for the method, believed that 312 days was a better yearly estimate for day wages in England, as he found fewer "non-working" holidays in his data than he had initially expected. Florentine workers, as we have seen, routinely received gold as compensation, which had important social and economic meaning beyond the wage rate. A shift from one currency to another in itself constituted a change in the nature of wages. But such issues were not discussed.

It is a marriage of convenience that has stood the test of time.[26] A basic scholarly goal has been to determine standards of living in the past: how people lived. The goal is laudable and strikes at the core of what makes history appealing. But it involves the additional epistemological leap of figuring a "basket of goods," the necessities of life, for which the salaries were used (Chapter 4). The composition of the basket has varied from scholar to scholar. Abel judged wages in terms of the price of wheat, which he saw as the basic staple of the medieval diet.[27] Many still follow Abel's lead. But van Bath (1960) found wheat inadequate, asserting that it would be better to express labor in terms of index figures, which included the entire cost of living, or at least all types of food consumed.[28] Allen disliked the use of grain "as a deflator," as he called it, because it did not work well for comparative study over time and space, as grain had a different meaning in different contexts. Giuliano Pinto's typical every day "budget" for Florence in the

[25] Pamuk, "The Black Death and the Origins of 'the Great Divergence,'" p. 292.

[26] Tognetti points out the limits of craft wages taken from large institutions that were subject to their own market forces. But he ultimately decided that it was "very likely" ("molto probabilmente") that the pattern of these wages was the same as those of other salaried workers. Sergio Tognetti, "Prezzi e salari nella Firenze tardo medievale: un profile," *Archivio storico italiano* 153 (1995), p. 305.

[27] Abel, *Agricultural Fluctuations in Europe*. He wrote the third preface in 1978. Allen, "The Great Divergence in European Wages."

[28] Slicher van Bath, *The Agrarian History of Western Europe*, p. 101.

fourteenth century consisted of 50 percent grain, 25 percent wine, 15 percent meat, and 5 percent each for oil and wood.[29] La Roncière's "budget type" consisted of a specific number of calories consumed.[30] Christopher Dyer stressed the many problems with the data and difficulties determining the basket of goods for medieval England and concluded that standards of living "cannot be measured exactly" because it was so variable with respect to social class.[31]

What is lost is the variable nature of nominal wage and the distinctions among labor forces. As scholars seek ever grander and more relevant conclusions, the danger is that the realities will recede further into obscurity.[32] The economist Gregory Clark in his popular *Farewell to Alms* traced wages back as far as Babylonia and as far forward as modern America. Clark saw the Black Death as a turning point in the "rise in real wages" which reached a level they "would not again reach until 1880."[33] From there Clark concluded that a "most obvious effect" of the improved wages and standard of living was "to make people taller."[34] Better wages led to better lifestyle, which led to well-nourished and taller people. The industrialized world was not only better off financially, but physically more imposing. Allen made the same claim: "The wage data would seem to confirm the relationship between income and height for the eighteenth century."[35] As a short-statured person raised in the industrialized West, I find it difficult to accept such conclusions.

In any case, assumptions are built on assumptions. The authors of the *History Manifesto* scolded economists for this very tendency: for treating historical data as fixed and available for insertion into ready equations. But as the quotes at the beginning of this epilogue show, historians have themselves felt uncomfortable discussing the details of their data sets apart from their possible *longue durée* implications. Thorold Rogers called such detailed investigation "necessarily repulsive."[36] Bloch said much the

---

[29] Giuliano Pinto, *Toscana medieval: paesaggi e realtà sociali* (Florence: Le Lettere, 1993), pp. 129–130.

[30] La Roncière, *Prix et salaires*, pp. 381–396.

[31] Christopher Dyer, *Standards of Living in Later Middle Ages:Social Change in England, 1200–1320* (Cambridge: Cambridge University Press, 1989), pp. 274–277 (quote p. 274).

[32] Phelps Brown and Hopkins, "Consumables," p. 196.

[33] Gregory Clark, *A Farewell to Alms* (Princeton, NJ: Princeton University Press, 2007), p. 40.

[34] Clark, *Farewell to Alms*, p. 55.

[35] Allen, "The Great Divergence in European Wages," p. 413.

[36] Thorold Rogers addresses his reader directly also in *Six Centuries of Work and Wages*, saying that if he has patience with his "dull account," he will see that "our ancestors" [the English] were not "without hopes," pp. 183, 179.

same thing, but added, unapologetically, that this was "tough luck" for the beleaguered reader.

A truly constructive dialogue has not yet been established. Economic historians whose main field is history interact surprisingly little with economic historians whose main field is economics. The distinguished economic historian Naomi Lamoreaux suggested a reason for this. She noted a "painful naiveté" among historians with regard to economic concepts and an inability to understand theoretical models.[37] This is undeniably true. But, conversely, models, however sophisticated, are only as good as the data they are based on. And suppositions such as those of Allen for Europe – that problematic data can be rendered more usable by adjustment of an equation – is fantasy. It represents a fundamental misreading of the past.[38] "The subject matter of economics," as the economist Joseph Schumpeter asserted, "is essentially a unique process in historic time."[39] The professional incentives for economists and historians to work together and conduct a serious dialogue with each other do not yet exist.

The role of the *Annales* school in the scholarly status quo must again be stressed, particularly in light of recent calls by historians to return to the methodology of Fernand Braudel.[40] The *Annales* interest in quantification owes much to Braudel and Le Roy Ladurie and the "second generation" of *Annalistes*, who encouraged the practice.[41] But the initial impulse toward quantification, as Braudel himself noted in his essay on the *longue durée* (1958), derives from the research of Francois Simiand and Ernest Labrousse in the 1930s, who saw in numbers "the conviction of scientific

---

[37] Naomi R. Lamoreaux, "Economic History and the Cliometric Revolution" in *Imagined Histories*, edited by Anthony Molho and Gordon S. Wood (Princeton, NJ: Princeton University Press, 1998), p. 75.

[38] There is among economists the stirrings of dissent; see J. Humphries and J. Weisdorf, "The Wages of Women in England, 1260–1850," *Journal of Economic History* 75 (2015), pp. 405–447.

[39] Joseph Schumpeter, *History of Economic Analysis* (Oxford: Oxford University Press, 1954), p. 14.

[40] Guldi and Armitage, *History Manifesto*, pp. 15–19.

[41] Iggers sees Braudel as paving the way for quantification in the 1960s and 1970s. Le Roy Ladurie does quantification in his *Peasants of Languedoc* in 1966. Georg G. Iggers, *Historiography in the 20th Century: From Scientific Objectivity to the Post-Modern Challenge* (Hanover, NH: Wesleyan Press, 1997). *Annales* took off in terms of long-term quantification in the 1960s and 1970s. See John Day, "Francois Simiand and the *Annales* School of History" in *Money and Finance in the Ages of Merchant Capitalism* (Oxford: Blackwell, 1999), pp. 139–150. See also F. Braudel, and F. Spooner, "Prices in Europe from 1450 to 1750" in E. E. Rich and C. H. Wilson, *The Cambridge Economic History of Europe* (Cambridge: Cambridge University Press, 1967), pp. 378–486: Emmanuel Le Roy Ladurie, "Motionless History," *Social Science History* 1 no. 2 (Winter 1977), pp. 120, 121.

study of past societies."[42] Labrousse said pointedly that "in order to be a historian, you need to know how to count" ("pour être historien, il faut savoir compter").[43] Peter Burke linked the "explosion of quantification" in the work of these scholars to the economic conditions of their day, specifically to the hyperinflation that struck Europe in the 1920s and the stock market crash in 1929.[44] Wilhelm Abel, writing in 1935, cited the work of Simiand and Labrousse as inspiration for his *Agricultural Fluctuations in Europe*. Beveridge, although following most nearly Thorold Rogers, began his quantitative researches at the same time as Simiand and Labrousse. Florentinists have, as noted in the introduction, been particularly influenced in this regard for study of their city.[45] La Roncière specifically cited the *Annales* school as inspiration for study of Florentine wages, and Christiane Klapisch-Zuber, co-author of *Tuscans and Their Families*, which assessed the statistical data of the *catasto* of 1427, was a student of Braudel. Le Roy Ladurie enthusiastically endorsed Cliometric trends that had become popular among American economists in the 1960s and 1970s.[46]

The problem with the search for long-term answers and the use of numbers as "empirical" devices is that it not only leads scholars, often unwittingly, to teleological analyses, but inclines them also to cherry-pick examples to prove a point. Indeed, Braudel did precisely this in his discussion of "labour markets" in his famous *Civilization and Capitalism*.[47] He told us at the outset of the discussion that he intended to show how the historical "transition to wage earning in the west" developed "earlier than we suppose."[48] The statement was uncontroversial. But Braudel then proceeded with a series of brief bullet point examples, starting with Paris in the thirteenth century, then the "curious contracts" of brick workers in contemporaneous Piacenza, then wage earners in the Portuguese countryside in the thirteenth and fourteenth centuries, followed by wage earners in Burgundy in 1393, from which we

---

[42] John Day, "Money, Credit and Capital Formation in Marc Bloch and Ferdinand Braudel" in *Money and Finance in the Ages of Merchant Capitalism* (Oxford: Blackwell, 1999), p. 127. For discussion of Simiand see F. Crouzet, "The Economic History of Modern Europe," *The Journal of Economic History* 31 (1971), pp. 135–152.

[43] Peter Burke, *The French Historical Revolution, 1929–2014* (Cambridge: Polity Press, 2015), p. 128.

[44] Burke, *The French Historical Revolution*, p. 129.

[45] Jacob Burckhardt, *The Civilization of the Renaissance in Italy*, translated by S. G. C. Middlemore (New York, NY: Penguin, 1954), pp. 61, 63.

[46] Claudia Goldin, "Cliometrics and the Nobel," *Journal of Economic Perspectives* 9 no. 2 (Spring 1995), pp. 191–208.

[47] Guldi and Armitage, *History Manifesto*, pp. 9–10, 15–19, 124.

[48] Fernand Braudel, *Civilization and Capitalism, The Wheels of Commerce*, vol. 2, translated by Sian Reynold (New York, NY: Harper and Row, 1979), p. 52.

learned that there existed a foreman to organize laborers. Braudel advanced a hundred years forward to Hamburg in 1480, where there was a "transient labor market." He went on to say that labor markets began to appear "more official with clearer rules," and cited the examples of a French treatise of the seventeenth century, Tudor England, and the seventeenth century Hanseatic league and activities in the city of Stralsund, where wage earners were about half the population.

The progression is contrived and effectively meaningless. For Italianists it is simply not true. We have already seen a foreman at Scarperia in 1350. Florence's wool cloth industry had many types of wage earners, as did the city's armies – and as did armies everywhere in Europe, which Braudel, like others, did not treat as part of the labor market. The deployment of examples from entirely different traditions over many years creates a sense of linear progression, allowing Braudel to conclude that "as years went, the labour markets became more official and their rules clearer."[49] The statement is true, but holds little scholarly value.

The importance of Braudel's work is manifest and raises larger questions about capitalism in a global framework that have been immensely influential in scholarly discussions – far more than this present study will be. Braudel's *longue durée* approach to geography and climate, as the authors of the *History Manifesto* pointed out, remains an important paradigm for future study. And one of the great virtues of *Annales* long-term quantification studies has been their ability to provide glimpses, in broad strokes, of the "faceless" crowd in the countryside, which constituted the vast majority of people in pre-modern society about whom we would otherwise know little.[50] But the present volume strongly rejects the all too pervasive tendency to extrapolate large trends from a single and often quite limited set of data. The dangers are so great because the impulse is so visceral. Severio La Sorsa in his study of the Florentine confraternity of Orsanmichele pointed out that in 1329 notaries employed by that institution earned 4 lire a month. Immediately after the Black Death, however, salaries rose to 100 florins. He concluded that the plague brought dramatic wage hikes – evidence based on a couple of men – that does not match that found in this study for the same profession at the same time. The conclusion may apply to Orsanmichele, but to generalize is clearly misguided.[51]

[49] Braudel, *Civilization and Capitalism*, pp. 49–54.
[50] See Emmanuel Le Roy Ladurie, *The Peasants of Languedoc*, translated by John Day (Urbana, IL: University of Illinois Press, 1974).
[51] Saverio La Sorsa, *La Compagnia d'Or San Michele, ovvero una pagina della beneficenza in Toscana nel secolo XIV* (Trani: V. Vecchi, 1902), pp. 97–98.

Regardless of the scope or subject matter of inquiry, a proper under-standing of context lies at the core of the historians' task. Whether that takes the form of long-term study or short-term study is irrelevant. As noted in the Introduction, in avoiding the tendency to "fetishize" archives (as some scholars have accused others of doing), historians run the alternate risk of fetishizing their scholarly predecessors, whose meth-ods, though laudable, invariably have weaknesses, as do all methods. The latter impulse is particularly troublesome because it is embedded in the very fabric of academe and offers much in the way of potential professional rewards. The point is worth repeating because along with reverence often comes caricature and misunderstanding. Indeed, if we take, as Guldi and Armitage suggest, Braudel as our scholarly model for long-term study, it is well to remember that Braudel himself treated historical time according to different scales, both short and long.[52] Guldi and Armitage's distinction is not one that the great scholar himself would necessarily recognize.

The criticisms expressed here are not new or unique. Critical views of the use of numbers are indeed deeply rooted in the historiography, should scholars take care to look closely. Already in the fourteenth century, the Muslim writer Ibn Khaldun, a contemporary of Giovanni Villani, and to some modern scholars was a "father of economics," saw numbers as "a good opportunity for false information" in historical writing.[53] In the preface to his universal history *Muqaddimah*, Khaldun warned historians, much like Bloch centuries later, about the facile use of the present day to understand the past. Writers who did this were guilty of being "lost in the desert of baseless assumptions" and did better to study "the nature of existent things, and the differences among nations, places, and periods with regard to ways of life, character qualities, customs, sects, schools." "The condition of the world and of nations," Khaldun argued, "does not persist in the same form or in a constant manner."[54] Khaldun may well deserve the economist's rank, as his conclusion corresponds to Karl Polanyi's notion of social embeddedness, Joseph Schumpeter's call for "historical context," and John Maynard Keynes' invocation that we must avoid putting "more order in the system" than there was.

But the current pull of scholarly imitation is powerful and appears in unexpected places. Thorold Rogers stated, for example, that England possesses the richest of all European archival sources – "more copious

---

[52] Francesca Trivellato, "Is There a Future for Italian Microhistory in the Age of Global History?" *California Italian Studies* 2 no. 1 (2011).

[53] Ibn Khaldun, *The Muqaddimah*, translated and introduced by Franz Rosenthal, abridged and edited by N. J. Darwood (Princeton, NJ: Princeton University Press, 2005), pp. 4–5.

[54] Ibn Khaldun, *The Muqaddimah*, pp. 5, 11.

and more continuous than those of any other people."[55] The statement, which Thorold Rogers offered in the spirit of blatant and undisguised nationalism, has nevertheless made its way into many subsequent works. Abel, who was not English, restated it (without attribution) in his comparative study of Europe, and the Nobel laureate Douglass North repeated it in his New Institutional Economic study of the rise of the western world. "The quantitative evidence from England," he says," is the most complete."[56] Clark said that England has a "uniquely well-documented wage and price history."[57] This permitted him to use England as the basis for his universal statements about the course of all of western history.

Florentinists will smile at such egregious overstatement, knowing the richness of their own archival data. But there are archives throughout the Italian peninsula that contain more complete numerical data than Florence. Meanwhile, the influence of Thorold Rogers, explicit and implicit, on subsequent studies cannot be overstated. When Beveridge found in his study of craft wages in Winchester that there was in fact no increase in rates from 1349 to 1350, contrary to the patterns set forth for those years by Thorold Roger for Oxford ("of panic and compulsion" in markets), Beveridge explained the difference as a "delayed concession to the change in labor conditions begun by the Black Death." If the patterns do not correspond to those of the great master, we must try to make them fit. Beveridge identified increases only after 1352 and most notably in 1362 and 1370, when other studies showed stabilization of wage rates.[58]

Recent scholarship continues to follow the nineteenth-century model of evaluating long-term wage movements by decade. Thorold Rogers, Phelps Brown and Hopkins, and Beveridge do this for England; La Roncière and Tognetti do the same for Florence; Paolo Malanima and Giovanni Federigo for Italy more generally, and numerous other scholars for other places.[59] Arranging wages by decade is convenient and useful. But the technique can also be employed to accentuate trends or

---

[55] Thorold Rogers, *A History of Agriculture and Prices in England*, vol. 1, p. v. "There is no European country, I believe, except England, the archives of which could supply satisfactory evidence of prices." Thorold Rogers states this again in *Six Centuries of Work and Wages*, p. 15. "The archives of English history are more copious and continuous that those of any other people."

[56] Douglass C. North and Robert Paul Thomas, *The Rise of the Western World: A New Economic History* (Cambridge: Cambridge University Press, 1973), p. 74.

[57] Clark, *Farewell to Alms*, p. 40.   [58] Beveridge, "Winchester," pp. 26–27.

[59] Phelps Brown and Hopkins, *Seven Centuries of Building Wages*, p. 205; Beveridge, "Winchester," pp. 38–43; La Roncière, *Prix et salaires*, pp. 280, 348; Tognetti, "Prezzi e salari," pp. 302–305.

deaccentuate them. Thorold Rogers divided English wages into the years 1341–1350 and 1351–1360. He placed the sharp rises he found for craftsmen (and threshers) for 1349–1350 in the first grouping, thus highlighting the impact of the plague. William Beveridge, on the other hand, divided his wage data into the years 1340–1348 and 1349–1359. The alteration appears minor, but it is important. It effectively disguised the surprising lack of wage movement Beveridge found for 1349–1350 and allowed him to add the unexpected rises he found after 1352 to his second grouping, thereby enhancing the immediate impact of the plague.[60] Thus Beveridge's data falls into line with that of Thorold Roger, and troublesome stickiness is smoothed over. La Roncière, as we have seen, cited "spectacular rises" in nominal rates of craftsmen in Florence in 1349–1350. But he grouped his craft wages under the years 1340–1348 and 1350–1360, effectively missing the years of critical change.[61] It is not entirely clear why, but his groupings were repeated by Sergio Tognetti.

Are we, in the preceding instances, really comparing wage rates? Bloch, in his review of Françios Simiand's *Les fluctuations économiques à longue période et la crise mondiale,* warned that while Simiand's graph of salaries from 1900 to 1920 showed a rise in rates that could easily be attributed to World War I, closer examination, including a look at prewar trends, might reveal still other variables.[62] The imprecision applies also to the language used by scholars. In one place, they speak of bricklayers as the prototypical day laborer/craftsmen. Elsewhere they refer to carpenters and stonemasons. These are not equivalent terms.[63] Meanwhile, even the periodization used by scholars is inconsistent. Allen's Middle Ages included the fifteenth century; Abels' Middle Ages went no further than 1300. Malanima took as his goal bringing together diverse local Italian wage and price studies to make a broad "national" analysis. But the goal, however laudable and work intensive, is teleological insofar as Italy was not then a nation, but a collection of city-states. Is it proper to read "nation" into Italy's distant past?

The remarks are not intended to deride the larger goals of scholars or the importance of "big" study. The argument is only that it is necessary to refine our methodologies, deal with dry detail, and acknowledge, rather

---

[60] Beveridge, "Winchester," pp. 38–43.

[61] La Roncière, *Prix et salaries,* pp. 280, 348. Tognetti, "Prezzi e salari," pp. 302–305.

[62] Bloch, "Le salaire et les fluctuations économique à longue periode," pp. 3–6.

[63] Giovanni Federico and Paolo Malanima, "Progress, Decline, Growth: Product and Productivity in Italian Agriculture, 1000–2000," *Economic History Review* LVII no. 3 (2004), p. 441.

than ignore, anomalous and contradictory information. Careful short-term study provides the foundation for long-term investigation.

In this spirit, and by way of conclusion, we may – owing to the copious cameral budget records – prospectively extend our wage data both before and after the Black Death, to the familiar ten-year span (1345–1354). This is done cautiously and with all attendant qualifications. Soldiers' wages are from banner units of twenty to twenty-five men, the common element in armies in the budgets.[64]

The longer view confirms the patterns outlined for 1349–1350. The nominal wages of infantrymen rose (and ultimately fell), following the general outline of building workers' wages (Tables E.2 and E.4). The salaries of mercenary cavalrymen were sticky (Table E.1). Italian captains and their men received exactly the same pay for the ten-year period (40 lire and 20 lire a month, respectively). German mercenary captains and their men earned the same rate from 1345 to 1351 (30 florins and 8 florins, 10 soldi respectively a month). The value of German wages, cited in gold, increased slightly during this time on account of changes in the exchange rate between gold and silver (Table E.4). In 1351, however, Florentine officials changed the citation of German cavalry wages to lire and set them at the rate of 96 lire a month for captains and 27 lire and 4 soldi a month for cavalryman (Table E.1), where they would remain until 1354.

The shift in 1351 is notable because it occurred when the price of gold began to rise with respect to silver (Table E.3) and when Florence embarked on a full-scale interstate war against Milan from 1351 to 1353, which involved much of northern and central Italy.[65] The city recruited an army of between 5,000 and 7,000 men – larger than that raised for the Ubaldini.[66] Thus, as the demand for soldiers increased, Florentine officials effectively froze the wages of its most skilled and mobile military workforce. The value of German captains' wages remained exactly the same from 1350 to 1351 (1,920 soldi), while the rank and file in their bands received a small raise (522 soldi to 544 soldi). If Florence had left the citation of wages in gold, the salaries would have risen substantially more throughout the war. Captains' wages would have

---

[64] The sample uses budgets of May/June from 1345 to 1354.

[65] Carlo Cipolla, *The Monetary Policy of Fourteenth Century Florence* (Berkeley, CA: University of California Press, 1982), pp. 49–54; Mario Bernocchi, *Le Monete delle Repubblica Fiorentina*, vol. 1 (Florence: Leo S. Olschki, 1974), pp. 118–126; Bernocchi, *Le Monete delle Repubblica Fiorentina*, vol. 3 (Florence: Leo S. Olschki, 1974), pp. 67, 252; ASF, balìe 10 fols. 24r–24v.

[66] C. C. Bayley, *War and Society in Renaissance Florence: The De Militia of Leonardo Bruni* (Toronto: University of Toronto Press, 1961), p. 20.

risen to 1,980 soldi and 2,040 lire in 1351 and 1352, respectively; Cavalrymen would have received 560 soldi by 1354.

The freeze therefore had the effect of lowering cavalry pay and insulating Florence from the increasing value of gold. Whether Florence paid the soldiers in silver currency is unclear and requires much more research (and the data may not exist for all the years). But the shift in citation alone meant that such payment was now possible, and the value of the wages would in any case no longer respond to the ratio between the two currencies.

Table E.1 *Nominal Monthly Wages of Banner Units of Italian and German Mercenary Cavalry, 1345–1354*

Year	Italian Captain	German Captain	Italian Cavalrymen	German Cavalrymen
1345	40 lire (*800 soldi*)	30 florins (*1860 soldi*)	20 lire (*400 soldi*)	8 florins, 10 soldi (*506 soldi*)
1346	40 lire (*800 soldi*)	30 florins (*1860 soldi*)	20 lire (*400 soldi*)	8 florins, 10 soldi (*506 soldi*)
1347	40 lire (*800 soldi*)	30 florins (*1830 soldi*)	20 lire (*400 soldi*)	8 florins, 10 soldi (*498 soldi*)
1348	40 lire (*800 soldi*)	30 florins (*1890 soldi*)	20 lire (*400 soldi*)	8 florins, 10 soldi (*514 soldi*)
1349	40 lire (*800 soldi*)	30 florins (*1920 soldi*)	20 lire (*400 soldi*)	8 florins, 10 soldi (*522 soldi*)
1350	40 lire (*800 soldi*)	30 florins (*1920 soldi*)	20 lire (*400 soldi*)	8 florins, 10 soldi (*522 soldi*)
1351	40 lire (*800 soldi*)	**96 lire** (*1920 soldi*)	20 lire (*400 soldi*)	**27 lire, 4 soldi** (*544 soldi*)
1352	40 lire (*800 soldi*)	**96 lire** (*1920 soldi*)	20 lire (*400 soldi*)	**27 lire, 4 soldi** (*544 soldi*)
1353	40 lire (*800 soldi*)	**96 lire** (*1920 soldi*)	20 lire (*400 soldi*)	**27 lire, 4 soldi** (*544 soldi*)
1354	40 lire (*800 soldi*)	**96 lire** (*1920 soldi*)	20 lire (*400 soldi*)	**27 lire, 4 soldi** (*544 soldi*)

Notes: Wages are listed first as in the budgets, then converted to *soldi di piccioli*. Changes in nominal rate are in bold.

Sources: ASF, Camera del comune, camarlenghi uscita 14 fols. 512r–529r; camarlenghi uscita 26 fols. 591r–604r; camarlenghi uscita 33 fols. 723r–732r; Scrivano di camera uscita 1 fols. 16r–20r; Scrivano di camera uscita 6 fols. 2r–10r, 17r–41r; Scrivano di camera uscita 9 fols. 2r–9r, 17r–45r camarlenghi uscita 80 fols. 237r–271r; camarlenghi uscita 89 (1352) fols. 478r–501r; camarlenghi uscita 90 (1353) fols. 102r–129r; Scrivano di Camera uscita duplicato #5 fols. 12r–52r; camarlenghi uscita 96 fols. 14r–66r; camarlenghi uscita 102 fols. 289r–342r; camarlenghi uscita 104 fols. 3r–24r.

Table E.2 *Nominal Monthly Wages of Banner Units (20–25 Men) of Shield Bearers, 1345–1354*

Year	Shield Bearer Captain	Ligurian Crossbow Captain	Shield Bearer	Crossbowmen
1345	10 lire (*200 soldi*)	4 florins (*248 soldi*)	5 lire (*100 soldi*)	2 florins (*124 soldi*)
1346	10 lire (*200 soldi*)	4 florins (*248 soldi*)	5 lire (*100 soldi*)	2 florins (*124 soldi*)
1347	10 lire (*200 soldi*)	4 florins (*244 soldi*)	5 lire (*100 soldi*)	2 florins (*122 soldi*)
1348	10 lire (*200 soldi*)	4 florins (*252 soldi*)	5 lire (*100 soldi*)	2 florins (*126 soldi*)
1349	10 lire (*200 soldi*)	7 florins (*448 soldi*)	6 lire (*120 soldi*)	3 florins, 15 soldi (*207 soldi*)
1350	17 lire (*340 soldi*)	8 florins (*512 soldi*)	8 lire/10 soldi (*170 soldi*)	4 florins (*256 soldi*)
1351	20 lire (*400 soldi*)	8 florins (*528 soldi*) 18 lire (360 *soldi*) 11 lire, 10 soldi (*230 soldi*) (*average*) = 373 soldi	10 lire (200 *soldi*)	4 florins (*264 soldi*) 12 lire (*240 soldi*) 9 lire (*180* soldi) (*average*) = 228 soldi
1352	20 lire (*400 soldi*)	8 florins (*544 soldi*) 18 lire (*360 soldi*) 11 lire, 10 soldi (*230 soldi*) (*average*) = 373 soldi	12 lire (*220 soldi*)	4 florins (*272 soldi*) 12 lire (*240 soldi*) 9 lire (*180 soldi*) (*average*) = 231 soldi
1353	16 lire (*320 soldi*)	24 lire, 10 soldi (*490 soldi*) 20 lire (*400 soldi*) (*average*) = 445 soldi	9 lire, 5 soldi (*185 soldi*)	12 lire, 10 soldi (*250 soldi*) 10 lire, 10 soldi (*220 s*) (*average*) = 235 soldi
1354	15 lire, 10 soldi (*310 soldi*)	20 lire (*400 soldi*)	9 lire, 5 soldi (*185 soldi*)	10 lire (*200 soldi*)

Note: Wages are listed first as in the budgets, then converted to *soldi di piccioli*.
Sources: ASF, Camera del comune, camarlenghi uscita 14 fols. 512r–529r; camarlenghi uscita 26 (1346) fols. 591r–604r; camarlenghi uscita 33 (1347) fols. 723r–732r; Scrivano di camera uscita 1 (1348) fols. 16r–20r; Scrivano di camera uscita 6 fols. 2r–10r, 17r–41r; Scrivano di camera uscita 9 fols. 2r–9r, 17r–45r; camarlenghi uscita 80 (1351) fols. 237r–271r; camarlenghi uscita 89 (1352) fols. 478r–501r; camarlenghi uscita 90 (1353) fols. 102r–129r; Scrivano di camera uscita duplicato #5 fols. 12r–52r; camarlenghi uscita 96 fols. 14r–66r; camarlenghi uscita 102 fols. 289r–342r; camarlenghi uscita 104 fols. 3r–24r.

The evidence reinforces the importance, as argued in Chapter 5, of currency in the formulation of wages. Cavalry rates appear to have depended more on monetary forces than on strictly market ones. There was otherwise no ostensible change in the conditions of employment of the cavalrymen. The soldiers remained on four- to six-month contracts, as did infantrymen. And, as argued earlier, Italian and German

Table E.3 *Average Yearly Exchange Rate*

Year	Rate (1 florin=)
1345	62 soldi
1346	62 soldi
1347	61 soldi
1348	63 soldi
1349	64 soldi
1350	64 soldi
1351	66 soldi
1352	68 soldi
1353	68 soldi
1354	70 soldi

Source: Same as Tables E.1 and E.2.

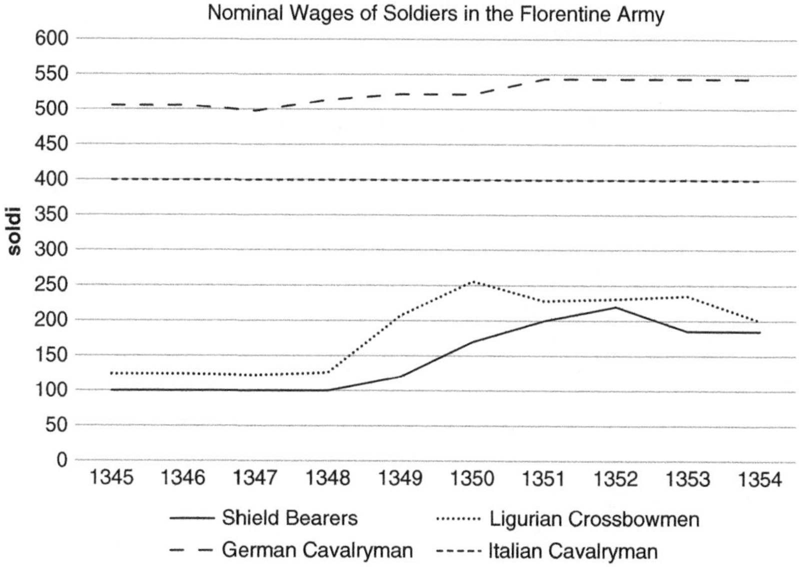

Figure E.1 Nominal Monthly wages of soldiers in the Florentine army, 1345–1354 (banner units)

cavalrymen cannot be neatly fitted under the generic rubric of "mercenary." City officials allowed a modest increase in German cavalry wages as gold fluctuated in price, but they set Italian cavalry rates for the whole period.

Table E.4 *Nominal Daily Wages of Construction Workers, 1345–1354*

Year	Skilled Construction	Unskilled Construction
1345	7 soldi	4.3 soldi
1346	8 soldi	3.7 soldi
1347	—	—
1348	12.5 soldi	6.9 soldi
1349	13.4 soldi	8.4 soldi
1350	16.8 soldi	10 soldi
1351	18.3 soldi	9.5 soldi
1352	17.8 soldi	10 soldi
1353	17.8 soldi	8.7 soldi
1354	17.0 soldi	9.4 soldi

Source: Richard Goldthwaite, *The Building of Renaissance Florence*. Baltimore, MD: Johns Hopkins University Press, 1980, pp. 436–437.

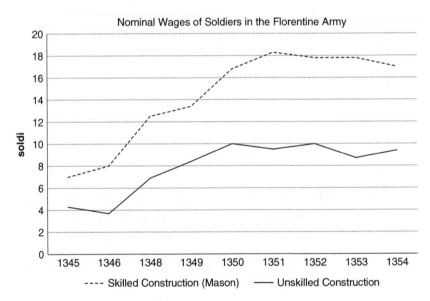

Figure E.2 Nominal daily wages of Florentine construction workers, 1345–1354

In any case, the data provides further support (Chapter 4) against the simple equation of mercenaries with greed. Machiavelli's statements notwithstanding, the "allegiance" of the men was not solely to the "size of their stipend," which remained fixed and decreased during the period of greatest demand. Although we cannot exclude the possibility that there was a glut of such men as a result of the contagion (Chapter 4), it is nevertheless likely that the soldiers perceived themselves and their craft quite differently than modern scholars have assumed. They accepted incentive-based contracts with the understanding that good service brought its own reward and that war itself was ennobling. The two hypotheses are in any case not mutually exclusive.

It is important to stress again that the evidence is preliminary. There remains communal legislation to examine, and additional *balie, consulte e pratiche,* and cameral budget records, where available, to inspect. But the extension of our data reinforces the difficulty with making broad assumptions based on a single wage pattern. Florentine trends were divergent and do not tell a single tale. The wages of Ligurian crossbow-men, for example, respond to the plague. But, in 1351, at the start of the major war, they did not increase, and, like German cavalry captains' wages, shift from citation in gold to citation in lire. The shift was accompanied by lower nominal wages and, for the first time, a proliferation of rates (Table E.2). The wages of some crossbowmen continued to be cited in gold, while others were cited in lire. Meanwhile, the salaries of shield bearers increased at the start of the war in 1351, but remained the same in 1352. The pay of the captains of their units did not rise until 1353.

The lack of upward movement of military wages after 1351 corresponds in basic outline to construction wages (Table E.3), which remained relatively flat over the same period, and may perhaps be taken as additional evidence of the importance of monetary factors in determining wages. But the most fundamental pattern of all in our data is wage stickiness. It was then, as Paul Krugman says of today, a "glaringly obvious feature of the real world." Indeed, infantry wages differed from those of craftsmen in that they remained the same from 1345 until the plague. Meanwhile, an examination of the forty-four additional public jobs discussed in Chapter 4 reveals that only five saw rate changes from 1345 to 1354. They include the now familiar policemen of the palace of the priors and civic musicians, whose nominal rates increased from 1349 to 1350, and also town criers, servants of the priors (*donzelli*), and the podestà (Table E.5).

The patterns are again not in synch. The nominal wages of the podestà and the servants of the priors increased in 1351, just as other wages stabilized or declined. The podestà's wage supported his *comitiva* of

Table E.5 *Nominal Wages of Public Employees that Change, 1345–1354*

Year	Podestá	Policemen/ Prior	Town Criers	Musicians	Servants/ Donzelli
1345	26,667	120	95	73	80
1346	26,667	120	95	62	80
1347	26,667	120	95	62	80
1348	26,667	150	140	80	80
1349	26,667	150	140	80	80
1350	26,667	170	140	100	80
1351	26,667	200	121	100	100
1352	40,000	200	121	100	100
1353	40,000	200	210	100	100
1354	40,000	200	168	100	100

Note: Wages are in *soldi di piccioli*, rounded to the nearest *soldo*.
Sources: ASF, Camera del comune, camarlenghi uscita 13 (1345) fols. 496r–511r; camarlenghi uscita 25 (1346) fols. 576r–590r; camarlenghi uscita 32 (1347) fols. 706r–711r; Camera del comune, scrivano di camera uscita 1 (1348) fols. 1r–15r; camarlenghi uscita 81 (1351) fols. 372r–380r; camarlenghi uscita 79 fols. 671r–678r; camarlenghi uscita 88 fols. 400r–403r; camarlenghi uscita 90 fols. 102r–129r; camarlenghi uscita 96 (1353) fols. 32r–58r; scrivano di Camera uscita duplicato 5 fols. 12r–52r; camarlenghi uscita 102 (1354) fols. 289r–344r; camarlenghi uscita 104 fols. 3r–24r.

judges and other officials. The size of this is not known for most of the period, but a cameral budget for 1346 gives the podestà's entourage as sixty-six men (thirteen judges, three "associates," thirty-eight notaries, and twelve *donzelli*), and a budget for 1354 lists the *comitiva* as consisting of only forty-nine men (eleven judges, three "associates," twenty-six notaries, and twelve *donzelli*). The podestà thus received 33 percent higher pay in 1354 for a workforce that was 26 percent smaller than in 1346. The reasons for this, and the increase in servants' wages, is unclear.

The wages of musicians and town criers confirm the importance of communal budgeting noted in Chapter 5. The two professions were paid a lump sum, distributed among the whole workforce. Florence allotted 40 lire a month to its troupe of musicians and 42 lire to its town criers. The practice accounts for the volatility of the wages, which both decreased and increased before and after the plague. In 1345–1346 the city increased the number of musicians from eleven to thirteen men, thus lowering the wage from 72 soldi a month to 63 soldi a month for each man. The plague in 1348 reduced the troupe to six men, causing Florence, as we have seen (Chapter 4), to specifically raise salaries to attract more *tubatores*, the most important of musicians to civic ceremonies. The number of players increased to nine, where it remained until 1354. Florence now paid 45 lire overall for its troupe of musicians, only 3 lire more than prior to the plague.

Florence never altered the rate (42 lire) for town criers. Nominal wages therefore increased and decreased depending solely on the size of the force. The city employed nine men from 1345 to 1347 (at 95 soldi a month). The number fell to six men during the plague in 1348, moving wages up (142 soldi a month), where they remained until 1351. In that year, the number of employees increased to seven, thus decreasing wages. In 1353 the city reduced its cadre of town criers to a mere four men. The reason for the shift awaits further study. But it caused the most dramatic increase in individual wages for our entire period (57 percent), more so than at the outset of the plague. The rate declined the next year, when the workforce increased to five men.

Fuller answers await the type of close contextual reading advocated throughout this book. The evidence supports the assertions of the modern economists Richard Freeman and Robert Solow regarding the complexity of investigating wage labor, the numerous factors at play, and the importance of eschewing the tendency to view numbers as "empirical" without a proper understanding of their context. If, as the economist Claudia Goldin has argued, the past is a "giant experimental station for economic ideas," then it is all the more important that we approach it with an open mind and a willingness to pay attention to often contradictory data.[67] The Middle Ages is neither a blank slate upon which we can inscribe modernity, nor an "other" to be used as a straw man for broader and more "relevant" hypotheses. It had its own ethos – if that is the right word – that in many ways is foreign to us, which differed from place to place, but which needs to be acknowledged by those who wish to quantify. Numerical data from the distant past should not be set on Procrustean bed to fit preformed attractive models. "Troublesome" data culled from archives tell a richer, more accurate and ultimately more "usable" and interesting tale.

---

[67] Claudia Goldin, "Cliometrics and the Nobel," *Journal of Economic Perspectives* 9 no. 2 (Spring 1995), p. 191.

Bibliography

Archives

Archivio di Stato di Firenze
Balie, 6, 7
    Camera del comune
    Camarlenghi entrata, 32–42
    Camerlenghi uscita, 53–72
    Camerlenghi uscita duplicato, 5
    Scrivano di camera entrata, 5, 7, 8, 10
    Scrivano di camera uscita, 1, 5–10, 13–14, 25, 26, 32–33, 80, 81,
    88–90, 96, 102, 104
Consulte e pratiche, 1
Miscellanea Repubblicana, 120
Provvisioni, registri, 36–38
Signori, Missive I Cancelleria, 10
Ufficiali delle Castella, 5

Primary Sources

Boccaccio, Giovanni. *Trattatello in laude di Dante,* edited by Pier Giorgio Ricci. In *Tutte le opere di Giovanni Boccaccio,* edited by Vittore Branca. Milan: Mondadori, 1974.

The Decameron, translated by Mark Musa and Peter E. Bondanella. New York, NY: Norton, 1977.

Epistole e lettere, edited by Gianetta Auzzas. In *Tutte le opere di Giovanni Boccaccio,* edited by Vittore Branca. Milan: Mondadori, 1992.

Cicero. *Epistulae ad Quintum Fratrem et M. Brutum,* edited by D. R. Schackleton-Bailey. Cambridge: Cambridge University Press, 2004.

Codice diplomatico dantesco, edited by Renatto Piattoli. Florence: Libreria Luigi Gonnelli e figli, 1950.

Commissioni di Rinaldo degli Albizzi per il comune di Firenze (1339–1433), edited by Cesare Guasti. Florence: Tipi di M. Cellini, 1867–1873.

Cronaca malatestiane, edited by Aldo Massèra, *Rerum Italicarum Scriptores* 15. Bologna: Zanichelli, 1922–1924.

Dante. *De Vulgari Eloquentia,* translated and edited by Steven Botterill. Cambridge: Cambridge University Press, 1996.

The Divine Comedy, translated and edited by Robert M. Durling. 3 vols. Oxford: Oxford University Press, 1997–2011.

Documenti storici del secolo XIV, estratto dal Archivio di stato Fiorentino, edited by Agostino Pepoli. Florence: Arnaldo Forni, 1884.

Francisci Petrarcae epistolae de rebus familiares et varie, edited by Giuseppe Fracassetti. Florence: Le Monnier, 1859–1863.

Francisci Petrarchae Poemata minora quae extant Omnia, or *Poesia minori del Petrarca*, vol. 3., edited by D. Rossetti. Milan: Societas Tipografica, 1831–1834

I Capitoli del Comune di Firenze, inventario e regesto, edited by C. Guasti and A. Gherardi. 2 vols. Florence: Cellini, 1866–1893.

Ibn Khaldun. *The Muqaddimah*, translated and introduced by Franz Rosenthal; abridged and edited by N. J. Darwood. Princeton, NJ: Princeton University Press, 2005.

Keynes, John Maynard. *The General Theory of Employment, Interest and Money*. New York: Harcourt Brace, 1936.

La cronica domestica di Messer Donato Velluti, edited by Isidoro del Lungo and Guglielmo Volpi. Florence: G. C. Sansoni, 1914.

Machiavelli, Niccolò. *The Discourses*, translated by Leslie J. Walker and edited by Bernard Crick. New York, NY: Penguin, 1970.

   The Discourses on Livy, translated by Harvey Mansfield and Nathan Tarcov. Chicago, IL: University of Chicago Press, 1996.

   The Art of War, translated by Christopher Lynch. Chicago, IL: University of Chicago Press, 2003.

   The Prince, translated and edited by David Wootton. Indianapolis, IN: Hackett Publishing Co., 1995.

   The Prince, translated by Peter Bondanelli, with introduction by Maurizio Viroli. Oxford: Oxford University Press, 2005.

Montaigne, Michel. *Journal de voyage*, edited by Louis Lautrey. Paris: Hatchette, 1906.

Petrarch, Francesco. *Le familiari*, edited by Vittorio Rossi. 4 vols. Florence: Sansoni, 1933–1942.

   Rerum familiarum libri, I–VIII, vol. 1, translated and edited by Aldo S. Bernardo. Albany, NY: State University of New York Press, 1975.

   Rerum familiarum libri, IX–XVI, vol. 2, translated and edited by Aldo S. Bernardo. Baltimore, MD: Johns Hopkins University Press, 1982.

   Rerum familiarum libri, XVII–XXIV, vol. 3, translated and edited by Aldo S. Bernardo. Ithaca, NY: Italica Press, 2005, 2nd edn.

   Petrarch's Lyric Poems, translated by Robert M. Durling. Cambridge, MA: Harvard University Press, 1976.

Pucci, Antonio. *Centiloquio in Delle poesie di Antonio Pucci*, edited by Ildefonso di San Luigi. Florence: Gaet. Cambiagi, 1772–1775.

Sacchetti, Franco. *Novelle*. Turin: Einaudi, 1970.

Smith, Adam. *An Inquiry into the Nature and Causes of the Wealth of Nation*, edited by Edwin Cannan. New York, NY: Modern Library, 1937.

Sonetti editi ed inediti di Ser Ventura Monachi: Rimatore fiorentino del XIV secolo, edited by Adolfo Mabellini. Turin: G. B. Paravia e comp, 1903.

Statuti della Repubblica fiorentina. Statuto del Capitano del Popolo degli anni 1322–1325, vol. 1, edited by Romolo Caggese. Florence: Tip. Galileiana, 1910.

Statuti della Repubblica fiorentina, Statuto del Capitano del Popolo:1322–25, edited by Giuliano Pinto, Francesco Salvestrini, and Andrea Zorzi. 2 vols. Florence: Leo S. Olschki, 1999.

Statuti dell'Università e Studio fiorentino dell'anno MCCCLXXXVII, edited by Alessandro Gherardi. Florence: Arnaldo Forni, 1973.

Statuti e legislazione a Firenze dal 1355 al 1415, Lo Statuto cittadino del 1409, edited by Lorenzo Tanzini. Florence: Leo S. Olschki, 2004.

"Statuto della Parte Guelfa di Firenze, compilato nel 1335." *Giornale storico degli archivi toscani* (1857): 1–41.

Stefani, Marchionne di Coppo. *Cronaca Fiorentina*, edited by N. Rodolico. In *Rerum Italicarum scriptore*, edited by L. A. Muratori. Città di Castello: S. Lapi, 1910.

Tutte le opere di Giovanni Boccaccio, vol. 3, edited by Vittore Branca. Milan: Mondadori, 1974.

Villani, Giovanni. *Nuova Cronica*, vols. 2–3, edited by Giuseppe Porta. Parma: Fondazione Pietro Bembo, 1991.

Villani, Matteo. *Nuova Cronica*, vol. 1, edited by Giuseppe Porta. Parma: Fondazione Pietro Bembo, 1995.

Secondary Sources

Abel, Wilhelm. *Agricultural Fluctuations in Europe: From the Thirteenth to the Twentieth Centuries*. London: Metheun, 1980 English edn.

Albanese, Gabriella. "La corrispondenza fra Petrarca e Boccaccio." In *Motivi e forme delle "Familiari" di Francesco Petrarca*, edited by Claudia Berra. Milan: Cisalpino, 2003, 39–99.

Allen, Robert C. "The Great Divergence in European Wages and Prices from the Middle Ages to the First World War," *Explorations in Economic History* 38 (2001): 411–447.

Antognini, Roberta. *Il progetto autobiografico delle Familiares di Petrarca*. Milan: Edizioni Universitarie di lettere economica diritto, 2008.

Arfaioli, Maurizio. *The Black Bands of Giovanni*. Pisa: Pisa University Press, 2005.

Ascoli, Albert and Unn Falkeid, eds. *The Cambridge Companion to Petrarch*. Cambridge: Cambridge University Press, 2015.

Auzzas, Gianetta. "Studi sulle epistole: L'invito della signoria fiorentina al Petrarca." *Studi sul Boccaccio* 4 (1967): 203–240.

Baldasseroni, Francesco. "La Guerra tra Firenze e Giovanni Visconti." *Studi storici* 11 (1902): 361–407.

Baranski, Zygmunt G. and Lino Pertile. *Dante in Context*. Cambridge: Cambridge University Press, 2015.

Baranski, Zygmunt G. and Theodore J. Cachey, Jr., eds. *Petrarch and Dante: Anti-Dantism, Metaphysics, Tradition*. Notre Dame, IN: University of Notre Dame Press, 2009.

Barbadoro, Bernardino. *Le finanze della repubblica fiorentina. Imposta diretta e debito pubblico fino all'istituzione del Monte.* Firenze: Leo S. Olschki, 1929.

"Finanza e demografia nei ruoli fiorentine d'imposta del 1352–1353." *Atti di Congresso internazionale per lo studio dei problemi della popolazione* 9 (1933): 624–629.

Barducci, Roberto. "Politica e speculazione finanziaria a Firenze dopo la crisi del primo Trecento (1343–1358)." *Archivio Storico Italiano* 137 (1979): 177–219.

Barlucchi, Andrea. "I centri minori delle conche Appenininiche (Casentino e Alta Valtinertina)." In *I centri minori della Toscana nel medioevo*, edited by Giuliano Pinto and Paolo Pirillo. Florence: Leo S. Olschki, 2013, 57–95.

Barolini, Teodolinda. *The Undivine Comedy: Detheologizing Dante.* Princeton, NJ: Princeton University Press, 1992.

"'Only Historicize': History, Material Culture (Food, Clothes, Books), and the Future of Dante Studies." *Dante Studies* 127 (2009): 37–54.

Baron, Hans. "The Evolution of Petrarch's Thought: Reflections on the State of Petrarch Studies." In *From Petrach to Leonardo Bruni in Studies in Humanistic and Political Literature.* Chicago, IL: University of Chicago Press, 1968, 7–50.

"Franciscan Poverty and Civic Wealth in the Shaping of 'Trecento' Thought: The Role of Petrarch." In *In Search of Civic Humanism.* Princeton, NJ: Princeton University Press, 1988, 172–175.

Bayley, C. C. *War and Society in Renaissance Florence: The De Militia of Leonardo Bruni.* Toronto: University of Toronto Press, 1961.

Berardi, D., Cassi Ramelli, A. E. Montevecchi, G. Ravaldini, and E. Schettini, eds. *Rocche e castelli di Romagna.* Bologna: University Press of Bologna, 1970–1971.

Bernardo, Aldo S. "Letter-Splitting in Petrarch's Familiares." *Speculum* 33 (1958): 237–241.

Bernocchi, Mario. *Le Monete delle Repubblica Fiorentina*, vols. 1, 3. Florence: Leo S. Olschki, 1974.

Beveridge William. "Wages in the Winchester Manors." *Economic History Review* 7 (1936): 22–43.

Westminster Wages in the Manorial Era." *Economic History Review* 8 (1955): 18–35.

Prices and Wages in England from the Twelfth to the Nineteenth Century. London: Frank Cass, 1965.

Billanovich, Giuseppe. *Petrarca Letterato: Lo scrittoio del Petrarca.* Rome: Edizioni di Storia e letteratura, 1947.

Blastenbrei, Peter. *Die Sforza und ihr Heer.* Heidelberg: Winter Universitätsverlag, 1987.

Bloch, Marc. "Le salaire et les fluctuations économique à longue period." *Revue Historique* 173 (1934): 1–31.

"Le maçon médiéval: problèmes de salariat." *Annales* 7 (1935): 216–217.

Boli, Todd. "Boccaccio's Trattatello in laude di Dante, or Dante Resartus." *Renaissance Quarterly* 41 (1988): 395–398.

Böninger, Lorenz. *Die Deutsche Einwanderung Nach Florenz Im Spatmittelalter.* Leiden: Brill, 2006.

Bothwell, James, P. J. P. Goldberg, and W. M. Ormrod, eds. *The Problem of Labour in Fourteenth-Century England.* Woodbridge, Suffolk: York Medieval Press, 2000.

Bowsky, William M. "The Impact of the Black Death upon Sienese Government and Society." *Speculum* 39 (1964): 1–34.

The Finance of the Commune of Siena, 1287–1355. Oxford: The Clarendon Press, 1970.

"Italian Diplomatic History: A Case for the Smaller Commune." In *Order and Innovation in the Middle Ages: Essays in Honor of Joseph R. Strayer,* edited by William C. Jordan, Bruce McNab, and Teofilo F. Ruiz. Princeton, NJ: Princeton University Press, 1976, 55–74.

A Medieval Italian Commune: Siena under the Nine, 1287–1355. Berkeley, CA: University of California Press, 1981.

Branca, Vittore. *Giovanni Boccaccio. Profilo biografico.* Florence: G. C. Sansoni, 1997.

Braudel, Fernand. "Histoire et sciences sociales: La longue durée." *Annales. Économies, Sociétés, Civilisations* 4 (1958): 725–753.

The Mediterranean and the Mediterranean World in the Age of Philip II, vol. 1, translated by Sian Reynold. New York, NY: Harper Books, 1966.

Civilization and Capitalism: The Wheels of Commerce, translated by Sian Reynold. New York, NY: Harper and Row, 1979.

Brucker, Gene. *Florentine Politics and Society, 1343–1378.* Princeton, NJ: Princeton University Press, 1962.

"An Unpublished Source on the Avignonese Papacy: The Letters of Francesco Bruni." *Traditio* 19 (1963): 351–370.

Civic World of the Early Renaissance. Princeton, NJ: Princeton University Press, 1977.

"Bureaucracy and Social Welfare in the Renaissance," *Journal of Modern History* 55 no. 1 (March 1983): 1–21.

Brunetti, Mario. "La Battaglia di Castro, 1350." *Rivista marittima* 43 (1910): 269–282.

"Contributo alla storia delle relazioni veneto-genovesi 1348–50." In *Miscellanea di storia veneta,* 3rd series IX. Venice: Viella, 1916.

Burckhardt, Jacob. *The Civilization of the Renaissance in Italy,* translated by S. G. C. Middlemore. New York, NY: Penguin, 1954.

Burke, Peter. *The French Historical Revolution, 1929–2014.* Cambridge: Polity Press, 2015.

Caferro, William. *Mercenary Companies and the Decline of Siena.* Baltimore, MD: Johns Hopkins University Press, 1998.

John Hawkwood, an English Mercenary in Fourteenth Century Italy. Baltimore, MD: Johns Hopkins University Press, 2006.

"Continuity, Long-Term Service and Permanent Forces: A Reassessment of the Florentine Army in the Fourteenth Century." *Journal of Modern History* 80 (2008): 219–251.

"Warfare and Economy of Renaissance Italy, 1350–1450." *Journal of Interdisciplinary History* 39 (2008): 167–209.

"Honor and Insult: Military Rituals in Late Medieval Tuscany." In *Ritual and Symbol in Late Medieval and Early Modern Italy*, edited by Samuel K. Cohn Jr., Marcello Fantoni, and Franco Franceschi. Turnhout: Brepols, 2013, 125–143.

"Petrarch's War: Florentine Wages at the Time of the Black Death" *Speculum* 88 (2013): 144–165.

"Military Enterprise in Florence at the Time of the Black Death, 1349–50." In *War, Entrepreneurs, and the State in Europe and the Mediterranean, 1300–1800*, edited by Jeff Fynn-Paul. Leiden: Brill, 2014, 15–31.

"Le Tre Corone Fiorentine and War with the Ubaldini." In *Boccaccio 1313–2013*, edited Francesco Ciabattoni, Elsa Filosa, and Kristina Olson. Ravenna: Longo editore, 2015, 43–55.

Campbell, Bruce. *The Great Transition: Climate, Disease and Society in the Late Medieval World*. Cambridge: Cambridge University Press, 2016.

Canestrini, Giuseppe. "Di alcuni documenti risguardanti le relazioni politiche dei papi d'Avignone coi comuni d'Italia Avanti e dopo il tribunato di Cola di Rienzo e la calata di Carlo IV." *Archivio storico italiano* 7 (1849): 347–446.

"Documenti per servire alla storia della milizia italiana dal XIII secolo al XVI." *Archivio storico italiano* 15 (1851): i–549.

Capini, Stefania and Paolo Galli. "I terremoti in Molise." In *I terremoti in Molise, Guida alla mostra*, edited by R. De Benedittis, A. Di Niro, and D. Di Tommaso. Muccilli Campobasso: Ministero per i Beni e le Attivita` Culturali, Campobasso, 2003.

Cardini, Franco. *L'Acciar de cavalieri*. Florence: Le Lettere, 1997.

Casini, Bruno. "Note sul potere di acquisto dei salari a Pisa nei primi anni della signoria gambacortiana." In *Studi in onore di Leopoldo Sandri*, vol. 1. Rome: Ministero per i beni culturali e ambientali, 1983, 227–275.

Cherubini, Giovanni. "I lavoratori nell'Italia dei secoli XIII-XV: considerazioni storiografiche e prospettive di ricerca." In *Artigiani e salariati. Il mondo del lavoro nell'Italia dei secoli XII–XV*. Bologna: Centro Italiano di Studi di Storia e d'Arte, 1984, 1–26.

L'Italia rurale del basso medioevo. Rome-Bari: Laterza, 1996.

Chiappelli, Luigi. "L'amministrazione della giustizia in Firenze durante gli ultimi secoli del medioevo e il periodo del Risorgimento, secondo le testimonianze degli antichi scrittori." *Archivio storico italiano* 15 (1885).

Chittolini, Giorgio. *La formazione dello stato regionale e le istituzioni del contado. Secoli XIV e XV*. Turin: G. Einaudi, 1979.

"Signorie rurali e feudi alla fine del Medioevo." In *Storia d'Italia*, edited by G. Galasso. Turin: UTET, 1981, 597–613.

"City-States and Regional States in North-Central Italy." *Theory and Society* 18 (1989): 689–706.

Ciappelli, Giovanni. "Il cittadino fiorentino e il fisco alla fine del trecento e nel corso del quattrocento: Uno studio di due casi." *Societa e Storia* XLVI (1989): 828–844.

Cipolla, Carlo. *Documenti per la Storia delle relazioni diplomatiche*. Venice: A spese della Societa, 1907.

Franceco Petrarca e le sue relazioni colla corte Avignonese al tempo di Clemente VI. Turin: Vincenzo Bona, 1909.

The Monetary Policy of Fourteenth Century Florence. Berkeley, CA: University of California Press, 1982.

Clark, Gregory. *A Farewell to Alms*. Princeton, NJ: Princeton University Press, 2007.

"The Long March of History: Farm Wages, Population and Economic Growth, England 1209–1869." *Economic History Review* 60 (2007): 97–135.

Cochin, Henri. *Un amico del Petrarca: lettere del Nelli al Petrarca*. Florence: Le Monnier, 1901.

Cohen, Deborah and Peter Mandler, "The History Manifesto: A Critique," *American Historical Review* (April 2015): 530–542.

Cohn, Samuel K. *The Cult of Remembrance and the Black Death: Six Renaissance Cities in Central Italy*. Baltimore, MD: Johns Hopkins University Press, 1997.

Creating the Florentine State: Peasants and Rebellion. Cambridge: Cambridge University Press, 1999.

"After the Black Death: Labour Legislation and Attitudes towards Labour in Late-Medieval Western Europe." *Economic History Review* 60 (2007): 457–485.

Connell, William and Andrea Zorzi, eds. *Florentine Tuscany: Structure and Practices of Power*. Cambridge: Cambridge University Press, 2000.

Contamine, Philippe. *War in the Middle Ages*, translated by Michael Jones. Oxford: Blackwell Publishing, 1980.

Coulton, G. G. *Black Death*. London: Ernest Benn, 1929.

Covini, Maria Nadia. "Political and Military Bonds in the Italian State System, Thirteenth to Sixteenth Century." In *War and Competition between States*, edited by Philippe Contamine. Oxford: Oxford University Press, 2000, 9–33.

Crouzet, F. "The Economic History of Modern Europe." *Journal of Economic History* 31 (1971): 135–152.

Dale, Sharon. "'Contra damnationis filios:' The Visconti in Fourteenth-Century Papal Diplomacy." *Journal of Medieval History* 33 (2007): 1–32.

Dalton, Amy H. "A Theory of the Organization of State and Local Government Employees." *Journal of Labor Research* 3 (1982): 163–177.

Davidsohn, Robert. *Storia di Firenze: Le ultime lotte contro l'impero*. Florence: G. C. Sansoni, 1960.

Storia di Firenze IV I Primordi della civilta fiorentina, part 1 impulsi interni, influssi esterni e cultura politica. Florence: G. C. Sansoni, 1977.

Davies, Jonathan. *Florence and Its University during the Early Renaissance*. Leiden: Brill, 1998.

Day, John. "Francois Simiand and the Annales School of History." In *Money and Finance in the Ages of Merchant Capitalism*. Oxford: Blackwell, 1999, 139–150.

Money and Finance in the Age of Merchant Capitalism, 1200–1800. Oxford: Blackwell, 1999.

Dean, Trevor. "Lords, Vassals and Clients in Renaissance Ferrara." *English Historical Review* 100 (1985): 106–119.

Del Treppo, Mario, ed. *Condottieri e uomini d'arme nell'Italia del Rinascimento*. Naples: Liguori Editore S.R.L., 2001.

Dini, Bruno. "I lavoratori dell'Arte della Lana a Firenze nel XIV e XV secolo." In *Artigiani e salariati. Il mondo del lavoro nell'Italia dei secoli XII–XV, Pistoia, 9–13 ottobre 1981*. Bologna: Centro Italiano di Studi di Storia e d'Arte, 1984, 27–68.

Doren, Alfred. *Die Florentiner Wollentuchindustrie*. Stuttgart: Cotta, 1901.

Le arti fiorentine, translated into Italian by G. B. Klein. Florence: F. LeMonnier, 1940.

Dotti, Ugo. *Vita di Petrarca*. Bari: Laterza, 1987.

Dyer, Christopher. *Standards of Living in the Later Middle Ages: Social Change in England, 1200–1320*. Cambridge: Cambridge University Press, 1989.

Ehrenberg, Ronald. *The Demand for State and Local Government Employees: An Economic Analysis*. Toronto: Lexington Books, 1972.

"The Demand for State and Local Government Employees." *American Economic Review* 63 (1973): 366–379.

Eisner, Martin. *Boccaccio, and the Invention of Italian Literature: Dante, Petrarch, Cavalcanti and the Authority of the Vernacular*. Cambridge: Cambridge University Press, 2013.

Emiliani, Paolo. *Storia dei Comuni italiani*. Florence: Le Monnier, 1866.

Epstein, Stephan R. "Cities, Regions and the Late Medieval Crisis: Sicily and Tuscany Compared." *Past and Present* 130 (1991): 3–50.

"Town and Country: Economy and Institutions in Late Medieval Italy." *Economic History Review* 46 (1993): 453–477.

Freedom and Growth: The Rise of States and Markets, 1300–1700. London: Routledge, 2000.

Epstein, Steven A. "The Theory and Practice of the Just Wage." *Journal of Medieval History* 17 (1991): 53–69.

Wage Labor and Guilds in Medieval Europe. Chapel Hill, NC: University of North Carolina Press, 1991.

Falsini, Alberto Benigno. "Firenze dopo il 1348: Le consequenze della peste nera," *Archivio storico italiano* 129 (1971): 425–503.

Farmer, D. L. "Prices and Wages." In *The Agrarian History of England and Wales, vol. II, 1042–1350*, edited by H. E. Hallam. Cambridge: Cambridge University Press, 1967, 716–817.

"Crop Yields, Prices and Wages in Medieval England." *Studies in Medieval and Renaissance History* 6 (1983): 331–348.

"Prices and Wages, 1350–1500." In *The Agrarian History of England and Wales*, edited by Edward Miller. Cambridge: Cambridge University Press, 1991, 431–525.

Federico, Giovanni and Paolo Malanima. "Progress, Decline, Growth: Product and Productivity in Italian Agriculture, 1000–2000." *Economic History Review* 3 (2004): 437–464.

Filosa, Elsa. "To Praise Dante, To Please Petrarch ('Trattatello in laude di Dante')." In *Boccaccio: A Critical Guide to the Complete Works*, edited by

Victoria Kirkham, Michael Sherberg, and Janet Smarr. Chicago, IL: University of Chicago Press, 2013, 213–220.

Fiorilli, Carlo. "I dipintori a Firenze nell'arte dei Medici, Speziali e Merciai." *Archivio storico italiano* 78 (1920): 5–74.

Fischer, David Hackett. *The Great Wave: Price Revolutions and the Rhythm of History*. Oxford: Oxford University Press, 1996.

Fiumi, Enrico. "Fioritura e decadenza dell'economia fiorentina." *Archivio storico italiano* 115 (1957): 385–439.

Flexner, Abraham. "The Usefulness of Useless Knowledge," *Harper's Magazine* 179 (June/November 1939): 544–553.

Folena, Gianfranco. "La tradizione delle opere di Dante Alighieri." In *Atti del Congresso Internazionale di Studi Danteschi*, edited by Centro di studi e documentazione dantesca e medievale. Florence: G. C. Sansoni: 1965, 54–56.

Foresti, Aldo. *Annedoti della vita di Francesco Petrarca*. Padua: Antenore, 1977 reprint.

Franceschi, Franco. *Oltre il "tumulto": i lavoratori fiorentini dell'Arte della Lana fra Tre e Quattrocento*. Florence: Leo S. Olschki, 1993.

"The Economy: Work and Wealth." In *Italy in the Age of the Renaissance, 1300–1550*, edited by John M. Najemy. Oxford: Oxford University Press, 2004, 124–144.

Francovich, Riccardo. *I Castelli del contado fiorentino nei secoli XII e XIII*. Florence: CLUSF, 1976.

Francovich, R. and M. Ginatempo, eds. *Castelli, Storia e archeologia del potere nella Toscana medievale*. Florence: All'Insegna del Giglio, 2000.

Freedman, Paul and Gabrielle Spiegel. "Medievalisms Old and New: The Rediscovery of Alterity in North American Medieval Studies." *American Historical Review* 103 (1998): 677–704.

Freeman, Richard B. *Labor Economics*. Englewood Cliffs, NJ: Prentice-Hall, 1979.

"How Do Public Sector Wages and Employment Respond to Economic Conditions?" In *Public Sector Payrolls*, edited by David A. Wise. Chicago, IL: University of Chicago Press, 1987, 183–216.

Friedman, David. *Florentine New Towns: Urban Design in the Late Middle Ages*. Cambridge, MA: Harvard University Press, 1989.

Frigo, Daniela, ed. *Politics and Diplomacy in Early Modern Italy: The Structure of Diplomatic Practice, 1450–1800*. Cambridge: Cambridge University Press, 2000.

Fubini, Riccardo. "L'istituzione diplomatica e la figura dell'ambasciatore nel XV secolo (in particolare riferimento a Firenze)." In *L'Italia alla fine del Medioevo: I caratteri originali nel quadro europeo*, edited by Francesco Salvestrini. Florence: Florence University Press, 2006, 333–354.

Galassi, N. *Dieci secoli di storia ospitaliera a Imola*. Imola: Galeati, 1966–1970.

Galli, Paolo Antonio Costantino and José Alfredo Naso. "Unmasking the 1349 Earthquake Source (Southern Italy): Paleoseismological and Archaeoseismological Indications from the Aquae Iuliae Fault." *Journal of Structural Geology* 31 (2009): 128–149.

Garbini, Paolo. "Francesco Nelli." In *Dizionario Biografico degli Italiani*. Milan: Treccani, 2013, 173–183.

Gasquet, Francis Aidan. *The Great Pestilence*. London: G. Bell, 1893.

Geremek, Bronislaw. "I salari e il salariato nelle citta del Basso Medio Evo." *Rivista Storica Italiana* 78 (1966): 368–386.

    Le Salariat dans l'artisanat parisien aux XIIIe–XVe siècles. Etude sur le marché de la main d'œuvre au Moyen Âge. Paris: Mouton et Cie, 1968.

    Salariati e artigiani e nella Parigi medievale. Florence: G. C. Sansoni, 1975.

Gessler, Eduard A. "Huglin von Shoenegg. Ein Basler Reiterfuhrer des 14. Jahrhunderts in Italien: Ein Beitrag zur damaligen Bewaffnung." *Basler Zeitschrift fur Geschichte und Altertumskunde* XXI (1923): 75–126.

Gherardi, Alessandro. "L'antica camera del comune di Firenze e un quaderno d'uscita de' suoi camarlinghi dell'anno 1303." *Archivio storico italiano* 26 (1885): 313–361.

Gilli, Patrick. "La fonction d'ambassadeurs d'après les textes juridiques italiens du XVe siècle et le traité de Martino Garati da Lodi: une impossible representation." *Mélanges de l'Ecole française de Rome-Moyen Âge* 121 (2009): 173–187.

    "Il discorso politico fiorentino nel Rinascimento e l'umanesimo civile." In *Firenze e la Toscana. Genesi e trasformazioni di uno stato (XIV–XIX secolo)*, edited by Jean Boutier, Sandro Landi, and Olivier Rouchon. Florence: Mandragora, 2010, 255–271.

    "Ambasciate e ambasciatori nella legislazione statutaria italiana (secc. XIII–XIV)." In *Il laboratorio del Rinscimento: Studi di storia e cultura per Riccardo Fubini*, edited by Lorenzo Tanzini. Florence: Le lettere, 2015, 7–26.

Gilson, Simon. *Dante and Renaissance Florence*. Cambridge: Cambridge University Press, 2005.

Ginatempo, Maria. *Prima del debito. Finanziamento della spesa pubblica e gestione del deficit nelle grandi città toscane (1200–1350 ca)*. Florence: Leo S. Olschki, 2000.

Goldin, Claudia. "Cliometrics and the Nobel," *Journal of Economic Perspectives* 9 no. 2 (Spring 1995): 191–208.

Goldthwaite, Richard A. *The Building of Renaissance Florence*. Baltimore, MD: Johns Hopkins University Press, 1980.

    The Economy of Renaissance Florence. Baltimore, MD: Johns Hopkins University Press, 2009.

Goldthwaite, Richard A., Enzo Settesoldi, and Marco Spallanzani, eds. *Due libri mastri degli Alberti: una grande compagnia di Calimala, 1348–1358*. Florence: Cassa di Risparmio, 1995.

Gordon, Robert J. "A Century of Evidence on Wage and Price Stickiness in the United States, the United Kingdom, and Japan" in *Macroeconomics, Prices, and Quantities*, edited by James Tobin. Washington, DC: Brookings, 1983, 85–133.

Green, Louis. *Chronicle in History*. Cambridge: Cambridge University Press, 1972.

Grillo, Paolo. *Cavalieri e popoli in armi: Le istitutioni military nell'Italia medievale* Bari: Editori Laterza, 2008.

Grohmann, Alberto. "Economia e società a Perugia nella seconda metà del Trecento." In *Società e istituzioni dell'Italia comunale: l'esempio di Perugia*. Perugia: Deputazione di storia patria per l'Umbria, 1988, 57–87.

Guidi, Guidubaldo. *Il governo della città-repubblica di Firenze del primo quattrocento*. 3 vols. Florence: Leo S. Olschki, 1981.

Guldi, Jo and David Armitage. *The History Manifesto*. Cambridge: Cambridge University Press, 2014.

Hale, John. *War and Society in Renaissance Europe*. Baltimore, MD: Johns Hopkins University Press, 1986.

Harriss, G. L. *King, Parliament, and Public Finance in Medieval England to 1369*. Oxford: Clarendon Press, 1975.

Shaping the Nation: England 1360–1461. Oxford: Clarendon Press, 2005.

Hatcher, John. "Plague, Population and the English Economy, 1348–1530." In *Studies in Economic and Social History*. London: Macmillan, 1977.

"England in the Aftermath of the Black Death." *Past and Present* 144 (1994): 3–35.

Henderson, John. *Piety and Charity in Late Medieval Florence*. Chicago, IL: University of Chicago Press, 1994.

Henneman, John Bell. "The Black Death and Royal Taxation, 1347–1351." *Speculum* 43 (1968): 405–428.

Royal Taxation in Fourteenth Century France: The Development of War Financing, 1322–1356. Princeton, NJ: Princeton University Press, 1971.

Herlihy, David and Christiane Klapisch-Zuber. "Direct and Indirect Taxation in Tuscan Urban Finance, c. 1200–1400." In *Finances et comptabilité urbaines du 13e au 16e siècle*. Brussels: Centre "Pro Civitate," 1964, 385–405.

Tuscans and Their Families: A Study of the Florentine Catasto of 1427. Chicago, IL: University of Chicago Press, 1985.

Hollander, Robert. Dante: A Life in Works. New Haven, CT: Yale University Press, 2001.

Houston, Jason M. *Building a Monument to Dante*. Toronto: University of Toronto Press, 2010.

"Boccaccio at Play in Petrarch's Pastoral World." *Modern Language Notes* 127 (2012): S47–S53.

Humphries J. and J. Weisdorf. "The Wages of Women in England, *1260–1850.*" *Journal of Economic History* 75 (2015): 405–447.

Iggers, Georg G. *Historiography in the 20th Century: From Scientific Objectivity to the Post-Modern Challenge*. Hanover, NH: Wesleyan Press, 1997.

Jones, P. J. *The Malatesta Lords of Rimini*. Cambridge: Cambridge University Press, 1974.

Kallendorf, Craig. "The Historical Petrarch." *American Historical Review* 101 (1996): 130–141.

Kaueper, Richard W. *Medieval Chivalry*. Cambridge: Cambridge University Press, 2016.

Kirkham, Victoria and Armando Maggi, eds. *Petrarch: A Critical Guide to the Complete Works*. Chicago, IL: University of Chicago Press, 2009.

Kirkham, Victoria, Michael Sherberg, and Janet Levarie Smarr, eds. *Boccaccio: A Critical Guide to the Complete Works*. Chicago, IL: University of Chicago Press, 2013.

Klapisch-Zuber, Christiane. *Ritorno alla politica: I magnati fiorentini, 1340–1440*. Rome: Viella, 2009.

Knapton, Michael. "City Wealth and State Wealth in Northeast Italy, 14th–17th Centuries." In *La ville, la bourgeoisie et la genise de l'etat moderne (xii–xviii siecles)*, edited by Neithard Bulst and J.-Ph. Genet. Paris: Éd. du CNRS, 1985, 183–209.

Kohl, Benjamin G. *Padua under the Carrara, 1318–1405*. Baltimore, MD: Johns Hopkins University Press, 1998.

Kuhn, Thomas S. *The Structure of Scientific Revolutions*. Chicago, IL: University of Chicago Press, 1962.

La Roncière, Charles M. de. "Indirect Taxes or 'Gabelles' at Florence in the Fourteenth Century: The Evolution of Tariffs and the Problems of Collection." In *Florentine Studies: Politics and Society in Renaissance Florence*, edited by Nicolai Rubinstein. London: Faber and Faber, 1968, 140–192.

"La condition des salariés à Florence au XIVe siècle." In *Tumulto dei Ciompi: un momento di storia fiorentina ed Europea*, edited by Atti del Convegno internazionale. Florence: Leo S. Olschki, 1981, 13–40.

Prix et salaires à Florence au XIVe siècle, 1280–1380. Rome: Palais Farnese, 1982.

La Sorsa, Saverio. *La Compagnia d'Or San Michele, ovvero una pagina della beneficenza in Toscana nel secolo XIV*. Trani: V. Vecchi, 1902.

Labrousse, Ernest. *Esquisse du mouvement des prix et des revenus en France au XVIIIe siècle*. Paris: Librairie Dalloz, 1933.

Lamoreaux, Naomi R. "Economic History and the Cliometric Revolution." In *Imagined Histories*, edited by Anthony Molho and Gordon S. Wood. Princeton, NJ: Princeton University Press, 1998, 59–84.

Landes, David S. "The Statistical Study of French Crises." *Journal of Economic History* 10 (1950): 195–211.

Lane, Frederic C. *Venice and History*. Baltimore, MD: Johns Hopkins University Press, 1966.

Venice: A Maritime Republic. Baltimore, MD: Johns Hopkins University Press, 1973.

Langholm, Odd. *Economics in Medieval Schools: Wealth, Exchange, Value, Money, and Usury According to the Paris Theological Tradition, 1200–1350*. Leiden: Brill, 1992.

Lanza, Antonio. *Polemiche e berte*. Rome: Bulzoni, 1989.

Larner, John. *Lords of the Romagna*. Ithaca, NY: Cornell University Press, 1965.

"Crossing the Romagnol Apennines in the Renaissance." In *City and Countryside in Late Medieval and Renaissance Italy: Essays Presented to Philip Jones*, edited by Trevor Dean and Chris Wickham. London: Bloomsbury, 1990, 147–170.

Law, John E. *The Lords of Renaissance Italy, the Signori, 1230–1300*. London: Davenant Press, 1981.

Lazzarini, Isabella. *Communication and Conflict: Italian Diplomacy in the Early Renaissance, 1350–1520*. Oxford: Oxford University Press, 2015.

Le Roy Ladurie, Emmanuel. *The Peasants of Languedoc*, translated by John Day. Urbana, IL: University of Illinos Press, 1974.

"Motionless History." *Social Science History* 1 no. 2 (Winter 1977): 115–136.

Lepore, Jill. "Historians Who Love Too Much: Reflections on Microhistory and Biography." *Journal of American History* 88 (2011): 129–144.

Levi, Giovanni. "On Microhistory." In *New Perspectives on Historical Writing*, edited by Peter Burke. Cambridge: Polity Press, 1991, 97–117.

Magna, Laura. "Gli Ubaldini del Mugello: una signoria feudale nel contado fiorentino." In *I ceti dirigenti dell'età comunale nei secoli XII e XIII*. Pisa: Pacini, 1982, 13–65.

Magnati e popolani nell'Italia comunale. Pistoia: Centro Italiano di Studi di Storia e d'Arte, 1997.

Mainoni, Patrizia. "Capitali e imprese: Problemi di identita del ceto mercantile a Milano nel XIV secolo." In *Strutture del potere ed elites economiche nelle citta europee dei secoli XII–XVI*, edited by Giovanna Petti Balbi. Naples: Liguori, 1996.

Le radici della discordia: Ricerche sulla fiscalità a Bergamo tra XIII e XV secolo Milan: Edizioni Unicopli, 1997.

"Finanza pubblica e fiscalità nell'Italia centro-settentrionale fra XIII e XV secolo." *Studi Storici* XL (1999): 449–470.

Malanima, Paolo. *L'economia italiana dalla crescita medievale alla crescita contemporanea*. Bologna: Il Mulino, 2002.

"Labour, Productivity, Wages in Italy, 1270–1913." Paper presented at Towards a Global History of Prices and Wages, Utrecht, Netherlands, 19–21 August 2004.

Mallett, Michael. *Mercenaries and Their Masters*. Totowa, NJ: Rowman and Littlefield, 1974.

"Ambassadors and Their Audiences in Renaissance Italy." *Journal of the Society for Renaissance Studies* 8 (1994): 229–243.

Marzi, Demetrio. "Notizie storiche intorno ai documenti e agli archivi piu antichi della repubblica *(secc. XI–XIV)*." *Archivio storico italiano* 20 (1897): 74–335.

La Cancelleria della Repubblica Fiorentina. Rocca San Casciano: Cappelli, 1909.

Masi, G. *Il sindaco delle magistrature comunali nel secolo xiv con speciale riferimento a Firenze*. Rome: Attilio Sampaolesi editore, 1930.

Mattingly, Garrett. *Renaissance Diplomacy*. New York, NY: Penguin Books, 1955.

Maxson, Brian. *The Humanist World of Renaissance Florence*. Cambridge: Cambridge University Press, 2014.

Mazzoni, Vieri. *Accusare e proscrivere il nemico politico. Legislazione antighibellina e persecuzione giudiziaria a Firenze (1347–1378)*. Pisa: Pacini, 2010.

Mazzotta, Giuseppe. "Petrarch's Epistolary Epic: The Letters on Familiar Matters." In *Petrarch: A Critical Guide to the Complete Works*, edited by Victoria Kirkham and Armando Maggi. Chicago, IL: University of Chicago Press, 2009, 309–320.

The Worlds of Petrarch. Durham, NC: Duke University Press, 1993.

McGee, Timothy. "Dinner Music for the Florentine Signoria, 1350–1450." *Speculum* 74 (1999): 95–114.

The Ceremonial Musicians of Late Medieval Florence. Bloomington, IN: Indiana University Press, 2009.

McNeill, William H. *The Pursuit of Power.* Chicago, IL: University of Chicago Press, 1982.

Medin, Antonio. "I Visconti nella poesia contemporanea," *Archivio Storico Lombardo* 28 (1891): 784–785.

Meek, Christine. *Lucca 1369–1400: Politics and Society in the Early Renaissance State.* Oxford: Oxford University Press, 1978.

The Commune of Lucca under Pisa Rule, 1342–1369. Cambridge, MA: The Medieval Academy of America, 1980.

Meiss, Millard. *Painting in Florence and Siena after the Black Death: The Arts, Religion, and Society in the Mid-Fourteenth Century.* Princeton, NJ: Princeton University Press, 1979.

Mercuri, Roberto. "Genesi della tradizione letteraria italiana in *Dante, Petrarca e Boccaccio.*" In *Letteratura italiana, Storia e geografia,* vol. 1, edited by Roberto Antonelli, Angelo Cicchetti, and Giorgio Inglese. Turin: Einaudi, 1987, 229–455.

Michaud, François. "Apprentissage et salariat à Marseille avant la peste noire." *Revue historique* 589 (1994): 3–36.

Milner, Stephen. "Fanno bandire: Town Criers and the Information Economy of Renaissance Florence." *I Tatti Studies in The Italian Renaissance* 16 (2013): 107–151.

Molho, Anthony. *Florentine Public Finance in the Early Renaissance, 1400–1433.* Cambridge, MA: Harvard University Press, 1971.

"Città-stato e i loro debiti pubblici: Quesiti e ipotesi sulla storia di Firenze, Genova e Venezia." In *Italia 1350–1450: Tra crisi, trasformazione, sviluppo. Tredicesimo convegno di studi, Pistoia, 10–13 maggio 1991.* Pistoia: Centro Italiano di Studi di Storia e d'Arte, 1993, 185–215.

Mucciarelli, Roberta, G. Piccinni, and G. Pinto. *La costruzione del dominio citta-dino sulle campagne. Italia centro-settentrionale, secoli XII–XIV.* Siena: Protagon, 2009.

Mueller, Reinhold. *The Venetian Money Market: Banks, Panics, and the Public Debt, 1200–1500.* Baltimore, MD: Johns Hopkins University Press, 1997.

Munro, John. "Industrial Transformations in the North-West European Textile Trades, c. 1290–c. 1340: Economic Progress or Economic Crisis?" In *Before the Black Death: Studies in the "Crisis" of the Early Fourteenth Century,* edited by Bruce M. S. Campbell. New York, NY: St. Martin's Press, 1991, 110–148.

"Urban Wage Structures in Late-Medieval England and the Low Countries: Work Time and Seasonal Wages." In *Labour and Leisure in Historical Perspective, Thirteenth to Twentieth Centuries,* edited by Ian Blanchard. Stuttgart: F. Steiner, 1994, 65–78.

"Wage-Stickiness, Monetary Changes and Real Incomes in Late-Medieval England and the Low Countries, 1300–1450: Did Money Really Matter?" In *Research in Economic History,* edited by Alexander J. Field, Gregory Clark, and William A. Sundstrom. Amsterdam: JAI, 2003, 185–297.

214   Bibliography

Muzzi, Oretta. "Un castello del contado fiorentino nella prima metà del Trecento. Certaldo in Valdelsa." *Annali dell'Istituto di Storia della Facoltà di Magistero dell'Università di Firenze* 1 (1979): 67–111.

Najemy, John M. *Corporatism and Consensus in Florentine Electoral Politics 1280–1400.* Chapel Hill, NC: University of North Carolina Press, 1982.

A History of Florence, 1200–1575. Malden, MA: Blackwell Publishing, 2006.

"Dante and Florence." In *The Cambridge Companion to Dante,* edited by Rachel Jacoff. Cambridge: Cambridge University Press, 2007, 245–253.

Nef, John U. "War and Economic Progress, 1540–1640." *Economic History Review* 12 (1942): 13–38.

War and Human Progress. Cambridge, MA: Harvard University Press, 1950.

North, Douglass C. and Robert Paul Thomas. *Rise of the Western World: A New Economic History.* Cambridge: Cambridge University Press, 1973.

Olson, Kristina M. *Courtesy Lost: Dante, Boccaccio and the Literature of History.* Toronto: University of Toronto Press, 2014.

Ormrod, W. Mark. "The Crown and the English Economy, 1290–1348." In *Before the Black Death: Studies in the "Crisis" of the Early Fourteenth Century,* edited by Bruce M. S. Campbell. Manchester: Manchester University Press, 1992, 149–183.

"England in the Middle Ages." In *Rise of the Fiscal State in Europe,* edited by Richard Bonney. Oxford: Oxford University Press, 1999, 19–52.

Edward III. New Haven, CT: Yale University Press, 2011.

Özmucur, Süleyman and Şevket Pamuk. "Real Wages and the Standards of Living in the Ottoman Empire, 1469–1914." *Journal of Economic History* 62 (2002): 293–321.

Pampaloni, Guido. "Gli organi della Repubblica fiorentina per le relazioni." *Rivista di studi politici internazionali* 20 (1953): 261–296.

Firenze al tempo di Dante. Documenti sull'urbanistica fiorentina. Rome: Ministero dell'Interno, 1973.

Pamuk, Şevket. "The Black Death and the Origins of the 'Great Divergence' across Europe, 1300–1600." *European Review of Economic History* 11 (2007): 289–317.

Paoli, C. "Rendiconto e approvazioni di spese occorse nell'esercito fiorentino contro Pistoia nel Maggio 1302." *Archivio Storico Italiano* 6 (1867): 3–16.

Park, Katharine. *Doctors and Medicine in Early Renaissance Florence.* Princeton, NJ: Princeton University Press, 1985.

Pelli, Giuseppe. *Memorie per servire alla vita di Dante Alighieri.* Florence: Guglielmo Piatti, 1823.

Penn, Simon A. C. and Christopher Dyer. "Wages and Earnings in Late Medieval England: Evidence from the Enforcement of the Labour." *Economic History Review* 43 (1990): 356–376.

Persson, Gunnar. "Consumption, Labour and Leisure in the Late Middle Ages." In *Manger et Boire au Moyen Age,* edited by Denis Menjot. Nice: Les Belles Lettres, 1984, 211–223.

Preindustrial Economic Growth. Social Organization and Technological Progress in Europe. Oxford: Basil Blackwell, 1988.

Pezzolo, Luciano. "Government Debt and State in Italy, 1300–1700." Working paper, 2007, University of Venice "Ca' Foscari," Department of Economics. www.dse.unive.it/en/pubblicazioni (last accessed February 2016).

Phelps Brown, E. H. and Sheila V. Hopkins. "Seven Centuries of Building Wages." *Economica* 22 (1955): 195–206.

"Seven Centuries of the Prices of Consumables, Compared with Builders' Wage-Rates." *Economica* 23 (1956): 296–314.

Piccini, Daniele. "Franceschino degli Albizzi, uno e due." *Studi petrarcheschi* 15 (2002): 129–186.

Pieri, Piero. "Alcune questioni sopra fanterie in Italia nel periodo comunale." *Rivista storica italiana* (1933): 561–614.

Rinascimento e la crisi militare italiana. Turin: Einaudi, 1952.

Pini, A. I. "Dal Comune città-stato al Comune ente amministrativo." In *Storia d'Italia*, edited by G. Galasso. Turin: UTET, 1981, 509–515.

Pini, E. "Alcuni dati sui prezzi e i salari nell'età dei comuni (Italia settentrionale e centrale)." In *Studi economico giuridici pubblicati per cura della Facoltà di giurisprudenza*, edited by R. Università di Cagliari. Cagliari: Presso la R. Università degli Studi, 1914, 65–91.

Pinto, Giuliano. "Persone, balie e salariati dell'ospedale di S. Gallo." *Ricerche storiche* 2 (1974): 113–168.

ed. *Il libro del biadaiolo carestie e annona a Firenze della metà del 200 al 1348*. Florence: Leo S. Olschki, 1978.

"I livelli di vita dei salariati cittadini nel periodo successivo al Tumulto dei Ciompi (1380–1430)." In *Il Tumulto dei Ciompi. Un momento di storia fiorentina ed europea*, edited by Atti del Convegno internazionale. Florence: Leo S. Olschki, 1981, 161–198.

"L'organizzazione del lavoro nei cantieri edili (Italia centro settentrionale)." In *Artigiani e salariati. Il mondo del lavoro nell'Italia dei secoli XII–XV*. Bologna: Centro Italiano di Studi di Storia e d'Arte, 1984, 69–101.

"I lavoratori salariati nell'Italia bassomedievale: Mercato del lavoro e livelli di vita." In *Travail et travailleurs en Europe au Moyen Âge et au début des Temps modernes*, edited by Claire Dolan. Toronto: Pontifical Institute of Mediaeval Studies, 1991, 47–62.

Toscana medievale: paesaggi e realtà sociali. Florence: Le Lettere, 1993.

Pirillo, Paolo. "Tra Signori e città: I castelli dell'Appenino alla fine del Medio Evo." In *Castelli dell'Appennino nel medioevo*, edited by P. Fosci, E. Penoncini, and R. Zagnoni. Pistoia: Società Pistoiese, 2000, 15–29.

Costruzione di un contado: I fiorentini e il loro territorio nel Basso Medioevo. Florence: Casa Editrice le Lettere, 2001.

"Signorie dell'Appennino tra Toscana ed Emilia-Romagna alla fine del Medioevo." In *Poteri signorili e feudali nelle campagne dell'Italia settentrionale fra Tre e Quattrocento: fondamenti di legittimità e forme di esercizio*, edited by Federica Cengarle, Giorgio Chittolini, and Gian Maria Varanini. Florence: Firenze University Press, 2003, 211–226.

Le Terre nuove fiorentine ed il loro popolamento: ideali, compromessi e risultati. Florence: Leo S. Olschki, 2004.

Forme e strutture del popolamento nel contado fiorentino, gli insediamenti fortificati (1280–1380). Florence: Leo S. Olschki, 2008.

Polanyi, Karl. *The Great Transformation*. Boston, MA: Beacon Press, 2001.

Queller, Donald. "The Development of Ambassadorial Relazioni." In *Renaissance Venice*, edited by J. R. Hale. London: Faber and Faber, 1973, 174–196.

Razi, Z. "Family, Land and the Village in Later Medieval England" *Past and Present* 93 (1981): 31–33.

Repetti, Emanuele. *Dizionario Geografico Fisico e Storico della Toscana*. Florence: Firenze libri, 1839.

Ricci, Pier Giorgio. "Studi sulle opera latine e volgari del Boccaccio." *Rinascimento* 10 (1959): 1–39.

Ricotti, Ercole. *Storia delle compagnie di ventura in Italia*. Turin: Pomba, 1844–1845.

Rizzi, Fortunato. *Francesco Petrarca e il decennio parmense, 1341–1351*. Turin: G. B. Paravia & Company, 1934.

Robins, William. "Poetic Rivalry: Antonio Pucci, Jacopo Salimbeni and Antonio Beccari da Ferrara." In *Firenze alla vigilia del Rinascimento*, edited by Maria Bendinelli Predelli. Fiesole: Cadmo, 2006, 319–322.

Romby, G. C., ed. *Una terra nuova nel Mugello: Scarperia: popolazione, insediamenti, ambiente, XIVXVI secolo*. Scarperia: Comune di Scarperia, 1985.

Roover, Raymond De. "Labour Conditions in Florence around 1400: Theory, Policy and Reality." In *Florentine Studies: Politics and Society in Renaissance Florence*, edited by Nicolai Rubinstein. London: Faber and Faber, 1968, 277–313.

Rossi, Aldo. "Dante nella prospettiva del Boccaccio." *Studi Danteschi* 39 (1960): 63–139.

Rossi, Vittorio. "Dante nel Trecento e nel Quattrocento." In *Scritti di critica letteraria, Saggi e discorsi su Dante*. Florence: G. C. Sansoni, 1930, 198–227.

"Un archetipo abbandonato di epistole di Petrarca." In *Studi sul Petrarca sul Rinascimento*. Florence: G. C. Sansoni, 1930, 175–193.

Le familiari, 4 vols. Florence: G. C. Sansoni, 1933–1942.

Rubinstein, Nicolai. "Florence and the Despots: Some Aspects of Florentine Diplomacy in the Fourteenth Century." *Transactions of the Royal Historical Society* 2 (1952): 21–45.

The Palazzo Vecchio, 1298–1532. Oxford: Oxford University Press, 1995.

Rutenburg, Victor I. "La compagnia di Uzzano." In *Studi in onore di Armando Sapori*, vol. 1. Milan: Instituto editoriale cisalpino, 1957, 689–706.

Salvemini, Gaetano. *Magnati e Popolani in Firenze dal 1280–1295*. Florence: G. Carnesecchi, 1899.

Schäfer, Karl Heinrich. *Die Ausgaben Apostoliche Kamera (1335–1362)*. Paderborn: F. Schöningh, 1914.

Schumpeter, Joseph. *History of Economic Analysis*. Oxford: Oxford University Press, 1954.

Scott, Joan. "Gender as a Useful Category of Historical Analysis." *American Historical Review* 91 (1986): 1053–1075.

Scott, John A. *Dante's Political Purgatory*. Philadelphia, PA: University of Pennsylvania Press, 1996.

Selzer, Stephan. *Deutsche Söldner im Italien des Trecento*. Tubingen: Niemeyer, 2001.

Sestan, Ernesto. "I Conti Guidi e il Casentino." In *Italia medievale*. Naples: Edizioni scientifiche italiane, 1968, 356–378.

Settia, Aldo. A. *Comuni in guerra: Armi ed eserciti nell'Italia delle citta*. Bologna: CLUEB, 1993.

Proteggere e dominare. Fortificazioni e popolamento nell'Italia medievale. Rome: Viella, 1999.

"Gli 'Insegnamenti di Teodoro di Montferrato e la prassi bellica in Italia all'inizio del Trecento." In *Condottieri e uomini d'arme nell'Italia del Rinascimento*, edited by Mario del Treppo. Naples: Ligouri, 2001, 11–28.

Simiand, François. *Le salaire, l'évolution sociale et la monnaie*. Paris: Felix Alcan, 1932.

Slicher van Bath, B. H. *The Agrarian History of Western Europe, 500–1800*, translated by Olive Ordish (London: E. Arnold, 1963).

Solow, Robert M. "Insiders and Outsiders, Insiders and Outsiders in Wage Determination," *Scandinavian Journal of Economics* 87 no. 2, Proceedings of a Conference on Trade Unions, Wage Formation and Macroeconomic Stability (June 1985), pp. 411–428.

Sombart, Werner. *Der Moderne Kapitalismus*. Leipzig: Verlag von Dunker und Homblott, 1920.

Sorbelli, Albano. *La Signoria di Giovanni Visconti a Bologna e le sue relazioni con la Toscana*. Bologna: Forni, 1902.

Sterpos, Daniele. *Comunicazioni stradali attraverso i tempi: Bologna-Firenze*. Novara: De Agostini, 1961.

"Evoluzione delle comunicazioni transappenniniche attraverso tre passi del Mugello." In *Percorsi e valichi dell'Appennino tra storia e leggenda*. Florence: Arti grafiche Giorgi & Gambi, 1985, 7–22.

Stuard, Susan Mosher. *Gilding the Market: Luxury and Fashion in Fourteenth Century Italy*. Philadelphia, PA: University of Pennsylvania Press, 2006.

Tanzini, Lorenzo and Sergio Raveggi, eds. *Bibliografia delle edizioni di statuti toscani (secoli XII–XVI)*. Florence: Leo S. Olschki, 2001.

Taylor, F. L. *The Art of War in Italy, 1494–1529*. Westport, CT: Greenwood Press, 1921.

Thorold Rogers, James E. *A History of Agriculture and Prices in England from the Year after the Oxford Parliament (1259) to the Commencement of the Continental War (1793)*. Oxford: Clarendon Press, 1866.

Six Centuries of Work and Wages: The History of English Labour. London: Swan Sonnenschein and Co., 1884.

Tocco, Francesco Paolo. *Niccolò Acciaiuoli: Vita e politica in Italia alla metà del xiv secolo*. Rome: Isime, 2010.

Todeschini, Giacomo. *Ricchezza francescana. Dalla povertà volontaria alla società di mercato*. Bologna: Il Mulino, 2004.

Tognetti, Sergio. "Prezzi e salari nella Firenze tardo medievale: un profile." *Archivio storico italiano* 153 (1995): 263–333.

Trexler, Richard. *Public Life in Renaissance Florence.* New York, NY: Academic Press, 1980.

Trivellato, Francesca. "Salaires et justice dans les corporations vénitiennes au XVIIe siècle: le cas des manufactures de verre." *Annales: H.S.S.* 54 no. 1 (1999): 245–273.

"Is There a Future for Italian Microhistory in the Age of Global History?" *California Italian Studies* 2 no. 1 (2011), http://escholarship.org/uc/item/0z9 4n9hq (last accessed February 2017).

"Microstoria/Microhistoire/Microhistory," *French Politics, Culture & Society* 33 no. 1 (2015): 122–134.

Van Zanden, Jan Luit. "Wages and the Standards of Living in Europe, 1500–1800." *European Review of Economic History* 2 (1991): 75–95.

Varanini, G. M. "Castellani e governo del territorio nei distretti delle città venete (XIII–XV sec.)" In *De part et d'autre des Alpes: Les châtelains des princes à la fin du Moyen Âge,* edited by Guido Castelnuovo and Olivier Mattéo. Paris: Flammarion, 2006, 25–58.

Verlinden, Charles. "La grande peste de 1348 en Espagne: Contribution à l'étude de ses conséquences économiques et sociales." *Revue Belge de Philologie et d'Histoire* 17 (1938): 17–25.

Vigueur, Jean-Claude Maire. *Cavaliers et citoyens. Guerre et société dans l'Italie communale, XIIe-XIIIe siècles.* Paris: Fondation de l'École des hautes etudes en sciences sociales, 2003.

Waley, Daniel. "The Army of the Florentine Republic from the Twelfth to the Fourteenth Century." In *Florentine Studies,* edited by Nicolai Rubinstein. London: Faber and Faber, 1968, 70–108.

"Condotte and Condottieri in the Thirteenth Century." *Proceedings of the British Academy* 61 (1975): 337–371.

The Italian City Republic, 3rd edn. London: Longman, 1988.

Westfall Thompson, James. "The Aftermath of the Black Death and the Aftermath of the Great War." *American Journal of Sociology* 26 (1921): 565–572.

Westwater, Lynn Lara. "The Uncollected Poet." In *Petrarch: A Critical Guide to the Complete Works,* edited by Victoria Kirkham and Armando Maggi. Chicago, IL: University of Chicago Press, 2009, 301–308.

Wickham, Chris. *The Mountains and the City. The Tuscan Apennines in the Early Middle Ages.* Oxford: Clarendon Press, 1988.

Wilkins, Ernest H. *The Prose Letters of Petrarch: A Manual.* New York, NY: S. F. Vanni, 1951.

The "epistolae metricae" of Petrarch. Rome: Edizioni di Storia e Letteratura, 1956.

The Life of Petrarch. Chicago, IL: University of Chicago Press, 1961.

"Petrarch's Last Return to Provence." *Speculum* 39 no. 1 (January 1964): 75–84.

Winter, Jay M., ed. *War and Economic Development: Essays in Memory of David Joslin.* Cambridge: Cambridge University Press, 1975.

Wojciehowski, Hannah Chapelle. "Petrarch and His Friends." In *The Cambridge Companion to Petrarch*, edited by Albert Ascoli and Unn Falkeid. Cambridge: Cambridge University Press, 2015, 16–34.

Wood, Diana. *Medieval Economic Thought*. Cambridge: Cambridge University Press, 2002.

Zak, Gur. *Petrarch's Humanism and the Care of the Self*. Cambridge: Cambridge University Press, 2010.

Index